EX LIBRIS

PRINCIPLES
OF TEACHING

Earl A. Johnson

*Professor of Education and
Head of Department,
Ball State Teachers College*

R. Eldon Michael

*Professor of Education and
Director of Extended Services,
Ball State Teachers College*

PRINCIPLES

OF TEACHING

BOSTON

ALLYN AND BACON, INC.

First printing .... *January, 1958*

Second printing .... *August, 1958*

Library of Congress Catalog Card Number: 58-6345

Printed in the United States of America

Preface

The great problem in the task of preparing teachers for the schools of America is making sure that each teacher is professionally dedicated to one purpose—helping each youth to understand the society in which he lives and to achieve his highest potential in that society. The goal of this task is to produce personnel who will live and work in accordance with their interpretation of what it means to be a good teacher.

The professional teacher, like all learners, is in a constant state of "becoming." Professional growth evidences itself in several areas of behavior. The teacher's concept of teaching expands to include the possibility of both positive and negative curricular influence of all experiences of children in relation to the school's goals. He has a growing recognition of the roles of administrators, supervisors, and other staff personnel in achieving goals of education with boys and girls.

Because of this expanding concept of teaching, it is the belief of the authors that the distribution of the teacher's time among the various facets of his art should be re-examined. Crowded classrooms and schedules make it difficult for the teacher to see beyond the immediate problems of teaching his particular branch of studies. Yet children's immediate behavior patterns clamor for attention to their causes. Confusion and misunderstanding arising from the needs of parents and laymen to know more about their schools adds to the burdens of teachers. The teacher needs to appreciate fully the importance of work with parents and laymen. Child study and community relations require their just share of the teacher's time, thought, and energy.

Teachers need to understand the importance of constantly increasing their skill in the art of teaching. They need to realize that teaching skill includes coming to know each pupil as an individual, discovering the best ways of organizing educative experiences adapted to the learner, and evaluating the results of teaching in terms of each learner's individual growth.

Professional growth evidences itself in the community life of the teacher. He consistently shares his time and talent in support of community improvement. He is keenly aware of the urgency of such improvement because he understands the educational impact of life in the community upon boys and girls. Thus, he lends his support to all institutions that educate, even though he maintains a special professional interest in schools.

Throughout the teacher's professional life, growth is accelerated in proportion to his ability to evaluate himself as a person and as a practitioner of the art of teaching. Self-evaluation is productive of growth, of course, only when followed with modification in practice where such is indicated.

The good teacher will become a member of appropriate professional associations, working always within the ethical code of the teaching profession. Early identification with the profession is encouraged; the profession now falls short of the respect it deserves, partly because of the lack of professional activity and self-discipline among a minority of its members.

The "teacher" in this book is the growing professional person to whom it is addressed. Although the book is specifically directed to the student who will be approaching some of his first classroom experiences, all teachers are invited to consider the concept of teaching it presents. It has been written in hope that it will contribute to the growth of teachers aspiring to the highest ideals of the profession.

The authors are keenly aware that the ideas contained in this book have resulted in part from many contacts with hundreds of colleagues and students for more than a quarter of a century. It is impossible to acknowledge all. However, special acknowledgment is due the following students, whose class reports have provided illustrations: Kathryn Boots, John Bowyer, Frances Brubaker, Charles Collins, Thelma Dawes, Leola DeFreece, Margaret Dorton, Spurgeon Ernie, Elizabeth Figert, Eunice Hartman, George U. Heeter, Cleo Hunter, Mary Knapke, Carolyn Langston, Nancy Linson, Gladys Lynn, Lois Mannix, Charles Meyer, Emily Meyers, Helena Miller, Frances Modlin, Lela Niles, Martha Norris, William Peterson, Paul Pierson, Roy Rankin, Hildegarde Riedel, Wilda Robinson, Harriett Robson, Enid Rogers, Ralph Ross, Vernon Shores, and Gladys Streib.

Sincere thanks are expressed to our colleagues Dr. Joseph Hollis, Dr. Merle Strom, Dr. Victor Lawhead, and Mr. John Snedeker, who read and offered valuable suggestions on portions of the manuscript.

We wish also to thank the many publishers, organizations, and services who have kindly granted us permission to use needed materials, and we are indebted to the many authors to whom footnote references are found throughout the book.

Special acknowledgment is due Ball State Teachers College Photo Service, *The Indiana Teacher,* and *The Muncie Star* for permission to use photographs from their files for illustrations.

Finally, to our wives and families, who have borne with us through the busy months of preparation of this manuscript, we tender this expression of thanks and affection.

Earl A. Johnson

R. E. Michael

Contents

Part Four

DEVELOPMENT THROUGH ASSUMING RESPONSIBILITY

Part Five

EVALUATION AND REPORTS AS PART OF THE TEACHING PROCESS

Part Six

THE CONTINUING DEVELOPMENT OF THE TEACHER

Part Seven

INITIAL EXPERIENCES IN WORKING WITH CHILDREN

PRINCIPLES
OF TEACHING

Part One

A concept

of

teaching

Introduction

Young men and women choose teaching as a profession because they sincerely desire to help youth mature. They enjoy working with children and young people, and they have discovered that there are personal rewards in the act of being helpful that transcend any other type of activity. This resolve to be a professional worker in the field of teaching precedes the attainment of becoming a dedicated person—dedicated to the profession of teaching.

The basic purpose of professional education is to help the prospective teacher think through the full meaning of working with learners. It gives a picture of the worker in education dealing with the complex problems that are involved in the teaching process. Teaching is one of the more complex of the several professions.

As his concept of the professional teacher expands, the prospective teacher identifies himself with accepted considerations, selecting some characteristics and rejecting others, but all in harmony with his own potentialities and compatible with his own growing set of values.

The broad areas of concern deemed essential portions of his professional heritage come to his attention. This over-all picture gives him the opportunity to see more clearly the various aspects of his own professional task. He begins to appraise his own skills and to identify his own problems in terms of his personality, interests, and abilities.

The prospective teacher discovers special areas of competence that would otherwise have been overlooked, as he works with learners and studies their behavior. He also becomes aware of the important role that the community behind the learners plays in their total developmental patterns. All of the things that learners do demand the teacher's attention, and none can be omitted from his training program.

As the individual's concept of teaching and his identification of himself in a professional role grow, he finds himself in need of filling many challenging new roles he had not anticipated. But as a professional person he keeps himself open-minded to the needs of youth and is aware that the needs of society change. The direction of his growth will be determined by his capacity to be continuously aware of the needs and interests of youth and also by his own desire to be increasingly helpful.

The extent to which the teacher can actually discover his own power through his own experience in working with learners will be the determining factor in his ultimate effectiveness in the schools. Such self-discovery leads to an ever-expanding and developing concept of the role of the teacher and of what teaching really means.

1

What it means
to be a teacher

Mary was the second child in a family of four children. Her parents were owners of a farm in a prosperous agricultural community. Mary had helped on the farm both in the home and in the field. She could drive a tractor as well as anyone, and hard work neither frightened her nor made her tired. She knew many things about the habits of farm animals, and had been around chicks, calves, lambs, and pigs as long as she could remember. Insects and worms had always interested her greatly, as did the honeybee, busily at work gathering nectar from hedges and flowers.

Mary attended church school regularly and helped in the primary department for several years because she could play the piano, and read and tell stories to delight little children. Mary had *always* liked children. Mrs. Wright, the department superintendent, said that Mary was her best worker because she could do so many things well and that children knew she liked them because she was so very kind and gentle with them. Mary was an active member in 4-H work and specialized in sewing. One of her best friends always came out ahead of Mary in the annual 4-H style show but Mary was generous in her feelings toward her competition and rejoiced with those who excelled.

Mary did better than average in high school. All of her

classmates knew she was destined to be a teacher because she spent much of her free time in the primary grades as a member of an organization called the Future Teachers of America, working as a teacher's helper. When Mary took a monarch butterfly to school one day to show the children, she had anticipated all the questions and was prepared to answer them. Her very enthusiasm was contagious and children were always glad when Mary came because she always had an interesting story to read and knew how to talk to them. All the teachers who came to know Mary said that surely Mary would become a good teacher.

She now has finished her pre-service education at State College and is ready to begin her first school. She is to be a teacher of first grade in West Elementary School. Mary's college record is excellent

Children are eager to bring their problems to one who appears kind and sympathetic to their needs and interests.

Courtesy of *The Indiana Teacher*

and she was a leader in the Association for Childhood Education during her senior year. Mary should be a good teacher.

Jim lived two blocks from North High School in the city of Gamma. His older brother graduated from college majoring in business administration. Jim's father is a machine operator in the largest factory in the city. Both parents finished high school but neither went to college. Jim's mother is not employed outside the home. She is a good and thoughtful mother; her children dress well and are always clean. The parents have always hoped that the children would attend college. Each child has understood fully that attending college will present financial problems so a savings account has been maintained in each child's name. Summer employment adds substantially to these accounts. The family car is shared by all and money is not spent on "jalopies." The members of the family all understand that wise spending is the only way that personal goals can be reached.

Jim, now in his junior year in college, is majoring in mathematics and science. Since Jim was a young boy he has been interested in mathematics. He mastered arithmetic easily and was eager to learn algebra, geometry, and advanced algebra in high school. His father gave him a chemistry set for Christmas when he was in the eighth grade. With that as a beginning he built up a keen interest in science that has carried through chemistry and physics in high school and on into college.

Jim has a big decision to make at this point. He has been unusually successful in all his courses in his chosen fields, and, interestingly enough, these fields seem to point to open doors of opportunity into industry where it appears that financial rewards may be greater than in teaching. However, Jim has been a junior Scout leader and has helped several of the boys earn merit badges in science. He has felt the thrill of helping younger boys learn things, and above all he knows that younger boys like him. They come to him with questions and he has been able to help them find answers. This all means much to Jim, and he knows that the decision whether he is going to work with people or with things will have to be made by him.

He has been able to make his decision since his college teacher sent him out an hour each day to work in a classroom with ninth-grade boys and girls in algebra. There he has found out that he has strong powers in helping boys and girls in mathematics; through this relationship he has been able to affect their lives favorably in other ways at the same time. Boys and girls have become important to him in a way that he had never known before, and his problem is no longer whether or not to teach, but rather how to become a really strong teacher. All who have worked with Jim are sure he can achieve a most satisfying career.

Sarah lived in a suburb of a medium-sized city. She had never given much thought to whether or not she would go to college—it had always been taken for granted. Both her father and mother are college graduates, and her elder sister was in college, so why should Sarah debate the subject in her mind? Sarah's choice was a strong private college, and she organized her high school program to meet its entrance requirements.

Sarah has a great variety of interests. She likes to read; she likes music and was a member of the high school band, playing the clarinet quite well without too much effort. She wasn't interested in working hard enough to be one of the better players. It would have taken more time than she wanted to devote to practice. She was in the Y-Teens and attended faithfully; she boasted that she had not missed a meeting in over two years. She had never been chosen as an officer, but here again she did not want to go to the trouble to work for an office. Moreover, she did not like all of the girls and they knew it, because she showed her dislikes in the way she dealt with them.

She liked physical education most and was usually chosen first when teams were being formed, because the girls respected her athletic skill and her team nearly always won. She was a competitor with a will to win. Boys liked her because of her personality and her ability to add to the fun of a party. She got along better with boys than with girls, and some girls readily admitted that they didn't like Sarah because the boys liked her so well.

When Sarah arrived at college things were very much the same. She left her clarinet at home because she knew it would take more work to make the college band, and she frankly didn't want to put in her time that way. Her interest moved quickly into physical education and dates. She was willing to give the time necessary to excel in all physical activities, both class and intramural, that were open to women. Her interest in sports was really so intense that her instructors were not sure she could become a good teacher. She seemed not to be able to see that the really superior physical education teacher must be seriously concerned about the physical development of all children, and that games and activities are chosen with specific development in mind for specific pupils. Because she was physically strong and highly skilled, she thought all people should be strong. All people looked alike to her and when one was not strong or did not have good coordination, Sarah lost her patience quickly; she had little time for those who could not succeed in a game.

When Sarah graduated from college she had no difficulty in getting a teaching position in physical education. But her teachers hoped that the challenge of her position would cause her to see that physical education in the school is far more than athletic skill, and that girls are more important than winning games.

Bill is the oldest of three children. His father was killed in an accident when Bill was fourteen years old. Although the family was left in moderate circumstances, the mother found it necessary to work to supplement what was left of the estate in order to give the children the essentials of a normal home life. The family lived in a small but modern home that was debt free. They disposed of the family car because it was not a necessity and public transportation was easily available. Bill's friends were kind and considerate of him but it was hard for Bill to reconcile himself to the fact that the family did not have a car. They did have a television set, and the gang could come to Bill's home for television programs.

As soon as Bill was sixteen a job at the gasoline station enabled him to earn his own money and provided him with the opportunity to be around cars. From his wages he clothed himself and had his own spending money. He was kind to his mother and gave her little gifts to show his affection.

Bill did satisfactorily in school but by the time he did his work at the filling station, he did not have time to engage in athletic activities with the other boys in the high school. Bill was only slightly above average in intelligence, and owing to the necessity of working after school and on week ends, he graduated just below the middle of a class of 195 pupils.

However, his average scholastic rating did not keep him from entering college in the town where he lived. He could live at home and still keep his job at the filling station. Bill had not decided what he wanted to become, and his restricted high school program did not help him greatly in making a decision. This fact led his college advisors to suggest that he take a general course and come to some conclusions about specializing by the end of his sophomore year. But at the end of his sophomore year one of Bill's closest friends joined the Navy so Bill decided to go with him and finish his college education after completing his military service.

At the end of his enlistment Bill returned to college. By that time he had decided to be an elementary teacher. He saw that the need for teachers was acute and his chances for immediate employment were good. He had not been particularly interested in younger children—in fact he had taken very little interest in his younger brother and sister. On the other hand his personal habits and discipline had been excellent, and his two years in college and his Navy service had given breadth to his general culture. He felt that he could do quite well in the field of education.

His college instructors, however, faced a big task because the drive of expediency was operating more strongly than the inner urge to help young boys and girls. He has now graduated and has accepted a position as sixth grade teacher in a small community school not far outside his home town. Time alone will tell what kind of teacher Bill will become. The odds favor him because he has reached sufficient maturity to want to succeed.

Who becomes a teacher? Mary, Jim, Sarah, and Bill are like many of your classmates—maybe somewhat like you. They entered college with various urges and purposes within themselves. Time and learning experiences helped each to mature in his own way. College opened up new possibilities to them, made stronger the professional urges that were present when they came, and gave meaning to some that they didn't know they had. Their backgrounds were vastly different, so the ways college education affected them were greatly tempered by what had happened to them before they entered college and by the way they felt about themselves as students planning to be teachers.

To these four cases might be added hundreds more but they would differ only in backgrounds of experience, intensity of desire to be helpful to boys and girls, or in the economic circumstances that controlled the activities of each individual and became strong determinant factors in each one's destiny as a person. Against these varying forces in the life of the individual, each person who enters college resolves his own purposes and his own way of thinking about children and learning, as he goes through the process of becoming a teacher. Out of all these factors a teacher is made.

What are the powerful influences in a person's educational experiences that aid him in becoming a teacher? He has already felt many of these experiences in a teacher education program before he reaches the junior year of college. His freshman and sophomore courses have broadened his cultural background and have given strength to the purposes which he brought with him. The books he has read, the courses he has taken, the personalities that have made impressions upon him—even the years that he has lived—have made an impression. He is moving ahead; he is in the process of becoming a person with serious responsibilities.

This chapter proposes to present a brief overview of the major areas of concern to the person who is intimately responsible for a teaching situation. Each person will need to decide where he stands in the progression of experiences toward becoming a teacher. The final achievement, of course, will be the attainment of full status in the profession, skill in the art of teaching, and civic leadership in the community.

Studying children. One of the early shocks that comes to the young teacher is the vast and evident range of difference in the potentials of various pupils. He finds himself coming to grips with the problems of the child with strong intellectual ability and equally strong work habits, as well as the one who lacks ability and has no particular zeal to overcome intellectual shortcomings through effort. Differences in interest in his well laid plans and purposes overwhelm him. He remarks in astonishment, "I never knew there could be such wide differences in a group of pupils who are alike in age and assigned to the same grade level." He learns early that being assigned to a particular grade has little bearing on the actual power of the pupil.

The more effective teacher recognizes these differences and makes radical adaptations in the goals that are set for each learner. But this in itself is a major challenge. While he as a teacher is aware of the differences, many parents either cannot recognize the inadequacies of their own children or refuse to accept them in the light of what they hope and dream about for their child. So he faces not only differences in children but differences in parents to whom he has a professional responsibility for interpreting the school's purposes and goals in terms of their children's purposes and activities.

This problem of knowing more about each pupil leads the teacher into many situations where he must re-evaluate not only how he feels about learners but also how he feels about his own professional philosophy and objectives. It challenges him to come to grips with the reality of taking a pupil where he is and working with him from that point. It causes the teacher to accept the question and realize that he must find an answer to what learning and growth, as applied to each child, really mean. He will come to realize the way inner factors are involved in changed behavior in terms of the problems, activities, and experiences that make up the learner's total environment, of which the school is only one part. But this capacity to see each child in terms of all the forces that have influenced him, tempered by his intellectual power to cope with whatever faces him, makes the teacher a master in his profession.

Working with the community. One seldom stops to think how a school becomes a reality. Each school—even any classroom in a school—had its beginning in an idea. That idea had to be put into action. Responsibility for a good idea had to be assumed and faith in it had to be strong enough to cause men to believe enough in it to take the proper legal steps. Responsible persons had to see that each move was made in compliance with the law. Each school that exists does so because law was in existence that made its establishment possible. Similarly, once the school exists, it is not possible to close the school without specified legal procedure. Society is protected against forces that would destroy the opportunity for youth to be educated; the right to make such vital decisions is vested in the rule of the greater number. In the United States this safeguard of democracy is called majority rule.

Each community determines through legally established procedures what kind of education it will provide, and how much. Some districts begin formal education with kindergarten and are willing to pay for it. Nursery schools may be publicly supported in the not too distant future. Other districts either do not know of the value of nursery school and kindergarten education or are not willing to make the additional sacrifice in cost that would be incurred. Special education is provided in many communities for the children of low mentality and those deficient in hearing and vision or otherwise handicapped. Many communities go beyond the years of secondary school and extend public education two years through junior college. On the other hand many communities offer a very

The community, through the school, helps its children by seeing that all of them are protected against polio.

Courtesy of *The Indiana Teacher*

restricted program of general education—little beyond what was commonly found forty years ago. Failure to recognize the great variation of needs in mass education causes many children to drop out of school. This condition of widely varied programs represents briefly the range of willingness of individual communities to provide education at public expense, and is perhaps the greatest disadvantage of leaving education largely to the decision of a local community. Willingness and ability to pay for education do not always go together. Neither do ability and need always coincide. A broader tax base and leadership possessed of greater vision of the needs of youth may be the answer.

The teacher who is employed to teach in these schools is required to meet the standards for certification set up by law in the particular state where he chooses to work. Hence, there are responsibilities which the state assumes such as certification of teachers, transportation standards, minimum curricula, teachers' minimum salaries, and minimum facilities. Accreditation and support are predicated on meeting certain standards aimed at bringing all public education to an acceptable level. Compulsory education laws place restrictions on parents who might otherwise choose not to send their children to school. Within quite radical limits, it is determined even where they will send the child.

The school exercises considerable authority over the life of the child. Parents are subject to the regulations governing age, curriculum, transportation, and length of day and term. The very fact that the school operates with legal authority may cause some teachers to appear authoritarian to those whom they are privileged to serve. But the teacher who desires to accomplish most will bear in mind that more is accomplished in a better way if he works *with* people instead of *over* or *for* people. Cooperative solutions to problems are far more effective than authoritarian solutions. One of the early discoveries of the beginning teacher is that parents have a much greater stake in the child than he has. He may be shocked at the way a minority seem to ignore that responsibility, but he will come to recognize that most parents wish for their children the same benefits that he aspires to help them gain. This commonality of goals makes it possible for the school and the home to become an effective team. Through teamwork the level of educational opportunity is raised.

So the community, under the authority given to it by the state, provides educational facilities for its youth. The state, in most cases, insures the youth some degree of equality of educational opportunity through standards for a minimum program and financial support. The local community goes beyond that minimum depending on its financial ability and whether or not it enjoys that kind of leadership, in both school and community, that brings about widespread understanding of its educational needs, goals, and purposes. The responsibility to determine what educational opportunities its youth will have rests firmly on the community.

Widening the role of the teacher. The teacher should be an accepted leader in the group of learners. He does not need to stand apart but can work with and among his pupils so closely that he is respected for the wise suggestions he makes and the good ideas

Helping pupils to gain the most from their many activities and interests is what is properly called teaching.

Courtesy of Ball State Teachers College Photo Service

he has. In the classroom good ideas are important. As a person of maturity and experience the teacher is expected to use his resources to be helpful to learners.

Out of this respect that pupils develop for him, and from the accumulated knowledge he is able to gather about each individual pupil, the teacher is in an ideal position to serve as an advisor when pupils need help in making decisions. He need not tell the pupil what to do but he should give alternative suggestions and point out all the courses for action. From this the pupil is able to make a wiser choice and one in which he has confidence.

The teacher also is simply a friend—but how much is implied in that one word "friend"! A friend is one to whom you take your troubles, who can say the things that make you feel better, who takes the time to listen to your doubts and fears. A friend is one who gives you a helping hand—maybe a dime for bus fare. All of these things the teacher is to his boys and girls.

But beyond this role the teacher is the one who by his expert help leads the pupil to be a learner. After all, teaching is his greatest skill, and the art of being a counsellor, guide, and friend is supplemental to the art of teaching. How he will work with each learner to accomplish the most is his responsibility. The extent to which he is skilled will determine his effectiveness in teaching.

Having served as a skilled craftsman in teaching he must appraise the results; his role in appraisal and acquainting pupils with the problems of self-analysis is his greatest role. Only by helping learners make adaptations necessary to meet new situations can the teacher serve his most important function.

Principles of learning that affect teaching. The problem uppermost in the mind of the teacher is how to bring about efficient learning. While engaged in this process the ultimate effective use of the things learned is always a consideration. Principles of learning are related and it is difficult to package them into neat, discrete bundles. However, the professionally trained teacher will recall principles of learning having to do with at least the following areas: readiness, individual differences, motivation, effect, complex and multiple outcomes, security, activity and experience, meaning and understanding, multi-sensory approach, whole–part–whole learning, and transfer of learning.

A review of the above areas of learning from time to time will bring the teacher up to date on developments that may modify his approach to children. For example, there is a trend in work in individual differences that gives increasing importance to cultural impact among the causal factors, whereas native intelligence received most emphasis only a few years ago. Research in progress constantly gives new interpretations to problems of human learning.

Along with experimental evidence in learning there has developed a vast body of scientifically documented information about all areas of human growth and development. These findings cannot be said to be unrelated to learning. In fact, without adequate developmental progress many areas of learning cannot be undertaken. Particular concern in this volume, however, is with those conditions enumerated above which suggest the conditions under which learning goes forward most advantageously. Developmental qualities are implied or assumed.

Principles of teaching that promote learning. Parallel to the learning principles mentioned above is the behavior or characteristic practice of the teacher that brings about the desired conditions for learning. Just as the pupil has the responsibility for ultimately making use of the things he has learned, so is the teacher responsible also. Professional behavior on the part of the teacher is not impulsive. Rather it is deliberately selected, controlled behavior. The teacher constantly checks his impulse to favor action that he knows will bring better results. He says, "John, why are you doing this?" rather than "Stop that, John!" By so doing he begins to place the responsibility on the boy for his actions. He refrains from negative criticism of unacceptable work from the child who is already oversensitive. He decides to try tracing difficult spelling words when aural and visual means do not bring results. He constantly strives to reach a common experiential background with the child for words used to assure meaning instead of trusting to luck that the words have meaning to children.

The teacher has a responsibility for making the transfer of professional knowledge about human learning to his teaching practices. It is this controlled, selected professional behavior related to conditions for learning that differentiates the teacher, in reality, from laymen or other professionals.

The teacher's planning and the curriculum. The fate of a child's school education is finally in the hands of the teacher. The real curriculum, as far as each child is concerned, is made up of the learning experiences he has under the supervision of the school; this means, in the final analysis, his interaction with the teachers and pupils who are assigned to the program in which the child is placed.

The learning experiences the child has—the curriculum, then—isn't what the state department, the central superintendent's office, the curriculum council, the board of education or other level in the educational heirarchy publishes and hands down to the teacher. The curriculum is what finally comes out at the classroom level in terms of learning activities.

Learning activities are sometimes planned for children, sometimes planned with them. In the latter case the planning experience becomes in itself a means of learning certain processes and techniques. The activities utilized in classroom learning and the products of these activities are determined by the teacher. The selection he makes and the degree to which he utilizes the ideas of his pupils in the planning process will reflect the goals of learning and the teacher's interpretation of those goals.

Evaluation is a part of any learning process. The desired outcomes of learning are not all of the kind that yield to techniques of "measurement." The goals will determine the kinds of evaluative processes to be used. In addition, the teacher's beliefs about goals will determine the plans he makes for evaluating outcomes.

It becomes clear, then, that the curriculum of the class and of the individual is the direct result of the teacher's interpretation of his job. As this interpretation takes form in the plans he develops, the die is cast. Planning is the final determinant of the curriculum—even of education.

Giving importance to lesson planning. Lesson planning should mean to the teacher just what the name implies—the organization of the pupils' activities and materials they need for a period of time in such a way that the maximum learning will result from the experience. Any person gets work done more efficiently and effectively if planning has been done; teaching is no exception. To the extent that effective planning is accomplished, teaching approaches excellence. The teacher takes into consideration permissiveness as well as direction. In other words, as the director of learning activities he considers whom he will permit to do certain things as well as whom he will ask to do certain things.

Lesson planning may involve only daily lesson planning or it may cover the work for a longer period. Plans that reach beyond a few days are best considered as unit plans, described later. Both kinds of planning are necessary if the teacher desires to make the most of his and the learners' time. The daily plan is often only a portion of a larger plan, or it may be one in a sequence which combine to carry out a project of work.

The lesson plan serves as a guide to the teacher and may take any of a number of forms. Most teachers agree that it should be as brief as is compatible with giving maximum help to the teacher in directing his work. The teacher needs, as a first step in planning, a sufficiently well formulated idea of what he wants pupils to learn, which he can write down. However, that is not what he needs most in his outline. Once the objective or aim is stated the remainder of the plan will contain a brief outline of the activities in which pupils will engage in order to learn. These activities are always chosen and adapted in the light of the interests of the pupils and their needs. The outline may include an introduction or pre-test, some strong or leading questions, or warning of possible digressions. It will be helpful if it contains a summary and the summary may well be the review of the last period's plans. It is essential to include a well-thought-through assignment so that pupils will have direction for future work. The assignment is the real teaching opportunity in daily planning and teaching. Thus we see that the plan serves as the teacher's guide for effective teaching.

Unit planning as a significant approach. Unit teaching attempts to improve the organization of learning experiences into a whole. It strives to emphasize interrelationships of the outcomes of learning. The improved organization may involve content or subject-matter organization; it may involve the experience activities that have their setting in useful content areas; or it may be focused upon problem solving. Regardless of how one wishes to apply the term "unit"—whether it be subject matter or activity experience—unit teaching rests upon the principle that learning takes place most effectively when the relationship of the facts to the whole have been established.

Besides contributing to relatedness among learnings, units built around needs and interests of children have greater meaning to them. The fact that learning is taking place in a situation where the driving force is interest and the unifying force is purpose—the solution of real problems—gives totality to the whole series of related experiences.

The larger purpose of education is to affect behavior, develop personality, sharpen skills, alter attitudes and thus bring about growth. The more nearly the nature of all experiences can be related, the nearer one can achieve unification of learning and thus bring about the desired change. This then is the function of the unit approach to teaching.

Pre-planning in teaching. For purposes of keeping one's self clear in the whole area of planning, it is helpful to take limited views of its several phases—pre-planning, lesson planning, unit planning, and planning with learners. Pre-planning is the learner's guarantee that the teacher has given careful consideration to the purposes and goals so that skillful direction can be assured if there happens to be any confusion in the minds of the learners in the course of a program of action.

Pre-planning will of necessity take the teacher into the area of possible selection of activities that will be most fruitful. Closely related to this will be a careful thinking through of the materials needed in the development of a particular activity. Once topics and materials are thought through, methods that are adaptable and efficiently usable will come in for consideration. After this has been carefully worked out the logical next step will be evaluation and necessary adjustment with possible subsequent action.

Geared to all pre-planning is the consideration of attaining greatest value to each member of the group and how this will be of significance to the community. Only those purposes are valid or those activities important that are measurable in terms of adaptability to the group of learners, or acceptable to the community in which the learners live. Thus we see that pre-planning is the forerunner of teacher-pupil planning as a guarantee that all efforts on the part of teacher and pupil will be possible and valuable.

Sharing plans with learners. The teacher must assume responsibility for guidance in selecting and planning a unit because he knows the individual members of the group and must be guided by the strengths and interests of the learners. Skilled work on his part is required because the status role he plays can so dominate the entire situation that effective sharing is greatly reduced. However, he has available to him all school records needed to supply him with necessary information regarding mental maturity and home background, as well as other data that the school collects regarding its pupils.

Once the teacher has acquired all the information regarding the individual children of his group, he considers such limitations as may result from the state or local courses of study. There may be restrictive influences in the community because of the customs or prejudices of the people. Facilities provided may be quite limited.

Having considered all factors that relate to the probable success or failure of the project, the teacher is ready to begin. The teacher will understand the natural interests of the children of his particular age and grade level. The interests of the pupils often lead to projects that may be selected and activated through the energies of teacher and pupils. The skillful teacher knows that his success is dependent upon the degree of harmony between his objectives and the learner's objectives.

In its simplest interpretation, planning in the classroom is the pooling of ideas about both what is to be done and how it is to be done. It may involve reasoning why one way of doing something is preferred over another. It may involve a sharing in pointing out the reasons for doing certain things or determining the sequence of events in carrying out a particular activity.

In order for pupils to maintain an active interest in a piece of work, they must see evidence that their ideas have been fully considered and, if found valuable, have been used. Each idea must be respected, otherwise the child who finds his help rejected will cease to have concern either for participating or passing judgment on the contributions of others in his group. This is extremely important. If the teacher is to have full participation in planning, the pupils must feel that the problem is wide open to the efforts of all and that the teacher is searching sincerely for ideas that can solve the problem. They must likewise feel that the teacher is confidently honest in

are to the learner and the more nearly the teacher meets the aims of his teaching. He feels he is reaching his highest goal in teaching when he sees his pupils searching out solutions to the problems that arose from their own interests. If he finds them searching on his bookshelves, through the files, in the library, or in later years in the laboratory, he looks on with pride because he sees therein the fruits of his greatest hope—self direction through an inner urge to learn.

The antithesis of the picture just described is the child or group of children who seem not to be able to find anything worthwhile to do; the teacher must constantly be urging, guiding, or even punishing in some manner in order to get direction for the learner at all. Every teacher wishes for himself that glorious situation where he can leave the room and expect work to go on just the same, trusting leadership within the group to take care of any condition that may appear in his absence. This cannot happen where the pupil's responsibility for his own actions is either not accepted or has had no chance to be developed. The teacher must have as one of his goals the situation where children have been given an opportunity to share responsibility, where leadership has had a chance to function, and where the greatest reward is in total sharing of all that goes on and everyone respects the rights and ideas of others. When this situation exists both teacher and pupil are working at the highest level of accomplishment; good citizenship is in full operation.

Techniques of evaluation and measurement. The area of evaluation is one of heavy responsibility and importance. It should help the learner to take the next steps and open the way to further development. Unfortunately, too frequently the evaluative process does quite the opposite because it encourages undesirable competition between those who are stronger and discourages the weak student to the point where effort seems futile. Evaluation at its best solicits the cooperation of all who have any stake in the progress of the learner. These include certainly the learner himself, the teacher under whose direction he works, and the parent who bears the burden of rearing the child for a normal productive life.

Evaluation should have its focus on the learner himself without any reference to comparison with either the peers of the learner or a standard for learners of his age or grade. The practice of comparing the work of the learner to a norm results in the error of shifting attention from the strengths or weaknesses within the learner himself to attempting to extend the efforts of the learner to attain certain goals that he may not understand or even care about. In addition he takes the risk of encountering that state of discouragement and frustration which blocks even more hopelessly the path of progress.

If the teacher and the parent can join hands to measure constantly, in terms of the child's own strengths, interests, and accepted outcomes, and if the child himself has been skillfully and carefully encouraged to accept a share in determining these goals, learning can be elevated to its highest level. The way will be open to attain a climate for growth that will reach the optimum level for the learner, the parent, and the teacher. Then society will reap the reward for the confidence it bestowed on its two powerful forces—the school and the home. Evaluation must be a way and not a goal.

Responsibility for reporting to parents. Thousands upon thousands of times every day throughout America, the parent asks the teacher, "How is my child getting along?" This is an unfortunate question if the teacher and the parent have been unable to sit down together to discuss what progress means or what goals are worth while and desirable. They may have taken for granted that each understands the other when in reality they speak different languages. Many parents seem to be satisfied if the answer is favorable and many teachers are happy if the parent is not too pressing. If the teacher should ask the simple question, "What do you mean by getting along?" or if the parent should pinpoint her question by asking, "How is my child getting along with his reading?" or "Does my child work happily with other children?"—then the answer can no longer be made in generalities. Fortunate indeed are the teacher, the child, and the parent if early in their association understandings regarding outcomes, methods, and responsibilities have been mutually worked out. They then can converse without danger of discovering differences of purpose, and disappointments and frustrations because of these differences.

Schools and homes have long been searching for a language that conveys meaning. Symbols that denote success or failure have been created, used enthusiastically for a while, and finally discouragingly discarded. Even cycles in the use of these symbols have occurred. They are used for some time, thrown away, and then picked up again later because no better way of reporting has seemed feasible. This probably is best illustrated in the use of *A, B, C,* and similar marks on report cards. Both the school and the home have long known that marks of this kind have meaning only if child, parent, and teacher all know for what they stand. Even then it is hard to be objective and meaningful because each must be tempered in terms of the ability of the one being evaluated. Simply stated, an *A* for one may not be the same as an *A* for another in the same room in the next seat, yet such marks are treated by many parents as if they were as standardized as the can of peas on the grocery shelf.

It is highly probable that optimum results in getting the home to understand what is taking place at school, and in helping the teacher to know what is taking place in the home, will come about through a series of frank discussions, in which the teacher can discuss with the parent realistic expectancies in terms of the child's potential, interests, and purposes. This is not easy because it takes time, patience, and consideration. It involves a mutual respect for ideas, and is based on the integrity of each working toward a single high purpose—what is best and possible for the child. It means that the teacher will find ways to say things to the parent that the parent will not be pleased to hear, but because of the way they are said they will command respect and admiration for the teacher. It means that the parent will find ways to say things to the teacher that will be straightforward and significant, but they will be clothed in such sincerity and respect that the teacher will welcome her visit. If possible, simple exchanges of notes can be used as supplementary devices to aid in helping each to work for the best interests of the child.

Practicing self-appraisal. Just as the child is always in the state of becoming—that is, "growing"—so is the good teacher always in the state of becoming. One often hears of the teacher who has taught twenty years as contrasted with the teacher who has taught one year twenty times. The problem of one's growth depends upon his ability to really look at himself in terms of both strengths and weaknesses, in terms of both ideals and practices, and in terms of his ultimate professional goal. It involves a critical self-analysis of methods, and a constant reviewing of one's professional and personal behavior. It means that one searches within himself as to how he acts as a member of his community. One must answer to his own conscience as to his relation to his church, or at least must be aware of what society thinks about him if he fails to recognize the influence of the church as an integral force in the society he is helping to mold. The teacher must with hardened objectivity examine himself continually on how he feels toward youth. He will need to find out what the relationship is between his attitude toward youth and youth's attitude toward him. He will need to determine the relationship between knowledge in a field of subject matter and his ability to help children become educated in terms of their own knowledge in the field. He will have to think through for himself the remark that he often hears that *"He must know something in order to be able to teach something."*

Beyond this, although he may be working primarily with children of a rather limited age-grade group, he will need to examine himself constantly to determine how fully he does understand the problems in human growth from birth to age twenty, in order that he may more fully and intelligently work with the problems that he faces at any given age level. He will need to recognize the fact that he is dealing with a social being in a social world and no mere biological being in a physical world. He must examine himself to determine whether he is giving emphasis to attitudes and ideas; if he is not he must shake himself violently, because he is missing his prime function in the classroom.

He will need to see whether he deals with boys and girls in a permissive way or a compelling manner. He will need to examine his hand to see if it is a "fist" or a "kindly palm." In short he will need a constant re-examination of how he deals with people in order to help them grow fully. This is his task of self-evaluation.

Importance of professional organizations. Each person entering the field of teaching has at least two choices. He may look upon his work as primarily a means of livelihood until he can find something more to his liking, or he can enter it with his eyes focused primarily on the service he can render. He is fully aware that the service he can render will be dependent upon his skill in rendering service. Whether or not his pay will be commensurate with the service he renders may be open to question. One of the foremost problems of the members of any organization where membership is limited to those of similar skill is to elevate the importance of the organization in the esteem of general society, so that the services of its members merit remuneration comparable to the period necessary to acquire the needed skill. This places the emphasis on personal status, but one cannot lose sight of the fact that status is acquired by skill or ability, service rendered, and membership in the group.

Some groups set themselves apart not only by the training that is required for membership but by the oath that they take. The medical group, upon being granted the degree of Doctor of Medicine, take the Hippocratic oath, which embodies the duties and obligations of physicians. A similar oath setting forth the general ethical obligations of persons admitted to the practice of law is taken. The intent of such an oath would seem to be to establish in the mind of the one taking the oath the moral code under which he is obligating himself to work, and also to elevate the individual in the eyes of a possible clientele as to his integrity, morals, and ideals.

It can easily be agreed that a profession is an occupation the preparation for which involves a specialized education based upon a general liberal education. The service itself relates to skilled social service rendered for the benefit and welfare of man, either direct or implied. Upon being admitted to render such a service by certification or otherwise, those so admitted associate themselves in an organization, the purpose of which is to help the members. Thus we arrive at the point where we look upon membership in the organization as being a mark of responsibility for one's self and others of similar occupation to help improve the general welfare of the group. One easily arrives at the conclusion that he has both a social and moral obligation to such membership if he wishes to work at that particular occupation.

So it is with teachers. Each teacher has had special education to qualify him to render a service. He is certificated under the laws of the state in which he works. Immediately upon being admitted to the group he will wish to share in the respect and honor of that group. To do so he must seek membership, and share in the cost of the organization and in the labors of promoting and strengthening the organization. This association is what those engaged in teaching call an association of teachers, and comes to be known as the National Education Association, the State Teachers Association, or the Local Teachers Association. The principal function of any of these associations is to improve its members to the end that they can render a higher service to those whom they teach.

Looking ahead. The really good teacher never ceases to be a learner. It is his cherished hope that he will be able to locate in a community in which he can render a valuable service, establish a home, and become a valuable citizen. In order to do this he must be able to contact that community and have those who represent that community see that his services will be valuable.

Once contacted through the placement services of the teacher education institution he must decide that all the facilities that he feels are necessary are available and that the remuneration will be ample to provide him with the necessities of life. He knows that teachers do not get wealthy but he does feel that he should be able to live respectably and with suitable security. This can be ascertained by making a study of the salary schedule and the retirement program.

He will come to know that permanent certification is usually dependent upon a certain number of years of experience and a graduate degree. Experience and graduate work will make the teacher stronger only if he is analytical of his experience and takes graduate work to bolster his felt deficiencies. Having done this and rendered successful service he is worthy of tenure and should have the security that a continuous contract gives. If a community is unwilling to reward the able teacher by such treatment then he should go elsewhere.

The teacher who would become strong as he works sees great opportunity for helping those with whom he works. He makes stronger those who would supervise him by his cooperation and his own willingness to discuss problems in teaching with them. They learn from him; he learns from them. The teachers who are his fellow workers all benefit from the suggestions that he gives of the methods that work for him, and he in turn learns from them in the same manner. Watching each other work, finding out what is good from one's fellow teachers, is a treasured way to gain power in teaching.

Then as one becomes a mature person, citizen, parent, and leader in the community, he has the great opportunity and responsibility of making the school strong and helpful. The teacher-educated citizens are the community's strongest assets for interpretation, direction, and leadership to insure that the school may be able to serve the purpose for which it was created. This is one of citizenship's great rewards.

Beginning to work with learners. At this point it would be well to glance into the immediate future. The young teacher usually faces his first classroom experience with great apprehension and yet great enthusiasm. He has had courses in psychology, methods, general education, and academic content. He may have had many experiences as leader and may have observed learners with varying concerns. However, he may not yet be sure that he wants to be a teacher. He is going into a situation where he is not fully responsible, but he is responsible for ideas that represent his thinking about the task of teaching. He wants to succeed; his inner feeling about how well he succeeds in these early experiences will probably have a heavy bearing on what he does or becomes in the years immediately ahead.

The challenge of working in a classroom is met more calmly by a feeling of preparation and readiness. The teacher can have faith in his academic background and in his ability to work with children of the age-grade where he is assigned. His college advisor will try diligently to assign him where he is most likely to succeed and where his supervisor can be effective. He can condition his feeling by his attitude toward those whom he teaches. Simple kindliness and effort at understanding go a long way. Pupils feel the warmth that the teacher has for them and this tends to bring out the very best that is in them. They want the teacher to succeed and they are harmonious and cooperative. Success, at least from the standpoint of control, is almost sure to follow.

But success in teaching doesn't just happen. It takes hard work. An excellent start each day can be made by arriving ahead of the children and being ready to receive them. If children have purposeful things to do upon arriving their first few moments will be exceedingly effective. On the other hand, starting behind quite often upsets the time schedule for the entire day. It destroys poise, makes for irritations, and produces tensions. Teaching climate is quite unfavorable when such conditions exist. If the teacher is at ease by virtue of his own confidence, enthusiasm, and manner he has a positive effect on pupils. The stage is set for pupils to come into the classroom in a quiet, business-like manner, ready to get work done.

A cheerful greeting, a kindly remark, an inquiry about a sick member of the family, a complimentary word, an encouraging smile all make for a good start and pleasant relationships. Knowing each pupil's name early and addressing the pupil by name in a cordial manner adds strength to the teacher's relations with pupils. Quite often the young person is at a loss to know what to say or do if pupils call him by his first name. Children should be taught to exhibit the same relation that they have with the supervisor.

Sincerity and modesty are strong attributes of the good teacher. The teacher strives to be the best resource person possible, but should not be embarrassed if he finds it necessary to admit that he doesn't know the answer to a question. Children respect the teacher who frankly admits his inability in such instances and welcomes the pupil's help in sharing the responsibility for learning together. The teacher should be well equipped with basic skills necessary for the age-grade he is teaching. He cannot afford to be found lacking in skills, and should be sensitive to errors in spelling, reading, numbers, or other skills that are deemed important in the particular community where he is working.

Most of all he must come to know early just how he feels toward children, and learn to analyze the children's behavior so that he will know just how they feel toward him. Thus, feeling for children, sympathy toward their concerns, patience with their noise and flutter, and even an affection for the "silliness" of the younger generation make the person the kind of teacher that both parents and pupils can work with and honor when they refer to him as "teacher."

2

Studying children

Every teacher wishes daily for a crystal ball—a special kind of crystal ball that would reveal the causes of the characteristic behavior of certain children. The wish is most fervent in relation to those patterns of behavior which get in the way of the regular activities of the school. Stubbornness, laziness, bashfulness, deceitfulness, meanness, and indifference are some of the categories that one is tempted to use. On the positive side of the ledger are helpfulness, honesty, smartness, enthusiasm, and vigorousness, categories which are made up of desirable behavior—the kind that makes the teacher's work a joy. In either category, however, there are deep-seated and complex causes which do not consist of the child's innate qualities; behavior patterns are viewed as the result of conditions operating in the lives of children. The study of children directed toward the identification of these conditions that stand in the way of maximum potential development then becomes a significant area of the teacher's task. Once identified, some conditions can be modified by an inventive-minded teacher, and fundamental changes can be wrought in desired directions.

How a classroom teacher studies children. The actual case of a seventh grade boy who will be called John will illustrate a way of studying pupil behavior. It will show how a public school teacher's concern about behavior, his observations, his guesses as to its causes, and his verification of those guesses led to a modified reaction to the pupil. Through greater understanding of the causes of his behavior the teacher was able to serve him better.

It was noted that John did not walk into the room like other children. Sometimes he "marched" in, raising his feet high and with pronounced rhythm. Sometimes he slid into the room; at other times he came in at a near run. After he got inside the room, though, he would go to his seat in a normal fashion unless there were several boys grouped about the room talking. In this case he would try to join the group, usually without success.

During class periods he listened attentively and frequently raised his hand; his answers were almost always irrelevant. When, upon rare occasions, he did give a correct answer, he would grin and look around the room—beaming, so to speak, upon the others. He laughed easily at almost anything that was said in the class.

The above patterns of behavior were reported by the teacher as a result of observation and note-making over a period of several weeks. They were of sufficient regularity to cause the teacher concern as to their cause. From his knowledge of the general needs of children, the teacher guessed the reason to be a lack of sense of belonging, of being accepted by classmates and teachers. The following account of an incident seemed to bear out the teacher's tentative conclusion.

> At the close of school one day, I happened to be watching the children leave the building and I noticed John standing alone, hands in pockets, near the sidewalk in front of the school, looking back toward the school. The children left in twos or threes and no one spoke or seemed to notice John. Every so often he would turn around and kick at some imaginary something, then turn again toward the building. Finally, after ten minutes or so, when all the other children had gone, John gave one long final look at the school door, then, running across the street and down the hill, he went leaping on his way home. No pal had showed up to walk home with him.

The indication of need for teacher attention is revealed through a further observation: "When the class left on Wednesday evening before the Thanksgiving vacation, John was the last to leave the room and the only child to say, 'I hope you have a happy vacation.' "

This over-simplified example traces the process of studying children from the teacher's awareness of significant behavior to a reasonable certainty of its cause. The steps may be reviewed and found to be:

1. A recognition of behavior out of the ordinary as a symptom of a more deep-seated problem.

2. An accumulation of examples of the behavior causing the teacher concern.

3. The identification of patterns. The reports of John's behavior given in the beginning described patterns which were derived from the accumulation of notes on separate incidents.

4. A research of known principles of child behavior to find suggestions of a possible cause. The teacher knew from his study of child psychology that a lack of acceptance by peers and recognition by adults may be compensated by overt acts such as the things John did. He accepted this need as his best guess at the cause of John's actions.

5. Further observation to validate the assumed cause or to suggest other hypotheses. The after-school incidents offered good evidence that John was seeking satisfying relationships with peers and teacher alike.

The teacher's observations of John included some notes of a positive nature. In spite of the fact that he was a slow learner and was, in fact, repeating the seventh grade, he was never observed cheating. Neither did he attempt to have other pupils do his work for him. There was evidence that his mother helped him with his reading although she would allow him to go without wearing his glasses because he did not like to wear them. It was noted above that he was attentive in class, outwardly at least, and would try to contribute.

Acting upon a clearer insight into the causes of his behavior and observations of his positive qualities, the teacher exercised his inventiveness in an effort to provide the kinds of activities in which John could succeed. Sometimes books that were easy enough for him to read were found. If housekeeping jobs that would obviously help the group came along, John was given the opportunity to do some of them. When there were projects that involved simple construction he was given the opportunity to work with groups and thus contribute something worthwhile to the general activity. The teacher tried to find his level in skill subjects such as arithmetic and give him tasks that he could do. In this way John was able to experience feelings of success more frequently and increase his sense of well-being. Every opportunity to recognize real service was capitalized. Along with this program some counselling was done with John about the way he could best react to success. At least a start on what would be a long process of reconstructing behavior had been made.

How teachers select and organize useful information. The materials needed for simple studies of behavior may be selected by teachers from daily contacts with their pupils. Psychologists, social workers, and psychiatrists, working under favorable laboratory conditions, have blazed trails and have provided help to the busy teacher. It is not intended that the gathering of information or its interpretation by teachers will be as comprehensive as that which is possible with clinical facilities. The education of children will be improved, however, through whatever child study the teacher can find time to do. Inevitably any increase of pupil growth will be accompanied by professional growth of the teacher who invests a certain portion of his time in child study.

The kinds of information and the types of incidents which regular public school teachers have felt were significant enough to record will be illustrated below. As an aid to interpretation, experts advise some effort at classifying information as it is obtained. One group of teachers used three categories:

1. The child as a physical being
2. The child's relationships with others
3. The child as an individual personality

These teachers were influenced in setting up their pattern of organization by the excellent report of a committee headed by Daniel Prescott.[1] In the lists which follow, the incidents and types of information have been selected from several reports and consequently do not comprise a study of one particular child. The intent is to illustrate the kinds of things which the teacher may be able to observe. At the same time the first step of interpretation, the organ-

[1] American Council on Education, *Helping Teachers Understand Children* (Washington, D.C.: The Council, 1945), pp. 430-32.

ization of information under a framework, will be illustrated. Possible disagreement with the placement of some items will only illustrate the impossibility of classifying all information into neat compartments. Indeed, some items ought to be placed in more than one:

1. The child as a physical being

I.Q. 79, overweight (common condition in family).

Sinus difficulty—seldom free of cold during winter.

Quick of movement and response.

Each task finished quickly. Eager to read aloud; volunteers in class but answers not very accurate.

Volunteered to wash boards—did a good job.

Eats well in cafeteria; doesn't seem to have many food prejudices.

Is never still a minute, and is very loud. He waves his arms and shrieks.

He has sparkling black eyes and black hair—a clean attractive child.

His mother says he has what the doctor calls "battle fatigue."

He wakes up in the night and cries. She asked that I be patient with him.

2. The child's relationships with others

Parents: loving but careless; spend money for entertainment, neglect necessities; food, sufficient in quantity but poorly balanced; father, a railroad section man.

Child: fourth of six children, three of school age.

Wants own way in games; plays with small group of intimates.

Liked by other children, friendly, takes part in all play.

Volunteered to learn verse to substitute for ill member of the group.

Took care of small child for visitor during lunch hour.

Bought candy for a friend.

Divided clay with three first graders during intermission so they could share in her play.

Readily subordinated her choice to that of group without loss of enjoyment.

Parents and children do things as a family unit—attend school functions and church together.

Went with other boys to gymnasium instead of staying in room at noon. Stood around edge of play, bounced basketball back when it came out of bounds.

Father a farmer. I had occasion to interview him. He didn't know ages, size of clothing, or color of eyes of two children or wife.

Mother pleasant, shy, neat.

Related obviously untrue story (attempt to gain importance in eyes of other children).

Told involved story of visit from cousin and sleigh riding. Because I listen and appear interested he favors me with considerable attention during intermission.

Sociogram [a chart showing persons one would prefer as friends, partners in an activity, etc.] shows two picked from room, one of them a neighbor boy and the other seated near him. The third boy he picked is about four years older, on the basketball squad and very aggressive, actually somewhat of a discipline problem in junior high school.

3. The child as an individual personality

Tomboyish, loud.

School attendance regular, not punctual in getting to room after bell at rest or noon periods.

Volunteers for duties, happy.

Never complains, though seldom free of cold in winter.

Picked up crying child on playground, took her to rest room, bathed her face and got her to smile.

Tried out for yell leader, was defeated. Took defeat without show of envy or resentment and entered into yells quite happily.

Frequently acts as spokesman for a group of pupils who are too shy to ask or doubtful of the answer to requests.

Takes part in play period but soon drops out of games.

Copied arithmetic work from neighbors.

Lost library book—said someone took it from desk. Search made and book found in his desk. I do not suspect dishonesty but rather that he jumps into self-justification as protection because of the kind of discipline he gets at home.

Tim will not sing before the class.

Today Tim said, "Mrs. A——, don't you think I'm doing better?" He wasn't, except that at least he had the desire to read, which is something!

How the teacher summarizes information about a child.
In order to make it clear how both recorded and incidental information are drawn together, the report of a classroom teacher about a child has been analyzed. The left-hand column of parts two and three are generalizations stated by the teacher. The column at the right contains anecdotal reports of behavior leading to these generalizations. Some general information is appropriately given in part one.

1. The child as a physical being

I.Q. and achievement low.

Frequent colds. Tonsils and adenoids removed recently.

Overweight—common to father's family.

Clothing of good plain quality—clean when she gets to school —gets disheveled quickly.

Youngest of three motherless children—reared by well-meaning but indulgent aunt.

Father, a farmer—rather prosperous, thrifty.

2. The child's relationships with others

Stubborn; not well-liked by associates; irritable.	Statement of classmates, "Sue likes to play but won't work. If she makes up her mind, she's stubborn as a mule."
	Was peevish when game she wanted to play was not selected by group.
	Has few friends; keeps to a few chosen companions (see segment of friendship sociogram). Shows Sue as a member of a clique of four, and chosen by two as best friends.
Rude; greedy about food; does not share, even with sister.	When a child in the last row asked for a reversal in the order in which they go to the lunchroom, Sue objected rudely, although the others took it as fun. When I did allow the reversed order she said she wouldn't eat, but she did.
	During her illness, children sent her valentines, flowers, and a magazine. When asked if she got them

she answered, "Sure, I got them; what did you think?" No thanks or expression of appreciation.

Got two candy bars, ate both greedily, not even offering to share with sister who is quite opposite in attitudes.

Grumbled when asked to wait until another group was served.

3. The child as an individual personality

Can't or won't concentrate.	Disturbs others; always turning around; does poor work; slow to get work in and then only partially complete.
Avoids all extra duties.	Almost never volunteers to take part.
	Cheats if pressed to improve work.
	Agreed to put on skit; next day asked to be excused from it.
	Said she would help clean erasers; "forgot" it.
	Scattered papers about desk—responded reluctantly when reminded to pick them up.
Resents her sister in next grade who is much prettier, slim, and well-liked by others.	Sister was overheard to say, "Oh Sue is like the _____'s (father's family); I'm like the _____'s (dead mother's family).
	Overheard Sue tell another pupil, "I hit Alice (the sister) in the back with a baseball yesterday." Her companion asked why she did it and she answered, "Oh, she thinks she's so smart!"

The teacher has drawn certain conclusions about Sue on the basis of the things she has said and done over a period of time. These incidents did not occur in the order presented in the summary. It is probable that other similar incidents went by unrecorded. The teacher seems justified in concluding that Sue's behavior reveals a pattern of stubbornness and irritability. Likewise there is lack of consideration of others and a tendency to be selfish. These qualities may account for the limited acceptance shown by her friendship sociogram, although there is acceptance in a very small group.

Conclusions relating to work habits are likewise supported by recorded incidents. Sue evidently isn't a good worker and shows some evidence of not wanting to work. So far the conclusions only describe behavior patterns. There is nothing in the information up to this point to suggest causes. In the conclusion that she resents a more attractive sister, however, is a clue to the cause of part of the trouble.

Among the things that Sue wants and strives for are the common satisfactions needed by all persons. She needs self-respect, affection, and respect from others, and a sense of belonging in her peer group. Sue is no different from other people in these regards. However, she finds herself falling short by comparison with her sister. The sister's remark suggests that Sue has been made aware of her shortcomings in the family generally. Failing to find love and affection in her home has been a blow to the foundations of her self-respect and self-confidence. She has attached herself to a very small circle of three other girls for such mutual security as they can provide.

The teacher seeking causes of Sue's behavior has one possible clue provided by knowledge of basic human needs. That clue is her need for acceptance and affection both within and without the family. If the teacher is reasonably sure that this deficiency exists, it suggests one approach in helping Sue; the teacher can at least notice her from day to day and let her know that he is doing so. Opportunities to afford minor successes may be capitalized upon when the teacher is fully aware of their importance. Time may provide opportunity to help the girl with her physical appearance. Knowledge of her friendships with even a small number of girls makes it possible to allow them to work together at times, thus adding to the pleasure of the total school experience. Likewise, the teacher may find it possible to help the family accept Sue by letting them know he accepts her with all her faults. Thus, another long process of rehabilitation will get under way.

The above materials represent an admitted over-simplification of the process of identifying behavior patterns and seeking causes. Likewise, the emphasis has been upon observations made by the teacher as he works with pupils day by day. There are other sources of information of a useful kind, some of which will be pointed out later. The method of reporting incidents illustrated above deserves some further comment, however.

Making accurate observations of the behavior of pupils is not an easy task. Not every incident can be recorded and not every one is significant. Recorded observations should not be undertaken for more than two or three pupils at a time. First, it is necessary to select the incidents about which reports will be written. Only those that seem to have possible future significance should be selected.

It is not easy to describe just what was said and done by a pupil without including some judgment and evaluation. If the teacher wishes really to know a child as a basis for doing something for him, he cannot begin by forming the judgments which he should normally reach *after* his study. He may be helped by carefully identifying

Student preparations for social events offer opportunities to observe emerging leadership and important behavior.

Courtesy of *The Muncie Star*

whatever preconceptions he has formed to help him reduce the danger of bias in his later findings. This is followed by systematically writing down from day to day just what was done and said in apparently significant incidents, being careful not to evaluate or judge. After this process has gone on for a time and an effort has been made to include information on many areas of the child's life, the several facts that have been obtained are reviewed to see whether any patterns are present. If previously formed hypotheses about the child's behavior are then brought out, the factual data may serve to validate or refute these hypotheses. Practice of this technique will help the teacher to avoid erroneous conclusions in other instances than those under study because of his increased sensitivity to superficial evidence.

Other methods of studying children. The preliminary use of the school records as an initial step in getting acquainted with students has been suggested in an earlier section. Helpful facts will be found in them that should not be overlooked. Wiles suggests numerous other devices which will contribute to the desired end.[2] For certain groups, first-day activities of the get-acquainted type are recommended. Activities and games are useful both in yielding information and in creating a relaxed atmosphere, permitting the teacher to make better observations of individuals and group relationships than would otherwise be possible. Depending upon the maturity of the group, discussions or reactions to community and world events and chats that center around hobbies and interests may be incorporated in these first-day events and at later times. As the teacher works with the group, indirect questionnaires may be used to supplement the information available in the records or obtainable in conversations, playground and classroom observations, home visits, casual meetings with parents, and other similar sources. Observation of the free choices a pupil makes tends to verify some of the teacher's initial conclusions. The things the children do creatively in the way of stories told or written, the pictures they draw, or the projects they construct using different media are valuable supplements to the other types of information in getting to know pupils.

[2] Kimball Wiles, *Teaching for Better Schools* (Englewood Cliffs, N.J.: Prentice-Hall, Inc., 1952), pp. 270-73.

Group meetings of teachers. Teachers' meetings have been used for many years to try to find ways of coping with general problems of pupil behavior. In more recent times, deans and guidance directors have used the plan of calling meetings of teachers for the purpose of pooling information and developing suggestions for helping certain pupils. The plan has a place in the program of a school that is emphasizing child study.

In a meeting of the kind suggested above, one person—a teacher, dean, counsellor, or principal—presents the problem and the information he has about a particular child or group. This presentation is followed by contributions of other teachers familiar with the situation. The meeting is then opened for discussion of the problem and for suggestions of possible ways of working with it. Out of the discussion a plan is devised that each person agrees to implement in his particular relationship.

Prescott points out that there are two advantages of such meetings.[3] The more obvious advantage, of course, is the additional information that is brought to bear upon the problem through pooling by all the teachers. The second advantage lies in the pooling of psychological knowledge possessed by various members of the group. The pooling of information not only suggests possible explanations and solutions but also serves as in-service teacher re-education, a necessary part of the program.

Some helpful instruments. The teacher will have been made aware during his professional training of numerous aids developed for use in studying and guiding student behavior. Many of these devices are useful, if their limitations are fully realized and if they are looked upon as aids and not as infallible measures.

One of the interesting devices used to reveal some of the relations of individuals within the group is the sociogram. In brief, the sociogram is a chart showing graphically the choices each person makes within a group indicating those with whom he would prefer to be associated. For example, each pupil may be asked to indicate the two people whom he would most prefer as partners in a class project, in a game, in dancing, or on a picnic. Any choice related to the type of attribute the teacher wishes to have revealed may be used.

[3] American Council on Education, *Helping Teachers Understand Children,* p. 165.

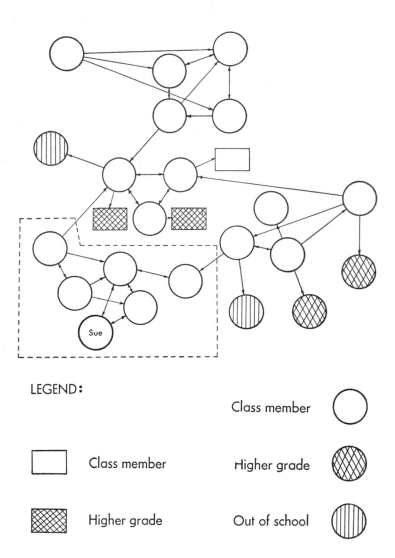

LEGEND:

Class member ◯

⬜ Class member   Higher grade 🔵

▦ Higher grade   Out of school 🔵

Friendship Sociogram, Grades 5 and 6

(Boys are represented by rectangles, girls by circles.)

Not only does such a chart reveal the persons who possess the attribute under study, but it may show the social aspirations of certain other pupils as well. An indication of mutual acceptance is also possible. Since choices will vary according to the situation, the results of the sociogram should be followed up by the teacher for checking and interpretation.

Another device is the problem checklist, useful in determining some of the concerns of children and youth. Such checklists are constructed by asking many pupils to write down, under proper conditions, the problems which concern them most at the time. If the results are to be used in constructing a checklist the problems are obtained from as representative a group of children of that age as possible. The problems that are found to be typical are then listed and a device for checking is worked out. The checklist is a helpful device, providing the teacher with tentative hypotheses and providing the pupil with a valuable experience in responding. The pupil should have the opportunity to talk over the checklist after it is completed, and the teacher should give as much help as possible in interpreting the experience.

Problem checklists have another use that ought not to be overlooked: they tend to help isolate the developmental tasks that are uppermost in the minds of the pupils of a particular class or school at a particular time. Different teachers will find different ways to contribute to the solution of these problems, thereby effecting curriculum adjustment of the most vital kind. For the faculty group that is looking for ways to improve the curriculum, these indications of current concerns have much to offer.

Observing group behavior. The teacher will be aided in his efforts to know children by following up group interaction as best he can. One of the first things to observe is what happens when the direct control of the teacher is replaced by self-control of the pupils. On occasions the supervisor will be called out of the room. The situation under the teacher's direction will reveal the ability of the pupils to control themselves. On other occasions, when study is to be done, the extent to which the teacher can free himself from direct control while assisting various pupils and small groups with their work is an indication of self-discipline.

If the sociogram has been used, it will be interesting to observe what behavior bears out the patterns on the chart. Look for pupils who pair off day after day. Notice also children who seem to avoid each other. It is instructive to note the effect certain pupils have upon one another. This is often observable in informal discussions of a point of common interest, during corridor sessions between classes, and in like situations.

Closely related to the observations suggested above is the apparent effect of the teacher upon the group and that of the group upon the teacher. There is often an attitude of expectancy pending the arrival of the teacher and evidence of warmth and acceptance when he does arrive. Children often reveal their feelings about the teacher by teasing, and the pupil-teacher relationship is revealed by the confidence they seem to feel that their teasing will be accepted in the spirit in which it is given. Evidence of an attitude of mutual understanding and respect will be present in the better situations.

Studying home backgrounds. Rounding out the program of knowing pupils with information about their home situations is strongly recommended. Some schools make provision in the teacher's schedule for this work, while others encourage the use of afterschool hours. It may be said that a child is never the same after the teacher meets his parents. This is because the teacher's interpretation of the child's behavior will be modified, usually in favor of the child. Likewise, the child will feel a little closer to the teacher because of this acquaintance.

Teachers working on special problems of behavior find it especially helpful to know as much about the home as possible. The extent of tragedy borne by children of all ages because of home conditions is common knowledge of teachers who know some of the intimate facts of their pupils' family relationships. Only as the school acquires a reputation for keeping the confidence of its clients for professional uses will the causes of many disturbed conditions be revealed.

Even with small children it is not always easy to devise ways of visiting the home and meeting the parents. One instance concerned a small boy whose learning rate was slow. The teacher, seeking to find ways of adjusting the work to his needs and interests, had tried for several months to get an easy acceptance from him for a home call. The child was apparently reluctant to have the teacher contact his mother. Finally, he came to school excited over the arrival of a litter of puppies. By a little careful display of interest the teacher managed to gain an invitation to see the puppies. In this particular case there was nothing in the home situation that need have worried the boy. There was illness and lack of material wealth. However, there was pride, cleanliness, and love, to a degree that the family situation was not a deterrent to school work. The case illustrates the tact that is sometimes necessary in dealing with the child when the home is to be contacted. As a rule this contact is not difficult before junior high school. The development of home contacts at the secondary level is still another matter. The complication here is caused by the children's maturity and by the division of their time among the teachers of several departments.

Planning home visits involves tact and honest consideration of the other person. The problem will vary with the community and the kind of school practices to which it has become accustomed. It is as much a reflection on the school as upon the parent if the first question is, "What has Johnny done now?" It simply means that the school has not made a business of contacting parents and vice versa.

If a telephone is available it is good procedure to call to arrange a convenient time for a short visit to get acquainted and talk about ways teacher and parent can be mutually helpful. Then, too, a note may be sent home and the parent's reply returned by the child. In some ways this is better because it makes the child a part of the whole procedure. Some parents will be a little timid about meeting the teacher because of the possible difference in educational experience and real or imagined cultural accomplishment. The home may not be attractive; it may be definitely otherwise. For all of these reasons, the very least one can do is remove as many sources of embarrassment as possible. To call at a pre-arranged time, when the family can be at its presentable best, is a matter of kindness as well as convenience.

The purpose of the visit is to establish a friendly contact that will enable the teacher and parents to do the most they can for the welfare of the child. This is the sole purpose of the call, and as long as it is evident that this is its purpose there is no cause for uneasiness on the part of either teacher or parent. It is best not to take notes or mark checklists during the call. If the parent is reticent, avoid the use of questions. Let the parent do most of the talking and asking questions. The techniques of home visitation are pretty much contained in the Golden Rule. At the first opportunity following the visit, the teacher should make notes of all the pertinent observations he can recall for later study.

Prescott listed several outcomes for teachers resulting from home visitation.[4] Some of the more significant things included teacher recognition of individual personalities of parents; learning the kinds and degrees of expectancies which parents impose upon particular children; observing the different ways employed by parents in dealing with boys and girls; learning more of the effects of temporary family disturbances on the behavior of children; observing the kinds of emotional ties that unite the family; and learning about the different sets of values and ways of behaving of different groups of families. Each teacher owes it to the children in his charge to be sufficiently familiar with the community to hold the above understandings. The resulting increments in teaching effectiveness, multiplied by the number of children benefited through this added understanding, adds weight to former pleas for widened horizons for teachers.

In analyzing one's reactions to children there are two points that must not be overlooked. In the first place, nearly every child comes to school as a bright child in the eyes of his parents. Teachers who are parents can appreciate this point more easily than college students who do not have children of school age. It is helpful to picture as far as possible the parent-child relationship in trying to perform the full duty of the teacher. No matter how unattractive or unpromising the child may seem, he has parents who, in their own way, cherish that child and have great faith in him. That faith of a well-meaning parent in the potential of a child must not be underestimated.

The second point growing out of the family relationship which must ever be respected by the teacher is the child's deep devotion to his parents. Little children, uninhibited by social comparisons, frequently express this pride in the most ordinary parent. As chil-

[4] American Council on Education, *Helping Teachers Understand Children*, pp. 42-66.

dren grow up they become more conscious of the clothing, the automobiles, the business associations, and the social and community prominence of parents. Nevertheless, there is a loyalty to parents for their own sakes which must be regarded by the teacher as he makes up his mind about children.

How the teacher interprets available information. Teachers study children in many ways. Their observations and gathered information help them to know their pupils. The whole purpose is to enable them to work more effectively with children. Teachers recognize child study as a function to which a share of their time is regularly allotted. However, information does not become assimilated in the blood stream of teaching-learning experiences benefiting children until it has been processed. The processing that is required is accomplished by teachers who strive to find in their professional knowledge clues to understanding their own pupils' problems. The cases of John and Sue early in this chapter illustrated this process of attempting to understand children's behavior as a first step in dealing more effectively with them.

The job of interpretation involves making preliminary guesses at the reasons for extraordinary behavior patterns and problems of learning as they are identified. The teacher turns to his knowledge of psychological principles as the source of such guesses or hypotheses. As the facts about a particular child are examined against such principles, cause and effect relationships often emerge. It will be recalled in the case of Sue that facts about the family relationship fitted together with the principles of need for affection, self-respect, and peer status in such a way as to explain part, if not all, of her behavior.

Educational psychology provides the teacher with many principles of child development and learning which may provide clues to the understanding he seeks. Some of these essential principles will be reviewed here as aids to interpretation of what has been learned about children.

Some psychological needs and developmental tasks. The study of needs is the study of motivation, of drives, of urges to act, in human beings. A comprehensive listing of needs is impossible in the scope of the present chapter. It is the purpose of this section to recall some of the general categories of need, for the teacher's use in forming hypotheses as to causes of behavior in his pupils.

The study is complicated by the fact that there is a progression of needs associated with development. The needs of an infant are at least different and possibly fewer than those of an adolescent. As development progresses, needs emerge and change in their expression and satisfaction.

Further complications are found in the orientations and purposes of authorities who have attempted to write down the needs of people. From one point of view, needs may be considered as "built-in" features of an organism. Hunger is an expression of need in the physiological organism of human beings and animals alike. Protection against the elements and natural enemies is another example of a physical requirement. Some psychologists, including Ruch, consider motivation as related to basic drives resulting from needs of the body for ". . . food (including a variety of specific substances), water, air, rest, sleep, warmth from cold, cooling when hot, relief from pain and relief from visceral tensions."[5] Motivation also finds its source, according to this group of authorities, in appetites and aversions. Among this group of motivating influences is the sexual appetite, which is credited with great force. Some other appetites include sounds having musical quality, colors in pleasing array, tastes, and smells. Aversions may be roughly identified as opposites of appetites. Drives, appetites, and aversions are "built-in" sources of behavior.

There are many other kinds of needs which human beings experience growing out of their development in a cultural environment. It is probable that many forms of need are founded in those "built-in" qualities suggested above. The exact relationship and manner in which the needs develop is not clear in all cases. For practical purposes it is not necessary to trace this process of derivation. The teacher has to be aware of what some of the more common needs of growing people are, for uses stated earlier.

In addition to the physiological needs described above, Prescott listed two other categories that have seemed to hold up quite well.[6]

[5] Floyd L. Ruch, *Psychology and Life*, 3rd ed. (New York: Scott, Foresman and Company, 1948), p. 125.

[6] Daniel A. Prescott, *Emotion and the Educative Process* (Washington, D.C.: American Council on Education, 1938), pp. 110 f.

One category is referred to as the "social or status needs." As the term implies, these needs have to do with the individual's relations to other people. Another category is described as "ego or integrative needs." Such needs have to do with the environmental situation with which he comes in contact and his experience resulting from such contact. The teacher will realize, of course, that there are interrelationships among needs which make it impossible to classify them fully.

More recently, Eiserer and Corey have stated, ". . . The most important things to the individual are his needs, first to preserve himself from harm, and secondly, to improve his perception of himself as worthy and important."[7] These authors seem to carry forward the idea implied in Prescott's last group of needs that the environmental situation has an important part in the individual's feeling and expression of a need. They emphasize further the matter of the situation as it looks to the individual as causing behavior when they say, "Our point is that the interplay of internal need and perceived external forces determines behavior at a given moment."[8]

Low expresses this same functional view of needs in the following manner: "It is reasonable . . . to consider needs as an expression of the interactions between the individual-with-his-feelings-of-need and society-with-its-imposition-of-tasks."[9]

The consideration of needs in the light of the above quotations shows their relationship to the conception of developmental tasks, a very helpful source of hypotheses about behavior causes. Havighurst, the originator of the concept of developmental tasks, says, "A developmental task is midway between an individual need and a societal demand. It partakes of the nature of both."[10]

For the practical purposes of the teacher a brief review of the more common needs usually listed as such and the more frequently mentioned developmental tasks is offered below. For greater understanding and special uses additional reading is suggested in the bibliography.

[7] Paul E. Eiserer and Stephen M. Corey, in *Adapting the Secondary School Program to the Needs of Youth*, 52nd Yearbook of the National Society for the Study of Education (Chicago: The University of Chicago Press, 1953), I, 51.
[8] *Ibid.*
[9] Camilla M. Low, in *ibid.*, p. 25.
[10] Robert J. Havighurst, *Human Development and Education* (New York: Longmans, Green & Co., 1953), p. 332.

Psychological needs:

1. Need for love and affection.

2. Need for belonging, for acceptance and understanding from others, for affiliation with family and peer groups. These first two groups of needs add up to a need for security.

3. Need for approval, for recognition of status, for attention.

4. Need for self-respect, for a sense of worth to his group, his community, a sense of being valued for what he is.

5. Need for freedom to learn, for a climate suited to trial and error without fear of punishment, rejection, or ridicule.

Developmental tasks. A precise definition of the developmental task has been postponed to this point. According to Havighurst, who has brought the concept into wide use, "A developmental

Many skills are required in a modern school to provide young people with opportunities for full self-realization.

task is a task which arises at or about a certain period in the life of the individual, successful achievement of which leads to his happiness and to success with later tasks, while failure leads to unhappiness in the individual, disapproval by the society, and difficulty with later tasks."[11] The fact that needs and developmental tasks alike progress with maturity and cultural influences has been mentioned in earlier sections. As a means of further help to the teacher, two lists, one for later childhood and one for adolescence as given by Havighurst, are given here for convenient reference.

Developmental tasks of middle childhood:

1. Learning physical skills necessary for ordinary games.
2. Building wholesome attitudes toward one's self as a growing organism.
3. Learning to get along with age-mates.
4. Learning an appropriate masculine or feminine social role.
5. Developing fundamental skills in reading, writing, and calculating.
6. Developing concepts necessary for everyday living.
7. Developing conscience, morality, and a scale of values.
8. Achieving personal independence.
9. Developing attitudes toward social groups and institutions.[12]

Developmental tasks of adolescence:

1. Achieving new and more mature relations with age-mates of both sexes.
2. Achieving a masculine or feminine social role.
3. Accepting one's physique and using the body effectively.
4. Achieving emotional independence of parents and other adults.
5. Achieving assurance of economic independence.
6. Selecting and preparing for an occupation.
7. Preparing for marriage and family life.
8. Developing intellectual skills and concepts necessary for civic competence.
9. Desiring and achieving socially responsible behavior.
10. Acquiring a set of values and an ethical system as a guide to behavior.[13]

[11] *Ibid.*, p. 2.
[12] *Ibid.*, pp. 25-41.
[13] *Ibid.*, pp. 111-58.

These are the tasks which face nearly all children in growing to adulthood. They are helpful reminders to teachers that these educational goals must receive their fair share of attention among the school's objectives. Obviously, not all of the education of youth toward the accomplishment of these tasks can be provided at school, but the conditions for accomplishing them may be improved through the controlled environment which the school provides. Modification of curriculum content following study of the tasks has been carried out in some schools. If the teacher will allow himself to be reminded of these generalized areas wherein youth find themselves obligated to achieve, he will find many opportunities to lend a hand to individuals and groups that might otherwise be overlooked.

SUMMARY

By practicing the suggestions in the discussion of studying children the teacher's professional competence can be enhanced. The acceptance of certain premises is assumed. First, that pupils have reasons for the things that they do and say, related to the situation as they see it. Second, that the identification of these reasons for acting, when possible, will make for more effective teaching. Third, that behavior patterns rather than single incidents are the best objects of study.

The teacher should have a sense of increasing competence in the following areas of teaching as a result of practicing the things that have been suggested:

1. The ability to view each child's behavior objectively and to select incidents that have significance.

2. Efficiency in making objective records of the things children say and do.

3. Use of an increasing number of supplementary tools for accumulating helpful information, including office records, conversations with pupils, home visits, sociograms, checklists, and group meetings of teachers.

4. Ability to make simple summaries of information about a pupil so as to facilitate interpretation.

5. Use of principles of educational psychology as a source of hypotheses about children's behavior.

6. Ability to see more clearly what the situation demands of the pupil when viewed from his position.

7. Greater skill in selecting and carrying out teaching-learning activities as a result of better understanding of children's problems.

PROBLEMS

1. *Arrange to observe a group of children regularly for several weeks. Select two or three pupils with whom you will plan to work closely. Describe in objective terms the things they do and say, being careful to select significant incidents and to avoid forming judgments prematurely. At the end arrange incidents to support conclusions reached on basis of observations.*

2. *Plan with your supervisor to secure data from a group of pupils on their three best friends. Construct a sociogram from these data and write your interpretation of the sociogram. Follow the indications of the sociogram through for verification or change.*

3. *Procure a copy of a problem inventory such as the Mooney Problem Checklist or Science Research Associates Youth Inventory. Go through it giving your own reactions. Write up a summary of the results as if it had been done by pupil "X." What would be your next step in dealing with "X"?*

4. *Arrange to use the school record on a pupil whom you are studying and list (using code, not names) the facts which might help explain his response to school or his learning problems.*

5. *Arrange a meeting of teachers who have regular contact with one or more of the pupils whose behavior you are studying. Exchange and record incidents in order to pool information and psychological knowledge. List possible causes of behavior together with psychological principles that suggest these hypotheses.*

6. *Seek an opportunity to visit a parent-teacher meeting, preferably involving parents of pupils with whom you work. Talk with parents and later recall and write up the things you talked about, how you felt during the interview, and how well you think you did as a teacher.*

7. *Read the two references in the NSSE 52nd Yearbook listed in the bibliography. Write up what you would look for in a situation (a real situation if you have made such an observation) that would color a pupil's behavior because of his interpretation of it.*

BIBLIOGRAPHY

American Council on Education, *Helping Teachers Understand Children.* Washington, D.C.: The Council, 1945.

Bernard, Harold W., *Psychology of Learning and Teaching.* New York: McGraw-Hill Book Company, Inc., 1954. Chaps. iv, v, and vi.

Eiserer, Paul E., and Stephen M. Corey, "How Youth Learn to Meet Their Needs," in *Adapting the Secondary School Program to the Needs of Youth,* Part I, 52nd Yearbook, National Society for the Study of Education. Chicago: The University of Chicago Press, 1953.

Havighurst, Robert J., *Human Development and Education.* New York: Longmans, Green, & Company, 1953.

Hilgard, Ernest R., and David H. Russell, "Motivation in School Learning," in *Learning and Instruction,* Part I, 49th Yearbook, National Society for the Study of Education. Chicago: The University of Chicago Press, 1950. Chap. ii.

Low, Camilla M., "Determining the Nature of the Needs of Youth," in *Adapting the Secondary School Program to the Needs of Youth,* Part I, 52nd Yearbook, National Society for the Study of Education. Chicago: The University of Chicago Press, 1953.

Mooney, Ross L., and Leonard V. Gordon, *The Mooney Problem Checklists* (1950 revisions). New York: The Psychological Corporation, 1950.

Ohlsen, Merle M., *Guidance.* New York: Harcourt, Brace & Company, Inc., 1955. Chap. ii.

Prescott, Daniel H., *Emotion and the Educative Process.* Washington, D.C.: American Council on Education, 1938.

Remmers, H. H., and Benjamin Shimberg, *SRA Youth Inventory.* Chicago: Science Research Associates, 1949.

Ruch, Floyd L., *Psychology and Life,* 3rd ed. New York: Scott, Foresman and Company, 1948. Chaps. iv and v.

Warters, Jane, *Techniques of Counseling.* New York: McGraw-Hill Book Company, Inc., 1954. Chap. xii.

Wiles, Kimball, *Teaching for Better Schools.* Englewood Cliffs, N.J.: Prentice-Hall, Inc., 1952. Chap. xii.

3

Working with the community

The nature of the teacher's work places him in the dual role of public servant and citizen. He renders community service as a public employee. When he leaves the school at the end of the day, he carries with him many professional responsibilities; however, all other professional people do likewise. He lives in a community and is not exempt from responsibilities as a citizen. Teachers in general are community-minded and perform many services; however, young teachers often find themselves confused, and through misunderstanding resist normal participation in community life. A teacher can lend assistance in any type of activity he prefers. A change to something not related to classroom teaching is often satisfying. The community generally appreciates one type of participation in community life as much as another. The fact that the professional educator does share his talents along with other citizens toward community betterment is the important thing. The teacher gains as much as he gives through such participation.

Teacher competences in community relations. One of the most exciting opportunities offered tomorrow's teacher lies in learning the skills needed to work with the community. School-community relationships are becoming matters of serious study and are of the utmost importance in the total operation of teaching. These important matters clamor for a reasonable share of the teacher's time. Just as a redistribution of the teacher's working hours was urged for child study in the preceding chapter, so now a plea is entered for a further redistribution of time and energy to provide for working with parents and laymen on school problems. Many new and growing competences are needed.

A list of competences toward which the growing teacher works will clarify the kinds of things which he may be called upon to do, and suggest areas in which to begin the development of skills and techniques that will continue to grow throughout his professional career. Further discussion and development of each of these competences will be the objective of this chapter. The list follows:

1. Sensing the way people in a community feel about the school, its purposes, and achievements.

2. Making informal observations to learn about the community.

3. Using school records to learn about the community.

4. Locating persons and places in the community to use as resources in teaching.

5. Talking to people who have questions about the school.

6. Conducting group discussions with parents and laymen to improve communication between school and community.

7. Using special programs to help the community understand teaching.

8. Recognizing opportunities for the school to provide needed community service.

9. Lending professional assistance to the program planning of other worthy community institutions.

10. Establishing good personal relations with pupils and their parents.

11. Communicating with homes through daily contacts with pupils.

12. Using teacher-parent conferences in teaching.

13. Taking an effective part in organized parent-teacher activities.

14. Using mass media of communication in teaching.

15. Fostering good personal relations with other teachers and all school employees.

Before going further into the detailed development of these

abilities, it may be well to consider briefly what we mean by a community.

Meaning of community. A layman intuitively defines a community in terms of a group of people or a geographical area with somewhat indistinct boundaries. One dictionary defines a community thus: "A number of people having common ties or interests and living in the same locality."[1] Another definition is found in the Dictionary of Education: "A group living in one locality or region under the same culture and having a common geographical focus for their major activities."[2]

These definitions are satisfactory in a general sense, but lack the precision, for teachers' purposes, found in the Cooks' definition:

> *Community: A Definition*
> 1. A population aggregate
> 2. Inhabiting a delimitable, contiguous area
> 3. Sharing a historical heritage
> 4. Possessing a set of basic service institutions
> 5. Participating in a common mode of life
> 6. Conscious of its unity
> 7. Able to act in a corporate way[3]

A school community is generally made up of an attendance unit having definite boundaries and incorporated under the laws in such fashion as to carry on the necessary business of education. Some of the characteristics implied in the phrase "integrated through common experience" seem to be in the embryonic stage in a number of our more rapidly growing suburban neighborhoods. Even here, however, integration does occur around common types of work, similar educational and cultural backgrounds, similar religious practices, and common goals for themselves and their children.

In any community many differences are apparent in the behavior of its individual members. As a group in a geographical area becomes a community, however, a certain portion of its members' behavior has to do with their living together. In this connection Brook-

---

[1] *Thorndike-Barnhart Comprehensive Desk Dictionary*, ed. by Clarence L. Barnhart (Garden City, N.Y.: Doubleday & Company, Inc., 1951), p. 181.

[2] Carter E. Good, ed., *Dictionary of Education* (New York: McGraw-Hill Book Company, Inc., 1945), p. 86.

[3] Lloyd Cook and Elaine F. Cook, *A Sociological Approach to Education* (New York: McGraw-Hill Book Company, Inc., 1950), pp. 48-49.

over points out, "Only that portion that has reference to the common life can properly be designated as community behavior."[4] The teacher, therefore, is careful to recognize behavior of individuals or small groups that really does not have any implications for the common life, when formulating opinions about a community.

Sensing the way people feel about school. An automobile trip of some length will provide varied evidence of the way people feel about their schools. External observation of the age, shape, and size of school buildings and the care of school grounds is an indication, though not infallible proof, of the concerns of the people for the education of their children. A look inside at the operation of the school is, of course, a better way of finding out what the program is really like. The average teacher going to a new community increases his chances of success as he learns what people think about religion, politics, controversial issues, government and world affairs, sex education in schools, modern teaching methods, and the proper content of curriculum. The 1954 Yearbook of the Association for Supervision and Curriculum Development states the problem as follows: "Although a teacher may create a beautiful physical environment to bring understanding and skills to the classroom, the children's learning is conditioned as much or more by the world outside the four walls of the classroom as by that within."[5] That is, the teacher takes into consideration the influences and attitudes to which the child is subjected outside the school as they relate to his learning. These serve also as a base for predicting the response which he may expect from the homes.

It is not uncommon for community expectations for education to differ considerably from the things that the teacher has learned through previous experience or from his training in the teachers' colleges and universities. The recognition that community beliefs differ from his own influences the manner in which the teacher will go about the job.

The importance of sensing the community's feeling about edu-

[4] Wilbur B. Brookover, *A Sociology of Education* (New York: The American Book Company, 1955), p. 372.

[5] Association for Supervision and Curriculum Development, National Educational Association, *Creating a Good Environment for Learning* (Washington, D.C.: The Association, 1954), p. 150.

cation is pointed out in a survey conducted by *Life* magazine, which states:

> In this welter of indecision one thing is certain: today's parent is inclined to feel that the school, good or bad, is just as responsible as he is for most of the upbringing of his child. In the old days it was felt that the schools' job was to teach reading, writing, arithmetic, and little else; but now the surveys show some ninety per cent of the general public feel that it is also the schools' business to train the whole child—even to the extent of teaching him honesty, fair play, consideration of others, and a sense of right and wrong. Most of them feel that sex should be taught in the schools. And in rural farm areas and in the south a majority feels that the schools should go on to teach religion as well.[6]

A generalization of this type may be drawn from a nation-wide survey, but it is necessary to determine the extent of such a belief in each local community.

A teacher needs to be aware of the manner and attitudes expected of him in his dealings with pupils. Brookover concludes that teachers are expected to maintain dominance, social distance, and respect in the classroom.[7] The opinion polls, reported by Koopman, on what one midwest community expects of its teachers and the role they play indicate that 85 per cent of the persons interviewed expect the teacher to act in a democratic fashion.[8] However, less than 50 per cent of the teachers were actually observed to take the democratic approach in teaching procedures. The two studies might be interpreted to mean that people do expect the teacher to be in full control of the situation at all times as the leader, but not necessarily to go about it in an authoritarian manner. Checking similar questions in the community by informal means can be helpful in getting the pulse of the local situation.

Making informal observations to learn about the community. While it is not anticipated that the teacher will often make extensive and systematic studies of the community in which he

---

[6] Elmo Roper, "What the U.S. Thinks about Its Schools," *Life,* October 16, 1950, p. 11.

[7] Brookover, *A Sociology of Education,* pp. 232-37.

[8] Margaret O. Koopman, "What One Midwest Community Expects of Its Teachers," *Educational Research Bulletin* 25:34-41, Feb. 13, 1946; and "The Teacher's Role in One Midwest Community," *Educational Research Bulletin* 25:91-97, April 10, 1946

works, it will be helpful to consider some points used by sociologists conducting such studies. A list of such points is given by Brookover:

1. General impression.

2. Demographic characteristics.

3. Ecological pattern.

4. Historical background—growth cycles and significant developmental events.

5. Life activities: making a living, home and family life, health and physical well-being, training the young, spending leisure time, giving information, religious behavior, politics, law and order, social class, and the world outside.

6. Value system.

7. Power system.

8. Impact of regional and national culture.

9. Community "characters."

10. Miscellaneous.[9]

Such a list as this may serve well as a guide to the teacher in making informal studies of the community to accumulate useful information.

Every community is made up of numerous organized groups which, to some degree, become pressure groups. Pressure groups may reflect in the activities of the school and in the manner in which the school is operated. Some of the more common ones found in all communities are church, patriotic and labor organizations, political parties and tax payers associations, Chambers of Commerce, parent-teacher associations, and local teachers' organizations. It is important that the teacher recognize and identify these influences in the community and understand how the balance of power among them is maintained. Every group has its objectives and purposes and they often are related to the welfare of its membership. Some are entirely devoted to the welfare of children. Others provide outlets for individuals who wish to be of service to others. The information obtained from observations made in the normal activities of teaching requires some attention, organization, and analysis if it is to be productive.

Using school records to learn about the community. School records are convenient sources of helpful information about the community. Using a map of the area, the teacher locates the homes

[9] Brookover, A Sociology of Education, p. 380.

of his pupils in preparation for making a trip into the neighborhood. The general economic status of the family can often be estimated from the occupation of the father or the probable combined incomes if both parents work. The school records will usually reveal the size of the families in the neighborhood, and possibly the recreational interests of the family group.

Having located as many homes as possible on the map, the teacher uses every opportunity to walk along the streets to observe the attractiveness and adequacy of the homes, the places where children play, the availability of shopping centers, and the places where children and youth congregate. One of the advantages of walking through the community stems from the chance that children and their parents may be seen together either near the homes or in the shopping centers. Thus, from a simple start with school records, a surprising amount of information and contact with the parents may be developed.

Locating persons and places that might serve as resources in teaching. The goal of all school-community relationships is the improvement of educational experiences for children. Parents, especially, are eager to cooperate with those who are working for the best interests of children. Outstanding teachers and administrators are making increasing use of parents and laymen in deciding what kinds of school programs will be developed, and discussing with them ways and means of implementing the good ideas that are brought forth. While the teacher is a participant in this broader aspect of education, his principal opportunity will be with the parents of the children for whom he is directly responsible. As Mort and Vincent point out:

> Parents are librarians, trip arrangers, transporters, club sponsors, and chaperones and their groups have also been extremely valuable in studying and organizing, for better effect, many informal educational influences such as radio and movies. In fact, most good schools not only vigorously promote the assistance of parents and parent groups, but welcome the continual presence of parents in the school.[10]

[10] Paul Mort and William Vincent, *Modern Educational Practice* (New York: McGraw-Hill Book Company, Inc., 1950), p. 359.

Continuing the thought of direct utilization of the abilities of people in the community, Hymes makes this statement:

> Sitting at home in every community are photographers, cabinet makers, tennis players, trumpeters, cellists, square dancing enthusiasts, story telling experts. These people go under the name of mother, father, grandparent. Some way must be found to bring this richness of skill, training, and profession into the classroom. The community must educate its children; the teacher should not be alone in this responsibility.[11]

Hymes goes ahead to point out that two other groups of people have much to offer in the educational picture by way of talent and

Many industries bring resource personnel and teaching materials into classrooms to enrich the school program.

Courtesy of *The Indiana Teacher*

11 James L. Hymes, *Effective Home–School Relations* (Englewood Cliffs, N.J.: Prentice-Hall, Inc., 1953), p. 171.

skill; these are the young married women, childless at this stage of their married life but not employed full-time, and older people who are retired and who would welcome an opportunity to do something useful with the skills they have spent a lifetime accumulating.

The teacher who is aware of these resources may find ways to use them in his teaching situation. In some situations he can bring them into the picture as guest speakers for a one-day stand; in others, it will be feasible to arrange some kind of continuing relationship in which these persons work in the classroom with some regularity.

Teachers derive many satisfactions from their jobs. People in other walks of life often engage in teaching activity in Sunday schools and other programs because it yields personal satisfaction to them. The pleasure that comes from helping is illustrated in the experience of one teacher who used six mothers to transport a group of children to a local factory. In addition to being very helpful to him in handling the children, it was obviously a very pleasurable outing for the mothers who did it. Utilization of people of the community need not be considered an imposition on them, for they often derive more in personal pleasure and satisfaction than they give in time and service.

In order to acquire functional knowledge of community resources, the teacher does two things: In the first place, he keeps in mind that this is a type of information that he wants. Secondly, he maintains some simple record, a card file or notebook, of such resources as come to light. Within the period of one school year the results of keeping alert to these possibilities and maintaining a simple record of them will be most gratifying. Having located possible sources of help, the teacher is then in a position to consider the most appropriate manner of utilizing them in the classroom.

Talking to people who have questions about the school. The importance of this competence may well be illustrated by excerpts from some diaries kept by active classroom teachers who were members of a graduate class. These items are typical of the experiences of all teachers.

> Exchanged ideas with a mother whose child was afraid to come home after school.
> Listened sympathetically to a grievance of the milkman.

Chatted at the neighborhood grocery to clear some school problems of new patrons, such as tardy bells, safety patrol, and park day.

Helped answer questions of a parent about school boundary lines where a problem of transportation was involved.

Explained to a mother how to help her child who was slow to learn.

Explained to a parent why a child can't be in the room he and his parents prefer.

Referred to the superintendent a patron who asked why bus driver's contract had not been renewed.

Listened to a parent who objected to having his child walk one-eighth of a mile after leaving a bus.

Explained the rental system to a parent unable to pay book rental, who came to school to see why his child could not have all the books he needed.

Was introduced by a grocery clerk to a room parent whom he had not met before.

These are the normal responses which classroom teachers may expect to make as they meet and talk with the parents of their pupils. These are significant points in school and community relationships because they are the most pressing problems of the parents at the moment. The parents, in turn, constitute the most interested group as far as school improvement is concerned.

It becomes abundantly clear, then, that every teacher shares with the administration the responsibility for providing information to parents, and through the discussion of parents' questions provides for their participation in school affairs. It is also clear that in order to discharge this responsibility the teacher needs to have information about the school and the way it operates. Not only does he need information on a wide variety of topics, but also he must be aware that there are areas in which he should refer inquirers to the principal or superintendent. This practice of referring certain questions to administration is not designed to withhold information from the public. The administrator generally operates in a wider circle of acquaintances and certainly has a broader view of all the problems that relate to the school. He is, therefore, able to provide information in such a way as to bring it into proper perspective with the whole situation. As in all other dealings, if a teacher is uncertain about his facts, it is best to be honest and not pretend or guess.

Assuming that the administrative climate is favorable and that other things are equal, the teacher can contribute to the amount of parent participation in a study of school problems by providing opportunities for the parents of his own roll room or grade room to discuss problems of common concern. These opportunities will be further elaborated in the next section.

Conducting discussion meetings with parents and laymen (and high school youth) to improve communication between school and community. The average layman carries in his memory a picture of education as he experienced it. All people did not have satisfying and successful experiences with school; many of them dropped out before completion of all minimum requirements. Unless the layman is provided the experiences through which to reconstruct his perception of the school and its activities, he will use this memory picture as a standard of evaluation. Thus, when his children bring home reports that deviate from his expectations, he has much the same reaction as when his wife brings home an unfamiliar brand of coffee. The new brand may be good, but being unfamiliar it immediately arouses suspicion. When new practices in school come to his attention without his having had an opportunity to understand them, he is very likely to react with disfavor.

Providing opportunities for discussion of information about new or different ways of teaching or new content is an important means available to teachers for helping the layman to modify and improve his conception of school work. Through such discussion and improvement of the layman's understanding of what schools attempt to do, the standards by which he will inevitably evaluate the results are brought into harmony with the goals toward which the school is working. The importance of this step is further realized when it is considered that the parents and laymen are going to evaluate the school one way or another, whether their evaluations are sought or not.

The importance of discussion of school problems was forcibly brought home to a principal who was suddenly confronted with an attendance report showing an alarming amount of tardiness. Pursuing a rather common authoritarian approach, he drew up a drastic program of controls involving rather severe penalties. This program was then presented to the student council for their consideration and discussion. When the suggestion was reported back to the senior class, they called a meeting and invited the principal in to discuss the problem. The seniors felt that altogether too much severity was involved in the principal's suggestion, and asked for reconsideration. A further study of the problem, including attempts to get at its causes, was suggested. The student council was authorized to elect a number of representative parents to meet with the principal, deans, and a special committee of the student council for discussion. This group met three or four times over a period of approximately six weeks and worked out some of the causes for the unfavorable tardiness situation and a much improved plan for controlling tardiness. By that time the next attendance report came out indicating that the problem had virtually disappeared. Throughout the discussions the homerooms had been kept informed of progress, and with the increased understanding of the problem on the part of parents, pupils, and the principal, everyone had put his shoulder to the wheel and had nearly eliminated the tardiness situation.

Faced with the important opportunity to hold discussion meetings with pupils and parents, the teacher is confronted with the desirability of improving his skill in discussion leadership. Some references are offered at the end of this chapter to assist the teacher with knowledge of these techniques. A few suggestions are offered here to the teacher-leader.

In the first place, the teacher who meets with parents for discussion learns to present the problem to be discussed to the group in as simple and concise a manner as possible. In some cases it is well to provide the opportunity for other problems to be placed on the agenda for discussion along with those which seem to require immediate attention. Following the identification of the problem, it is extremely important that the teacher-leader devote his effort to bringing forth suggestions and expressions of opinion from as many of the group as possible. A difficult task for the leader is to endure sometimes as much as one minute of silence while people collect their thoughts and muster up the courage to express them. If the leader will wait until people are ready, he can be assured that they will talk. Throughout the discussion, he does everything he can to encourage further statements and to accept each contributor, for each one who speaks is trying to add to his own understanding as he verbalizes his thoughts.

When a point has been thoroughly discussed, the teacher-leader attempts to summarize what has been said, including differences of opinion. It should be emphatically stated that discussion meetings for the purpose of studying problems are not action meetings, and consequently do not call for parliamentary procedure. Eventually, a group that is in a position to take action may wish to pass certain resolutions. Generally, however, much study and discussion is needed prior to the time when an action meeting is appropriate.

Everyone who attempts to lead a discussion faces the same feelings of inadequacy and experiences moments of desperation in which it seems that all is lost. Occasionally someone becomes angry and raises his voice in a fashion that makes such discussions seem futile. All too many times teachers and administrators have had this happen in the first effort and have felt that further efforts were destined to failure. This is undoubtedly a fundamental error, for if second opportunities are provided it is unlikely that these things will be repeated.

The teacher who has the courage to try discussion methods with parents will find his confidence rising very rapidly with each successive trial. He will be helped by reading about the role of the discussion leader. Experience, supplemented by some study of the function of symposiums, panels, lectures, buzz sessions, role playing, and other techniques of group discussion, will develop confidence in the teacher in his ability to perform this very essential function.

Using special programs to help the community understand teaching. Establishing communication with parents and bringing them into situations where it is possible for them to understand the school is not easy. Parents often feel insecure in the school and in the presence of teachers. There is the additional fact that many of them have heavy demands upon their time. Many schools operate special parents' nights through the various seasons of the year, for which elaborate plans are often made and strong efforts expended to bring about parent attendance. These special nights are usually well supported, and a majority of teachers and administrators feel that they are very worth while.

Many times attendance at an open house meeting where many other parents are present is the opening wedge to later contacts. One serious difficulty with such meetings is getting the general public to understand that these are not the times for lengthy discussions of problems of individual children. This understanding can be accomplished by the parent organization as it is brought into the planning for these events. With the assistance of members of the parent-teacher association during the open house, the teacher can make appointments for teacher-parent conferences to be held later.

These special open house programs take many forms. The teacher's part will sometimes be participation in the general session, but more often it will consist of preparing his own classroom to exhibit the work of his pupils in various ways. Attractive bulletin boards and table displays are sometimes possible. These displays include the work of the poor pupils as well as that of the best. Some teachers use a folder, into which children place many items of their regular work, as a part of the mechanics of the daily teaching program. Tests,

Class plays are always an appealing and creative means of bringing the school and the community closer together.

Courtesy of *The Muncie Star*

spelling lists, drawings, written compositions, and other similar materials which show progress from one point of time to another provide most interesting studies for parents when placed upon the
individual desks in the room.

In some forms of the open house an abbreviated schedule is provided; short sessions of classwork are planned to give a first-hand
view of the school in action. A variation of this type of program
consists of setting up the schedule so that the parents themselves
follow the child's schedule through ten-minute classes, during which
each teacher provides a discussion of what the pupils are doing.

Open house programs such as those described above are a common part of the school's recognition of American Education Week.
American Education Week occurs early in November each year and
receives national publicity through all channels of communication.
The teacher should not overlook this special opportunity to encourage parent visitation. As each building unit supplements the wide
general publicity for American Education Week by announcements
and invitations to attend its own particular programs, parents find it
easy to follow their neighbors and their children back to school.
Efforts expended during American Education Week lead to many
fruitful small-group and individual contacts throughout the school
year.

**Recognizing opportunities for the school to provide needed
community service.** One of the more easily recognizable opportunities for the school to identify itself with community activities is to
make it possible for groups to hold meetings in the building when
classes are not in session. Modern school building design often reflects the needs of the community for this kind of assistance. The
need varies from the rural school district, which has little or no
urban facilities within its bounds, to the larger towns and cities
where many municipal auditoriums, union halls, and church recreation rooms may be available.

When community resources are utilized in the classroom instruction of children and when the classroom is extended into the community through field trips and work experiences, it sometimes
becomes a natural thing for a class or the school as a whole to undertake a project of community improvement. During the depression
following the financial crash of 1929 there were many places scat-

tered throughout the country where the school represented virtually the only hope of the community for lifting itself by its bootstraps. Through the efforts of the federal government, various foundations, and several state departments of public instruction, schools were encouraged to modify their traditional programs in the direction of community service and community development. As a result of this activity, the concept of the community school was extended—a concept which included the school as a resource for the community as well as the community being a resource for the more common purposes of the school.

Brookover points out that there are five main approaches by which the school can relate itself to community action programs:

1. Provide and develop leadership.
2. Provide facilities for community action groups.
3. Develop a community-centered curriculum.
4. Utilize community resources.
5. Serve as an agency of coordination in the community's educational efforts.[12]

Teachers have in their possession a great many skills that can be used in working with adults as well as children. The processes of thinking involved in problem solving are as valid in adult groups as with children. If, in addition to their knowledge of problem solving, they are informed on modern techniques of discussion, they may not only serve as discussion leaders but may develop the abilities of non-teaching adults to act as leaders.

Teachers likewise can be alert to the possibilities of building units of work around local problems. Thus this is an effective means of adapting the school's curriculum to community needs as they are observed. There are many instances where intelligent teachers have used problems of fighting insects, local health, and needed community improvements as a central core of studies. In these instances pupils have not only learned fundamental skills but have learned to use their skills of communication in dealing with people.

Olsen lists several types of direct service which high school students have rendered in various situations.[13] Among these services are

[12] Brookover, A *Sociology of Education*, p. 394.
[13] Edward G. Olsen, *A Modern Community School* (New York: Appleton-Century-Crofts, Inc., 1953), pp. 35-36.

such things as school-community newspapers, radio and television programs, serving in community surveys, assisting social service agencies, assisting community agencies, planning for community projects, assisting in the school nursery, and carrying on projects through student government of the school. There is considerable evidence that participation by students with adults in various kinds of services in the community is one of the best ways of developing leadership. Viewed in this way, the service projects provide laboratory experience for the development of responsible citizenship.

Being aware of the opportunities which community services will provide for good educational experiences for children and young people will help the teacher to be alert to these opportunities when they present themselves. In screening and selecting things to

The school that serves an agricultural community enhances its effectiveness through its farm shop facility.

Courtesy of *The Indiana Teacher*

be done, the combined experience and judgment of the teacher, administrators, and other staff members will be helpful. There are many problems to be considered relating to total time required, effect on work of other teachers, and liability in case of accident. There is no doubt, however, that as the school becomes conscious of the needs for community services it advances itself in good community relations.

Lending professional assistance in the planning of other worthy community institutions. An elementary teacher reported that she had been asked by the superintendent of a Sunday school primary department to help in making plans for activities to advise on the selection of new books, materials, and supplies that could be used with the younger children. In this way the professional ability of the teacher was utilized in the development of the program which was to be implemented by other people. It is not uncommon, nor is it undesirable, for school personnel to teach Sunday school classes. However, their abilities might be capitalized more effectively if they were asked to serve in the consultative role just described.

Adult organizations, desirous of helping their members accomplish educational goals, have often called upon persons in public schools and colleges for assistance in designing programs to meet their needs. Whether these activities are carried out on a grand scale or in the simplest situation, the skills of the teacher are needed and teachers need to recognize the helpfulness which they can lend to such programs.

Fostering good personal relations with pupils and their parents. One of the best ways for teachers to foster good relations with pupils and their parents is to be consistently helpful when problems present themselves. One teacher reported that a mother came to school, obviously nervous and embarrassed, to pay for a book which was supposed lost. The teacher checked the records and in less than four minutes found the book, because the name and number had been recorded at the time the book was loaned. The parent was pleased, of course, not to have to pay for the book, but especially by the care exercised by the teacher in caring for her interests and those of her child.

Health problems in the home often create tensions in the children.

A teacher reported that he was careful to show an interest in a child whose mother was confined to a tuberculosis sanatorium for a year of treatment. Obviously the personal attention which the teacher could give did not replace the mother's care, but it did go far towards creating in the child a feeling of security during this time.

Teachers frequently report parents coming to school to explain various physical handicaps of children which require special handling. These problems range from impaired vision and hearing to complete inability to engage in the normal activities of the room. Many disabilities, such as cardiac ailments, are not apparent on the surface and need to be reported to teachers. It is helpful to parents and adds greatly to their feeling about the school when teachers respond with obvious interest to these requests.

Teachers sometimes use classroom projects as a means of entertaining parents when they are invited to visit. For instance, one elementary teacher had made ice cream as a project in the classroom. Then the class and the teacher issued invitations to the mothers to visit school. A number of the mothers did come and a surprise snack consisting of the ice cream and cookies was served by their small hosts and hostesses. In this way the teacher and pupils joined hands in making the parents feel welcome, and in treating them as their guests. It is the reverse, one might say, of the home visit in which the teacher goes to the pupil's place of residence and becomes the guest of the family.

Communicating with homes through daily contacts with pupils. The parent is vitally interested in what his own child is doing. The inevitable question "What did you learn today?" when the child reaches home usually receives anything but a satisfactory answer. Children respond with the first thing that strikes their fancy, all too often with some comment such as "I don't know," "Nothing," "We had recess and played dodgeball," "We had reading groups today," or some equally vague expression as they dash outdoors to play. Parents really do want to know what their children learn, and a simple habit which the teacher can develop is very helpful. This is nothing more than periodically planning a list of the things that have been learned or to focus attention on the progress that has been made toward some kind of goal or goals. Summarizing or noting progress is a sound teaching practice. Learning is helped by having the pupil become aware of his progress, his improvement, or the point at which he is in the learning process.

The frequency of such summary would depend on what is to be learned, the developmental status of the learners, and other practical conditions inherent in the school operation. The elementary teacher could, near the close of the school day, call a halt and ask the question, "What are the things we have done today?" It would be wise to set aside a corner of the blackboard for listing these things in clear outline form where the pupils can see them as well as hear them described. It would seem desirable also to list important things that have been started but are incomplete. This list, left until the next day, would serve as a point of departure for the new day's work. Letters to parents could be written periodically by the pupils, listing a number of things that have been accomplished over a period of time. High school classes would probably be assisted in their learning if similar summaries were prepared periodically. Regardless of the maturity of the learner, this matter of noting progress as a means of reorientation and further planning is helpful.

Teachers have reported good results from the development of room newsletters distributed at various intervals of time. These newsletters are the product of the cooperative efforts of teacher and pupils and should be simple and to the point, making clear in language that all parents can understand what the teacher and pupils are doing about education. Obviously, not all children will have learned the same things or in the same degree. However, the school's program and the pupils' own evaluation of the progress of the group will be very helpful.

The most common means of distributing newsletters is to send them home with the pupils or to enclose them with periodic grade reports. Again, teachers have reported better results by using direct mail to the homes for these informational materials. There are many chances for pupils to forget to deliver them or lose them between the school and the home. The fact that the school takes the trouble to communicate by direct mail seems to make a favorable impression.

Teachers can perform thoughtful acts such as sending advance notice of times when the school will be in recess. These notices enable the parent to make preparation for the child to be at home. This is particularly important if both parents work. Even the more prominent holidays and the irregularities at the close of the school term justify some kind of communication so that the parent may know the hours at which dismissals are planned, how long the recess will last, and when school will be resumed. Many family plans are built around school schedules. It is only a matter of courtesy to make certain that the pupils and parents alike are reminded of these irregularities in time.

The things which have been said have to do with special communications. One other principle should be mentioned. The pupil inevitably communicates some kind of impression about the school to his parents as a result of his daily experiences. Often what the child does not say about school is more significant to the parent than the things he does say. Many parents will testify that children will appear troubled and sometimes even sick for no apparent reason. Under such circumstances they are justified in wondering how things are going at school. The child may express a sudden unhappiness or dislike for school, which again may cause the parent to wonder just what is the source of the trouble. Teachers are sometimes described as grouchy, mean, or unfair; at other times they may be characterized as pleasant, interested, nice, or "swell." It is inevitable that, through the children, parents are continually forming and reforming impressions of the teacher and the school.

Using teacher-parent conferences in teaching. There is a trend toward supplementing the usual report card with teacher-parent conferences. Successful use of this plan requires a careful build-up of such conferences in the minds of parents and pupils as well as teachers. The traditional reaction of parents to home visits of "What has Johnny done now?" suggests that through the years parents have been accustomed to teachers and administrators leaving them alone unless there was trouble at school. This, of course, is an unfortunate circumstance, and the school must share its responsibility for it.

A similar reaction may occur when the parents are requested to arrange an appointment with the teacher to talk about the pupil's progress. Even with careful groundwork the parents may feel that they are being called in to be told how to rear their children. In fact, teachers are accustomed to a great deal of directing, and sometimes find it difficult to place themselves in a frame of mind for a bona fide give-and-take discussion.

Parents have much to contribute to the school because they know so much about the child as a whole. Many teachers' problems in dealing with pupils are made easier when they know more about the home life and the past history of the child. They also depend upon parents to encourage the continuing development of skills which are initiated at school. One teacher reported an experience of having sent a note home about a child whose work she felt was not progressing as it should. The father came to explain that the child had suffered severely from an illness in early childhood and expressed great pride in what the child was accomplishing as contrasted with what they had expected. With information about the handicap under which the child was working, the teacher agreed that the present state of affairs did represent progress, and was happy therefore to go ahead and accept what the child was able to do.

The situation in reverse is indicated in the case of a pupil whose parents were dissatisfied with the progress he was making in reading and had applied considerable pressure for better results. When the teacher and parent were able to sit down together and come to a common understanding that the child was really trying but that he had real difficulties in learning to read, the acceptance of the situation on the part of the parent was greatly enhanced.

Some schools have experimented with less frequent reports supplemented by one or two planned teacher-parent conferences during the school year. This plan has great possibilities. Surprisingly enough, the parent actually learns more about his child and his work in school under this plan than he had under the more common formal reporting system.

The teacher constantly tries to develop a manner that makes it easy for parents to talk. A teacher-parent conference must feature the sharing of time for talking, ideas, and mutual respect. There is a natural barrier existing between teachers and parents which can be removed only through their becoming better acquainted with one another. The attitude that will prevail in successful teacher-parent conferences is that each one is trying to be helpful in the total job of educating the child.

Taking an effective part in PTA and other similar activities. Teachers in the local school and education in general have a powerful ally in the organized groups of parents across the country who devote their time, energy, and influence to improving the educational opportunities of children. The most famous of these organizations is the National Congress of Parents and Teachers with its state and local units scattered throughout the United States and its possessions. The Objects of the National Congress, which can be found in any of its publications, are as follows:

1. To promote the welfare of children and youth in home, school, church, and community.
2. To raise the standards of home life.
3. To secure adequate laws for the care and protection of children and youth.
4. To bring into closer relation the home and the school, that parents and teachers may cooperate intelligently in the training of the child.
5. To develop between educators and the general public such united efforts as will secure for every child the highest advantages in physical, mental, social, and spiritual education.

The local unit of the Parent-Teacher Association provides the teacher with a channel of communication with the parents of his pupils. He becomes a member of the Association if he subscribes to the objects stated above and pays the dues, which are ordinarily very low. Whether or not the local parent-teacher association is affiliated with the National Congress generally makes only minor differences in their stated objectives. The Objects of the National Congress are widely used for a basis of organization of independent units. These objects serve as criteria for the determination of proper efforts of the individual members and the organization as a whole.

In working with a parent-teacher association that is affiliated with the National Congress, the teacher identifies himself with a group that has no axe to grind. The organization constantly strives to devise activities that will result in progress toward the Objects as stated. The teacher can lend assistance to the group by helping to determine what constitutes real parent-teacher work. Too often the energies of the parent-teacher association are devoted to money-raising projects which may very well be reviewed as to their relation to the Objects. Money-raising projects do serve the purpose of developing unity in the organization. A tangible goal provides a basis for the unity which any organization needs. Money-raising projects devoted to the purchase of equipment and supplies for the school may be questioned on the ground that they replace the normal channels of taxation for the support of education. On the other hand, money-raising projects that are carried out for the purpose of improving communication betwen the school community and the school would be more clearly related to the Objects. Money-raising projects for the purpose of promoting the welfare of children, relieving suffering, and providing programs for the improvement of family living seem also to be in harmony with the Objects. Activities of the local parent-teacher association to provide leadership in the study of local school problems and efforts to bring about improved educational programs would likewise be interpreted as bona fide parent-teacher association work.

The parent-teacher association provides the teacher one opportunity, at least, for social contacts in the community, and often leads

Pleasant social activities help the interested and maturing teacher develop in his role in the life of the community.

Courtesy of Ball State Teachers College Photo Service

to other opportunities. The teachers may properly encourage meetings of room parents including both husbands and wives. The success of such meetings is enhanced by a social hour and good refreshments. It is not necessary that the teacher do all the work in these meetings. It is easy to enlist the cooperation of the parents, and the pleasure derived from these contacts does not detract from the help the teacher receives from knowing parents better.

The teacher who is familiar with the Objects of the parent-teacher association with which he works will find these Objects to be common ground on which to discuss plans with room representatives and other parents in carrying on organization work. Sometimes the parents appointed to positions as room representatives are not too clear about what they are supposed to do. The teacher will render a real service by working with such representatives on a basis of equality and against a background of common goals. It is often possible to coordinate room activities with parent-teacher association meetings in such a way as to be mutually helpful. Events occurring around special holidays such as Halloween can be designed in a cooperative fashion, to the great benefit of the children and in a manner advantageous to both the school and the organization.

The spirit in which the teacher approaches his relationship with the parent-teacher association will be the determining factor in the effectiveness of his part in its program. The PTA is a powerful ally of the teaching profession in efforts to advance the interest and welfare of children. The teacher can well afford to study its program and to lend every assistance toward making it more effective.

Using mass media of communication in teaching. The availability of newspapers, radio, and television, the principal media for mass communication, varies widely from one community to another. The editorial and management policies of each of these communication media vary somewhat, but one of the principal factors involved is the ability of teachers and school administrators to work effectively with them.

Nearly everyone recognizes that school is news. Schools deal with children, the dearest possessions of parents and grandparents. Interest and emotional involvement, therefore, run high. The question is, what makes good school news and how is it handled most effectively?

Some newspapers will be glad to have well written stories which they can reproduce almost verbatim. Other newspapers will prefer to have the information presented in concise form, and have their own staff write the stories. The teachers and administrators will first obtain a clear understanding of the preferences of the local editors. The responsibility for clearing up this matter is usually taken by the administrator.

The handling of school news is a matter of established policy in a school system. A clearing house is often set up to control the distribution of publicity so that all areas of the school are treated fairly. The teacher will want to understand the accepted channels and obtain a clearance before giving a story directly to a newspaper.

The amount of publicity the individual teacher receives may become a factor in his relations with other teachers in the school. If there is no established channel for news releases, it is good practice to confer with the principal before releasing a story to be certain that it will not boomerang upon him in his staff relationships.

In general, the use of news communicating media is thought of as a way to disseminate information about the school to the community. The reverse use of newspapers, radio, and television is a matter of importance to the teacher also. Information about matters of public interest taken from the newspapers provides a basis of discussion in the classroom and may lead to valuable work units.

For the teacher's own professional use, information about various meetings and the activities of important groups in community life may be very helpful. The teacher may select from such notices meetings in those neighborhoods where he would like to become acquainted. The fact that the teacher is present at some of these meetings indicates to the parents and laymen his interest in the things that concern them. Such meetings are often followed by discussion periods and social hours in which the teacher may have opportunity to meet many persons whom he would otherwise not come to know.

Increasing interest in developing the ability of school people to work with newspapers, radio, and television is in evidence. The National Citizens Council for Better Schools has inaugurated a column in its newspaper, *Better Schools*, which is designed to help teachers and laymen alike to do a better job with school news. This is a competence which involves many understandings, much applied psychology, and extensive experience in human relationships. A well informed public means strong support for education. Improving skill in using mass media of communication will help develop such a public.

Fostering good personal relations with other teachers and school employees. Staff agreement on policies affecting instruction is a bulwark in community relations. Parents and laymen develop the highest respect for a school in which there are well established areas of agreement. Good staff relations result from close personal acquaintance among the teachers and all school employees. These personal relationships are the result of many opportunities for social contact outside of school as well as opportunities for discussion of professional problems during the school day. An instance is cited where a principal and his wife expended much effort, time, and money in bringing the teachers and their families together in pot-luck suppers, picnics, and other enjoyable occasions. After many years and varied experiences, members of that faculty still number among their best friends former colleagues who shared in these activities. This experience illustrates the importance of encouraging and participating in programs designed to bring faculty members and their families into social contact.

What has been said above applies equally to relationships with the office force, custodians, cooks, bus drivers, the school nurse, and others who contribute to the total school program. In fact many schools now include all of these workers in their social affairs. Each school employee makes a significant contribution to the effectiveness of the school's program.

SUMMARY

Working with the community requires first of all an understanding that lay citizens are responsible for educating the children of the community. They have chosen to meet that responsibility by providing schools. They have an important stake in and serious concern for those schools. Teachers realize why they are concerned and work with them to make the schools effective instruments in the education of children.

To work effectively with the community requires the ability to do a great many things. This chapter has made suggestions for improving the competence of teachers in fifteen activities of teaching having to do with community relations. These competences, enumerated at the beginning of the chapter, are repeated here for emphasis. The teacher should recognize an increased feeling of security in this final reading, as compared to the first.

1. Sensing the way people in a community feel about the school, its purposes, and achievements.

2. Making informal observations to learn about the community.

3. Using school records to learn about the community.

4. Locating persons and places in the community to use as resources in teaching.

5. Talking to people who have questions about the school.

6. Conducting group discussions with parents and laymen to improve communication between school and community.

7. Using special programs to help the community understand teaching.

8. Recognizing opportunities for the school to provide needed community service.

9. Lending professional assistance to the program planning of other worthy community institutions.

10. Establishing good personal relations with pupils and their parents.

11. Communicating with homes through daily contacts with pupils.

12. Using teacher-parent conferences in teaching.

13. Taking an effective part in organized parent-teacher activities.

14. Using mass media of communication in teaching.

15. Fostering good personal relations with other teachers and all school employees.

PROBLEMS

1. *Seek permission to look at the school records for one group of pupils with whom you are familiar. Using this as a start, develop a five-page analysis of the community from which these pupils come.*

2. *Confer with your supervisor to ascertain the advisability of asking pupils to list specialties of their parents and neighbors which might be used in the school. If permission is granted design a procedure for obtaining the information and a way of keeping the information so that it will be readily available for future use.*

3. *Make an analysis of the learning progress and potential of one of your average pupils. Outline the points you would expect to discuss with the child's parents. Write an opening sentence for each point.*

4. *Secure a manual or text on group discussion leadership. Outline the duties of the moderator in a panel-forum type discussion situation.*

5. *Secure information about the most recent American Education Week theme. Write a proposal to your principal suggesting an activity that you would like to carry out in your situation at the next American Education Week.*

6. *Write a digest of as many services which schools have performed for your home community and the college community as you can find out about.*

7. *Write a suggestion directed to your local Sunday school superintendent suggesting how you and other teachers could be helpful in his program in ways other than teaching classes.*

8. *Observe a good teacher closely for one week and submit to him a summary of things he has done that might be appreciated by his pupils and their parents. Ask him to supplement the list and return it to you for your files.*

9. *Seek an opportunity to sit in on a conference or make a home call with your supervisor. Write up your analysis of the problems you would have had if you had been alone.*

10. *Ask your supervisor to get you a job helping with the program*

or refreshments at a PTA function. Write up the things you learned while working with the parents.

11. *Ask your supervisor to help you find out how news is handled in the school. Supplement this information by consulting the editor of your home town paper about how he would like school people to handle school news.*

12. *Arrange a short chat with the building custodian to find out what teachers do to help him give optimum service.*

BIBLIOGRAPHY

American Association of School Administrators, "Building Public Understanding," in *American School Curriculum* (1953 Yearbook). Washington, D.C.: The National Education Association, 1953. Chap. x.

——, *Public Relations for America's Schools.* Washington, D.C.: The National Education Association, 1950.

Bathurst, Effie, *How Children Use the Community for Learning.* Washington, D.C.: U.S. Government Printing Office, 1953.

Beauchamp, George A., "Fundamental Considerations for Curriculum Planning," in *Planning the Elementary School Curriculum,* Part II. Boston: Allyn and Bacon, Inc., 1956.

Bottrell, Harold R., *Applied Principles of Educational Sociology.* Harrisburg, Pa.: The Stackpole Company, 1954.

——, ed., "Developing Special Competencies," in *Educational Sociology: A Resource Book for Teachers and Community Workers,* Part IV. Harrisburg, Pa.: The Stackpole Company, 1954.

Brookover, Wilbur B., *A Sociology of Education.* New York: American Book Company, 1955.

Campbell, Roald F., and John A. Ramseyer, *The Dynamics of School-Community Relationships.* Boston: Allyn and Bacon, Inc., 1955.

Cook, Lloyd A., and Elaine F. Cook, *A Sociological Approach to Education.* New York: McGraw-Hill Book Company, Inc., 1950.

Gillin, John, "The School in the Context of the Community," in *Education and Anthropology,* ed. George D. Spindler. Stanford, Calif.: Stanford University Press, 1955. Pp. 62-72.

Hymes, James L., *Effective Home-School Relations.* Englewood Cliffs, N.J.: Prentice-Hall, Inc., 1953.

Lane, Howard, and Mary Beauchamp, "The Role of the Adult in the Child's Life," in *Human Relations in Teaching.* Englewood Cliffs, N.J.: Prentice-Hall, Inc., 1955. Chap. xiii.

Menge, J. Wilmer, and Roland C. Faunce, *Working Together for Better Schools.* New York: American Book Company, 1953.

National School Public Relations Association, *It Starts in the Classroom.* Washington, D.C.: The National Education Association, 1951.

National Society for the Study of Education, *The Community School,* ed. Henry B. Nelson, Part II (1953 Yearbook). Chicago: The University of Chicago Press, 1953.

———, *Citizen Cooperation for Better Public Schools,* (1954 Yearbook). Chicago: The University of Chicago Press, 1954.

Olsen, Edward G., *School and Community Programs,* 2nd ed. Englewood Cliffs, N.J.: Prentice-Hall, Inc., 1954.

Parker, Beatrice F., "The Parent-Teacher Conference," *Elementary School Journal* 53:270-74, 1953.

Stanley, William O., B. Othaniel Smith, Kenneth D. Benne, and Archibald W. Anderson, *Social Foundations of Education.* New York: The Dryden Press, Inc., 1956.

4

Widening the role
of the teacher

How would you have your pupils remember you? As one who worked with them using a kindly smile, a sympathetic touch, an understanding look, and an encouraging word with a gentle hand on the shoulder? One who helped them find answers to their questions, took them for a walk to see the flowers in the spring, the birds and insects in the summer, and taught them to enjoy the beauty of the leaves in autumn? Or helped them to gaze into the heavens at night and dream about the mysteries of the stars, or talked with them to the man in the moon? Or read them a story? Or believed them when a big brown bear almost caught one of them in the dark last evening? Or caused the fairies to dance on their bed covers and whisper sweet melodies until their eyes were closed by the sandman? These can be the memories that you leave with them if they are little children and you work closely with them.

When they seemed to have no close friend they found you always willing to listen to their story of trouble and reassure them that you and their mothers still loved them. That seemed enough at the time because you too filled a big place in their small world of home and school. And even a pat on a hurt or a button sewed on made them know that you more than almost anyone else outside of their own little home circle knew what to do when a person needed a friend.

With the older boys and girls in junior or senior high school it is just a bit different. Friendly understanding still counts. Would you have your pupils remember you for being always fair and honest? As one who had strong intellectual interests that they can look back upon, recalling that you started that first spark that led into the thing they do now? Or remember you because you explained things so well with such patience and clearness; or because you were willing to admit that you didn't know the answer, but said "Let's look it up together," and you found the answer together? Or because you took time just to sit down and listen; and they knew because you listened you understood?

All of the things above and many more you will find make up the opportunities that come to the teacher when he gets close to boys and girls and they bring their problems to him.

The teacher's role as a leader. The teacher works with boys and girls; they are always in the position of learners, and he in the position of leader. As the leader he takes the responsibility to determine the strength of each learner and directs him to those things that will teach him the most. His interest is squarely in the individual. The pupil learns through the experiences that are the most meaningful to him in the light of his background, interests, and ability. The teacher sees that he is faced with problems that he can complete, things he can do with the greatest benefit to him and to the group of which he is a part.

As a leader the teacher understands the part he must play to get the greatest amount of participation from each member of his group. He understands that he gets his strongest response when he demonstrates that he has faith in his pupils. Strangely enough, faith is an inter-active process. Faith is reciprocal; the teacher's faith in the pupil encourages the child to meet the teacher's expectations. He can't afford to let his teacher down.

The teacher attaches importance to every contribution that is made. Thus the pupils themselves make no serious differentiation in the importance of each person's contribution. The teacher as the leader puts extra stress on the importance of those contributions that might otherwise get a lesser tag on them. When the teacher puts a high price on each one's worth, the pupils themselves put high values on their contributions also.

The teacher as leader makes decisions because of his wider background of experience. The teacher will do well to share in decision-making, and where decisions of pupils are just as worth while as his it is excellent to use the pupil's decision. If he finds himself making too many decisions he stands the chance of having pupils want him to make the decisions for them, or refusing to make decisions, if they are criticized by either the teacher or their peers. But the leader must make decisions for the greatest good, and only he is able to decide in cases that involve the greater number. He must take the risk of being charged with being dictatorial at times. He will make sure that he feels displeased with himself when he is in that role.

It is essential that the individual and the group have important purposes. The purposes of the individual must not be harmful to the best interests of the group, while at the same time the group's purposes should be beneficial to each of its members. This setting up of purposes stems from all the members and the teacher, the leader working within the group in establishing those purposes. If he works faithfully within his group he holds steadfastly to democratic techniques that will tend to strengthen each member of his group. At the same time he insures cooperation from as well as within the group. This is true for the leader regardless of the ages of those with whom he works.

It is a well established fact that a person works more diligently if he has shared in the setting up of purposes and has taken part in the planning. The extent to which the individual members have shared in this will depend quite largely on the encouragement and permissiveness of the leader. It will be limited, of course, by the maturity or ability of the participating members, but that will be tempered only by the skill and ingenuity of the leader in causing the individuals to feel the significance and importance of having ideas too. If one is made to feel that he has good ideas he feels safe in expressing and sharing them. The teacher leads the pupil to have this confidence so essential to his development of faith in himself as well as in those with whom he works.

The principle of sharing in setting up purposes and carrying out plans can be illustrated in a trip to the corner grocery by a first grade group, or by a visit to a naturalization ceremony at the county courtroom by a senior civics class. In either case the idea was created by someone and was accepted by the members of the group. The trip itself was an idea put into action, but the purpose for the trip was tied to a general concern on the part of the majority to acquire more information about certain aspects of the grocery or the naturalization program. The more members there were who developed concern and were able to secure satisfactory answers, the more nearly the trip was successful. In order to accomplish this much advance planning and sharing in the planning had to take place. The teacher, no doubt, possessed the widest background for the experience, and as leader it was his responsibility to make sure that each pupil's concern was satisfied. But the ideas and suggestions which culminated in definite plans could and should come from the pupils. The extent to which they were the pupils' own suggestions made the difference in how well they were carried out. If pupils merely made suggestions that they knew or thought the teacher wanted them to make, the suggestions would not be their own. They could easily be thrown overboard once the trip was under way. Agreements are not so much commitments to the teacher as commitments to one's self. If the commitments are to one's self or even to one's peers they are more effectively kept.

Finally, to the extent to which the teacher as leader becomes an integrated part of the group, he will win their uninhibited response and encourage them to share with him the responsibility for the success of what is undertaken. The project becomes the concern of all, and there is harmony and agreement, and mutual understanding of motives, aims, and responsibility. It is in this condition that the teacher releases his own power and the power of each of those whom he teaches.

The teacher's role as counsellor. The teacher has the best opportunity of anyone in the school organization to build a relationship of faith with his pupils. He is with them every day and they come to understand him, and he them. Understanding is the underlying basis for confidence, and through confidence faith is built. Pupils go for advice to those people in whom they have faith. If the counsellor is approached by the pupil, he is in a far better position than when he is forced by circumstances to approach the pupil. The teacher is in an excellent position to have the pupils come to him.

An old sage once was quoted as saying, "If someone comes to me for advice, I first find out what he wants me to tell him and then I tell him to do exactly that. He then goes away thinking I am a smart man." Perhaps that kind of advising is a little fickle, but the advisor does have the real burden of making pupils do enough reflective thinking to come to conclusions that are free of prejudice and that will stand up under testing and opposition. In order to accomplish this the pupil must weigh all the evidence, examine all the possible consequences, and then arrive at his own conclusion. If the sage quoted above makes sure that his client has done all of these things before he comes, he can safely advise him to go ahead.

The teacher is admonished to consider the "whole child." No better way has been found to express totality in referring to all the factors that are to be considered in working with a pupil. He does grow physically as well as intellectually. He does develop socially, emotionally, and civically as he goes through the process of "becoming." Not one phase of this development can be neglected. Someone must take cognizance of this basic fact. The teacher is in an excellent position to do this—it is his profession.

But it should be pointed out that only the teacher who has accomplished this all-round development in his own life is in a good position to work with the child as a totality. The teacher who regards the intellectual or scholarly to the neglect of the other factors will do likewise with pupils. He will take great pride in academic accomplishments and may tend to deprecate the value of social stability, or even ignore it altogether. That kind of counsellor would be in jeopardy quite often but the number of pupils who sought his counsel would likely be negligible. "Bees tend to seek flowers that contain nectar."

One of the big issues for the young teacher is to examine himself continually to determine his attitude toward the problems of pupil development. It is relatively easy to overemphasize intellectual development, since by nature of his profession he himself is considered an intellectual by society. He feels he must play the role as expected. But the teacher, in order to accept the role of counsellor, should demonstrate balance. The teacher should be well educated and respected because of strong intelligence. Pupils are attracted to what is usually spoken of as common sense. Do you know whether or not you have common sense?

The counsellor-teacher works for the things in which youth is interested. Being *for* something immediately puts the teacher on the side of the one whom he would teach and counsel. It in a way makes him a member of the "gang." It makes him a "regular" fellow, a good sport, a "pal." That feeling of togetherness is essential to the teacher. His acceptance must be recognized by those whom he seeks to help.

The teacher is concerned about all of his pupils. It is relatively easy to concern one's self with the most maladjusted, and the maladjusted do take more than their share of the time. But the teacher as a counsellor recognizes that all pupils need guidance. He must be as concerned about the needs of the well adjusted as those of the maladjusted. It is a matter of the kind of help each one needs. They all need help, but not the same package; it is the individualizing that makes the teacher more valuable.

Through all of the facilities of the school, the teacher comes to know all he can about each pupil. He has access to all the files that may reveal the intellectual power and the educational profile of each of his pupils. Beyond this, and equally important, he sees his pupil in every situation in which he adapts himself to his school and social environment. Nothing can be omitted that has any bearing on revealing the pupil's true nature and his capacity for adjustment. Out of this totality of understanding the teacher can help the pupil toward becoming a mature individual. He helps the pupil learn to make his own choices and be responsible for them. After all, one must make his choices because, as he soons learns, he takes the consequences when the chips are down.

The role of the teacher as a citizen. The teacher is a member of his society. This makes him first a citizen, then a teacher. The teacher is in a position to be a highly respected citizen, and he must make every effort to fulfill that responsibility. He attains status by what he does as an adult person capable of doing many good things. Through these he reaches out into the community and gets to know the community he serves.

The effective teacher is keenly alert to the community needs and its expectations of him. He must be closely in touch with his community and in a position to lead. The attitudes of his clientele toward moral, social, and economic problems are of vital significance to him. He may not agree, but if he is to effect a change, or deal with the children, he must know what they are taught to believe in their homes.

In this fundamental area of approaching problems with an open mind, the teacher comes to be fully aware that many of the members of a community may have very limited views in their own philosophy of education. They may talk of freedom but have grave doubts about who should enjoy it. Through intimate contacts as a citizen the teacher comes to know not only his own limitations, but the limitations that the community would put upon him.

On the other hand, it should be remembered that the community may be even more liberal than the teacher. It may take great pride in its school and its accomplishments. Faith may have been so established that parents look to the teacher's judgments in most matters regarding their children's welfare. Under such conditions the teacher soon feels challenged by the weight of this confidence and responds by being conscientious, honest, and desirous of meriting that trust.

The teacher as a citizen in the community does all the things that other worth-while citizens do. He votes, seeks out those things that improve the general welfare, and lends his support in effort, finance, and voice. He becomes a church member and takes his responsibility as a lay member of his church. He is a member of some civic group and works diligently to make its purposes realized. He participates in social welfare drives and makes contributions in line with his income. He supports everything that will result in the cultural improvement of his community. He wants to own property and pay his taxes for the support of the government which serves him.

Through all this he is accepted and comes to know all that he should know in order to serve his community best as one of its good teachers. In this way he becomes a discerning citizen and is not forced to follow the dictates of the community, but can help lead the way. He can take the parents along with him in what he conceives to be good teaching, and because they know him, because he has worked among and with them, they accept him as the specialist in his field. They respect his judgment and he respects their confidence.

The role of the teacher as a specialist in teaching. The word "specialist" is intended here to emphasize the fact that teaching is a professional skill. The teacher needs to regard himself as possessing a skill acquired through patient years of hard work. This covers all the period from the very beginning of his professional course through all of his laboratory experiences in actual contact with children, including his internship as a student teacher, and through the years of teaching until he has reached his full stature. Then the general public can expect the teacher to be skilled in his art, and he is justified in taking pride in that skill. After all, no one need expect those about him to hold him in higher regard than he is willing to hold himself. That need not take the form of conceit but just good, solid self-confidence. The teacher should overpower all tendencies toward inferiority feelings. If people do not have faith in teachers it is the profession's fault. We cannot sell ourselves short.

The teacher, first of all, is a specialist in human relations. This is reflected in the way the pupils in the classroom regard one another and are at ease. It is portrayed in the way the teacher causes the timid parent to feel confident when she drops by to discuss Jimmy's difficulty in learning to read. It is demonstrated when the irate parent comes to the classroom to give the teacher a "piece of her mind." Or it is given articulation in the room mothers' meeting when by thoughtful and timely counsel the teacher helps the group to set up purposes that satisfy the concerns of every member of the group.

The human relations problem is most vital in the classroom, where teaching effectiveness is dependent on the climate for learning. The teacher helps each pupil feel able to make worthy contributions to the group. This takes the form of a feeling of security. Each contribution is highly regarded. Anyone talks without fear of embarrassment or being laughed at; mistakes are turned into contributions. The smallest contribution is accepted with the strongest. The parable of the widow's mite takes life again in the classroom, where the teacher turns each idea, however small, into a worth-while help. The meek must be helped to become stronger, and the strong are taught to respect the meek. All are taught to share their ideas and work together. This is human relations at its highest and best.

The teacher is called upon to show his strength in human relations as he works with other teachers in the building. His classroom becomes a place where teachers meet to share ideas and talk about the problems of teaching. It offers him the opportunity to make suggestions when the teacher across the hall says "What would you do?" He becomes a resource person for method, both in organizing and presenting material and in the art of pupil organization, and he shares that skill with his fellow teachers. Interestingly enough, in the sharing he becomes stronger and more essential to his professional group.

Beyond his function with pupils and with those in his professional group, he builds relationships with parents in the field of human relations, by getting them to believe in him and in themselves and assume the responsibilities of parenthood. He does this by pointing out his ways of working with children, and encouraging and complimenting them. The relationship with parents must be from a positive approach, and the teacher recognizes that he commends what he approves and avoids finding fault with what he cannot change. If his opinion is solicited he can express his views, but if he finds himself greatly opposed it is best to change the topic. Many a good teacher is right in his views but can get run over by the locomotive of mass opinion and go down in defeat. Here again he demonstrates his strength, in understanding human nature and avoiding issues where he stands a good chance of losing.

Parents naturally look to the teacher as the specialist in developing academic growth, and he is on ground where he feels secure. Here he gains the status from which he reaches out into the areas of social relations, mental hygiene, child development, child psychology, and home relations. The teacher cannot be an expert in all things, but he can develop any fundamental skills, such as teaching reading, and he can be a specialist in a secondary school area where he speaks as an authority. Thus he meets parents on ground where he knows his strength and can make helpful appraisals of each one's role in helping pupils attain their fullest development. Thus through his wise counsel he becomes an authority parents seek out, and if he guards his behavior he can retain that position with them.

In his role of specialist he retains his common touch, and talks at a level that is understood by those who may be weak in academic background but strong in the desire to have their children succeed. In this hope for their children they are often willing and anxious to subscribe to the teacher's suggestions and trust implicitly his ideas.

With such faith the teacher bears the major burden for the child's educational program. This is a burden that the teacher must assume with confidence, but with the added conviction that what he prescribes must be correct or he alone must accept the responsibility for failure in his judgments.

The teacher in the role of friend. Probably no position is as high in the mind of a boy or girl as that expressed in the simple word "friend." When a pupil says "He's my friend," no stronger bond can be expressed. The teacher who attains that position with his pupils has attained the ultimate so far as they are concerned. No greater or better reason seems necessary to the youth when asked why he did something than simply, "Because he was my friend."

The teacher who develops that relationship is in a position to talk to the pupil as he chooses, and be trusted, but as a friend he weighs carefully his friends' feelings. He knows that the pupil will talk over his troubles with him. The pupil really understands the common bond of mutual trust, because this is one of his first and warmest relationships. This cannot be overemphasized; it is the basis for good teaching and good relationship extending through the pupil to the family.

It is this kind of relationship that leads parents to say "Just drop in any time and have a cup of coffee." This is the way friends treat each other. It also leads the teacher to have no fears when parents drop by, because they will appreciate the teacher's problems and not expect more of him than he can really do. This kind of relationship causes the family circle, when talking about school problems, to be considerate of the teacher because they know him as a friend.

As a friend the teacher shows concern about all the things that concern the pupil. If the pupil has a close relative ill, or if the pupil himself has won some sort of award, the teacher expresses regret or pleasure. A card to the pupil on a birthday or when he has been out ill are signs of interest that are appreciated, and mark the teacher as a truly interested friend. A complimentary remark to the parent on some out-of-school interest marks the teacher as interested not only in school affairs, but in all the things that happen to people. To remark to a child that you are pleased because his father has been chosen for some position of responsibility pleases the pupil. Even an inquiry about a sick pet makes him know that you understand. All these are things a real friend does for a friend.

If a pupil has forgotten to bring bus fare or for some other reason can be helped to avoid embarrassment, the teacher can endear himself to both parent and pupil by helping him out in the pinch. The confidence generated by one so thoughtful draws teacher, pupil, and parent closer together.

These are just the ordinary things friends do for each other; and yet they are not so ordinary. To drop little words of encouragement, to give a friend a chance to lighten himself of a worry, to congratulate for an accomplishment, or to give someone a little lift— these are not ordinary in these busy times. They are marks of refinement and courtesy that bind people together and make life seem more important; they are signs of friendship and culture.

The role of the teacher in helping to establish purposes. Direction, and to a great extent drives, are determined by the learner's purposes. The purposes are the learner's, but the teacher, with the parents and anyone else who touches the learner's life, has a share in setting up those purposes. The purposes attached to learning are very largely directed by the teacher. The extent to which these purposes are carried out depends largely on the harmonious understandings that are developed by the school, the home, and the pupil himself; responsibility for that harmony rests squarely on the teacher. The teacher is one from whom skill in human relations is expected, and this skill will be shown by the teacher's care in seeing that the purposes are the pupil's own. The teacher is fully aware of the definite limits to the success that can be achieved by simply telling pupils what to do. Teachers are greatly frustrated when an assignment is made without giving the pupils any particular reason for doing it. They return the next day with varying degrees of work completed. Quite often the teacher shows his displeasure by making an even heavier assignment. The results are much the same. The difficulty lies in the fact that the pupils did not accept the assignment in terms of their own purposes, and as a consequence very little was accomplished.

The learning situation is for the most part a pupil-teacher responsibility. Planning is a part of learning, and success in learning depends upon the extent to which planning has been shared. Sharing in planning tends to insure that the purposes of both teacher and pupil are compatible. The teacher's purposes are seldom questioned by the learner, and this tends to make the teacher more authoritarian than he would otherwise be. However, the broad-minded teacher accepts challenges from his pupils with good grace. Rapport in which all work with the spirit of helpfulness, and honestly share in challenging, testing, and accepting purposes, should be one of his treasured accomplishments.

In the last analysis, the teacher's role is that of building a climate for learning where purposes are established and followed through with equal zeal by teacher and learners, and all agree that the purposes are worth while and satisfying. The climate is favorable for challenges from any source within the group, and the need is apparent when any participant questions the merits of the purpose, causing all concerned to participate in another appraisal. The teacher, by his maturity and experience, may have to make the decision to end the appraisal and say "This is it," but only after the process has operated fully enough for him to be convinced that no further important ideas are forthcoming. Challenges are important as long as they refine the purpose or cause the learners to weigh values. Then the teacher is in a position to accept the situation and direct the work.

The teacher's role in appraisal. Appraisal must be looked upon as a major teacher responsibility. The school quite often treats appraisal as an act of finality in which the teacher plays the major role. This excuses the learner from his share of the responsibility and leaves him with no road open ahead, especially if the appraisal results in a stamp of failure. The teacher's real problem is so to work with the learner that there is sharing of responsibility for making the appraisal.

In fact, the way the learner feels toward his entire school problem is tempered by the way he comes to look upon the appraisal process. Appraisal is made in terms of the individual himself, and the teacher has the task of convincing the pupil that it is a part of learning that he must do himself if he is to continue to grow after his formal educational program has been completed.

Many learners become so conditioned by appraisal techniques that something is bad or good only when the teacher rules it so. This causes the learner to resort to devices to appear favorable. So-called cheating on examinations, copying the other person's work, using other pupil's themes, accepting other pupil's help—all stem from the same source outside of the learner. They are learned responses taught the same as any acquired forms of behavior. Punishment seldom corrects the problem; it usually only makes the pupil more stealthy in concealment. The teacher cannot tell the pupil that he is only harming himself, when at the same time he is rewarding the one who does well and showing disapproval of the one who does poorly. The pupil often seeks to win approval at any price, and the teacher can change this attitude by utilizing the pupil's judgment in self-appraisal and, if marks are necessary, striving to use marks in terms of the learner's ability. This is a difficult task for most teachers, because they have been taught to measure with standards that do not take into account the learner's ability or efforts.

If the teacher firmly believes that the kind of attitude toward appraisal he wants to develop is one in which growth is of the greatest concern, he directs his attention toward keeping records that measure growth. Growth is what takes place from one measuring time to another. Even then whatever change does or doesn't take place is accepted without too much fanfare.

This can be illustrated by physical growth. Suppose a physical education teacher sets his standard in terms of height, with the ultimate goal of seven-foot men and six-foot women. Teachers quite frequently set just as ridiculous a standard for academic achievement. This standard may well be set without regard for height of either parent or remote ancestors. That is the standard, and each boy or girl must reach the height or get a low mark. All who reach it are to receive the highest grade and a gold medal besides. If the teacher made the punishment severe enough for failure to reach the standard, he would find himself faced with all kinds of devices for reaching the goal. Some ingenious boy would likely conceal stilts in his trousers, or girls would insist on being measured with excessively high-heeled shoes. Measuring sticks would be altered or reading of the measuring stick would be falsified; in short, every known way to beat the game would be used. This is really no more extreme than the extremes pupils go to on examination programs, when teachers make examination results the major factor in determining success.

The other approach of course would be to stress proper sleep, proper rest, proper diet, and proper recreation, with well understood definitions of the word "proper" and a mutual understanding that these should result in physical growth predetermined quite definitely by the pupil's characteristics in terms of the genes of both parents. With all of this understood the pupil should realize that his growth would result from how well he followed his rules. Furthermore, he or anyone else could measure the results and get the same figures, and even then the figures would be accepted in terms of how well he followed the rules, plans, and schedules.

In this situation the teacher clearly would carry a heavy burden of the responsibility for pupil attitude by the way he approached the problem and accepted the results in terms of the goals which he and the pupil shared in setting. Whether the growth be physical or intellectual, the responsibility of the teacher is the same. The teacher should provide the record for the changes that take place, but the data that appear in the record are samples about the pupils taken at various times—inches, pounds, themes, dates for measles, chicken pox, vaccinations, tests, letters from mother or father, or anything that takes place in boys' and girls' lives as they go to school. The way the teacher accepts these and the professional use he makes of them will determine their ultimate value.

The teacher's role in helping the pupil adapt to social change. The pupil, as the teacher finds him and works with him, has very few concerns about the demands of society. Our social structure is so set up that he is forced into the school and he doesn't object too strenuously because all of his peers are there. It is what everyone else is doing, and not only is he attracted by the fact but the school has consistently more things of interest to him than anywhere else he knows about. For that reason he registers very few complaints about being in school unless the school makes little effort to interest him. But the pupil and his parents place great faith in the teacher to make correct curricular prescriptions. The teacher recognizes that the classroom is only one of the places where the pupil learns. He also knows that to use the facilities in the community is his best way to help pupils make the adaptations that are to continue all through their lives.

The pupil, in the state of always becoming, uses the teacher as society's bridge from the best that has been experienced in the past to what is being done at the present. Although the past greatly influences the present, the imponderability of change makes any attempt to look into the future most difficult. Therefore the teacher's greatest problem hinges on his efforts to make his pupils analytical critics of what is now. The present is his workshop.

The teacher's role is to lead pupils to be critical of their total environment and selective of that which is best. This applies to every phase of environment, especially man's cultural core in which are found skills, knowledges, aesthetics, sentiments, and higher values. Upon these society is dependent for its stability, and the school is relied upon to maintain stability from one generation to another.

Change is inevitable and each generation views with alarm the dangers that are ahead for youth. But teachers should look upon the present as the golden age, confidently relying on youth to forge ahead. The complexity of the times makes the problem difficult, but no generation of teachers has had more to work with, both in the ability of those whom they teach and the percentage of the population presenting itself. Also, teachers have never before had the physical facilities they have today or the remarkable spirit of cooperation from the parents of those whom they teach. The challenge is great, but the profession will meet it.

The teacher's role in aiding pupils to be adaptable lies in the area of attitudes and values. He strives to help all his pupils make correct interpretations of all their environmental forces, to the end that they are able to distinguish between right and wrong, beauty and ugliness, truth and falsity, temporal and permanent values. This ability helps the pupil work out his own set of values and determines his attitude.

SUMMARY

The emphasis in this chapter has been upon maturation in the teacher's point of view and his expanding opportunities for service as he assumes more responsibility. The dedicated teacher sees these opportunities as ways of becoming increasingly professional. He attains the pinnacle of respectability as a professional person skilled in leadership, counselling, teaching, and being a good citizen and a good neighbor. This is the widening role of the teacher as he takes his place along with the other professional people in his community.

Some competences that are acquired through this expanding role are:

1. The ability so to work with all people—pupils, parents, and lay citizens—that they sense the sincerity of the teacher as a skilled practitioner.

2. The ability to know when to assume authority and when to delegate responsibility for the best interests of the total society.

3. The ability to consider the totality of the learner's interests.

4. The ability to practice strong citizenship in the community.

5. The ability so to work as a teacher that teaching is regarded by all as a learned profession.

6. The ability to demonstrate skill in bringing out the best in all with whom he works.

7. The ability to practice friendship and neighborliness at their best.

8. The ability to make appraisals in such a way that positive reactions are the natural outcome.

9. The ability to help people live with what they have but seek at the same time to make improvement.

10. The ability to listen to problems that are presented, and then to make helpful suggestions.

PROBLEMS

It is recognized that it will be hard to draw from the experiences of the young teacher in this expanding area, so problems have been set up to draw upon observation of experienced teachers. These may involve the supervisor, some teacher who has seemed to be outstanding, or an imaginary ideal.

1. *Select a teacher whom you have observed in action, who is, in addition to being a superior teacher, an outstanding citizen. Make a list of all the characteristics and actual activities as a functioning citizen that this person exhibits. Analyze yourself and deter-*

mine the ways in which you feel you can perform in like manner. If you find yourself deficient, how do you account for these shortcomings?

2. Select a teacher who you feel compares favorably with outstanding representatives of other professions in your range of knowledge and observation. Now determine in what ways they are similar and dissimilar. How does your ideal teacher show up even more favorably in the area of general service?

3. The real teacher is a sincere person with deep concerns for those whom he serves. Select an outstanding teacher of your acquaintance from this point of view and make a sketch of the person's general personality as it confirms your judgment of him.

The following problems may be applied to you:

4. Over a period of about a month make a list for your own personal analysis of the situations in which you have been a good neighbor. This may be with respect to the other people in your dormitory, fraternity, or sorority house, or in the community where you live. Select a typical month so as to be fair to yourself.

5. Pupils will come to you often with concerns which to them are serious. How well can you listen to their problems and then render a service that is not only satisfying to them but gives you a feeling of real spiritual uplift? Make a self-analysis of a few such experiences and then discuss them with your supervisor or your college professor.

6. It has been emphasized time and again that the total child is involved when we work with him. In several cases both with yourself and with your supervisor determine the extent to which you are made to realize such totality.

BIBLIOGRAPHY

Grambs, Jean D., and William J. Iverson, *Modern Methods in Secondary Education.* New York: The Dryden Press, 1952.

Hymes, James L., *Effective Home-School Relationships.* Englewood Cliffs, N.J.: Prentice-Hall, Inc., 1953.

Klausmeir, Herbert J., Katharine Dresden, Helen C. Davis, and Walter A. Wittich, *Teaching in the Elementary School.* New York: Harper & Brothers, 1956.

Lane, Howard, and Mary Beauchamp, *Human Relations in Teaching.* Englewood Cliffs, N.J.: Prentice-Hall, Inc., 1955.

Michaelis, John U., and Paul R. Grim, *The Student Teacher in the Elementary School.* Englewood Cliffs, N.J.: Prentice-Hall, Inc., 1953.

Moustakas, Clark E., *The Teacher and the Child.* New York: McGraw-Hill Book Company, 1956.

Wiles, Kimball, *Teaching for Better Schools.* Englewood Cliffs, N.J.: Prentice-Hall, Inc., 1952.

Part Two

Applying
principles of learning
to the
art of teaching

Introduction

A broad concept of teaching that reaches into many aspects of pupils' lives has been developed. The school is an institution devised by society to foster the growth of children into happy, well adjusted, useful citizens. It supplements the agencies and activities of the total community as they lend their many influences to mold and shape the boy and girl of today into the man and woman of tomorrow. The teacher is the professional person who makes the school effective in carrying out the intentions of the society that created it.

Learning is the business of the pupils in the school; bringing about learning is the business of the teacher in the school. Bringing about modifications in human response patterns is teaching whether the modifications take the form of increased self-control, skill in mathematics, communication, play, or increased knowledge. A growing body of knowledge of how human beings learn is at the disposal of the teacher. A consideration of the art of teaching must include this body of knowledge and the basic principles it contains.

When principles of human learning are utilized in relation to working with learners, many adjustments in the school program become necessary. Some of these adjustments have to do with surroundings in which learners work —physical comfort and beauty, the climate of relations with teacher and other pupils. It likewise includes the understanding of common purposes between teachers and parents and the community at large.

Other adjustments that become apparent include the expectations and requirements set up by the community and the school for the learners. The various kinds of learning experiences and the materials at hand with which learners may work likewise share in a scrutiny of the school's program under the criteria of learning principles.

The focal point of concern for adjustment in this discussion is, however, the teacher's own practices as he works with learners. One might say it is the teacher's own behavior that is under consideration as the effect of that behavior on learning is determined.

Teaching practices—the ways the teacher does things in working with learners—reflect the extent of his understanding of learning principles. Teaching behavior is controlled —not impulsive. The teacher works in a manner that is selected because of his knowledge of how it will affect learning. Principles of teaching that grow out of the accumulated knowledge of how certain practices affect learning represent a step in relating learning theory to working with learners. Guides to ways of doing things gradually evolve as the teacher thoughtfully considers his work.

In these chapters a brief review of some principles of learning is presented. Then follows the effort to make them take shape in the classroom as principles of teaching—as guides to the manner of working with learners. Much that will follow in Part Three, as well, is an effort to help the teacher with shaping classroom work in harmony with these principles.

5

Principles of learning
that affect teaching

The teacher's competence for his professional task is measured by his ability to bring about learning. For this reason, a review of some principles of learning related to teaching practice is desirable at this point. If the knowledge now available about learning is to make for more effective teaching, the teacher's classroom methods will be designed with this knowledge in mind. The application is far-reaching. It pervades the teacher's interaction with his students, his colleagues, and his profession.

Principles of learning related to teaching. The principles of learning, which will be reviewed as a background for developing teaching competence, are centered around the following eleven topics:

1. Readiness
2. Individual differences
3. Motivation
4. Effect
5. Complex and multiple outcomes
6. Security
7. Activity and experience
8. Meaning and understanding
9. Multi-sensory approach
10. Whole–part–whole learning
11. Transfer of learning

Each of these topics will be elaborated by a statement of the principle, an interpretation of its meaning, and some special considerations from psychological research influencing its use in teaching.

Readiness. *A learner must be sufficiently matured and skilled to be ready for a new learning experience.*

This principle recognizes the inevitable interdependence of maturation and learning in the process of growth. The child learns to walk only after his body has matured to a point that permits him to walk. Running comes later and is dependent upon both further maturation and the previously acquired skill of walking. There is a margin between what one has already learned, assuming sufficient maturity, and what one is about to learn. This margin, in most children, lies between walking with considerable skill and beginning to learn to run. School learning likewise requires the recognition of a point between what has been learned and what is to be learned. It is only at this point that learning can occur. Cronbach describes pupil readiness thus: "The pupil's readiness for any situation is the sum of all of his characteristics which make him more likely to respond one way than another. Readiness involves the pupil's equipment, his needs and goals, and his learned ideas and skills."[1]

Maturity, and a degree of physical health accompanying it, are necessary prerequisites to effective learning. The phenomenon of maturation in all its aspects occurs at its own rate in each individual child, and in general there is little that can be done to hasten the process. Maturation does not go on, however, without reference to the total environmental contacts of the child. Learning is aided by maturation and both contribute their share in behavior changes.

Previous experience is another factor of readiness frequently noted. Much has been said about the part parents and kindergarten, as well as the experience of living in the community, play in developing readiness for school living. The principle of readiness for reading is well established, and the same is true for arithmetic. The concept of readiness does not seem to receive as much consideration at the upper grade levels and in the secondary school as in the primary grades.

The experience factor might be expected to become acute in

---

[1] Lee J. Cronbach, *Educational Psychology* (New York: Harcourt, Brace & Company, 1953), p. 74.

readiness for the study of a subject such as algebra. Equally acute situations related to the language arts would be expected in literature and social studies. A pupil whose preparation and skill in arithmetic is adequate would be expected to succeed in algebra; his chances of becoming interested in the subject would be greatly multiplied for this reason. The situation would be paralleled in the other areas.

The interests of children play an important role in the readiness picture. Reading material that appeals to the interests of slow learners helps to exploit the general state of readiness that exists at the moment. Using such material becomes a part of the preparation of the pupil to learn. If a goal can thus be made attractive to the learner the first necesary step toward learning will have been accomplished. The learner has to feel a need for learning to be ready to learn. Whatever can be done to prepare the pupil for his learning is an essential part of the teacher's task.

Individual differences. *Different individuals learn at different rates in the same category of learning. The rate of learning of an individual may vary from one category to another.*

The teacher is familiar with the evidences of individual differences from his own observations of people and previous study of scores on many educational tests. He recognizes the problems of teaching and organization that are related to this phenomenon.

The tendency of educators is to describe individual differences in terms of some arbitrarily assigned degree of presence of a trait. Intelligence, for example, is described numerically as a trait possessed in greater or less degree than a one-to-one ratio of mental age to chronological age. The intelligence of a person is thus conceived as a quantity rather than a response pattern consisting of what the person does or does not do. Skinner challenges this approach on the ground that traits, as commonly conceived, upon close examination become "effects" rather than causes.[2] Since the function of education is to modify behavior, effective efforts must be directed at causes of responses rather than the manipulation of traits.

Increasing attention is paid to the influences at work upon children and adults that bring about the differences that we observe in

[2] B. F. Skinner, "Function versus Aspect," *Science and Human Behavior* (New York: The Macmillan Company, 1953), chap. xiii.

their responses. To a great extent personalities seem to be determined by outside influences. The responses that individuals make are the ones they have learned to make. As would be expected, personality and individuality of children show the effect of home and community life. The socio-economic status of the family and the neighbors is found more and more to have a causal relationship to many responses in which teachers are interested. There are marked differences in the responses of children from different economic levels of our society.

The greatest discrepancy between the social classes is found in the values to which they subscribe. Middle-class parents tend to place pressures upon children to conform and excel to a greater degree than do parents of either lower or upper classes. As a result children of the middle class tend to be more anxious in general, more concerned about the opinion of others. They learn to engage in unreasonable striving to move up in the social scale. The school is regarded by parents as the best avenue by which this rise can be accomplished; hence the emphasis upon school success.

The above discussion of social and cultural influences that make people respond differently to learning situations is not meant to detract from our knowledge of the more common evidences of variation. It suggests, rather, the need for further study of all possible causes of variation in such measures and observations as we have learned to make. To treat intelligently differences in response requires all possible knowledge of the causes of such responses.

Motivation. *More efficient learning takes place when it seems worth while to the learner.*

Increasing importance is attached to the way the learner sees a situation in relation to his own goals. His responses are selected in terms of what outcomes he perceives in the total picture and how these outcomes are related to the satisfactions he seeks. This fact suggests the desirability of studying the way in which concepts, goals, and needs may be engendered in the learner.

There is wide agreement that the learner must be motivated before learning will take place. Something which he understands must be related to his wants and seem worth trying to reach. Learning occurs when this thing he wants is out of immediate reach and requires him to act in ways that are new. Each person encounters somewhat different obstacles in this effort, and as a result is seen to behave in different ways. Likewise, each person brings with him a unique experiential background which influences his perception of the goal.

Behavior which is motivated as indicated receives a generous amount of the learner's energy. It is carried on persistently, and changes from one tactic to another if success is delayed. When success—that is, satisfaction—accompanies the learning of the new activity a liking for the activity is developed. This liking is then a new interest for the child.

It follows from what has been said that success feelings have an important bearing upon motivation. The learner can experience the satisfaction he seeks only as the activity he learns is successful. Success and failure in the mind of the learner are relative to the level of aspiration which he holds. The level of aspiration is determined by expected achievement. Furthermore, the level of aspiration shifts in such a way as to maintain a kind of balance between successes and failures of a given individual. In this way the level of aspiration becomes an important control factor in the mental hygiene of each person.

In classroom practice success and failure are often identified with praise and blame—reward and punishment. The significance of these incentives depends upon many things within the learner. The importance of a reward of any kind depends upon whether or not the reward satisfies some motive of the learner. Even the proper use of reward or praise can be overdone to a point of reduced effectiveness. The same is true for punishment or reproof.

Although general practice favors the use of positive forms of incentives, it is generally agreed that blame, reproof, or punishment will produce learning to a greater extent than a laissez-faire policy of no comment or reaction. The use of both positive and negative incentives, however, is related to the introversion-extroversion characteristics of the learner. Either praise or blame can be used unwisely where the teacher does not understand its effect on different personalities. In one study of fifth grade pupils, introverts responded with better performance under praise; extroverts responded better when blamed.[3] When there was no discrimination between personality types, praise and blame were equally effective.

[3] George W. Thompson and Clarence W. Hunnicutt, "The Effect of Praise and Blame on the Work Achievement of Introverts and Extroverts," *Journal of Educational Psychology* 35:257-66, 1944.

Effect. *Those responses made to a given situation which are accompanied or closely followed by satisfaction will, other things being equal, more likely occur when the situation arises again.*

The original law of effect included annoyers as well as satisfiers. However, the use of annoyers or punishment in teaching is less likely to produce consistently better results than the use of satisfiers or rewards. When used effectively, blame or punishment is related to special conditions.

Effect is related to the primary drives of human beings. The use of rewards is productive in learning to the extent that they fulfill a need of the learner. This point suggests the judgment to be exercised by the teacher in using rewards.

The most important element in the controlled use of effect is the temporal relation between the response of the learner and the reward he experiences.[4] The strongest reinforcement will be attached to the last response made before the reward is received. This is true whether the response had any place in a sequence of events leading to the reward or not. In fact, the response may be unrelated to that sequence. It has been found that responses occurring even after the reward was given have been reinforced. The proximity of the effect to the response is the crucial point. These points provide food for thought for the teacher and should modify his acts in teaching.

Related to the matter of temporal relationship between response and reinforcement, psychologists are finding special interest in the results of varied schedules of timing rewards. Possibly some future developments in this area of study may be used to improve the frequency of controlled effect in the classroom. At the present time there is feeling that classroom reward occurs at intervals too far removed from the responses to be reinforced and, in the over-all sense, too infrequently.

Classroom teachers have at their disposal at all times two powerful agencies of positive reinforcement. These are, first, the learner's satisfaction arising from the subject matter itself and, second, the good will and affection which teachers extend to their pupils.

The increased ability of a boy to swim, to play a game, to operate a tool, or to solve a problem as a result of instruction is rewarding

---

[4] Ernest R. Hilgard and Donald G. Marquis, "The Nature of Reinforcement," in *Conditioning and Learning* (New York: Appleton-Century-Crofts, Inc., 1940), chap. iv.

to him. It satisfies needs which he has recognized or which are inherent in his total situation. Status with peers is often related to the way games are played or the ability to perform some act such as swimming. Learning in such cases is its own reward. Even the slightest improvement may have its positive effect.

The good will and affection of the teacher are powerful sources of satisfaction, but their use is conditioned by the peer culture in which the group operates. For instance, open approval by the teacher in a slum-oriented group would be a serious threat to a pupil's status with peers and elders.[5] In adolescent society the teacher may show good will with discretion, but even in middle-class and upper-class groups it can easily be carried to a point where it backfires upon the status of the learner in the group.

It is not meant that the teacher will never show disapproval, but that aversive stimulation will be reserved until attempts at positive reinforcement have failed. It has been found that extroverts may be effectively stimulated by the use of blame, whereas the introvert would be less likely to respond and the danger of damaging results would be much greater. It should be recalled also that both praise and blame result in greater reinforcement than no response at all on the part of the teacher.

In conclusion, the use of both positive and negative forms of reinforcement is like using powerful drugs. There is no sure prescription that will cover all individuals with varied personalities and from many cultural backgrounds. The amount of reward must be geared to the group and the individuals in it. The overuse of reward and punishment will result in an immunity rendering them ineffective in the learning process.

Complex and multiple outcomes. *Learning of more than one type occurs at any one time. Outcomes such as behavior patterns consist of many separate learning products operating in a functional relationship. Different outcomes are acquired by different individuals in the same situation.*

These statements about learning center the teacher's attention upon ways in which more learning can be accomplished if he plans his work accordingly.

[5] Allison Davis, *Social Class Influences upon Learning* (Cambridge, Mass.: Harvard University Press, 1948), pp. 23-27.

Attention is first called to the fact that the products of a teaching-learning situation do not occur one at a time and alone. Furthermore, they are not limited to one type of learning.[6] For example, a man learning to play golf may, in addition to learning to like the game, find that he is learning a great deal about people, how to meet and communicate with them, and how to conduct business in informal situations. These things happen simultaneously with progress toward the initial objective of learning the game.

The various kinds of learning that go on together are not necessarily all on the positive side. The would-be golfer may learn to fear the professional and may learn to dislike certain individuals with whom he is thrown in contact or the pattern of behavior of a certain group.

Similarly, the pupil in school may increase skill in spelling and punctuation but not necessarily find reinforcement to do them well because of the teacher's method of handling the situation. He may integrate these skills into a pattern of good creative writing and a liking for it under more skillful professional handling. The way he feels about using the skills in the larger pattern is very important.

It may be surmised from the above paragraphs that the learning products which can occur are of many types. Attitudes toward school in general, teacher, and classmates, growing out of the experiences involved in learning a skill, are learned as a result of the teaching-learning situation as certainly as the skill itself. Pride in accomplishment, neat and accurate work, and in meeting standards, or indifference in these areas can result. One also acquires the abilities to evaluate and use what is learned in a broader sphere of activity and to persist to the completion of a task.

The possible variety of learning products is a promising aspect of teaching. These outcomes do not just happen; they are caused. The methods the teacher uses will determine most of these by-products. By consciously planning to bring about a majority of positive outcomes as by-products, the total educative value of a single learning experience is greatly increased.

The second point about learning outcomes refers to their complex functional nature. A game of basketball, for example, is made up of many skills and patterns tied together with information about the

[6] William H. Burton, *The Guidance of Learning Activities*, 2nd ed. (New York: Appleton-Century-Crofts, Inc., 1952), pp. 146-49.

rules of the games. A boy who turns in a creditable performance presents a pattern of behavior that puts each skill to work at precisely the right time along with several others. Footwork, dribbling, passing, fitting into position, looking for openings, and many other learned responses make up his play.

An equally complex learning has been accomplished by a girl who serves a dinner to her friends. The culinary skills of preparing the right combination of foods that makes a delightful meal are indeed complex. The artistic appearance of the table is a further combination of what has been learned about custom, materials, colors, and arrangements. But our hostess faces still the problem of seeing that her guests are properly received, comfortably and properly seated, and enjoyably entertained through pleasant conversation and gracious serving. To serve such a dinner to friends is a learning experience. To have done it successfully indicates that it has been learned—the many previous learning products were all functioning smoothly together.

The third point about learning outcomes is that they will vary from one individual to another in the same situation. There are many possible reasons for this. They stem not only from the inherent ability of the learners concerned; they are related to the values and motivations to which the learners have been exposed. The opportunity to serve a dinner as a learning experience would be received with enthusiasm by a girl accustomed to entertaining in the home. It might mean less—next to nothing, in fact—to a child reared in a slum section. The attitude of the parent toward the learning in question would have something to do with the amount of achievement. Finally, the personality of the timid and shy child would limit the benefits derived from such an experience.

Security. *Learning is most efficient in an atmosphere of security and belonging.*

Children may be inclined to develop fears and build phantasies around their school life to an extent that the progress of growth and learning is impaired. There are many fears that beset children and youth related to the school in general and the teacher in particular. Teachers accentuate these fears through unwise threats used to bring about compliance with their wishes. Common fears have to do with possibilities of failure in passing and punishment for failing to learn. For some children the fear of being unable to understand increases the chances that understanding will not come. There is always the parent-child relationship to be considered and many children have a fear that their parents will be disappointed in their school achievement. Parents often cause or increase the intensity of this fear by over-emphasis upon attainment of goals beyond the child's ability.

Carrying a heavy load of fear regarding school work may cause a child to elaborate in phantasy beyond the reality of a situation, with the result that he looks upon the teacher as a tyrant out of all proportion to the facts of the situation.[7] All kinds of exaggerated ideas of the teacher's lack of consideration and kindness may develop. The child has no desire to be dishonest. He has reached a point where reality and phantasy are blended and the difference is not clear to him. This is an unhealthful state of affairs and learning is impaired.

The teacher strives to keep from creating tensions of the type discussed above by making certain positive efforts. This is accomplished by sharing with the pupil in every way possible classroom responsibility, accepting him with all his faults, and striving to contribute as much as possible to conditions that are conducive to good general mental health.

In addition to being able to distinguish between fact and phantasy, there are other conditions which the learner must establish for himself with the aid of his teacher and the other significant adults in his life. One of these is a feeling of personal well-being. Given reasonably good physical health, the child achieves this feeling that he is important as a result of the attitudes his peers and the adults around him manifest toward him. The teacher is one of the most important adults in his life, and will want to contribute to the child's sense of well-being by being accessible as a friend and a counsellor.

A third condition which the learner will achieve with the help of the teacher is increasing tolerance for tension in everyday living. Conflicts arise in everyone's efforts to reach his goals; as a matter of fact, such tensions are a part of learning. A degree of tension brought about by striving to reach an unattainable goal, however, is

---

[7] Peter Blos, "Aspects of Mental Health in Teaching and Learning," *Mental Hygiene* 37:555-69, October 1953.

not conducive to good mental health; hence it is not helpful to learning. It is the teacher's function to assist both in the selection of attainable goals and in finding ways to attain them in some degree.[8] Through the experiences shared with the teacher in finding ways to relieve tension, the learner comes to accept it as a part of living.

Closely related to tolerance for tension is a fourth condition, the ability to accept one's role in life and find in it satisfaction in living. For example, no matter how hard a girl tries "to kiss her elbow" in the hope she can be a boy and play a boy's role in life, sooner or later she must accept the fact of being a girl and a woman. Most girls and women as they reach maturity find adequate expression and self-realization in this role. A few do not and an impaired state of mental health may result. The same adjustment is portrayed when physical disability such as blindness or loss of limbs occurs. The fact, though difficult, requires adjustment to a role within the realm of physical possibility. Each person strives to find satisfaction in living within the socio-economic level in which he is placed. If he cannot do so he may achieve a new economic status by extra effort and as a result added social recognition, coupled with new learned ways of responding to his new surroundings. These problems of accepting one's role and finding in it satisfactions are present in the lives of children. Therefore they are concerns of the teacher who would be of most help to them.

Certain facts about emotional disturbances are helpful to teachers in setting up their own attitudes and expectations with regard to children.[9] The first point is that an emotionally disturbed child is not just pretending to be sick—he is sick. The second point is that he did not choose to be that way. Third, if pain accompanies his illness it is not pretended—it is real pain. Fourth, he is not inherently a weak person who could be expected to get this way. Finally, emotional maladjustment appears in many forms, requiring an alertness to its possibility when unexplained behavior is manifested.

There are many sources from which a sense of security or lack of it may arise. Many of these sources are, of course, outside of the

[8] Celia B. Stendler, "Building Secure Children in Our Schools," *Childhood Education* 25:216-20, January 1949.
[9] C. H. Patterson, "The Classroom Teacher and the Emotional Problems of Children," *Understanding the Child* 21:67-72, June 1952.

school. The teacher can do little to relieve most of these outside conditions. The contribution which can be made at school, however, is sufficient to be significant.

Activity and experience. *Learning is accomplished by the learner for himself through first engaging in purposeful, conscious mental or physical activity, then continuing with the activity, undergoing its consequences to complete an experience.*

This statement of principle attempts to involve the complete cycle of a learning experience. Long ago Dewey said "When an activity is continued into the undergoing of consequences, when the change made by action is reflected back into a change made in us, the mere flux is loaded with significance. We learn something."[10] Our common expression, "learn by doing," is an over-simplification of the matter of activity and experience. The activity springs in the first place from some need or want in the awareness of the learner. The surrounding circumstances as well as the ready responses of the learner enter into the choice of the response to be made—what action to try. Without undergoing the consequences of the action the learner never knows whether he has achieved satisfaction of the want or failed.

The learning experience as described here involves the motivation of the learner and his readiness to learn. Some want or need that is important enough to him to justify taking action in the first place is necessary. Not only must he have such a goal for action, but he must be able to take action that will hold some promise of reaching the goal. For example, a boy is building a "machine" such as only boys know how to build. He wants a wheel heavy enough to serve as a flywheel. Not too far away is a junk pile, so he rides his bicycle to the junk pile and looks around. Sure enough, there is just what he wants. However, it is bolted to the frame of a large machine too heavy to move. In anticipation of such a situation, however, the boy has brought along an adjustable wrench. Try as he will he cannot loosen the rusted bolt which holds his wheel. Disappointed, he returns home, but later in the day when his father returns from work he explains the problem to him. The father suggests using a short length of pipe to lengthen the wrench handle, adding leverage. Re-

[10] John Dewey, "Experience and Thinking," *Democracy and Education* (New York: The Macmillan Company, 1916), chap. xi.

turning to the junk yard equipped with both the wrench and the gas pipe extension, this time the boy easily removes the bolt. Elated, he returns with the prized wheel and proceeds with his "invention."

This illustration points up the felt need which led the boy to cast about for a possible satisfactory wheel. He was large enough to go alone to the junk pile. He could ride a bicycle, had one to ride, and the distance was not great. Furthermore, he knew enough about machinery to equip himself with a suitable tool. Everything went fine up to the point of loosening the bolt. Here he reached a limit, for the wrench was designed for a man's use and in a less difficult situation. The disappointment resulted from finally having to return without the wheel. If satisfaction were to be gained it was obvious something else would have to be done. Using his father's advice and modifying his action led to success and satisfaction.

The consequences of both plans of action were significant in rounding out this experience. The decision to look for the needed wheel in the junk pile might have been abandoned before it was put into action, in which case the possibilities of a resource might not have been learned. The secondary problem, encountered because of lack of leverage, resulted in a modified action and success. Without this problem, the practical use of leverage would not have been learned, at this time, at least. The point that a change in plan of action may lead to success was an important learning for the boy. Otherwise disappointment and frustration would prevail and the whole experience of building the machine might be lost. The accompanying sense of failure would detract from the best conditions for mental health.

As implied in the statement of the principle, the situation relating to activity and experience is the same for mental or physical endeavor. Activity of both a mental and physical kind is illustrated above, with the emphasis on the physical. Other activity of an abstract nature could be drawn out in the same way. The same relationship to goal and consequences would be required to make of it an educational experience.

Meaning and understanding. *Purposeful, efficient, and functional learning is aided by meaning and understanding derived from experience, direct or vicarious.*

The section on activity and experience pointed up the necessity of a goal or purpose for initiating action by the learner. It is what the learner sees in a situation that determines the goal. The boy working on his "invention" could see hours of pleasure ahead in play with the machine. To him this would represent a satisfying result of his labor.

School learning requires goals too. They may be related to the child's personal plans for his future. For instance, a girl may envision herself as entertaining friends at the piano, and hence see value in long hours of practice. Another child may seek equal status with others in the school in the skills of arithmetic, spelling, or reading and see value in the work of learning these skills. Whatever the goal may be, it is determined by what the child sees in it.

The meaning attached to the situation is derived from experiences related to the matter at hand.[11] The girl at the piano may have admired the way her mother or a sister played for her or a group of friends. Perhaps a television artist had stirred her imagination. Possibly the approval of admiring friends or audience in the form of praise and applause is sought. In any event, the meaning she attaches to the learning situation comes from experiences related to it.

The crux of the problem of meaning and understanding is communication. For the teacher, the problem is to combine words and activities in such a way that learners derive from them the same thoughts that he puts into them. It is not possible to carry on school work without the use of words. Valuable as they are and much as they are to be encouraged, direct experiences cannot be provided in all areas of necessary learning. Where direct experience cannot be provided, an indirect experience, such as a television program, may help to clothe words and learning activities with meaning. The variety of means by which indirect experience can be provided includes films, television, radio, and dramatization.

Care to provide experiences that will give the pupil the same meanings for words as are intended by the teacher will add to the understanding of the learning situation. It will improve goal setting, reduce the amount of lost motion, and increase the probability of appropriate use. Thus, the great danger of verbalism, the parroting of words without knowing what they mean, is reduced. The principle is especially important in teaching reading where meaning of

[11] Lee J. Cronbach, "The Meaning of Problems," *Supplementary Educational Monographs*, No. 66 (Chicago: The University of Chicago Press, 1948), pp. 32-43.

words in context must be included with the ability to pronounce words.

Processes as well as words must be understood against a background of experience. Pupils do become able to perform the mechanics of arithmetical processes without being able to select the appropriate one in dealing with numbers. It is often necessary to develop basic number experiences with a child before he can progress in upper elementary arithmetic. Such things as are done by good parents in play with their children of pre-school age are implied. The actual use of blocks, sticks, or other objects to show accumulation or addition is sometimes required to give meaning to the process of addition. The important question of when to add requires such treatment if the process is not understood.

Meaning of processes in everyday life, likewise, causes confusion. A child who has never participated in choice making with a group has trouble with such a word as "vote." One child, whose father had gone to the polls to vote, associated the latter with "boat," the nearest thing to it he could think of. Add the confusion with "poles" which carry telephone wires, and the hopelessness of the situation is apparent. Children in modern schools vote on various questions. They are shown voting booths and machines and sometimes actually operate them. The full significance of the vote may require greater maturity, but the way voting is done has been made clear. There is now meaning where in the mind of the child in the example there was utter confusion.

Backgrounds of children vary in the extent of experience related to school learning. A child of active parents who take him about with them will attach meaning to more things because he has seen more. Likewise, the degree of intelligence and maturity of the learner will determine the need for supplemental experience. The less the education, maturity, and intelligence of the learner the more he will need direct experiences. Learners of higher intelligence will need less direct or vicarious experience and will have the advantage of speed and ultimate range in learning as their use of more and more abstractions develops.

Multi-sensory approach. *Learning experiences may be improved through ingenious use of each sense in combination with one or more other senses.*

The sensory avenues most commonly used in school learning are sight and hearing. The use of these senses can be effectively expanded beyond reading and listening to the teacher while he "tells" something to pupils. The combination of seeing and hearing with touch, taste, and smell to assist pupils in reproducing total direct experiences of others is a further means of improving learning.

An original experience often makes its impression through more sensory avenues than is realized at the time. Temperature, characteristic odors, and even tastes make up situations, and are impossible to reproduce through verbal means. Hence, a part of the impact of the original experience is lost. Take, for example, a visit to a dairy farm. The best written description cannot convey to the city-bred child the way the cows are fed and milked, the pleasant odor of good hay and feed in a clean barn, the sounds of the animals feeding, the animal heat inside on a cool day, and the refreshment of cool milk and buttermilk in the milkhouse.

Through the use of still pictures some improvement can be made upon the restrictions of verbal means of relaying the experience. A black and white sound film can add movement and sound, giving a far more realistic impression of the trip to the dairy farm. The addition of color film conveys an even more accurate visual experience. Thus the sense of sight has been used to great advantage in learning beyond its restricted use in reading alone. Yet so far it is in the realm of vicarious experience. Likewise the sound track brings some of the auditory impressions experienced in the direct visit. The sense of hearing is exploited beyond the restricted use in listening while the teacher "tells" the pupils something. The learner is not allowed free choice, however, for he must see only what the camera is pointed toward and hear only what is in range of the microphone. He is not able to select his sounds well because microphones have a way of picking up all extraneous noises without partiality. The learner has received an improved experience, even though it may be one that lacks all the impact of a real visit.

In spite of the limitations cited above, it is clearly desirable to consider any and all aids to exploit fully each sensory approach and to combine as many such approaches as are practical in the situation. In this way vicarious experiences are given added effectiveness in causing learning to be meaningful.

Whole–part–whole learning. *Learning by wholes derives its greater efficiency over part learning through the learner's perception of essential interrelationships in the material to be learned.*

An adage of teaching, "Proceed from the simple to the complex," has been taken at face value so long that no one is certain of its origin. On the surface it seems valid, carried to extremes in many kinds of learning, it is open to question.

Field theory psychologists have challenged the connectionist view that learning is additive in nature. Rather, they insist that initial learning experiences should expose the learner to unitary wholes rather than segments. Illustrations are drawn from memorizing poetry, learning to read, learning to swim, learning to comprehend historical documents, and many others.

Conclusive evidence that one method of learning is superior to the other is not available. Two important points to guide in the selection of the whole method, however, are:

1. Whether or not there is a relationship among the parts which gives meaning to the whole, and
2. Whether or not this relationship is such that it can be comprehended by the learner.[12]

Wholly unrelated items such as lists of words, numbers, and unrelated facts do not fall within the category of materials suited to whole learning.

On the other hand, words that can be learned together, that make up a whole sentence, do have a relationship to one another. Words carefully selected in keeping with maturity and experience of learners are learned effectively in relation to other words and to the sentence to which they gave and from which they derive meaning.

Learning a game is difficult unless one can see the game in its entirety. Unless one understands the advantage in having kings in checkers there seems to be little point in reaching the king row. A bid in contract bridge makes no sense if one knows only auction bridge. To learn to bid without comprehending the place of bidding in contract is next to useless.

In either game suggested above, the learner must be able to see

[12] Lee J. Cronbach, *Educational Psychology* (New York: Harcourt, Brace & Company, 1954), pp. 306-09.

the relationship of his action to the whole game. In the classroom the attempt to teach by wholes may as well give way to part teaching where the relationships between parts cannot be comprehended.

For the reasons indicated above there are differences in effectiveness of whole learning methods for children of different intellectual abilities. Children of superior intelligence tend to profit more from the use of whole methods because they are able to comprehend the pattern of the whole and the relationships among the various parts.

The length of the material or the operation to be learned determines practical limits for whole learning. Even though whole learning for poems and plays is recommended, there is a practical consideration when they are too long. In this case divisions of poems and acts of plays can become the wholes to be learned.

In summary, it may be said that there is belief and some evidence that whole learning has a more important place in modern education than it currently fills. With the emphasis on meaning and problem solving in present-day goals of education, the greater values of relationships in whole learning are to be sought.

Transfer of learning. *The chances that learned responses will be applied to new problem situations are increased by clear objectives, learning activities much like adult activities anticipated, and conscious effort by the learner to generalize so that new opportunities for application will be recognized.*

The ultimate success of any training program depends upon whether it improves performance in practice. The success of the school is related to the extent to which it accomplishes the purposes set for it in a given community and culture.

The transfer of school learning may be considered in terms of specialized learning, on the one hand, and personal growth or general learning on the other. Questions are frequently raised about the seeming lack of carry-over of arithmetical ability to a job situation. Less frequently, questions are raised about carry-over of school training when acts of poor citizenship are performed.

Questions of this type will always prevail because there are many factors, such as intelligence, social class values and attitudes, and health and parental care, over which the school has little immediate control. However, the school can improve the chances of transfer of learning by giving attention to some things which may not currently receive sufficient emphasis.[13]

Greater clearness as to what the school is supposed to teach children would go a long way to improve the probability of transfer. The community and the school working together can do much to make it clear what learners are supposed to learn. This is a prerequisite to any program of education.

The materials and methods by which learning is accomplished can be related as closely as possible to what learners will be doing later. That is, practice exercises in arithmetic, business training, and science will be couched in modern business terms. Some settings approximating the adult world will be provided. This likening to modern life with all its variety can, of course, go only so far.

The most important single effort that can be made is to generalize constantly so that the learner sees how the learning he is doing could crop out in other situations, and to create for him an awareness and an alertness to this possibility. The learner is finally responsible for the effort required to accomplish transfer from even the best of learning situations.

Many desired learning outcomes are integrated patterns of action. This characteristic of many important learnings has been emphasized earlier. The inherent relationships of skills included in the composite requires that these relationships be in evidence in the learning situation. Citizenship has been mentioned. Being an effective citizen brings many skills into focus. All the skills of good human relations are involved. The ability to share effectively in group study of problems is likewise a part of the pattern. Skill as a leader of discussion contributes to the latter function. Many other similar learned abilities enter into becoming an effective citizen. These skills cannot be learned effectively in isolation from conditions comparable to those in which they will find use.

Transferability of learning outcomes depends upon the teacher and the learner. Neither can be complacent in the teaching-learning situation. The learner sabotages all the opportunity he has been provided, if he becomes complacent about the matter after he leaves the school. The teacher has the responsibility of selecting materials

[13] For a good summary see: Thomas G. Andrews and Lee J. Cronbach, "Transfer of Training," in *Encyclopedia of Educational Research*, ed. W. S. Monroe (New York: The Macmillan Company, 1950), pp. 1483-89.

and methods that will bear some resemblance to later use. He has the further responsibility of clearing his own mind and that of the learner of any idea that transfer will occur without special effort. He owes it to the learner to let him know that what he is learning can be transferred, and to give him practice in recognizing old problems in new clothes. In return, the community and the school may reasonably expect the learner to make a continuous effort to recognize the old problems in new situations.

SUMMARY

It has been the purpose of this chapter to review the principles of learning related to the teacher's work. The teacher has presumably studied these matters in previous full-length courses in educational psychology. This review of learning principles complements what has already been treated in Part One of this book. Principles of learning provide a necessary foundation for the development of part of the principles of teaching by which the teacher selects the way he will teach. These principles of teaching, with illustrations, will be developed in the next chapter.

Learning principles likewise make up the background for planning lessons and selecting learning activities for pupils. These matters, too, receive attention in later chapters.

This chapter occupies a strategic position, therefore, in the total picture of developing competences in teaching. The teacher should feel, as a result of this study of learning principles, increased competence in the following areas:

1. Discussing classroom problems with his supervisor in terms of what psychology has taught us about learning.

2. Interpreting teaching and learning observed in the classroom.

3. Creating simple learning experiences for children illustrating principles of learning.

4. Evaluating his own efforts to help children learn.

Because of the interlocking nature of the two chapters of Part Two, the problems are placed at the end of Chapter 6.

BIBLIOGRAPHY

Anderson, G. Lester, "Quantitative Thinking as Developed under Connectionist and Field Theories of Learning," in *Learning Theory in School Situations,* University of Minnesota Studies in Education, No. 2, pp. 40-73. Minneapolis. University of Minnesota Press, 1949.

Blair, Glenn M., R. Stewart Jones, and Ray H. Simpson, "Maturation and Experience Together Determine Readiness," in *Educational Psychology.* New York: The Macmillan Company, 1954. Pp. 114-22.

Brownell, William A., and Harold F. Moser, *Meaningful vs. Mechanical Learning,* Research Studies in Education, No. 8. Durham, N.C.: Duke University Press, 1949.

Barker, Roger G., "Success and Failure in the Classroom," *Progressive Education* 19:221-24, 1942.

Coladarci, Arthur P., ed., *Educational Psychology: A Book of Readings.* New York: The Dryden Press, 1955.

Combs, Arthur W., "Intelligence from a Perceptual Point of View," *Journal of Educational Psychology* 47:662-73, July 1952.

Cronbach, Lee J., *Educational Psychology.* New York: Harcourt, Brace & Company, 1954.

Dewey, John, "Experience and Thinking," in *Democracy and Education.* New York: The Macmillan Company, 1916. Chap. xi.

Fullagar, William A., Hal G. Lewis, and Carroll F. Cumbee, eds., *Readings for Educational Psychology.* New York: Thomas Y. Crowell Company, 1956.

Hilgard, Ernest R., "Individual Differences and Their Testing," in *Introduction to Psychology.* New York: Harcourt, Brace & Company, 1953. Chap. xv.

——, and Donald G. Marquis, "The Nature of Reinforcement," in *Conditioning and Learning.* New York: Appleton-Century-Crofts, Inc., 1940. Chap. iv.

Koenker, Robert H., "Arithmetic Readiness at the Kindergarten Level," *Journal of Educational Research* 42:218-23, 1948.

Levinger, Leah, and Lois B. Murphy, "Implications of the Social Scene for the Education of Young Children," in *Early Childhood Education,* ed. Nelson B. Henry. 1947 Yearbook, The National Society for the Study of Education. Chicago: The University of Chicago Press, 1947. Chap. iii.

May, Mark A., "The Psychology of Learning from Demonstration Films," *Journal of Educational Psychology* 37:1-12, 1946.

National Society for the Study of Education, *The Psychology of Learning* (1942 Yearbook). Chicago: The University of Chicago Press, 1942.

Sears, Pauline S., "Levels of Aspiration in Academically Successful and Unsuccessful Children," *Journal of Abnormal and Social Psychology* 35:498-563, 1948.

Seidman, Jerome M., ed., *Readings in Educational Psychology*. Boston: Houghton Mifflin Company, 1955.

Skinner, B. F., "Function versus Aspect," in *Science and Human Behavior*. New York: The Macmillan Company, 1953. Chap. xiii.

———, "The Science of Learning and the Art of Teaching," *Harvard Educational Review* 24:86-87, Spring 1954.

Swenson, Esther J., "Organization and Generalization as Factors in Learning, Transfer, and Retroactive Inhibition," in *Learning Theory in School Situations*, University of Minnesota Studies in Education, No. 2. Minneapolis: University of Minnesota Press, 1949. Pp. 9-39.

Smith, Henry P., "Individual Differences in Ability to Learn," in *Psychology in Teaching*. Englewood Cliffs, N.J.: Prentice-Hall, Inc., 1954. Chap. x.

Stolurow, Lawrence M., ed., *Readings in Learning*. Englewood Cliffs, N.J.: Prentice-Hall, Inc., 1953.

Thompson, George W., and Clarence W. Hunnicutt, "The Effect of Praise or Blame on the Work Achievement of Introverts and Extroverts," *Journal of Educational Psychology* 35:257-66, 1949.

6

Principles of teaching
that promote learning

What has been said about principles of learning needs special interpretation. The teaching profession has not yet reached a point, and it never will, where the performance of certain rituals will guarantee a specified learning outcome. In the field of electrical engineering, it is possible to predict with precision, through mathematical computations, the result of operating certain equipment under controlled conditions. A splendid illustration of this fact can be observed if the teacher will but turn on his radio and reflect upon the exactness with which he can locate any station within the receiving range of the instrument. So precise is the outcome, in fact, that it is common to find sets with push buttons. Merely to push a certain button is a guarantee that a predetermined station in a distant city will be brought in.

Human learning cannot be predicted with such exactness. One can, however, repose a certain kind of confidence in the application of the principles of learning listed in Chapter 5. Experienced educators know that, when teachers control their practices in accordance with these principles, greater learning results in more cases than when learning activities are designed by chance. Other things being equal, therefore, the teacher will use, as an application of the principle of readiness, pre-tests of knowledge, skills, or attitudes in an effort to locate the approximate status of each individual pupil. On the basis of these observations the teacher will then decide what learning is best adapted to the group and what procedure to apply. The expenditure of effort in this practice followed by appropriate adjustment of the learner's program has a profound effect upon his perception of the situation. It may well result in higher motivation, better individual and group behavior, greater initiative on the part of pupils, and, in the final analysis, more rapid and lasting progress toward goals sought. Each principle of learning suggests a set of conditions, to be experienced by the learner and provided by the teacher, in which it may be confidently expected that increased learning will occur. Corresponding principles of teaching to assist the teacher in bringing about these favorable conditions will now be presented.

Readiness. *Teaching effectiveness is increased by predicting pupil readiness, providing tryout experiences under observation, and readjusting the program where predictions do not hold up. In the final analysis, readjustment is most effective as it relates to the individual.*

The teacher of the elementary grades will be familiar with the problems of readiness. Much is written about general school readiness for children who are entering school for the first time. A few of the common conditions of general readiness for school attendance include ability to take care of personal toilet habits, put on wraps, tie shoes, adjust to the school situation, and be separated from parents. Often children are started to school before they are really ready for it.

The prediction of pupil readiness for learning takes into consideration, first, the events of maturation incidental to the sequence of growth and development. That is, a process of maturing is going on constantly in the nervous system and in the other systems of the body, making possible learning outcomes of steadily increasing difficulty.

The developments along the way making possible a learning response such as reading may not occur simultaneously. The mental and muscular development involved, with other factors, constitute a "sequence of readinesses" for learning to read rather than a single state of readiness.[1]

In addition to the developmental aspects of readiness, experiences which children have, related to an area of learning, bring the powers they have developed into use in proportion to their breadth and frequency. For example, a child who has played number games and counted and accumulated objects has brought into use some of his potential arithmetical ability as it has developed. The knowledge that such experiences are in his background would suggest greater probable readiness.

Not all of the suggested contributing factors can be observed directly in predicting readiness. For example, some of the characteristics of a learner who is ready to read include background of experience, mental age of six and one half years, corresponding emotional maturity, the desire to read, and sufficient visual and auditory power to participate in the effort.[2] Therefore, the prediction must be made upon the basis of available observations, such as mental age through testing, sufficient vision and hearing through examinations of these senses, and possible inferences on experiential background from records and parental conferences. The necessity of assuming a great deal in other phases of development make necessary the "tryout" learning experiences described later.

Prediction of pupil readiness involves, secondly, a number of factors related to the learner's personality and his own personal goals. Again, some of these factors can be observed or determined through examination. The physical health of the learner can be ascertained through physical examination. Through opportunities to observe the activities of the learner in informal situations certain inferences may be drawn related to interests and hobbies, attitudes, and mental health. Through contacts with parents the attitude of the home toward learning may be guessed. Since much is left to inference and subjective means of assessment, a further reason for tryout experiences is evident.

In the third place, prediction is based upon the aptitude of the

[1] William H. Burton, *The Guidance of Learning Activities*, 2nd ed. (New York: Appleton-Century-Crofts, Inc., 1952), pp. 192-94.

[2] Paul Witty, *Reading in Modern Education* (Boston: D. C. Heath and Company, 1949), p. 55.

learner and prerequisite knowledge and skill. General learning aptitude is obtainable through the use of intelligence tests. Achievement
tests produce reliable evidence of information and skills in many
areas. In other areas such as music, athletics, and dramatics performance offers the best evidence.

To the extent that it is possible for the teacher to select information about learners from indications of development, goals, personality, and abilities, his predictions of readiness will be improved. It
is necessary to arrange tryout learning experiences, however, for
three reasons: First, the prediction could not involve data on some
important factors; second, there is a need to give tryout experiences
on the possibility that a greater degree of readiness than anticipated
has been attained through growth and development; and third,
should the tryout indicate a lack of readiness, readjustment of the
program can be made.

Providing tryout experiences has special importance, because the
readiness inherent in the individual must be challenged into action
to be productive of learning. The frontiersman no doubt often had
adequate maturity for reading. Since neither the necessity nor the
opportunity often presented itself, he did not learn to read. The
teacher does not wait until readiness is apparent. He tests by tryout
experiences at frequent intervals to see whether readiness is present.

On the basis of observations made carefully during the tryout, the
teacher decides whether the program can continue on this level or
whether readjustments must be made. The importance of readjustments made upon the basis of tryout cannot be overestimated. Readjustments are of two general types: those which have to do with
shifting the framework of operations to provide different series of
learning experiences for different groups of pupils; and those which
have to do with shifting the experiences of an individual learner
within the established framework for groups.

Readjustments of the first type might include placing initial
arithmetic experiences at fourth grade instead of second grade. Or
algebra might be moved from ninth grade to eleventh grade. The
real problem involved in such shifts is to find the place in the
learner's development "where certain types of understanding can be
developed."[3] The general progression of studies in the school pro-

[3] Lee J. Cronbach, *Educational Psychology* (New York: Harcourt, Brace &
Company, 1954), p. 226.

gram has resulted from years of effort to adjust to the usual rate of development of the average class. The teacher is responsible for carrying this adjustment on to the individuals in his class.

Other administrative devices of adjustment include efforts at homogeneous grouping, acceleration of superior pupils, and retention of slow learners. In general, these plans are ineffective in meeting the problems of readiness. Efforts at homogeneous grouping throughout the entire school program break down because there is insufficient relationship among the many factors contributing to readiness. Pupils grouped on the basis of one variable may be quite heterogeneous with respect to another variable.[4]

The grouping of pupils for particular activities on the basis of performance in that activity is especially advantageous in skill subjects such as reading, arithmetic, algebra, spelling, and grammar. The subgroups formed in an elementary classroom for purposes of instruction in reading are sometimes flexible to allow movement back and forth. The resultant interaction among pupils is beneficial. This form of grouping is quite different from the sectioning of an entire grade for the entire day's program.

There seem to be advantages in the acceleration of superior pupils at high school and college levels when there is an accompanying high degree of physical and social maturity.[5] The absence of enrichment opportunities increases the desirability of acceleration. The retention of slow learners in a grade level is of doubtful value, although when it seems that the pupil is capable of learning and has had an obvious interruption of opportunity that jeopardizes chances of success, retention may be advantageous. The preponderance of experience and research, such as Goodlad's study, gives cause to question the value of the practice.[6] Two groups of unsuccessful first graders were studied in a dozen schools. One group was promoted, the other retained. Both groups were maladjusted in their second year.

The teacher's activities in adjusting learning experiences to the

[4] *Ibid.*, p. 231.

[5] Merle R. Sumption, Dorothy Norris, and Lewis M. Terman, "Special Education for the Gifted Child," in Nelson B. Henry, ed., *The Education of Exceptional Children*, 1950 Yearbook, The National Society for the Study of Education (Chicago: The University of Chicago Press, 1950), p. 279.

[6] John I. Goodlad, "Research and Theory Regarding Promotion and Non-Promotion," *Elementary School Journal* 53:150-55, 1952.

readiness of the individual blend heavily with efforts to adjust teaching to individual differences. Most suggestions so far have to do with shifting pupils around from one group or grade to another. In spite of this effort, the teacher is faced with individual problems of readiness. The practices of adjusting instructional methods in the classroom will be discussed in the section on planning.

Individual differences. *Teaching effectiveness is improved as teachers seek causes of poor responses that make individuals different, treat such causes as are remediable, and adjust requirements for individuals where treatment is ineffective. On the other hand, good responses that make individuals different are nourished to the end that the range of differences becomes greater.*

Reflection upon his own experiences from early childhood will be sufficient to refresh the teacher on the extent of individual differences. He will recall the child who could run faster or climb higher than anyone else in his group of playmates. He will also recall that some children wanted to run faster than anyone else while others were satisfied just to run. As school days came along it was obvious that there were those who learned numbers more rapidly than others and those who got into fights more frequently than others, and in almost every area of activity similar differences soon became apparent.

The classroom problem of meeting wide variations in pupil response is one of making plans. Adapting to individual differences does not mean making individual plans for each child in the room. Given the right opportunity, children will to a surprising degree make their own individual plans. The same general type of activity may be suitable for a large number of children. Within a given type of activity the pupil will inevitably determine his own individual approach. Another consideration to be kept constantly in mind is the kind of goals for which teaching is being planned. For those types of learnings that might be roughly classified as skills or factual information, the organization of the material and the exercises will be developed by the teacher in such a way as to allow different rates of progress in learnings of increasing complexity and difficulty. Learnings of the type commonly found in arithmetic, high school mathematics, reading, spelling, or chemistry are of this kind.

The informational side of certain project activities likewise provides for the more able students to do research and designing. The unique abilities of all pupils, regardless of intellectual capacity, find expression. In projects, more than the skill or factual learning is involved. Very definite purposes of personal development, such as becoming a contributing member of a group, developing a feeling that one has group status, learning to cooperate with all levels of intelligence toward the accomplishment of a common goal, and similar competences of democratic living are considered. Often, through activities of this kind, persons who have not accomplished at more than ordinary levels in intellectual learning make contributions that cause them to be appreciated by other members of the group. This condition is beneficial for both those doing the appreciating and those being appreciated.

Each pupil should be encouraged to pursue his own interests and go as far as seems feasible and profitable.

Courtesy of *The Indiana Teacher*

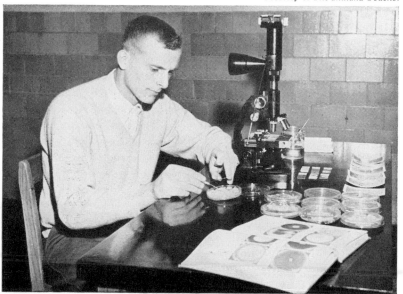

A good example of this kind of situation occurred in a junior high school English class. Many junior high school English courses involve a unit in letter writing. About the time the unit in letter writing was being opened in this particular instance, a convocation speaker showed films of some of the experiences that youth in Germany were undergoing in clearing up rubble after World War II. Upon return to class the pupils proposed that it would be interesting if they could obtain the names of some young people in Germany and correspond with them about the things they were doing. Through the United States Department of State arrangements for the correspondence were completed and the work of writing the letters was begun.

The teacher was surprised to find that some of those pupils who had not done particularly well with spelling, grammar, and punctuation did produce some very interesting and well organized letters. When the letters were read before the group the interesting quality of some was apparent to the pupils. The writers who generally did not do well in technical aspects of grammar but who had produced interesting letters achieved new status with the group. The opportunity to appreciate abilities other than spelling and grammar in their fellows was likewise a valuable experience for the pupils who normally handled the mechanics of writing with ease.

Opportunities for this type of recognition of individual achievement are greatest when classroom teaching is organized around problems and interests of pupils. The unit plan of teaching holds greater promise of meeting the needs of individual learners than any method of teaching so far developed. An extensive development of unit teaching is offered in Chapters 9, 10, and 11.

In any classroom organization the teacher can help pupils select goals which they can achieve. For the slow learner this is extremely important, since inability to reach a goal or repeated experiences of running out of time lead to continual feelings of failure. If possible, such a child should be allowed to complete a task, no matter how simple, before moving to another. Selection of appropriate goals for the more able pupils and provision for progress to new tasks should be a matter of equal concern for the teacher.

If the assign-study-recite formula is predominant in the classroom, assignments and questions may be varied with attention being given to individual capacities. Pupils can be required to report only those things that the teacher feels they can do successfully.

Modern concepts of worthwhile educative experiences and the availability of many forms of materials have led to wide use of independent work activities for a portion of the pupil's time. Originally conceived as "seat work" to keep pupils quiet while teachers did something else, the independent work activity is now stressed as productive of many desirable outcomes. Burton's summary of the nature of such activities follows:

> Practice work in reading, writing, arithmetic, and spelling is still useful when properly related to classwork and under legitimate motives.
>
> Recreational and informational reading of many types is easily available.
>
> Performing individual projects for the good of the group at work on a unit; finding and making available information and materials; arranging an exhibit; arranging an assembly; making pictures, posters, slides, models, and so forth.
>
> Creative work: writing prose or poetry; drawing; painting; modeling; arts and craft work generally; and many others. These may be purely individual or may be contributory to group enterprises.
>
> Constructing models, exhibits, play equipment, science apparatus, puppets.
>
> Listening.
>
> Collecting.[7]

Other ways in which teachers can adapt to individual differences are presented in seeking adjustments to meet physical size, auditory or visual handicaps, and the like. There are children and young people who lack feelings of security adequate for the best advancement in school to whom the teacher can offer a bit of extra warmth, friendliness, or a helping hand. The methods of control used in a classroom may drive certain already-disturbed children within their shells. A democratic, friendly approach will contribute most to the whole range of learning for which the school exists.

Motivation. *Teaching effectiveness is improved as the pupil is involved in setting goals for learning, as he encounters problems in reaching them, and as he relates his satisfaction in their solution to new goals.*

[7] William H. Burton, *The Guidance of Learning Activities* (New York: Appleton-Century-Crofts, Inc., 1952), pp. 280-81.

Teachers have the problem of making pupils desire what the school has to offer. Young children with a desire to read, for example, learn to read more rapidly than others. This desire often springs from the fact that the parents have read to children and thus caused them to equate reading with pleasure. Boys from middle grades upward aspire to play on a baseball or basketball team. Girls in junior high school often want to participate in group musical activities, such as school orchestras and quartets. Actual group participation is a second step removed from the direct learning necessary to make this participation possible. Nevertheless, it is sufficient motivation to make them willing to undergo the long hours of practice or vigorous exercise to accomplish the goal. The value of the learning is seldom doubted in these instances by the children.

Lessons in factual information, in writing, and in handling num-

The growing interest in the physically handicapped child often finds expression in specially designed facilities.

Courtesy of *The Muncie Star*

bers present themselves as arduous tasks to many pupils. Somehow a desire to know these things needs to be developed in the pupil. There must be within the youngster an acceptance of the goal toward which these learnings lead. Such goals have a wide variety of origins and often arise from the most surprising situations.

Today's school endorses such a wide variety of learnings that it is difficult to imagine a child who cannot be interested in some aspect of such a program. There are, however, many pupils who live amidst outside influences that make it difficult for them to feel kindly toward the program of the school at which attendance is mandatory.

Modern teaching procedures try to take into account the necessity of the pupil's understanding and acceptance of goals. Various devices are used to accomplish these ends. To the extent that it is possible to engage pupils in planning for the activities they will undertake as individuals and as a group, the purposes of the course or unit will be more in keeping with the needs and interests of the class. Children are encouraged, in classes planned this way, to ask the questions that concern them in a given area. The kinds of questions that fourth graders will ask about such things as weather will be different from those asked by seventh graders in the same subject. By the same token, more advanced questions will be expected from seniors. A constant alertness to the questions pupils have about day to day happenings in the community will provide a great many sources of fruitful study. Excellent units have been developed by teachers around spontaneous incidents. For example, an elementary unit resulted in one school because a flock of wild geese happened to fly over the school grounds. The unit was not purely accidental. This particular incident happened at a time that the teacher thought was right for beginning certain major studies. Many teachers plan for and await these sparks that set off a barrage of questions from children in an area such as science or social studies. In like manner, they often pass by, or reserve for the moment, questions that are not in accordance with their plans.

The effect upon children of carrying out a unit which springs from an interest that is spontaneous is almost miraculous. To them it is the most important thing in the world. They are impressed by the fact that school is a place to learn about the things they want to know. Being able to proceed with those things that are of great interest at the time makes for efficiency in learning.

Not all the learnings that the school must accomplish will be inspired by the incidents and the expressed curiosities of learners. It is necessary that things which they have not thought about be called to their attention, too. This is the function of the teacher. It is desirable to make every effort to have pupils accept these learnings as worthwhile.

Needs of children and developmental tasks of youth have been discussed in relation to earlier topics. These needs and basic sources of motivation have to be understood by teachers in order to interpret the requests which children make. The teacher unfamiliar with developmental needs of children and young people may not give proper attention to requested activities that contribute to status with their fellows or to a sense of security in the school or in the home.

The alert teacher finds a variety of original ways to develop new and lasting interests in the lives of pupils.

Courtesy of *The Indiana Teacher*

Learning to identify goals and purposes is like other learning for individual pupils and groups of pupils. A group that has been accustomed to having the teacher set all the goals and make all the decisions, and has had little, if any, part in the selection of ways of going about jobs in the classroom, will not immediately take up the ideas suggested above. It is necessary for them to be taught that, in order to accomplish the most learning for the amount of time spent, they must set clear objectives for themselves. It is not reasonable to expect a group of children to be able to do this immediately. It can only be accomplished through patient effort on the teacher's part to elicit from them questions of concern.

Effect. *Teaching effectiveness is improved by the prompt use of after-effects to responses, geared to the individual. Positive reactions following a response produce most consistent gains; negative reactions following a response are effective in controlled situations and are more productive than no reaction at all.*

The teacher is urged to emphasize the use of praise instead of blame, success instead of failure, approval instead of disapproval, attention instead of disregard, and affection instead of indifference in dealing with pupils in the classroom. These acts are the positive reactions to which the principle refers. They contribute much to a favorable climate for learning and pleasant human relations. Their importance extends beyond that, however. The correct use of these reactions to the responses of learners contributes much to the ultimate learning of the child and the likelihood of transfer of learning.

The complete law of effect as originally stated by Thorndike included negative stimulations as being equally effective in reducing the chances of recurrence of a response.[8] More recently, as a result of experimentation with human subjects, Thorndike modified his conclusions.[9] While satisfaction or positive forms of reaction were found to strengthen learning, the negative counterpart, annoyance, was credited with aiding learning through encouraging the learner to try a new approach. Some evidence was cited in the preceding chapter to indicate that negative stimulations may have a place with

[8] E. L. Thorndike, *Animal Intelligence* (New York: The Macmillan Company, 1911), p. 244.

[9] E. L. Thorndike, *Fundamentals of Learning* (New York: Teachers College, Columbia University, 1932), p. 311.

extroverted personality types. While this evidence is by no means conclusive, there is rather general agreement that even a negative aftereffect to a response is more effective than total disregard of the response.

Confusion is readily encountered in the relationship between an aftereffect and the response which elicited the reaction. Skinner points out that the reaction to a response does not cause that response but increases the *probability* that it will be made should a like situation arise in the future.[10]

In terms of classroom performance, then, what does the principle of effect mean for the teacher? Among other things, it means careful attention to the matter of success in children's school experiences. As stated earlier, satisfaction from making progress in a school subject is a great reinforcer. The boy who is "stuck" and discouraged with his mathematics problems is either going to be "stuck" and discouraged with the next new list or will attack with expectations of winning. Which response he makes will depend upon the outcomes this time. The role of success becomes clear. The success of the pupil is related to other principles already discussed, especially the matter of readiness. The teacher's role is to make adjustments that will enable the learner to succeed. This role is indirect, but very potent. The teacher, through adjustment of the situation surrounding the pupil, places him in a position to succeed.

More direct roles are also played by the teacher in implementing effect in the classroom. When a child is learning and knows that the *teacher knows* he is learning, he is anxious to keep on. The means by which he is assured of the teacher's recognition of the fact will vary. The teacher may only nod his head and smile, but to the child who has just made a new step in learning, this reaction is worth more than gold! The teacher may praise the pupil, in good taste so that the individual's security in the group is not threatened. Sometimes the accomplishment places the learner in a position to do something more to his liking or to join a group to which he aspires. Any of these aftereffects is conducive to a continuation of the activity that brought them about.

Teachers ask, "What do you do when pupils do not give the right answer or respond in other ways that cannot be praised?" It is not

---

[10] B. F. Skinner, *Science and Human Behavior* (New York: The Macmillan Company, 1953), p. 62.

to be expected that the "right answer" will be forthcoming in every response. It may be that the pupil's thinking is basically correct. In an atmosphere of security the pupil will feel free to give answers that represent his best effort. He will feel free to ask questions and make suggestions which represent the progress of his learning to date. He can be encouraged by the teacher's attention to his question or by the response which his classmates make to his suggestion. This is another reason why the group needs to be trained to give courteous attention to each pupil's problem. The effect of the peer group reaction in the adolescent years is more powerful than any reaction of the teacher.

If a learner responds in such a manner that no positive reaction can be mustered, a simple considered disapproval is better than no reaction. It is suggested, however, that negative reactions are habitually overdone by teachers. Since positive reactions are so much more reliable in increasing the probability of recurrence of a desired response, careful consideration needs to precede the use of any other kind.

Complex and multiple outcomes. *Teaching effectiveness is improved by selecting methods that control "by-products" that are sure to accompany the focal learning of any teaching effort.*

It is not uncommon to become so intent upon accomplishing a single teaching objective that the whole energy of the teacher is focused upon it. The goal of the teacher may be to have children learn a particular game. The object of the game is explained along with the rules and other ways in which the play is to be accomplished. The game begins and little by little the children learn to play it. While learning the new game, the children are comparing it with other games they know. If it does not compare favorably in fun derived, they may resent the imposition of this new game at this particular time. Fifth grade boys, for example, once grumbled about basketball being introduced in their gym classes when they would so much prefer playing dodge ball. There was a certain reaction against basketball because of this intrusion upon their preferred sport. A new game might prove to be more fun than the things they have been doing, in which case they would learn to like it.

Modern teaching methods accomplish many learnings in addition to the traditional goals of schools. They expect to develop competence in reading, numbers, writing, spelling, and grammar, along with learning socially acceptable effective ways of handling their relations with people. This is made possible by the fact that learnings do not occur as single units but in simultaneous combination. Teaching methods are being developed so that positive personal growth outcomes result as well as knowledge and skills. For example, a class studying history and government may be conducted in such a way as to provide opportunities for discussion of controversial issues, for cooperative research into local history or local government, for communication with adults having information that can be used, and for systematic procedures in solving problems. These activities are undertaken as ways to provide young people with opportunities to learn to work together, to learn to attack problems through the use of resources, and to learn to communicate with members of the adult community. When such teaching procedures are used, the informational items of learning are enhanced by growth from the experiences provided by the procedures themselves.

Security. *Teaching effectiveness is improved by sharing pupils' tensions and reducing them through problem solving, sharing their doubts about their roles in life, and helping them to see potential satisfactions.*

A disturbed class does not learn well; a disturbed teacher does not teach well. Neither situation helps the individual learner, who may be encountering all the problems of his own with which he can cope. The most efficient learning of the most acceptable types undoubtedly results when the pupils are engaged in activities that are well adjusted to their needs, interests, and degree of maturation, and are proceeding with these activities eagerly and in a happy, forthright fashion. It is not difficult to observe the wholeheartedness with which a group of children engage in the work at hand. In conditions marked by positive attitudes there will be a minimum of undesirable learnings growing out of resentment and feelings of frustration and domination.

The teacher undertakes to manage the classroom so that pupils will feel at home—be comfortable with the teacher and the boys and girls—and have a sense of personal well-being based upon their achievement and personal relationships. The factors that contribute to such an atmosphere are numerous and complex. Events in the immediate lives of the teacher, parents, and pupils have a great deal to do with it. Some events, such as those which occur at breakfast to upset parents and pupils alike for the day, are not left at home but are carried to school and mark the moods and responses of pupils. Occurrences of this kind are beyond the teacher's control. There are, however, many things he can do to offset the emotional effect of such occurrences.

The teacher contributes to the positive emotional climate of the room when he controls his behavior and displays positive attitudes. It is, for example, his business to minimize the effect which a head ache may have on his interaction with the class. Disappointments in pupil behavior or parent relations at a particular time are diminished by the teacher's knowledge that many things correct themselves.

The best teachers display good humor, an attitude of receptiveness, and unflustered good judgment a good portion of the time. They make it their business to be receptive to the questions and little confidences of their pupils. They try to seem eager to meet their pupils, to seem happy in their presence, and to enjoy the opportunity to work with them. In other words, they show evidences of liking their pupils. Because of their added maturity they may be expected to control their impulses and emotions in such a way that their innermost feelings remain concealed.

Most normal children experience some problems in carrying out school work. That child is rare indeed who has not found himself in need of help, or doubtful of the accuracy of his preparation or his knowledge of procedure. In an atmosphere where there is a high degree of consistent reaction favorable to the child on the part of the teacher, confidence in this reaction is built up. As a result, the learner does not hesitate to ask questions, nor does he fear the teacher if he should make an error. Unfortunately, pressures may be exerted upon children both at home and at school to do work which they do not know how to do. The results are the same as they have always been—frustration, undue anxiety, cheating, and dishonesty.

The teacher's consistent and characteristic attitude with regard to the learner's adequacies is a very important source of feelings of security that contribute to efficient learning. The feelings of greatest security in certain situations, however, are those which come from the reaction of the group, rather than the teacher. Many times behavior unacceptable to the teacher is exhibited by pupils who fear the ridicule or the unfavorable reaction of their peers. The development, therefore, of a positive pattern of group response when learners find themselves in error is an important responsibility of the teacher. Just as the teacher will refrain from ridicule, so will he try to train children to be sympathetic in their responses to those of their classmates who make errors. Some groups of children are so highly competitive that they fall into habits of being inconsiderate of their fellows' feelings. Other children tattle at the slightest excuse. The attitude of the teacher toward these unfavorable group situations and the consistency of his effort to alleviate conditions of this kind will determine the eventual atmosphere for security and belonging on the part of the individuals who make up the group. It is in a learning situation charged with positive emotional factors that children experience satisfaction. These satisfactions are the significant rewards or aftereffects essential for permanence of learning.

Earlier sections of this chapter have implied the importance of adapting learning exercises to the abilities of the children in the group. Such adaptations of learning activities lead to a greater number of children experiencing success more often. Everyone by nature enjoys success. School children are no different from adults in this regard. When they are able to succeed with their school work, they are inspired to greater efforts to add to their learning. Another regenerative outcome is that they learn to like school when they can have a reasonable share of success in it. The successes of children at all levels of ability should be recognized. The pupils themselves will appreciate even a simple task well done by a child who usually does not do well. Learning to appreciate the best efforts of their fellows is an important part of the education of all pupils—fast and slow alike.

Many children have gone to school for too many years with little or no feeling of success. They are entitled to an opportunity to tackle something that they can do. Unless they have this opportunity, nothing can be expected except a strong dislike for school, feelings of hopelessness, eventual behavior problems, and leaving school. The teacher not only recognizes the achievements they make, but helps them to select goals that they can reach.

Competition is another problem which teachers face. School learning is such that a certain amount of competition is inevitable. Most children like to run races and play games; many of them also enjoy running races in arithmetic, spelling, or reading books. They will naturally compete for certain places of leadership in room organization, in school activities, and, for that matter, in the teacher's favor. The question is, how much competition is wholesome, and with whom—one's self, or one's fellow pupils?

If competition is permitted to exist beyond safe limits it encourages the ridicule which has already been ruled out of a wholesome group situation. For example, when two children in the same classroom are in keen competition, the one who thinks he has the advantage may ridicule the other.

When the pupil can be induced to compete with his own record, competition is highly desirable and beneficial. An example of this would be the fifth grade boy who was not doing too well with spelling. When his parents learned about this they encouraged him to see if he couldn't improve his own record. The emphasis was not upon beating the others, but upon satisfying himself. The competition here was to see whether from one week to the next he could have all of his spelling words right, without regard to whether or not someone else had as many right as he did.

Inter-personal competition may have a discouraging effect upon those who are less able. Just as fear of the instructor leads to undesirable means of evasion through cheating or otherwise misrepresenting the case, so too much competition between members of the group may encourage dishonesty or, at best, ill feelings among the children involved. The situation would undoubtedly improve if pupils could choose others of similar ability with whom to compete.

In a highly competitive situation, the person who never wins usually does not develop feelings of security and belonging. In like manner, the pupil who has always won or the pupil who has always succeeded in academic learning will find it difficult to appreciate other virtues in less able fellows. Good education consists of making a classroom the kind of social and intellectual environment that will convey a sense of security with the group as well as with the teacher. Where the emphasis is on interpersonal competition, the development of a sympathetic nature is not encouraged. Children need to understand the importance of their feelings toward other people as they are taught to be considerate of their fellows and to respect their shortcomings, recognizing that no one is perfect.

Activity and experience. *Teaching effectiveness is improved by helping pupils identify wants and needs of sufficient importance to them to initiate activity, identify and feel its consequences, modify the activity, if need be, to bring about success, and to identify the change of activity as learning.*

An analysis of the teaching activity in any class reveals possibilities of things for pupils to look at, things to compare, things to measure, or things for which they may search. In addition, there are questions to discuss, disagreements to be reconciled, new ideas to be advanced, and alternate solutions for problems to be brought out. All of the things that pupils do that advance the kinds of learning in which the school is interested are properly considered learning activity.

Excellent use can be made of activity that involves organization in the modern classroom. Dependent upon the maturity of the learners, a class can be organized so that, to an appropriate degree, the pupils assume responsibility for management details. The very pertinent fact that high school students are approaching adulthood in many aspects of their being is often overlooked. It seems reasonable to say that much poor motivation and poor discipline is related to the fact that the school has not given the maturity of the learners the recognition that it deserves. That is, it is rather uncommon to find high schools operating in a fashion that would indicate that the approaching adulthood of students has been taken into consideration. Often high school seniors are subjected to the same degree of external control as upper elementary grade children. The activity involved in the proper organization of a class for effective problem solving and development of self-direction makes contributions toward certain goals of personal growth, equal at least to the more common activities of recitation and writing papers.

The same observation holds in the elementary grades. As indicated earlier, the teacher will expect pupils to assume responsibility commensurate with their maturity. Fourth grade pupils have been taught how to organize themselves and how to carry on appropriate phases of their school work on their own. These activities of organization are indeed important parts of the total learning process. Again it should be said that activity merely for its own sake is not enough. But if an activity is *selected* because of its promise for accomplishing learning, it is important.

The principle of activity can be implemented beyond the confines of the classroom. A teacher organized a civics class to do a clean-up job in a small town. The pupils undertook the project of community improvement through the disposal of unsightly objects and accumulated trash. They gathered on a Saturday morning with their equipment—tractors, wagons, and shovels. Needless to say, the project made the newspapers. This teacher was attempting to develop civic pride and a disposition favorable to public service through an activity which he and his class had jointly devised. Service to the community is highly commendable as educative activity.

Nothing that has been said is intended to depreciate the values of the more common kinds of classroom studies in which pupils engage. Certainly purposeful reading is a valuable activity in the learning process. Seeking, selecting, and using numerous kinds of resources—some in books and some in the community—have their place. In certain classes, personal records of the learning that is accomplished may be kept. Evaluations of the work of the group and of their own individual accomplishments may be made by the pupils. These activities of recording and evaluating are very valuable learning experiences. Recitation is often an appropriate activity, depending upon what is to be learned. The whole idea of this discussion is to suggest a wide variety of ways to incorporate into classroom practice the principle that learning is an active process.

The experience backgrounds of both teacher and pupil will have their effect upon the teaching-learning situations that are devised with the activity principle in mind. The teacher who has always studied and worked in classes where book assignments, recitations, and examinations predominated will find it refreshing to speculate upon the possibilities of increasing the scope of activities and the kinds of plans that are needed for this kind of teaching. Once a teacher has experienced a democratic teaching-learning situation in which the group really has the opportunity to establish its goals and to some degree assist the teacher to establish a way of working together toward these goals, he will appreciate the values of such experiences. In addition to desirable factual information, skills, and ability to do group work, there is frequently a wholesome shift in attitude toward learning and school in general. The extent to which the teacher has a wholesome attitude toward experimentation with new ideas will determine the frequency with which a learning activity will be varied. Teachers are urged to make repeated attempts, since first efforts often meet with limited success. Activity work is admittedly an advanced form of teaching.

From the standpoint of the pupil, the methods which are utilized at a given time must not be too far removed from his previous experience, or else he will not understand what is being done or why. Misunderstandings on the part of pupils with regard to the reasons why teachers are doing things in a different way often lead to dissatisfaction on the part of parents who likewise do not understand. The teacher should not undertake to change procedures rapidly with any group of pupils without making sure they understand his purposes. Relating this to the activity principle, the teacher will be well advised to work with the group, pointing up the desirability of new forms of activity and developing with the pupils the plans for this type of teaching. In like manner, the teacher who has not utilized these methods too often himself will find it to his advantage to make the transition in keeping with his own understanding and confidence. Finally, the teacher will make every effort to have the parents aware of new activities through discussions, observation, and appropriate participation.

Meaning and understanding. *Teaching effectiveness is improved by providing experiences that will insure the pupil's receiving the same thought as that intended by the teacher, and vice versa. Communication of both words and processes is thus enhanced.*

So much of school learning is tied up with words, both spoken and written, that the question of meaning takes on special significance. Meaning is closely related to experience. A high school science class may take a trip to a dairy preliminary to a study of sanitation and nutrition in milk. The opportunity to follow the process of milk production from the pastures and feed bins to the refrigerated storage before it goes to the bottling plant not only lends unity to the study, but it also provides experiences that add to the understanding of milk and the milk industry. Without seeing the pastures which have been developed with considerable care and expense, or the processing of the rations in the dairy barn, these aspects of the industry would have little real significance to many—even farm children whose families do not specialize in milk production. It is one thing to read in a book about sanitation in a dairy barn; it is quite another thing to see how it is accomplished. The whole problem of producing highly nutritive milk with a low bacteria count takes on added meaning to the class that has visited the source of supply. Added insight, of course, will be gained through a visit to the pasteurizing and bottling plant where the final packaging is accomplished.

Teachers of social science and literature encounter grave problems of understanding the terminology of their subject fields. A relatively simple concept such as voting has little meaning to the child of the upper elementary grades unless he has the experience of voting in a situation that he understands. Meaning is further enhanced if he is able to see how and why voting in the adult world is done. Even then he will have little insight into the thinking that goes into decisions that precede intelligent voting.

Unless care is exercised to make certain that a correct understanding of words is developed, teaching proceeds on a basis of superficial rote memorization without accomplishing its purposes. Memory spans being what they are, the symptoms of learning are slow to develop and the effects are short-lived. The teachers of elementary and high school grades cannot be too careful in providing direct or vicarious experiences which will help establish the meanings of the terms which they use. Discussion methods that provide pupils the opportunity to verbally exercise their understanding are a necessary part of this total communication process.

Learning number work has often been confounded by a lack of meaning. Pupils can and do memorize combinations of numbers without the slightest notion of what the combinations themselves mean. It is not uncommon to find learners who are confused as to whether they should add, subtract, multiply, or divide when confronted by a problem situation. They run into all kinds of difficulty with problems requiring the application of these four fundamental processes. Again, experience with real objects in establishing basic notions of numbers, in establishing the decimal system of numbers, and in gaining an understanding of number operations by actual accumulation of objects cannot be overemphasized. The pupil needs to be helped repeatedly to understand that when he multiplies he is merely accomplishing, more conveniently, a series of additions. By the same token, when he divides he is merely accomplishing a series of subtractions.

Teachers experience the same difficulties in understanding the terminology frequently found in books and in lectures on educational topics. Many misdirected efforts have resulted from lack of proper understanding of such ideas as socialized recitation, problem projects, units, core curriculum, and discipline. Verbal meanings depend upon a background of common experiences of pupil and teacher. It is the teacher's job to work to establish such a common background.

Multi-sensory approach. *Teaching effectiveness is improved by reproducing in combination as many sensory impressions as possible from an original experience. Using each sense in a variety of ways is likewise effective.*

The developments in recent years in availability and use of all types of visual and auditory materials have often enabled the learner to see the things about which he is learning as well as hear them described and explained by the teacher or read about them on the printed page. Everyone is familiar with the difficulties of writing in such a manner that the ideas intended by the writer are accurately conveyed to the reader. In like fashion, everyone is familiar with the difficulty of verbal explanation—especially the difficulty of an adult, with his broader range of experience, speaking to children, whose experiences have not yet been so broad. The difficulty encountered by one person in understanding the operation of canal locks illustrates this point very well. Although locks had not been a matter of special concern to this person, because he was of inland origin and had never lived near a great waterway, various persons had tried to explain their operation. The usual pictures of ships going through canal locks had been studied. However, it was a trip following college graduation that enabled him to see a lock in operation and to understand for the first time how ships can overcome problems of elevation through the use of these devices. Through the medium of motion pictures, this kind of thing can be very clearly explained, no matter how far distant from the locks. Seeing certainly is understanding, in many instances.

The use of recordings on both tape and wax is familiar to many people today. Through these devices the range of opportunity to listen has been greatly expanded. Excellent recordings of famous orchestras and famous speakers can be heard in the classroom at nominal expense of time or money. One's appreciation of the powers of a great symphony orchestra or of a great orator is not complete, however, without having seen the original in action. In modern schools films and television enhance the values of sound recording alone.

Visual aids of great value in teaching are not limited to pictures —motion or still. Any good teaching materials center will quickly demonstrate that there are other valuable visual aids. Costume dolls can teach quickly what the dress and customs of peoples of foreign lands are like. The typical black and white pictures in books can give only a limited impression of the colorful costumes often displayed. Many charts, diagrams, and illustrations, including scale models of all sorts of things provide insights otherwise not possible. A toy steam engine that can be dismantled to show the working parts can show a boy more about engines than he can learn by reading about them.

The senses of seeing and hearing have been, and are, the principal avenues of approach to the learner used by schools. The army, in its program of teaching, attempts to make use of all senses, including smell, taste, and touch. It is probable that schools could make greater use of these other senses than they do. Sensitivity of human touch has rarely been exploited. Early practitioners of medicine had to rely upon this sense to a very great extent. There are many skillful medical practitioners today who can diagnose with great accuracy through sensitive, trained hands. Many mechanics are more accurate in certain adjustments on machinery through touch than they are through the use of gauges. There are many avenues of learning in which we say that we have "to get the feel" of it. There is actually more to this than would seem at first glance. Work proceeds more efficiently in familiar and satisfying surroundings. A strange pen slows one down; a different typewriter doesn't perform quite as well. The reason is that in the skills of writing and typing we have partially learned through the "feel" of the instruments used. The sense of feeling makes for these differences in accomplishment; it is reasonable to expect that they have their effect upon learning.

The senses of taste and smell are limited in the realm of school work, but where applicable they certainly ought not to be overlooked. In the area of food selection and preparation wide use is made of these avenues of learning. Touch plays an important part in this area as well. Many chemical substances are identifiable by smell. The sense of smell alerts us to many unhealthful and un-desirable conditions—even dangers.

Another factor of teaching related to these various senses of the human body has to do with an impaired condition in any one of them. The teacher must know that there are limitations on the vision or hearing of certain children. By being aware of these things he will make arrangements so that the effects of the impairment will be minimized. A large number of schools report on the hear-ing loss of pupils and recommend seating accordingly. A teacher once experienced a feeling that a certain student strongly disliked him for some unexplainable reason. Finally, by accident, it be-came known that this girl could not see the blackboard and, re-senting this fact, became emotionally disturbed to a point of show-ing open resentment toward the instructor. When it was found that the child was having trouble seeing, a change of seats was made immediately. The instructor and the child became the best of friends and she became one of the best pupils in the class. Strange things like this occur as a result of impairment of the various senses and abilities of the body.

The teacher will do well to reflect upon those learning experiences which have made the most lasting impressions upon him. One teacher recalls a vivid experience with one of the very earliest uses of films for educational purposes. It was a silent film about the orange groves, the streams of water irrigating the orange groves, and the mountains in the background that provided the pure snow water to be stored in the oranges in the form of juice. Certain sani-tary advantages were pointed out. It was shown how the oranges were cleaned and packed, and then it was pointed out that no one's hands other than the consumer's need ever touch the edible portion of the orange. Although the informational part was in printed titles, the combination of the visual image and the printed word produced an effect that has outlasted hundreds of other impressions. As children are taught the proper use of such aids to learning they will come to make more effective use of the experiences these aids pro-vide. Children often look upon a motion picture film in school at first as a form of entertainment. Once they realize that it is not only a variation from the usual school routine but also a very effective way of learning, they look upon it with greater respect.

Whole–part–whole learning. *Teaching effectiveness is improved through the consideration of wholes when understandable relationships exist among the parts and the parts are dependent upon these relationships for their meaning. For unrelated items this advantage is not present.*

The question of whole or part learning is one which deserves the attention of each teacher in his planning activities. There was a time when nearly all learning, which was largely memorization, was undertaken on a part basis.

Memorization of a long speech or a long selection of poetry might be a formidable task. Most people will approach this kind of learning job in terms of what seems to be a practical amount of material to be memorized at once. Learning certain portions of the material will enable the individual to put the parts together, and thus recite the whole. The ultimate complete recitation, however, involves a concept of the whole in order to put the parts together in the proper order. If the parts themselves are considered as entities, they will be most easily memorized if they have obvious interrelationships for a certain completeness within each of the parts themselves. Memorization, however, is but one form of learning.

In a learning situation such as swimming the learner cannot *partly* learn. Until he actually swims he has not learned to do it. True, there is much to be learned *about* swimming after one has mastered the first simple strokes and the fundamental act of swimming. Refinements are produced through study of many phases of the total act. In this case, however, the learning of the original skill is accomplished as a whole.

If the teacher is aware of the superiority of whole learning methods in most learning situations, he will develop his plans accordingly. As a result a story will be taught in its entirety; a long division process will be demonstrated completely. Likewise, related exercises will be placed together in long unit assignments where the interrelationships will be obvious from the beginning and the unit goals will be developed before any of the intermediate steps are undertaken.

Insight into the unified learning to be undertaken can be accomplished in a number of ways. Teachers frequently give an overview of the work through a talk or general discussion at the opening of the unit. A class about to engage in a problem-solving unit can gain an understanding of the total unit by defining the numerous subproblems involved, and by discussing the ways in which the work will be undertaken.

Under the theory of whole learning, the parts comprising the whole that require attention are treated as this attention is needed. An example could be a game of baseball. Most teachers today would not spend a lot of time in the beginning trying to teach all the rules of baseball to a group of boys, nor would they spend a lot of time with pitching, catching, and batting, and training in other details of the game. Rather, after a little preliminary instruction, they would start a game, and as the boys play, different segments of the game would be taken up to bring about improvement. For example, rubber stands to hold a ball at proper height for batting might be brought into use, or other techniques known to good ball players and coaches would be applied as the parts needing attention were pulled out of the whole game. However, the wholeness of the activity would be preserved, and would be interrupted only for the study of those parts needing improvement in relation to the whole.

Another excellent example would be found in learning to play a piece of music. The pupil would play the composition as a whole to find its principal themes and over-all structure. Undoubtedly certain passages would present difficulties requiring special practice. When the problems represented by these passages had been solved the learner would proceed with the mastery of the entire composition.

Modern teachers approach creative writing from the standpoint of the idea to be expressed, and pupils are encouraged to get it down as a whole in the best possible form. As the writing progresses attention is given to the circumstances or problems relating to the central idea, and ways and means are found to improve the arrangement of these parts. Finally, each sentence is examined to see whether it does its part in the whole operation.

Transfer of learning. *Teaching effectiveness is improved by selecting learning experiences as much like life situations in which learning is to be used as possible. The teacher helps the*

*learner to see old problems in new situations and stimulates him
to be energetic toward and responsible for such identification.*

By various means the teacher strives to increase the chances that
one kind of behavior will occur rather than another. Attention to all
the other principles contributes to this increased probability of a
more adequate response in a new and later situation. What constitutes a "more adequate" response by the learner?

At this point it is necessary to recall the function of the school
in the community and the society of which it is a part, and the objectives of education toward which it strives. Teaching cannot be
effectively geared to the job of bringing about a certain kind of
response on the part of learners unless those goals which the community holds for its offspring are clear. The adequacy of learning
will ultimately be judged by the degree to which the learners attain
those goals.

It is clear, therefore, that teaching for transfer of learning must
be concerned with the kinds of responses desired and the areas of
living in which their use is anticipated. The goals are often not
sufficiently clear to give teaching a direction. Responsibility cannot
be placed upon learners until they in turn can be informed about
the learnings for which they are accountable. The first and continuing task is a constant clarification of objectives for education in the
society, if learning is to be reflected in the "more adequate" responses of the offspring. The professional group in the school and
the laymen of the community, therefore, work together for maximum
clarification. The next chapter gives more attention to the kinds of
objectives to be clarified.

As far as the teaching-learning situation is concerned the teacher
and learner have responsibilities to be met if transfer is to be accomplished. Neither party can relax his vigilance.

A teacher of bookkeeping once expressed dissatisfaction with the
results he had obtained the previous year. He found that a few of
the pupils were in bookkeeping jobs following graduation and that
they had to relearn most of what they were putting into practice
on the job. He determined to try to bridge the gap.

The procedure which this teacher settled upon involved a study
with the new class of the names, types, and locations of the businesses in the community. This was done while the basic operations of
bookkeeping were being developed, with the express purpose of

finding places where pupils could do some direct observation of accounting practices. The teacher called upon the businesses selected and was greatly encouraged by the generous offers of help he received when he made his purposes clear. The class made plans and discussed the things an individual should seek to learn, the kinds of courtesies he should extend his hosts, and other details. Pupils then made visits to various kinds of offices and obtained a first-hand view of different systems in use. In each case the pupil identified the basic steps in accounting procedure.

The program was successful beyond the dream of the instructor. Important among the outcomes was evidence that the things being learned could be found and put to work out of school. Likewise, the use of practice materials took on new meaning against the background of a real operation; the pupil knew how much the practice materials resembled certain types of businesses. An excellent way had been found to give these learners practice in identifying the old problems in a new situation.

In the above exercise the teacher had met several of his responsibilities in teaching for transfer. However, the conclusion as to the effectiveness of each individual's learning would have to await his entering into a job situation or assuming responsibility for his private affairs. If, in these situations, he expended the required amount of energy to see his old problems in the new setting, conclusive evidence would be at hand that teaching had been effective. In this case the learner likewise would have met his responsibility to the community, which had set up the opportunity for him to learn.

The ultimate effectiveness of learning in many areas often becomes evident only after a lapse of time or in a situation where direct relationship to training is difficult to observe. The transfer to out-of-school situations is like that. Teachers of elementary grades and junior high school have a better opportunity to observe the fruits of their labors in the restricted environment of the school. Arithmetic teachers can observe the outcomes of their teaching in shop and home economics laboratories. Children need to know that arithmetic will help them in these subjects, and ought to be shown how it will help them. The spelling lesson isn't unrelated to other things; children can see how it helps their older brothers and sisters who have to write themes and letters. They should be encouraged to write letters themselves at times.

The rules for transferability apply to making learning functional in school life as well as to making it functional in out-of-school life. Constant effort to generalize experience with the learner so that he gets in the habit of looking carefully at a new situation, plus an attitude favorable to this search, is required.

SUMMARY

The systematic study of principles of learning and principles of teaching in the two chapters just completed represents a pivotal point upon which a large segment of the development of teaching skill turns. The review of the principles of learning has suggested a group of principles of teaching. The competence of the teacher can be expected to improve as his practices in the classroom are brought into harmony with these principles.

The careful study of the principles of teaching outlined above should result in a sense of growing competence on the part of the teacher in the following areas:

1. Analysis of a teaching-learning situation with greater understanding of why it was carried on as it was and what made it effective.

2. Analysis of his own efforts to help pupils learn, and greater insight into what contributed to his success and how greater success might be achieved.

3. Planning activity with children in such a way as to bring about maximum application of the numerous principles in combination.

4. Meeting more effectively some of the special problems of teaching represented by each of the eleven areas of consideration in the principles.

5. Controlling his own reaction so as to provide progressively improved conditions for learning.

For the convenience of the reader, the two sets of principles are brought together in parallel columns to complete the summarization of Part Two.

Principles of Learning	Principles of Teaching
1. Readiness. A learner must be sufficiently matured and skilled to be ready for a new learning experience.	**1. Readiness.** Teaching effectiveness is increased by predicting pupil readiness, providing tryout experiences under observation, and readjusting the program where predictions do not hold up. In the final analysis, readjustment is most effective as it relates to the individual.
2. Individual differences. Different individuals learn at different rates in the same category of learning. The rate of learning of an individual may vary from one category to another.	**2. Individual differences.** Teaching effectiveness is improved as teachers seek causes of poor responses that make individuals different, treat such causes as are remediable, and readjust requirements for individuals where treatment is ineffective. On the other hand, good responses that make individuals different are nourished to the end that the range of differences becomes greater.
3. Motivation. More efficient learning takes place where it seems worthwhile to the learner.	**3. Motivation.** Teaching effectiveness is improved as the pupil is involved in setting goals for learning, as he encounters problems in reaching them, and as he relates his satisfaction in their solution to new goals.
4. Effect. Those responses made to a given situation which are accompanied or closely followed by satisfaction will, other things being equal, more likely occur when the situation arises again.	**4. Effect.** Teaching effectiveness is improved by the prompt use of aftereffects to responses geared to the individual. Positive reactions following responses produce most consistent gains; negative reactions following responses are effective in controlled situations and are more productive than no reaction at all.

5. **Complex and multiple outcomes.** Learning of more than one type occurs at any one time. Outcomes such as behavior patterns consist of many separate learning products operating in a functional relationship. Different outcomes occur with different persons in the same situation.

5. **Complex and multiple outcomes.** Teaching effectiveness is improved by selecting methods that control "by-products" that are sure to accompany the focal learning of any teaching effort.

6. **Security.** Learning is most efficient in an atmosphere of security and belonging.

6. **Security.** Teaching effectiveness is improved by sharing pupils' tensions and their successes in reducing them through problem solving; also, through sharing their doubts about their roles in life and helping them to see potential satisfactions in them.

7. **Activity and experience.** Learning is accomplished by the learner for himself through first engaging in purposeful, conscious, mental or physical activity, then continuing with the activity, undergoing its consequences to complete an experience.

7. **Activity and experience.** Teaching effectiveness is improved by helping pupils identify wants and needs of sufficient importance to them to initiate activity, identify and feel its consequences, modify the activity if need be, to bring about success, and to identify the change of activity as learning.

8. **Meaning and understanding.** Purposeful, efficient, and functional learning is aided by meaning and understanding derived from experience, direct or vicarious.

8. **Meaning and understanding.** Teaching effectiveness is improved by providing experiences that will insure the pupil receiving the thought intended by the teacher. Communication of both words and processes is thus enhanced.

9. **Multi-sensory approach.** Learning experiences may be improved through ingenious use of each sense in combination with one or more other senses.

9. **Multi-sensory approach.** Teaching effectiveness is improved by reproducing in combination as many sensory impressions as possible from an original experience and using each sense in a variety of ways.

10. **Whole-part-whole learning.** Learning by wholes derives its greater efficiency over part learning through the learner's perception of essential relationships in the material to be learned.

11. **Transfer of learning.** The chances that learned responses will be applied to new problem situations are increased by clear objectives, learning activities much like adult activities, and conscious effort by the learner to generalize so that new opportunities for application will be recognized.

10. **Whole-part-whole learning.** Teaching effectiveness is improved through the consideration of wholes when understandable relationships exist among the parts, and the parts are dependent upon this relationship for their meaning.

11. **Transfer of learning.** Teaching effectiveness is improved by selecting learning experiences as much as possible like the life situations in which learning is to be used. The teacher helps the learner to see old problems in new situations and stimulates him to be energetic toward and responsible for such identification.

PROBLEMS

1. *Select from your own experience some skill you have learned, such as typing or driving a car. Try to decide upon something in which details remain clear. Analyze this experience and write up each of the principles of learning reviewed in Chapter 5 in terms of how it affected your learning.*

2. *Observe carefully the work of a supervisor for a week and list under each of the eleven principles of teaching the things which stood out in his work with learners illustrating his recognition of the principle. Note indications of lack of recognition as well.*

3. *Select a teaching problem in your field. From this write a plan for teaching a small group of pupils. Show how the things you as a teacher will do are governed by principles reviewed in these chapters.*

4. *Describe a learning or teaching experience in which the principles of motivation and effect operate together.*

5. *Describe a recent effort of your own to teach a child something in a class with which you are currently working. Evaluate this*

effort in terms of the principles of teaching that were applied and those which might have been applied.

6. *Seek an opportunity to observe for a period of several days an elementary class or a core class (junior high schools sometimes are organized on a core curriculum which integrates the work in some fashion and places pupils under the direction of one teacher for a half day.) Evaluate what you see in principles of complex and multiple outcomes.*

7. *Observe the teaching of a new concept. Analyze the effort of the teacher to meet the requirements of adequate experience for meaning and understanding.*

BIBLIOGRAPHY

Bernard, Harold W., *Psychology of Learning and Teaching.* New York: McGraw-Hill Book Company, Inc., 1954. Chaps. iii and xv.

Burton, William H., *The Guidance of Learning Activities,* 2nd ed. New York: Appleton-Century-Crofts, Inc., 1952. Chap. vi.

Cantor, Nathaniel, *The Teaching⟷Learning Process.* New York: The Dryden Press, 1953.

Cronbach, Lee J., *Educational Psychology.* New York: Harcourt, Brace & Company, 1954. Chap. viii.

Educational Policies Commission, *Education of the Gifted.* Washington, D.C.: National Educational Association, 1950.

Dickson, George E., "Making Teaching a Satisfying Experience," *Educational Leadership,* February, 1956.

Gates, Arthur I., Arthur T. Jersild, T. R. McConnell, and Robert C. Challman, *Educational Psychology.* New York: The Macmillan Company, 1942.

Goodlad, John I., "Research and Theory Regarding Promotion and Non-Promotion," *Elementary School Journal* 53:150-55, 1952.

Melvin, A. Gordon, *General Methods of Teaching.* New York: McGraw-Hill Book Company, Inc., 1952. Chap. v.

National Society for the Study of Education, *Learning and Instruction* (1950 Yearbook). Chicago: The University of Chicago Press, 1950. Chap. xii.

Ojeman, Ralph H., "Identifying Effective Classroom Teachers," in *Bases for Effective Learning* (1952 Yearbook, Department of Elementary School Principals). Washington, D.C.: The National Education Association, 1952. Pp. 130-38.

Pressey, Sidney L., and Francis P. Robinson, *Psychology and the New Education.* New York: Harper & Brothers, 1944.

Simpson, Ray H., *Improving Teaching-Learning Processes*. New York: Longmans, Green & Company, 1953.

Sumption, Merle R., Dorothy Norris, and Lewis M. Terman, "Special Education for the Gifted Child," in Nelson B. Henry, ed., *The Education of Exceptional Children*. Chicago: The University of Chicago Press, 1950. P. 279.

Thorndike, E. L., *Fundamentals of Learning*. New York: Bureau of Publications, Teachers College, Columbia University, 1932.

Tyler, Ralph W., "Trends in Teaching: How Research is Affecting our Understanding of the Learning Process," *School Review* 59:263-92, May 1951.

Wiles, Kimball, *Teaching for Better Schools*. Englewood Cliffs, N.J.: Prentice-Hall, Inc., 1952. Chaps. i and xi.

Part Three

Planning

affects

learning

Introduction

The goals of education are achieved through the activities of the learners. Some of the goals of learning to which the community aspires for its youth are informational in nature —the cultural heritage, social mores, and philosophy of government. Some of the goals include the tools of learning and basic abilities in language and number. Still other goals have to do with the personal qualities, attitudes, health, and skills of social interaction necessary for participation in a democratic society.

The teacher is the designer of the particular activities and combinations of such activities needed for the education of a particular group of learners. He brings to focus upon the problem all that he has learned about the learners and the community, the facilities and resources available, plus his own knowledge of the learning process. This marshaling of resources and designing and selecting activities constitutes planning.

The teacher does not always work alone in planning, however. Neither does planning always reach finality in advance of his contact with learners. Pupils often enter into the planning in a direct sense. When this is the case the process is called teacher-pupil planning. A wider range of educational outcomes can often be procured from teacher-pupil planning. This is especially true when goals of personal growth are to be emphasized.

Much planning by the teacher in advance of meeting the learners is done in any event, even if teacher-pupil planning is to follow. Leadership is the teacher's responsibility together with knowledge of resources and possible activities. Pre-planning is done also when the learning is of the informational or skill-developing type. In these situations the content of lessons and units is often prescribed and the learning activities are predominantly selected by the teacher.

A trend in the planning and implementation of activities has been toward larger units of learning. Teaching itself that makes use of larger units takes on new forms and holds new opportunities. Unit teaching anticipates attention to a central problem over a longer period of time. Because of the time factor, the teacher can incorporate projects of research, construction, and enrichment into the total program. The opportunity to bring this kind of flexibility and variety into the work holds great promise in the area of motivation and individual differences. Advantages in keeping with other learning principles are to be found in unit teaching.

Planning for shorter periods of time is often necessary or desirable. Important lessons may need to be taught alone. Re-planning is often necessary when unexpected difficulties are encountered in the classroom, or when some new line of interest needs to be followed up. Even with the best of units, planning in relation to progress of individual pupils will occur almost daily. Teachers learn procedures of pre-planning, lesson planning, unit planning, and teacher-pupil planning, and use all of them in their professional activity. They come to know that good education doesn't just happen—it is planned.

7

The teacher's planning and the curriculum

Each day people are confronted with tasks to be accomplished. A task in itself contains a goal, and the goal may be reached in any of a number of ways. For each situation, however, there is a best order and timing of events. Mammoth construction projects such as the great irrigation dams in the western mountains might be contemplated as illustrations. Or one can meditate upon the construction of super-highways in progress, and the need for planning of thousands of miles more of such construction. These are evidences of the need for planning in the physical world.

The goals of teaching and education. Teaching aims and purposes in general are derived from two sources. One of these sources is the general opinion of experts as to what aspects of the culture must be transmitted to young people. That is, for a given age or grade level of children, there is continual revaluation and agreement by experts and lay citizens relative to informational content that should be learned by children. Furthermore, every society has developed certain mores that govern the behavior of children and adults, and strives to engender feelings favorable to such behavior as a part of the education of its members. Another source of teaching aims is found in the careful

171

consideration of the needs of children and youth. With the development of child study and a resulting increase in knowledge of the interests and the internal motivations of learners, additional insight into the means by which educational goals can be reached has been gained. The form teaching takes when the needs and interests of learners are prominent considerations in planning often differs markedly from earlier conceptions of classroom procedure.

A fundamental principle of curriculum construction and planning centers around the dual nature of desired outcomes of teaching. Outcomes are of two broad overlapping classes, which will be referred to in this text as "specialized" objectives and "personal growth" objectives. Examples that follow are offered in an attempt to make the distinction clear.

The objective of the teacher in the first example is to develop the skill and understanding involved in "carrying" in arithmetic. An understanding of carrying depends upon an understanding of the number system. It would seem very wise for teachers at various grade levels to utilize direct experience as a safeguard against possible misunderstanding in this important learning. Even though the best students in any class group do understand, it is quite probable that there will be many in the class who do not. Therefore, at any grade level where there is need to clarify the process in question, it is wise to use bundles of sticks, or some other objects that can be tied up in packets of ten, to work simple examples. In so doing the class applies the simple rule that any time ten units are found together a packet will be made. Skills in numbers and language arts are among the specialized goals of education. Many objectives relate to prerequisite knowledge or skill as a basis for entry upon an occupation or a program of further education. These, too, are considered goals of specialization.

Quite a different set of goals appears in the case of the seventh grade children who asked their teacher, "What is in the sky?" This question became the central problem of a rather extended series of plans and activities. The subproblems which were developed included information upon many aspects of atmosphere, stars and planets, and the weather. An important part of the whole set of learning experiences included the development of plans, the division of labor, the organization of study groups, and the survey of available sources of information with which to work. Each of these preparatory activities required a considerable amount of thinking and planning on the part of both the teacher and the pupils. Even though this kind of planning with pupils involved working with them from day to day, it still required a great deal of speculation and imaginative planning by the teacher to anticipate at least some of the problems which did arise.

One might believe at first glance that information needed to answer the original question "What is in the sky?" would be the most desired outcome. Indeed, such information is not to be overlooked or discounted. However, the children undoubtedly did learn many things besides facts about the atmosphere, the heavenly bodies, and the weather. They learned that their original problem was such that it had to be reorganized into subproblems to be studied effectively. They learned also that there were sources of information which they probably had not tapped.

Pupils having access to a weather observation station would proceed in a different manner from those who were in a more isolated spot. The resources of school libraries are vastly different. The disposition of the teacher to help by taking students to college libraries or to an observatory would make a difference in the procedure. The study of stars and planets under these conditions would take a different turn and would increase in significance to the pupils.

The activities involved in finding sources of information, in making arrangements to take trips, in making the observations on the trips that were made, and in formulating these observations into workable reports are considered by many educators to be the very best kind of learning experience. It is believed that the outcomes of such experiences necessitated by the problem-solving approach are the more long-lasting and more important learning products. Other educators, looking upon the scene from a more subject-centered point of view, would not attach this much significance to the elemental research activities of the pupils. Those teachers who have a social orientation to education would look upon the cooperative activities of the pupils in formulating group reports and in sharing sources of information as very desirable.

From what has been said it is apparent that there are at least two very broad classes of goals of education. There are those goals which are concerned with developing skills and acquiring information through practice and memorization. These are referred to as "specialized" learnings. They constitute a very important aspect of the total of education. Specialized goals carried to a high level of attainment by talented pupils provide us with artists, physicians, technicians, writers, musicians, and many other members of our society without whom we would find life very drab.

While applying the skills obtained through high level specialized education, however, physicians, lawyers, writers, musicians, and artists live alongside the other members of society. In meeting their responsibilities as citizens they all must agree upon certain courses of community action. They engage in discussions and they cooperatively seek information having a bearing upon their mutual concerns. They recognize each other's worth as citizens and as people—as parents, neighbors, friends, and relations. In short, they are con-

The development of new skills in relation to students' specialized interests adds greatly to personal growth.

Courtesy of Ball State Teachers College Photo Service

cerned with attitudes and actions relating to problems of common welfare.

Through living in a community and sharing with their parents and neighbors and friends, and through experiences in school as an organized society of young people, children gradually acquire in some degree the means of effective cooperation in a democratic society. While the school does not begin to replace the community and the home as educative influences in these regards, it can often— through the pursuit of such long range plans as that described above in relation to "What is in the sky?"—provide instruction in how to solve problems. Through similar experiences the school can point out what happens when people undertake to work together in a democratic fashion. A junior high school boy who serves as chairman of a committee can see what happens when he attempts to usurp the prerogatives of the group. He can have the effects of good leadership and of less competent leadership pointed out to him as part of the total experience. Young people who have many opportunities throughout their school experience to act in leadership capacities go about their adult responsibilities in an increasingly confident manner.

These products of the problem-solving approach in school learning may be referred to as "personal growth" objectives. They are the kinds of goals of education which, by and large, consist of changes in the way the pupil looks at things. They have to do with his values. They have to do with his attitudes toward his fellow pupils. They have to do with his ability to exercise self-control in a group situation and to discipline himself when outside direct controls are relaxed. They have to do with an ever-increasing insight into the psychology of relations with other people. They have to do with work habits and attitudes toward school work, toward home responsibilities, and toward responsibilities for the safety, welfare, and health of others.

If one reviews thoughtfully the famous Seven Cardinal Principles of Secondary Education enunciated in 1918,[1] he will agree that five of the seven are concerned largely with the growth of the pupil as a person. The pupil is to learn to control his living so as to enjoy good health; he develops values in an ethical relationship; he

---

[1] *Cardinal Principles of Secondary Education*, U.S. Bureau of Education Bulletin 35, 1918, pp. 10ff.

develops the skills of citizenship for a democracy; he establishes high standards for himself as a member of a home; and he learns to use leisure wisely. These matters of the growth of the individual occupied a prominent position in the thinking of the committee that established this famous set of principles.

The strategy of teaching. In what has been said, it is implied that the kinds of plans the teacher makes will be influenced by the predominance of one or the other of these types of goals. If it is the teaching of skills that is anticipated, plans will be made very largely in advance by the teacher. The selection of appropriate things to be learned and the expectation of degrees of accomplishment in keeping with the previous experience, achievement, and maturation of the learners will be in evidence. If the teacher is uncertain of the level of accomplishment of his charges, he will select tests or other suitable ways of finding out their status. This will give him the needed insight into the degree of difficulty with which his pupils can cope. Having selected these immediate goals, and knowing the work habits and speed of accomplishment of his pupils, he will then select numerous exercises which will help develop the skill desired. If the recognition of a new word is the problem at hand, the teacher will exercise all of his ingenuity to put meaning into the word. He will show how it is related to other words that are already known; he will try to explain the action, if it is an action word; or will try to show the object if it is the name of something. Then he will try to use the word and will provide experiences in seeing the word and reading it many times. To adults, elementary reading books sometimes seem a bit monotonous and repetitious, but it is known that a certain number of exposures to a word are necessary in order to accomplish recognition. Pupils differ in the amount of exposure necessary for mastery, and somehow the teacher's plan will have to take this into consideration. Even with the calculated number of exposures provided in the reading book, not every pupil will accomplish the desired learning. All of this involves the technique of teaching a new word in reading. There are many more ramifications, but enough has been said to point up the necessity of having a plan by which to proceed.

If the goal sought falls in the area of personal growth, however, different methods must be used. A well known educational film depicts the effort on the part of high school pupils to improve the lunchroom.[2] There was a feeling on the part of members of the student council that a great deal of thoughtlessness was in evidence. Their own conduct in handling food and throwing empty paper cups and plates was considered less than desirable by the pupils themselves. Also, poor food selection habits involving too much dessert and candy and not enough milk were obvious. The council therefore undertook to study the problem of how the lunchroom could be improved. Interestingly enough, they did not proceed to read books about how people should act in lunchrooms. Rather, they sought the causes of the behavior of those who ate there. Through numerous discussions, committee meetings, and other de-

[2] McGraw-Hill Textfilm, *Motivating the Class, Parts I and II* (New York: McGraw-Hill Book Company, 1950).

The desire to create beauty with one's own hands has long been a strong source of motivation for boys and girls.

Courtesy of Ball State Teachers College Photo Service

vices including a poster campaign, attention was called to the un-
desirability of the present type of conduct. The improvement of the
physical situation and food selection followed the development of a
different feeling on the part of the pupils.

This kind of educational program, springing from the pupils themselves to improve their own conduct, physical surroundings, and
health, was assisted by the guidance and experience of more mature
people. Sponsors, teachers, and principal had to know when to lead
and when to follow. There were no drills or exercises which would
take the place of exchanging opinions, proposing possible helpful
steps, and evaluating those proposals leading to final activity. The
desired outcome was accomplished through the cooperative planning of pupils, teachers, and administration, all seeking a common
goal.

Dual nature of teaching—emphasis on special goals. It
should be stated that no teaching-learning experience is ever completely a matter of specialized learning or completely one of personal growth. The subject of chemistry, if taught for college preparatory or pre-vocational purposes, is a good example of specialized
learning. The manner in which pupils use the laboratory equipment
and the manner in which they behave toward one another will vary.
As in the case of any other shop or special equipment situation,
much depends upon the consideration each worker has for the
others as he goes from one piece of apparatus to another. The
teacher has a good opportunity and a responsibility for developing
considerateness about the use of such equipment. Each person will
leave materials in such condition that the next user will not be delayed. It is to be expected in a class of high school age that there
will be numerous opportunities for this kind of teaching. It will be
found, however, that improvement in such attitudes and feelings
will require different strategy from that used in teaching the information and skills which commonly make up the school subjects.

A chemistry class also presents other opportunities for growth
in self-direction. It is not uncommon to find an occasional spurt of
water directed by a pupil toward one of his unsuspecting classmates. The very fact that water is available is too strong a temptation many times. Carried to extreme, such incidents could be the
ruin of a good learning situation. In a class of large size it will be

quite difficult for the teacher to carry on his work effectively, and to prevent such annoyances by sheer police action. The majority of pupils, however, will agree that this kind of interruption is really their loss, and will control themselves accordingly. When such interruptions do occur, an opportunity is provided for the teacher to engage in a reconstruction of the attitudes of the individuals involved. In so doing he may want to utilize the social pressure of the group. As the classwork is resumed, there will be further opportunity for the pupils to demonstrate their ability to control themselves. Given maximum possible pupil understanding and a consistently positive attitude on the part of the teacher, most pupils will respond and go forward without further serious delay.

To illustrate further the important principle that teaching-learning situations have a dual nature, consider the following diagrams. Figure 1 illustrates emphasis upon specialized learning. ("S" represents specialized learning; "P" represents personal growth.) The example of the chemistry class could be replaced with classes in arithmetic, reading, spelling, grammar, algebra, advanced art work,

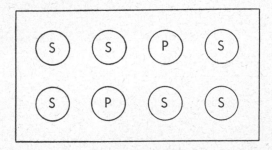

Figure 1

advanced shop work, or others. The circles in the rectangle may be thought of as the activities or learning experiences the pupil has in a typical class period. The bulk of his experience will be concerned with learning facts and skills related to the subject at hand. That is, in chemistry he will be memorizing atomic weights, symbols, and elements, and developing skills with chemical equations and apparatus. Scattered throughout the total experience, however, will be the activities and opportunities that have to do with self-control. That is, the equipment he uses will be replaced in a fit condition for the next person, the frequency of the surprise spurt of water will be diminished, and the sharing of discussion will improve.

An effort has been made to show that even in a class as highly specialized as chemistry there are some factors in the learning situation that have to do with personal growth. It is recognized that in a chemistry class the large majority of the activities and learning experiences will be in the direction of mastering course content and related skills. This overbalance on the side of specialization will cause the teacher to select methods of procedure that are designed to bring about good results in learning factual information and skills in the handling of apparatus and in the mathematical combination of the chemical elements. The utilization of these methods is in keeping with the kind of learning that is to be accomplished.

Emphasis on personal growth goals. Figure 2 represents the situation in a physical education class at elementary or secondary level. Again, physical education is selected because of the predominance of personal growth objectives. Other areas contribut-

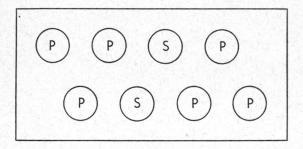

Figure 2

ing to personal growth include art in the elementary grades, crafts, dramatics, social studies, core curriculum programs, and newly developed secondary offerings in social living.

Physical education is taught in a modern school for a wide variety of personal growth purposes. It is true that a certain minimum skill in playing games is sought, and is highly desirable in bringing about the satisfactions to be derived from the total program. As the class engages in games on a free play basis, consistent with good organization, the physical education teacher has a better opportunity than any other teacher in the school to observe the behavior of children in an uninhibited situation. In all other school classes children are continually aware of the controls they must observe. When pupils engage in games in the gymnasium or on the playground, they are less aware of such controls, and often more nearly reveal their true personal characteristics. A physical education teacher who sees in his work this opportunity for greater development of self-control will find a way to free himself from the details of the game to a point where he can make mental note of the patterns of such behavior, both desirable and undesirable.

Balanced emphasis on goals. Figure 3 represents a teaching-learning situation in which there is not the extreme emphasis depicted above in either type of desired outcome. Such a situation is found in social studies, literature, general science, and arts at various levels. In this type of class there is often a near-equality in emphasis. Most teaching-learning situations are capable of such balance, if the teacher is aware of its desirability.

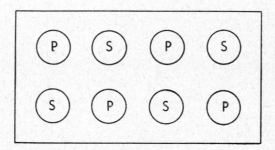

Figure 3

If Figure 3 is understood to represent a class of upper elementary pupils studying community health in science, the balance will be apparent. There are many items of information about the causes and prevention of illness that are appropriate knowledge for this age group. Likewise there is much to be known about foods that promote health, and the care with which foods must be handled and prepared.

Much of the information is to be found in books in school or public libraries. The equally significant aspect of the study, however, is to cause the pupils to feel strongly about community health. No better place to begin can be found than the classroom. Pupils can be encouraged to discuss the factors which are on the side of good health for the group and those which are against it. The importance of each person's washing his hands before eating can be brought out. Schools with lavatories or sinks in the rooms are increasing in prevalence. The habits of individuals who care about others are observed when coughs and sneezes are covered. Plans and suggestions to improve the room situation are developed.

The study can move into the special area of food preparation and handling, by a study of the school cafeteria. Here the cleanliness of the kitchen and the cooks, the refrigeration, and the disposal of waste can be observed and evaluated. In this way the pupils come to consider their own and others' welfare as they consider the factors that influence them personally.

All the while learning of factual information about the causes and prevention of illness is going on in a context of reality. The balance between specialized and personal growth goals is increased because of the broader activities of learning through observation and discussion. Studies of this kind by pupils often lead to suggestions for the real improvement of the situation itself.

Goals determine learning activities. The foregoing examples, in chemistry as an illustration of a highly specialized subject with goals of information and skill in the foreground, and the physical education class with its goals of personal growth and development stressed, have been used to bring out the differences in the kinds of plans which the teacher will develop. Much of the detailed planning of what the pupils will do in the chemistry class will be done by the teacher before the class convenes. He is dealing with an organized body of content that will determine somewhat the sequence from one topic to another. New and difficult understandings must be brought about for the learners at every turn.

This requires skillful development of new points, involving lectures, demonstrations, discussion, questions and answers, and opportunities for exercise. When the teacher feels that the learning has been accomplished or when the time allotted to a particular topic has been used up, a fairly precise measurement of the outcomes can be accomplished by using tests, and in some cases by requiring demonstrations. All of these things can be rather precisely planned by the teacher before the development of any given lesson or series of lessons. This does not mean that, in any good teaching, plans will not be modified to suit the occasion. However, in teaching a subject like chemistry or foreign language and many other specialized areas of the school curriculum, rather accurate predictions of what will transpire can be made and formulated into plans.

The physical education teacher's planning characteristically follows a different pattern. In the secondary school the games which are selected may, and often do, follow the sports seasons to a considerable extent. This is generally done because students left to their own choices will want to play games that are in season. Weather, of course, may have something to do with this in certain latitudes. However, the physical education teacher is not too concerned about what particular game is played on a particular day. He may be concerned with bringing about a well balanced program of exercise, but there are many games that would accomplish this purpose. Since this is true, within the very broad framework he may allow children to choose the games that they will play much of the time. Again, this does not mean that he will not from time to time introduce new games for the sake of variety and expanding the repertoire of possible activities. The very fact that children know that they will have the opportunity to choose is in itself a strong motivating factor. They will enter with enthusiasm into the games of their choosing that they like. For the teacher's purposes of bringing about a well balanced exercise program or observing characteristics of behavior on the playground, one game will serve as well as any other. Planning, therefore, becomes more of a cooperative situation with the pupils.

Another obvious characteristic of planning for physical education is the organization of groups and teams to carry on the program with maximum activity for everyone involved. Where playing space is available it is not uncommon to find three or four games going on at one time under the supervision of one teacher. In such a situation the opportunities to develop self-control and to assume responsibility for the present activity of the group are very great. It is to be expected that there will be interruptions in the smooth operation of such programs. Arguments will occur; tempers will flare; differences will need to be reconciled. When the difficulties are ironed out the group will resume its activity, presenting a new opportunity for finding out whether self-control has been advanced. Other characteristics of planning for this kind of learning will be pointed out later. The important thing at this point is to see that the kinds of goals sought will have a marked influence on the kinds of plans made.

Evaluation is controlled by goals. The influence of specialized goals or personal growth goals upon a given teaching-learning situation determines the nature of another important aspect of planning and teaching. That aspect is evaluation of pupil learning. Implied in what was said earlier about the chemistry class is the nature of the evaluative procedures appropriate for skill and informational learning. It is possible to measure according to good standards the extent to which a learner has acquired factual information. Great strides have been made in the last quarter-century in the improvement of this type of evaluation. Many very carefully constructed standardized tests are available and are recommended when measurement of this type of outcome is desired.

The difficulty in evaluation as related to the kind of learnings desired arises from the fact that no school subject is wholly directed at teaching information and skills. This point was developed in the preceding paragraphs, and in like manner it has been made clear that no school subject is wholly directed at personal growth objectives. Even in the physical education class, which was used as an example of this type, a certain body of content is required before the major activities can be carried out. The basic rules of any game must be understood and practiced before all members of the group can participate in it with maximum enjoyment and benefits. While the emphasis may be upon personal growth as gained through experiences in playing the games, a great deal must be known to carry out this program. Insofar as this kind of information and basic skill is required, the planning and teaching will be something like that of the specialized class. Likewise, so far as the information and skill are concerned, testing and demonstration may reveal the extent of learning.

It is rather obvious, however, that the physical education teacher will not be able to give pencil and paper tests that will reveal an increase in a boy's ability to hold his temper. The evaluation of this important type of learning will of necessity be based on observations of how the boy behaves. In a game in which he has lost himself, so to speak, such observations and evaluations are commonly called subjective estimates. The best that can be done is for the teacher to look systematically for signs of growth, or lack of it, in the individual's reactions to unpredicted incidents. Such evaluations are not easy to make, but they are extremely important indications of the kinds of growth that parents and educators alike consider very important.

The difficulties of valid evaluation are multiplied in those subjects where there is a need for emphasis on both information and personal growth. Social studies may be taken as an example of an area which lies between the extremes represented by chemistry and physical education. The distribution of emphasis between factual information and personal growth activities varies with the level of maturity. There are teachers who emphasize the informational side of history and government. If the announced goals of a social studies course are informational in nature, evaluation can be accomplished through measurement devices. On the other hand, there are teachers who feel that the important outcomes in the social studies are not factual details but rather the feelings the pupils develop toward their society and its institutions, toward their fellows, and toward other peoples of the world, coupled with experiences in the processes of government and democratic action.

Certain efforts to analyze and improve the teaching of citizenship have been made. The extent to which the individual assumes the responsibilities that befall him as a citizen of a democracy determines the quality of his citizenship. It is always difficult to determine the extent to which training in youth will transfer to adult life. The area of citizenship responsibility is no exception. Perhaps the best thing that can be done is to develop class activities for a portion of the class periods that will incorporate the principles of democratic action. In the elementary classroom, the lack of the pupils' maturity will limit to some extent their ability to carry on this type of procedure. Simple sharing situations, however, are observed at all levels. In the intermediate grades the beginnings of discussion and consensus and choice are in evidence in the activities of some successful teachers. In the secondary school, as children develop into youth and approach adulthood, it seems reasonable to expect that an increasing amount of activity designed around democratic processes could be undertaken. Participation with adults in the community on problems appropriate to the level of maturation is not out of the question. When this kind of community activity can be combined with selected but nonetheless real responsibilities assumed by young people, the nearest approach is made to what may be expected when individual and adult life is achieved. Observations, then, of the pupil's behavior in situations related to his inner feelings constitute a more valid basis for evaluation than almost any other source of evidence. Evaluation of personal growth is difficult, as has been previously stated. The point to be made is that in setting up learning situations of this kind, one must consider not only the possibilities for developing activities that contribute to these learnings, but one must consider also how evaluation will be carried out.

The teacher, in going about the process of planning, will decide what his major purposes are; that is, whether learning products that will be emphasized are specialized or whether they are of the personal growth nature. Any proposed class activity will fall somewhere between the two extreme points. The teacher will then select from literally hundreds of possibilities the things that he will have his pupils do in order to learn. Before finally accepting his statement of goals, he will consider the problem of evaluation; that is, he will face the question of how to determine when the learning has been accomplished and in what degree. It would seem that unless in his planning the teacher sees ways to evaluate a given objective, it might be wise to leave it out and teach toward objectives that can be evaluated. The kinds of learning activities and the kinds of evaluative devices used reveal the extent to which the teacher is aware of specialized and personal growth objectives appropriate to his offering.

SUMMARY

The relationship of the planning of learning activities to the curriculum has been emphasized in this chapter. The sources of educational goals in the transmission of the culture to the young and in the needs of children and youth have been pointed out.

Educational goals have a dual nature that has been characterized by specialized outcomes in combination with personal growth outcomes. The teacher recognizes the need for both types of outcomes and plans his work so that appropriate emphasis is placed upon both. The different emphasis of objectives from one subject field to another within the school program has been recognized.

This dual nature of educational goals leads to selection of learning activities bearing the greatest possible relationship to the type of outcome sought. Techniques of teaching and learning activities which will bring about learning of facts and skills are better understood than those which contribute to personal growth. The maintenance of proper balance of types of learning activities in keeping with goals has been referred to as "strategy" of teaching.

In the consideration of teaching-learning situations, notice has been taken that a single activity may contribute factors of personal growth and specialization at the same time.

Furthermore, the dual nature of goals of education requires the teacher to select different means of evaluation in accordance with the type of goals sought. Techniques of measurement for facts and skills are well known and well developed. The evaluation of personal growth requires the use of subjective estimate to a greater degree than the evaluation of skills or factual learning.

As a result of considering these principles, the teacher should sense increasing competence in the following aspects of teaching:

1. Recognizing the experiences in a teaching-learning situation that contribute to personal growth.

2. Identifying one's own area of specialization somewhere along a scale ranging from specialized goals to personal growth goals.

3. Recognizing the kinds of evaluation required to give appropriate coverage of the child's learning at school.

4. Planning short teaching activities in proper perspective to broader units.

Inasmuch as this chapter serves as an introduction for the chapters in Part Three, problems will be found in the chapters which follow.

BIBLIOGRAPHY

American Association of School Administrators, *American School Curriculum* (1953 Yearbook). Washington, D.C.: The National Education Association, 1953. Chaps. i, v, vi, and viii.

American Association for Health, Physical Education, and Recreation, *Developing Democratic Human Relations Through Health, Physical Education, and Recreation* (1951 Yearbook). Washington, D.C.: The National Education Association, 1951.

Association for Supervision and Curriculum Development, *Action for Curriculum Improvement* (1951 Yearbook). Washington, D.C.: The National Education Association, 1951.

———, *Growing Up in an Anxious Age* (1952 Yearbook). Washington, D.C.: The National Education Association, 1952.

Beauchamp, George A., *Planning the Elementary School Curriculum*, Boston: Allyn and Bacon, Inc., 1956.

National Council for the Social Studies, *Social Studies for Young Adolescents*. Curriculum Series No. 6. Washington, D.C.: The National Education Association, 1951.

National Education Association and American Association of School Administrators, Educational Policies Commission, *Education for All American Youth, A Further Look*. Washington, D.C.: The National Education Association, 1952.

National Science Teachers Association, *Physical Science Today*. Washington, D.C.: The National Education Association, 1951.

National Society for the Study of Education, "The Activity Movement," in Part II, 33rd Yearbook. Bloomington, Illinois: Public School Publishing Company, 1939.

———, *Modern Philosophies of Education* (1955 Yearbook, Part I). Chicago: The University of Chicago Press, 1955.

Rugg, Harold, *Foundations for American Education*. Yonkers, N.Y.: World Book Company, 1947. Pp. 540-70.

Smith, B. Othaniel, William O. Stanley, and J. Harlan Shores, *Fundamentals of Curriculum Development*. New York: World Book Company, 1950.

Spears, Harold, *The Teacher and Curriculum Planning*. Englewood Cliffs, N.J.: Prentice-Hall, Inc., 1951.

Stratemeyer, Florence B., and others, *Developing a Curriculum for Modern Living*. New York: Teachers College, Columbia University, 1947.

Thayer, V. T., Caroline B. Zachry, and Ruth Kotinsky, *Reorganizing Secondary Education*. New York: Appleton-Century-Crofts, Inc., 1939.

Warner, W. Lloyd, Robert J. Havighurst, and Martin B. Loeb, *Who Shall Be Educated?: The Challenge of Unequal Opportunity*. New York: Harper & Brothers, 1944.

8

Giving importance to lesson planning

A lesson plan is made up of the detailed sequence of events to be carried out with a specific group of pupils for a period of one to several days. "Daily teaching plans" refer to those modifications which are made for a day on the strength of the events of the previous day. Such daily plans are often necessary in all organizations of teaching.

To show the relationship of lesson plans to the whole of teaching a comparison with the planning of a vacation tour might be made. Assume that a family of five has planned such a tour for three weeks' duration. On such a tour, designed for recreational and educational purposes, one would expect to take various side trips along the way. The differences in interests within the family would lead to different activities in different places. This variety, provided for the sake of individual needs, does not necessarily detract from the values and over-all effectiveness of the tour.

To illustrate further the point of varied interests resulting in varied activities, consider a possible segment of the tour. As the family approaches the city of Denver, after two days of travel in the plains and prairies of the Middle West, they plan what they will do during the two days they will be there. Their guide book suggests numerous possibilities from which to make a choice. The gold-domed State Capitol, the mountain parks, the Colorado Museum of Natural History, the Red Rocks Theatre, Central City, and gold panning along Cripple Creek would make different appeals to people with different tastes. These are but a few of the many things from which activities might be selected.

Having talked over the possibilities, the family decides to go together to the Capitol and the Museum. It is the choice of the father and the boy to see a sports event at the University while the mother and girls decide to drive out to Central City and attend the Opera, taking advantage of offers of tickets from Denver friends. Such an arrangement would allow each member of the family to follow a course adapted to his needs and interests. Since the purpose of the tour is personal improvement and recreation, it is not necessary that each person do exactly the same things.

After a busy day, the family returns to the motel and plans the next day's activities. A change in the weather has reduced the chances for a pleasant picnic in the mountain parks, which had been originally considered in the two day plan. By an unexpected bit of good luck the mother has found that tickets for the entire family are available for the matinee in Central City. The enthusiasm of the girls and their mother for the experience of the first afternoon is contagious, and this alternative to a day of outdoor activity is chosen.

This illustration in travel helps show the relationship of various kinds of teaching plans. Without general planning of the tour as a whole the profitable experiences in this particular city might have been lost. The educational values were enhanced by the review of possibilities in greater detail by the family group as they approached this point selected for stopover. Unforeseeable conditions in the weather necessitated a bit of replanning that resulted in a continued experience of great value to the group.

Comparing plans in two situations. If plans for teaching may now be compared to the plans made for the tour, the necessity for all types of plans mentioned in the introduction to Part Three will become more apparent. The teacher of a sixth-grade room teaches the boys physical education. They have agreed upon a plan for dividing the class into teams, and are engaged during the physical education period in playing and related activities. The goals are pleasure and improvement in skills, teamwork, attitudes, and knowledge of play.

Early in the play the teacher has observed that the boys need a bit of instruction in batting. This need can be met through the use of special equipment designed to hold a baseball at the correct position for striking. Each boy is coached in the detail that he seems to need to make a more effective hitter. The other boys field the balls, thus gaining further help in the details of the game. As each team completes this activity to the satisfaction of the teacher, they return to the playing field while another team is given this special help. Planning this lesson has a very definite relationship to current games of baseball. The whole planned experience with baseball including special games after school and possibly a league play-off may be thought of as the unit teaching plan. The lesson in batting technique grew out of the observation that the boys needed this experience. Whether the lesson in batting will be repeated will depend upon the further observations of the teacher as the boys resume play.

COMPARISON OF TEACHING AND PLANNING
A FAMILY TOUR

Family Tour	*Teaching Baseball*
Unit: A three-week tour in the West. (Based on needs and interests of the family.)	*Unit:* A series of several weeks of activity in baseball. (Based on needs and interests of a class of sixth grade boys.)
Lesson: A two day stop in Denver. Some possible activities: Indoor activities: Capitol building Opera Sports Outdoor activities: Picnic Panning gold	*Lesson:* One or two days' special attention to batting techniques (based on observation by teacher while boys are at play). Use special equipment. Arrange maximum continuation for play. Determine effect.
Daily: Obstacle—the weather. The new plan for the day takes advantage of a new opportunity in the form of available tickets.	*Daily:* Obstacle—all teams but one showed desired improvement. This team is given a second round of instruction in batting.

The process of planning the lesson in batting technique involved a number of points. The decision to give the lesson and to try to accomplish certain things with the boys came first. Then came the selection of the available equipment, and arrangement of things the boys were to do and the order in which they would be done. The plan included preservation of the greatest amount of continued play possible at all times, since the teacher did not want to reduce the high motivation of the moment. It was necessary to consider how improvement would be noted as a result of the special instruction, and how the decision to have further batting instruction would be made. The planning process is present in all its essentials in the preceding schematic comparison.

What a good plan contains. Purposes of teaching and local conditions vary so widely that it is impossible to give satisfactory models of plans in the scope of this book. However, reference will be made to plans teachers have made and to the process of planning an effective lesson.

Examples of plans in the field of one's choice may be found sometimes in journals, books, and curriculum laboratory collections. Wide differences among contributors in the same subject will be observed. Possibly more important than examples is a set of criteria for a good plan. One such set of criteria follows:

1. The plan shows a clear relationship between what has gone before and what is to follow.
2. The plan indicates clearly what the pupils are supposed to learn.
3. The plan indicates clearly what the pupils will do to bring about the learning desired.
4. The plan shows some means by which differences among pupils' rate of learning and ability to comprehend will be cared for.
5. The plan reveals the teacher's thinking about evaluation of the learning which has been undertaken.

Throughout the discussion of planning in this chapter, an effort will be made to help the teacher develop a plan which will approximate these standards.

Relating the lesson to what has gone before. Teachers in the early phases of classroom work often do short lessons as a part of the total plan of teaching by the supervisor. A lesson plan prepared for such an occasion furnishes an illustration meeting this first criterion. The unit in progress concerned Greek drama and dramatists.

In introducing his part of the lesson the teacher said, "I've been interested in the discussions we have had in class concerning the Greek drama and Greek dramatists, especially Sophocles and his contributions to the Greek theatre. I thought you might be interested in knowing more about the physical aspects of the Greek stage. We will take up Greek make-up also, later in the period."

In this manner the particular things with which the class would be concerned for the short time he would work with them were fitted into the current scheme of things.

Pupil background. Any teacher undertaking work with a group of pupils for the first time must do a great deal of guessing. For example, if the new group is a third-grade class, he must start by assuming that the majority of the pupils, at least, have had some kind of success with the work of the preceding grades. Being generally familiar with what pupils have done prior to third grade, the teacher begins on the basis of these assumptions.

In every graded situation, however, it soon becomes apparent that certain assumptions are correct and certain ones incorrect, and that while an assumption may be safe for a portion of the group it is not safe for all the group. The reading vocabulary which the teacher may expect from third graders may be lacking in a large segment of the class. Learning is a continuous process; teaching is likewise continuous.

It is quite difficult to plan teaching activities without a clear conception of objectives. The best objectives, however, are those which are based upon the needs of the learners. The observation of needs requires time for obtaining information with regard to each individual of the kind described earlier. A lack of information about how the group works, the kinds of experiences it has had, and the success it has had with those learning experiences is, therefore, a serious handicap.

Another difficulty arises from insufficient knowledge of background; learning may degenerate to verbal memorization unless the teacher is careful to ascertain the experience background of the group so that instruction may have meaning. For example, the teaching of number concepts requires experiences involving the counting of real objects, accumulating objects beyond ten, and expressing the results according to our decimal number system. The teacher may find that pupils go through the motions and repeat the words but cannot pass tests of understanding. In many forms of learning, experience shared by pupils and teacher is necessary to insure understanding. The teacher considers means of checking to see whether experience has been shared and, if it has not, builds it into his plan.

Community impact. It has been implied above that knowledge of the immediate background of the learner in the study under consideration is of great importance in developing plans. It is helpful to know more than just the immediate subject-matter background. If the teacher can find out over a period of time the type of response to expect from each pupil; something of his relations with fellow pupils, parents, and relatives; his neighbors in the community; and his socio-economic status, physical health, and problems of mental health, which could affect his school behavior, a start will have been made toward better planning. Likewise, it is often important to know just how the pupil's group experience in this particular class has affected him. The matter of interaction within peer groups has been discussed earlier. The first thing that the planning process takes into consideration, then, is as much community background as can be obtained.

Stating clearly what the pupils are to learn. Brief mention has already been made of the necessity for a clear statement of what learning is anticipated. The determination of the objectives of a teaching-learning situation may be teacher-dominated, or it may be done in cooperation with pupils. Teachers of specialized subjects are often justified in establishing the objectives for a lesson or unit. Other teachers often do so even when a cooperative approach would be more appropriate and more effective. The teacher who set up the plan for teaching the Greek stage thought he was justified in setting up his own goals because he was bringing to the class special information and was restricted to a part of one class hour. The general aim in the Greek stage plan provides an opportunity to point out some problems in developing such statements. It was stated as follows: "To help the child to understand, interpret, and appreciate world literature."

Difficulties in using words. The words *understand* and *under-*

standing are trick words, and lead teachers into a false sense of security about their stated aims. If an understanding is intended of, for instance, the influence of Greek literature in our heritage, the aim should be stated something like this: "Help the child understand that literature from many lands is an integral part of our rich literary inheritance." Such "understandings" should be positive and clearcut statements using or implying the phrase "understand that."

Interpret is a broad general term. The real intent of the teacher becomes clear if a statement similar to the following is incorporated: "To help the child derive meaning from literature written against unfamiliar cultural backgrounds." In a statement such as this, the full impact of the objective is realized. The goal is to give meaning to literature. This clearly involves learning about the culture from which the literature is derived.

The words *appreciate* and *appreciation* are likewise trick words. They contribute their share to the teacher's false sense of security about his statements of aims. An aim stated in terms of appreciation without reference to the particular feeling that will be aroused is not helpful in later phases of planning. It is quite difficult to tie up such statements with learning activities and teaching procedures. It is likewise quite difficult to follow up with an evaluation. In this example it is probable that the teacher wants more than understanding; that is, he hopes to arouse a feeling on the part of the pupils that literatures of other countries hold promise of an enriched view of life. If such a feeling can be aroused, at least some of the pupils will be motivated to read the literatures of other lands. In such cases the goal of an aroused feeling is appreciation, but the emotional element involved can be made clearer and the creation of teaching-learning situations thus made easier.

The same general comments could be made with regard to specific aims, since they are stated in terms of the same three basic generalizations discussed above. The specific aims were stated thus: "To help the pupil in this understanding, interpreting, and appreciating of world literature by presenting the physical features of the Greek theatre as related to the present-day theatre, and by giving some idea of basic Greek make-up."

It is suggested that clearer statements regarding understandings would be:

1. That physical features of the theatre today were invented by the ancient Greeks.

2. That use of make-up by Sophocles provided the possibility of facial play not possible for earlier actors using masks.

A specific aim covering *interpretation* might consist of a statement like this: "To help the pupil attach meaning to play-acting of Sophocles' time as it tried to portray the life and feelings of the people who attended." Such a statement sets forth more clearly what is implied in the term interpretation.

To illustrate again the area of *appreciation,* a statement of aim could be: "To cause the pupil to feel that the theatre continues to be an outlet for men to express their deepest emotions, as it was for the Greeks two thousand years ago." This statement attempts to point out the feeling that the teacher hopes to arouse in the learner. Appreciation can be developed only as specific feelings are aroused. Effort thus expended will vastly improve the clarity of the objectives and will in turn simplify a choice of learning activities and evaluation techniques. These suggestions for formulating statements of objectives are equally important whether set up by the teacher alone or by pupils and teacher in cooperation

Objectives that pupils understand. Lesson planning attempts to excite in each pupil a purpose that makes sense for him; that is, the teacher puts himself in the place of the young learner and tries to see from that point of view just what the whole exercise is good for. It is not always readily apparent to children just why they should study their lessons. Insofar as it is possible to do so, a teacher tries to make things seem worth doing. Children have a natural desire to grow up and to be able to do things their parents and older brothers and sisters do. To many children it is not difficult to demonstrate that reading, for example, is an activity from which much pleasure can be derived. Some kinds of learning often seem to be worthwhile in themselves to children. Such claims are often made for work with numbers. Not every school task, however, can be easily justified or motivated, and the teacher will often be hard put to accomplish this phase of planning.

When planning is so arranged that young people have a direct part in selecting what is to be learned and how it is to be achieved, several advantages accrue. It is human nature to feel kindly disposed toward those activities with which we have a direct and responsible connection. When planning is so carried on that pupils have a part in choosing what they will learn and the means by which they will learn it, the task to be accomplished becomes to a greater extent their own. Such planning further guarantees that it will be in keeping with the maturity and abilities of the learners themselves. A very good indication of pupils' real goals in learning is found in the questions that they ask. Altogether too often pupils' aims appear to be mere restatements of a teacher's aims without any real significance. A goal cannot be a pupil's own unless he has had something to do with formulating it. One of the most promising devices for determining pupil aims is to establish a situation which encourages asking questions. Note should then be made of the questions actually asked, for these questions constitute an indication of pupils' real goals more nearly than almost any other signs.

After pupils have expressed concerns in a given area of learning it is the teacher's responsibility to demonstrate that these concerns have been considered in the plans that are developed. The entire advantage is therefore augmented when the teacher goes ahead to consider with the group how the teacher and the class can best accomplish the things they want. If the goals finally selected are clear, their relation to learning activities becomes easier. Likewise, greater common understanding of what is to be accomplished adds greatly to the ease of planning evaluation.

Cooperative development of goals results in cooperative and positive attitudes on the part of the pupils. Learning activities are not selected because they are hard or unpleasant; they are selected because they present a promising means of accomplishing things children want to accomplish. As a result, there is little if any fear in the situation. Threats are omitted from the scene entirely and mere busy work to fill up time has no place. This kind of planning, then, contributes to desirable conditions for teaching in which tension is reduced to a minimum.

Teacher-pupil planning is somewhat more common in elementary school classrooms where modern teachers have learned to capitalize upon the events of the day or upon new-found interests and sources of motivation. Secondary teachers are more and more turning to pupil needs and interests as sources of motivation. Even in such formally organized subjects as mathematics, chemistry, and foreign language some details relative to when and how subject matter shall be treated can be left to pupil decision. Although this is not the same kind of motivation as that resulting from the discovery of a new problem and the challenge of suggesting solutions, nevertheless those decisions which can be left to the pupils add greatly to their sense of belonging, and lend significance to the things they do.

Teacher-pupil planning limitations. The teacher needs to recognize that while teacher-pupil planning is a great addition to professional teaching practices, it has its place like everything else. The remoteness of goals and length of planning periods are directly related to the age and maturation of the pupils. The teacher in the lower or middle elementary grades cannot expect successful planning periods that are too long or in which the anticipated learning products will be too long delayed. At these levels, the teacher will use cooperative planning judiciously as needed. Planning periods will be more frequent but of shorter duration. The goals will be attainable in shorter time, and a greater percentage of time will be devoted to action that will move toward realization of the goals.

As the junior and senior high school years are approached with added maturation, the intellectual and cooperative activities of planning meetings will be more satisfying to children. Maturity enables a person to look farther ahead toward outcomes. Consequently learning units can be longer, with appropriately longer planning periods. These planning periods will not need to be so close together at these upper levels. This, in turn, creates a desirable situation for the secondary teacher in which the activities become increasingly self-sustaining, requiring less constant direction on the part of the teacher. This luxury the elementary teacher can also attain in some degree; but periods of self-sustained activity will be shorter and will require more frequent attention from the teacher. There is, nevertheless, a great advantage in planning so that everyone understands what is to be done and has a feeling that it is worth while. This frees the teacher to take care of numerous individual teaching jobs that continually arise.

Learning activities. Activity directed toward learning involves thoughtful "doing" of one kind or another. Every planning consideration of the teacher should be in terms of what will bring about the kind of thinking or responding that is desired. There is nothing wrong with physical activity; it often serves a useful purpose when accompanied by intellectual control and evaluation. There is no need, however, to have pupils jump up and down in the same place to be active. Mental activity goes on all during the class period. There is no such thing as separate activity periods in a teaching plan. The entire plan for teaching is set up in terms of mental response. It is highly desirable that the teacher provide for the involvement of the maximum number of learners in whatever activity is planned. That is, where possible, stimulation of a group as a whole will be preferred to direction to a single person.

Opportunities to design simple learning activities. In early classroom experience, planning may be limited to a very simple exercise. Teachers of industrial arts, fine arts, home economics, and physical education often have a small group of pupils assigned to them as their special responsibility. When the activities in a class are such that this may be done, the teacher is provided with an excellent opportunity to gain vital experiences in working with children without the burden of handling large numbers of pupils and the attendant organization and management problems. He is able to acquire an intimate knowledge of the pupils and to develop in them a sense of group belonging which helps to bring about an effective teaching-learning situation.

Plans for a small group of this kind can be of superior quality. In an arts program each pupil may be working on a different project. Having only four to six pupils enables the teacher to make a daily appraisal of each one, to evaluate his progress, and to anticipate some problems before they are actually encountered. This planning really amounts to an accumulation of individual plans. How Johnny is getting along with his bird box, how Mary is progressing with her clay dogs, how Jimmy made out with his tie rack and Sue with her book ends—such information helps the teacher plan for tomorrow's work. In a large group of pupils it is obviously not possible to make a detailed analysis every day of every learning situation. However, the teacher does gradually acquire skill in surmising the probable responses of the rest of the group from the responses of those who can be observed at any one time.

On the basis of probable reactions the teacher tries to guess what will happen the next day if these same pupils or others are confronted with certain activities. In the case of the arts, there is always the problem as to whether to anticipate an error a pupil is likely to make in the next step with his project and try to prevent it, or to allow him to proceed, make the error, and then solve the problem of what to do about it. In other, more formal, teaching situations, the pupil responses near the end of the class period may indicate that what the teacher thought he had taught that day had not been learned. Such a finding creates a problem of reteaching a segment of the group. The reteaching may even involve making up a new approach in the hope that it will be more effective than what was done before. It is always profitable to guess what is going to happen in a given class period and to anticipate as far as possible the problems and difficulties that are going to arise. Then, depending upon the nature of the youngsters and the expense of time, effort, and possible money involved in anticipated errors, the teacher determines upon the course of action to be followed.

In classes of more formal subject context there are frequent occasions in which a pupil requires extra individual attention. Doing special work with an individual provides the teacher with an opportunity to utilize his best techniques of planning just as does the problem of a small group of pupils. The simplicity of the situation under these conditions provides an excellent opportunity for real analysis of teaching and learning.

The teacher might have the opportunity to contribute something unique from his own experience and thus enrich the total learning situation. Contributions may consist of intimate pictures of unfamiliar places and peoples or incidents which he has witnessed not otherwise available to the class. Other examples of supplemental teaching include the preparation of bulletin boards and displays of various kinds, the preparation of special materials or devices for use by the group, contributions from recent study in college classes, or special research for a specific purpose. Planning to make these short contributions is excellent experience.

Examples of activities selected to meet goals. The teacher who planned the lesson on Greek theatre wanted the pupils to learn about its physical features and about the origin of facial make-up. To accomplish this learning he first had a short biography of Sophocles read aloud. Questions then brought out the fact that it was he who introduced painted scenery and facial make-up. Later activity involved sketching of arrangements of the theatre bringing out the basic principles of perspective drawing. By doing these things the teacher hoped the pupils would achieve the learning goals which had been established.

A teacher of French found among his pupils some who had traveled in Europe and several who planned to do so. It seemed desirable to give some special instruction in the language commonly used on railroads and in restaurants, hotels, and markets. This became the objective of a lesson which lasted for five or six days.

As activities for the accomplishment of this objective, the teacher planned to have two students each day read a page of conversational French dialogue dealing with the subjects of railroads, restaurant menus, hotels, and markets. Following the reading of such material the teacher planned to ask the pupils questions about what had been said.

Accompanying this exercise, new words and phrases were to be placed upon the blackboard with explanation and discussion of each one. Study sheets were also provided each day dealing with different aspects of the problem, including vocabulary and idiomatic expressions often encountered.

Through these activities in which the pupils engaged it was expected that some facility with the common language needed for touring French-speaking countries would be developed. The lesson was related to and a part of the current course in French.

The teacher strives to develop skill in the selection of learning activities related to the goals which have been established. This skill is very closely integrated with skill in making assignments and introducing new activities to pupils. Because of the importance of this phase of teaching, special attention is directed toward it in the paragraphs that follow.

The assignment. In developing daily lesson plans the teacher makes important decisions that determine characteristics of the assignment. In the first place he determines whether he will continue within the limits of the textbook and within the classroom proper, or whether the educational program to be enjoyed by his pupils will utilize the textbook as only one source of information and regard the classroom as the hub of a wider circle of activity.

The teacher will also decide, wittingly or unwittingly, whether the assignment will be good because of the energy he has expended upon it, or whether it will be mediocre because energy has not been expended. The development of good assignments is the essence of the teacher's work. Time, effort, imagination, and initiative are involved. What is done in planning the assignment really determines what teaching will be done. In the assignment new work is developed. It is here that the stimulation and the groundwork for understanding are to be found. If one must neglect any phase of his planning for teaching, it should not be the assignment that suffers.

A common difficulty, and one which tempts every teacher with large numbers of pupils and several preparations a day, is the improper use of the textbook. Its proper role is an aid to learning, and it should be so considered. It really provides a quick view of the things to be learned. It can be looked upon as a reference, or it may be considered a definite minimum for which poorly motivated pupils will be held responsible. In no case should it be followed slavishly to the point where making the assignment merely consists of turning the pages in the book. In such cases, the teacher is abdicating his responsibility for determining the sequence of topics and selecting the learning activities. Such practice amounts to leaving it to the textbook writer to make these decisions. No textbook writer ever presumed to make such decisions for any teacher. Allowing the assignment technique to fall into this pattern completely ignores the principle of adjusting the problems and their solutions to the backgrounds and needs of the class at hand. The possible use of real materials and resources in the immediate environment which might be brought to bear on their educational program is also lost.

The assignment is the teacher's greatest opportunity to do good teaching. It provides the opportunity to grasp indications of interest when it is at its peak. There is also the possibility of receiving genuine help from pupils' suggestions for action. It provides one of the teacher's excellent opportunities to adapt work to individual abilities. Special chores and responsibilities and special bits of investigation and research can be awarded to those whose ability is known to be high. It is the teacher's opportunity to select from his wider experience a range of activities that will more nearly meet the needs of the group with which he works.

Aids in improving assignments. The foregoing paragraphs have indicated some ways in which planning can improve the assignment in teaching. Another suggestion related to the background of pupils to be used when beginning a new phase of a subject is the use of a pre-test procedure. The pre-test is not to be confused with a final test of achievement, and pupils need to have this brought clearly to their attention. Results of pre-tests are for the teacher's guidance and do not have anything to do with the final mark. Pre-tests may be of the same form as final tests, or they may take the form of conversational inquiry into what the group knows about the phase of work about to be opened. The purpose of a pre-test activity is to find out an individual's status or the status of a group with regard to learning under way. This may be illustrated in the case of a project in the arts area. A girl may be making a garment or a boy may be making a knapsack. In either case they are using fabric and will undoubtedly be using a pattern. The work is at the stage where the material is to be cut. The teacher may wish to call together several children who are in approximately the same stage of progress and review with them the procedure in laying patterns on the material and the necessary checks to be made before cutting begins. If, however, the class involved happens to be an advanced group which has had considerable experience with using a pattern and cutting materials, this extensive review of procedures may be greatly modified or may be deemed wholly unnecessary. If, in either case, preparation and knowledge of procedure are found to be inadequate, it will be very much in order to make an assignment involving reading and demonstration work on this particular phase of work.

It is hard to say which is the more discouraging experience for a teacher—completion of a carefully prepared assignment only to have children say, "Well, gee, we did all that last year and know how to do it," or the presentation of a new topic only to have children say, "We don't know what you are talking about." In either case the assignment is poor and the difficulty could have been avoided by some kind of preliminary effort to find out the present status of learning.

Another suggestion for improving of the assignment is to develop additional enrichment work for those who are expected to finish basic requirements early. In some cases, children can demonstrate proficiency with a new list of spelling words or a set of mathematics exercises without further study. In such a case it is highly desirable to have some kind of extra work that will be worth their while. This idea is closely related to individual differences as they affect lesson planning, found in later paragraphs in this chapter.

Still another suggestion that helps make assignments definite and somewhat self-supporting is the use of study guides. A study guide is often a duplicated sheet which contains an outline of the things to be done, showing where the topics are to be found in the textbook and suggesting other sources of information. It provides a sequence of activities so that every person may proceed through the assignment, without becoming confused as to what to do next, and may find just the touch of supplemental help needed to keep him going. Study guides may contain added suggestions of things to look at or things to compare, and directions for making observations and stating hypotheses, as part of a total built-in process designed to improve reflective thinking. Carefully worded questions will lead the pupil along, step by step, through activities which he can carry out at his own rate of speed. Usually the teacher should go through the activities contained on study guides with the whole class, so that the meaning of the questions and the intent of the instructions is clear, whether or not every detail is absorbed in the preliminary demonstration.

Study guides can be expanded to include directions for searching for added resources. There can be suggestions for activities of a service kind related to the lesson at hand. The desirability of certain constructional projects can be pointed out with some general suggestion as how to proceed. Through the use of questions and carefully drawn directions, pupils can be led to expand their use of resources; they can be encouraged to outline, to read rapidly, and to engage in numerous other activities which are quite difficult to get across when only an oral assignment is made.

These suggestions comprise only a partial list of those which might be made for improvement of this very important teaching activity. No teacher can afford to overlook the importance of that portion of the lesson plan which may be listed under the assignment. If skill is developed in pre-test activities so as to find, as nearly as possible, a margin between what is learned and what is to be learned, the assignment may then be geared to that point. If this is the case, this portion of the teacher's work is more likely to result in learning than almost any other phase of classroom activity. Since it does occupy a crucial spot in the teaching-learning situation, teachers whose teaching pattern is largely a day-to-day procedure cannot afford to cut short the time given to it in their daily planning activity.

Provision for individual differences. Always a troublesome problem in planning, caring for individual differences is especially difficult when lessons are planned on a daily basis. The wide variety in achievement level and rate of learning is more readily cared for in a situation where more time can be expended with a group in the study of a broader unit of activity. For example, a project in any of the arts has several advantages for making adjustments over the situation of trying to teach required skills in arithmetic, unless the latter is organized in a larger block of related experiences. The problem of individual differences is one point at which unit planning and unit teaching hold definite superiority over daily planning. These matters are further discussed in Chapters 9 and 11. However, some suggestions that may be helpful in lesson planning will be made at this point.

Heterogeneous group. A junior high school teacher reported an experimental effort in a geography class of seventh-grade pupils. Actually he was using unit teaching, but the illustration will serve to clarify the use of committees of pupils of all ability levels in meeting the problem. Teacher-pupil planning activity first brought out the topics in geography in which the pupils were interested. Thirteen areas were listed as follows:

Manufacturing
Communication
Transportation
Animals
Construction
Power
How people live
Fishing
Nature
Natural resources
Foods
Farm crops
Weather

Finally, it was agreed to select five areas from the list and to have committees of five pupils each study them. Pupils indicated first, second, and third choices and the teacher helped arrange the committees. This plan resulted in each committee having various ability levels. Each group selected a chairman who, interestingly enough, was neither the fastest nor slowest learner in that particular group.

Pupils worked on the reports in the ways in which they could make the greatest contribution. At the reporting stage were found the points of illustration desired. One slow learner held pictures while another member of the committee discussed it in relation to their problem. Another slow learner announced the names of people as they made their reports. In another case a slow learner made a report after having been helped with some reading by a more able pupil. The important thing here was that each pupil had a part in the report geared to his ability, which in these cases was very low. The resultant feelings of success and belonging motivated them to some learning. The social studies lend themselves well to this kind of whole-group participation.

A fourth-grade teacher reported an interesting experience growing out of study in social studies. A part of their study included rug weaving, which the children wanted to do. Not having room enough to bring in a big loom, the teacher suggested that each child make a small loom. Simple cardboard looms using the kind of yarn familiar to elementary teachers were constructed, and the yarn matts were woven as planned. Useful pads for hot dishes or decorative purposes resulted.

The interesting observation by the teacher was that two of the slow learners in her grade did better work on the weaving and enjoyed it more than her superior students. The fast learners felt that it took up too much time. The slow learners, however, felt a great sense of accomplishment in that they really had finished something and that they really had made it with their own hands. This is an illustration showing how a broadened base of learning activity provides a slow learner with an occasional opportunity to feel success.

Teachers of arithmetic are making use of some projects to assist the slow and fast learners alike. There is enough interest in the arithmetical number system and processes to challenge the ingenuity of even the brightest pupil. The design and construction of aids to learning and understanding may be used to involve learners of all levels of ability. Physical objects such as the abacus can be designed by the more able members of a group and can be constructed and used by the slow learners, giving both satisfaction of belonging and aid in learning. In such projects the research and design become the challenge to the fast learners.

In all subjects the careful planning of assignments makes it possible for everyone to have something he can do and at the same time avoid unnecessary duplication of effort. A list of basic exercises, for instance, can be selected for initial study. The successful completion of certain ones permits the pupil to proceed to the next. If, however, difficulty is encountered at one point, restudy of the matter with further practice is required. The more able pupil will then be permitted to work at the application of the principle at a higher level or to pursue an interest of his own growing out of the lesson. The less able pupil will study at a level more nearly geared to his needs. This type of assignment is complemented with appropriate evaluation procedures which will be discussed later in connection with the recitation.

Some principles by which teachers can be guided in teaching pupils in heterogeneous groups will be given at this point.[1] To the extent that a lesson can be planned so as to incorporate these principles, a better adaptation to individual differences will be possible.

Principles relating to slow learners:

1. Be especially careful to ask the student to do things which you are reasonably sure he can do.

2. Through your own activity and through the development of consideration on the part of the class, provide an increasingly sympathetic atmosphere.

3. Provide group work for a part of the time in which the slow learner shares with a representative group of the entire class. This adds greatly to his sense of belonging and serves as a stimulation to do the best he can.

4. Try to report progress to the slow learner as regularly as possible. Discuss his situation with him frankly but do not omit opportunities to comment on strong points.

5. In setting up evaluation procedures and plans, use a broad enough base that at least sometimes a pupil will experience a feeling of success.

[1] Jean D. Grambs and William J. Iverson, *Modern Methods in Secondary Education* (New York: The Dryden Press, Inc., 1952), pp. 271 and 278 ff.

Principles relating to fast learners:

1. Fast learners ought, as nearly as possible, to be given an opportunity to develop all of their talents.

2. All possible materials written on an adult level dealing with the problem at hand should be provided.

3. The teacher needs to guard against giving the fast learner an undue share of his time. It is pleasant to work with these able children and a strong temptation is to give them more time than they really need. Actually what they need is challenge and stimulation with a minimum of assistance.

4. Provide opportunities for them to do research on the more involved phases of the lesson under consideration.

5. As an outgrowth of extra studies and activities, practice in writing reports of their observations is good.

6. Leading group discussions and assuming responsibility for discussion of controversial issues often challenges these children.

7. Opportunities for leadership in assisting groups of pupils or suggesting and following up problems of personal and group interest should be provided.

Caution to provide for all pupils. Lest the importance of the large group of average-ability pupils be minimized, a few statements of principle for dealing with them in a heterogeneous group are indicated:

1. There should be provided clearly recognizable activities that are designed to help learn what is to be learned.

2. There should always be an opportunity equal to that of any other member of the class to raise questions and to have help from the teacher and from the rest of the class in deriving ways to find the answers.

3. There should be plenty of opportunities to undertake tasks that do not require too complex solutions involving a principle that is learned.

4. There should always be an opportunity to participate in activities with the faster learners when proficiency in the middle-group activities has been demonstrated.

The above list of suggestions is by no means exhaustive and the application is not easy. It is not likely that any one lesson plan will provide an application of all these principles. However, the quality of a lesson plan will be improved distinctly as it does incorporate some of these ideas. A majority of lesson plans are especially weak in differentiation for pupils having different types and different degrees of competence.

Evaluating the recitation. Nearly every daily planning procedure anticipates a situation in which at least a part of the period will be devoted to some kind of pupil performance. This performance will vary greatly from a physical education class, on the one hand, to a chemistry class, on the other. It will differ distinctly from the reading group activity of an elementary room to the written lesson on spelling, and will further differ as the activity moves into the area of art or physical education. A large part of the planning effort of a great many teachers is directed toward this portion of the teaching-learning period.

Unfortunately, the recitation has degenerated in the American school to a kind of oral quiz period. The idea of providing an opportunity for exchange of opinions, sharing of information and ideas, and bringing out differences with a view to increasing learning has become lost in lesson-hearing procedures. Recitation has become a time when pupils literally march up to the front of the room to recite from memory what they have learned at their seats or what their parents have taught them the night before. In a large number of schools today, the period of pupil activity in academically oriented subjects is a period devoted to question and answer.

In making lesson plans looking toward a recitation period, a teacher should attempt to create as frequently as possible situations where communication between pupils will be in order. Encouragement of pupils to raise serious questions and to volunteer responses of various kinds should be a part of planning. Suggestions as to how the group can best proceed with the work under way go along with the idea of voluntary responses. By the same token, a well founded disagreement of such quality as to elicit a favorable reaction from the class and the teacher is highly commendable. The purpose of teacher questions should be to elicit intelligent discussion from the pupils and lead to a situation in which communication between pupils will be in evidence.

A recitation period in which there is an honest interaction among the pupils themselves and with the teacher, with everybody participating and contributing to the best of his ability, gives the teacher an excellent opportunity to observe the extent of learning resulting from the assignment. In a discussion period in which there is a fine interchange of ideas, with suggestions coming from first one side and then the other, with the teacher playing the role of guide, new and interesting problems are bound to arise. While every tangent of discussion cannot be undertaken in the new assignment, there are certainly many times when such new problems are appropriate for continuation. Under such conditions the next logical step is for the group to decide what needs to be done and how to do it, thus developing a new assignment. A class that has found stimulating problems in a period of good discussion, and has found it permissible to work upon them, has experienced motivation of a high order. The satisfactions derived by the pupils from this experience have notable effects upon the learning.

In order for this kind of work to be fruitful, the teacher must have an appreciation of the value of such occasions and be willing to adjust his program accordingly. It is necessary to realize that education occurs in many different ways and that the motivation to pursue a problem having its origin in pupil discussion will, in all probability, more than compensate for the necessity of passing quickly over some portion of the text material that normally would be given more time.

In addition to the observations made possible by the discussion type of recitation period, the evaluation may proceed in other ways. A short test, demonstration, or bit of creative work on the part of a pupil is suggestive of some of these variations. Adaptation of these techniques to the immediate situation is recommended as they become appropriate.

Closing activity. Class periods should not end with the ringing of the class bell in the middle of a sentence by either pupils or the teacher. A little time should be reserved at the end of the period which will enable the group to re-assess its work and determine just what the state of progress is before leaving the room. Such a bit of time is necessary because pupils may not clearly perceive what they have accomplished unless this is done. Likewise, they may not have as clear conceptions of what needs to be done as they should have in order to proceed into the next day's work.

A most helpful practice is that of making a few notes—two or three sentences will be enough—at the close of the period before other activities make the teacher forget important observations on a particular lesson. In many teaching situations these few notes made at the end of the period will serve as an emergency plan if, for some reason, time for more adequate planning is not available. If the teacher and pupils combine forces and write these notes on the blackboard they provide the pupil with a take-off point for the next day's work. In many cases they may serve a good purpose as a summary to help pupils answer parents' questions about the progress of school work for the day.

SUMMARY

An attempt was made in this chapter to outline procedures involved in making superior lesson plans. The functions of unit plans, lesson plans, and daily plans and their relationships have been described.

Five criteria for evaluating lesson plans were set forth and the organization of the chapter focused attention upon means of approximating those standards in the preparation of lesson plans:

1. To relate the lesson to what has gone before and what is to follow, the teacher was urged to consider pupil backgrounds and the impact of the community. Further assistance is to be had in pre-testing, discussed later in the development of assignment techniques.

2. To state clearly what pupils are to learn is the process of formulating objectives. To make statements of learning objectives that will help to guide the choice of learning activities and evaluative techniques requires careful use of language. An effort has been made to point out some ways to express the goals of a lesson more adequately. Inherent in the kinds of objectives that mean something to pupils is the manner in which they are established. Although there are goals for learning that originate with the teacher's superior knowledge and wider experience, many goals of learning are best derived from cooperative efforts with pupils.

3. To select the things pupils will do to learn requires insight into the predominant characteristics of the objec-

tives. If there are more goals of a specialized nature, the use of procedures that improve memory and skill is desirable. If, on the other hand, the goals are more of the personal growth type, procedures involving cooperative planning, group work, and projects that lend themselves to creativity and originality are indicated. A proper balance of both types of activity is a first consideration in planning. The ingenuity of the teacher in setting up activities appropriate to the needs and maturity level of the pupils is reflected in good planning.

The assignment was given special attention under this criterion of a good lesson because it is in this aspect of lesson-type teaching that the pupils are made aware of the learning activities in which they will engage. The cooperative development of the assignment is a recognized possibility. Numerous suggestions for the improvement of the assignment are offered.

4. To provide for individual differences requires the use of every bit of skill the teacher can muster. The limitations of the lesson plan and day-to-day teaching in this regard are admitted, and the greater adaptability of unit teaching is suggested. Learning activities in which groups of pupils cooperate, each contributing at his level of ability, are among the more promising ways to adapt teaching to heterogeneous groups. Graded activities that allow each pupil to reach a level commensurate with his ability are also suggested.

As a further aid to the teacher, lists of principles for teaching slow, fast, and average learners in heterogeneous groups are given.

5. To evaluate the results of learning the teacher sometimes uses an improved recitation period as an opportunity to make subjective estimates of pupil growth. The necessity for the teacher developing this ability cannot be overemphasized. Other means of evaluation developed in a later chapter are recommended for adaptation.

Little attention has been given to the form of the lesson plan. The view is held that a plan which meets to some degree of approximation the five criteria set forth will serve the teacher well. The nature of the material will dictate the form of the plan. The degree of the teacher's experience and the training supervisor's expectation will determine the amount of detail to be involved. Above all things a plan should be useful to the teacher in preparing the lesson, as well as in teaching it.

Through the study and application of the matters set out in the foregoing chapter, the teacher should grow in at least these areas of competence:

1. Writing lesson plans that are effective parts of a larger concept in teaching.

2. Sensing the desirability of daily planning and making daily plans to meet changing conditions.

3. Developing teaching plans that achieve a balance in learning experiences commensurate with the goals to be approached.

4. Developing teaching plans that are of greater benefit to all pupils in a heterogeneous group.

5. Making more effective use of teaching time through the proper use of assignments and recitation.

6. Making lesson plans that are focused upon the learning activity of the pupils rather than upon the teaching behavior of the teacher.

PROBLEMS

1. *Using a group of learners with whom you are familiar as a point of reference, write a list of objectives for a lesson of your choice.*
   a. *List some information and skills.*
   b. *List some understandings.*
   c. *List some appreciations.*
   d. *List some attitudes you hope to reinforce.*
2. *Write in some detail a description of four learning activities, each focused at one of your objectives in each type a, b, c, and d above.*
3. *Follow through from objective to activity described above and write four paragraphs indicating how you will proceed to evaluate the learning that has been done. Be specific, giving guides to observation or test items as required.*
4. *Explain how you meet needs of slow and fast learners in the situation you have chosen.*

BIBLIOGRAPHY

Bossing, Nelson L., *Teaching in Secondary Schools,* 3rd ed. Boston: Houghton Mifflin Company, 1952. Chaps. x and xi.

Burton, William H., *The Guidance of Learning Activities,* 2nd ed. New York: Appleton-Century-Crofts, Inc., 1952. Chap. xi.

California Committee on Developmental Reading, "Suggestions for Teaching Slow Learners Found in Regular Classrooms," *National Association of Secondary School Principals Bulletin* 35: 23-40, February 1951.

Crawford, T. J., "Lesson Planning for Typewriting," *UBEA Forum* 9: 14-16, January 1955.

Curtis, Dwight K., "Planning Your Work," in Grim and Michaelis, *The Student Teacher in the Secondary School.* Englewood Cliffs, N.J.: Prentice-Hall, Inc., 1953. Chap. iii.

———, and Leonard O. Andrews, *Guiding Your Student Teacher.* Englewood Cliffs, N.J.: Prentice-Hall, Inc., 1954.

Doane, Kenneth R., "Working with Individual Pupils," in Grim and Michaelis, *The Student Teacher in the Secondary School.* Englewood Cliffs, N.J.: Prentice-Hall, Inc., 1953. Chap. iv.

Dodes, I. A., "Planned Instruction," in *The Learning of Mathematics,* 21st Yearbook, National Council of Teachers of Mathematics. Washington, D.C.: The Council, 1953. Pp. 303-34.

Elmer, M. S., "Planning in the Rural School," *Instructor* 59:72-73, September 1950.

Garrison, Noble Lee, *The Improvement of Teaching.* New York: The Dryden Press, 1955. Chap. vi.

Goller, M. S., "Teaching Accrued Expenses," *Journal of Business Education* 26:117-18.

Grambs, Jean D., and William J. Iverson, *Modern Methods in Secondary Education.* New York: The Dryden Press, Inc., 1952. Chaps. iv and xi.

Harbison, C. R., "Lesson Planning As a Valuable Aid in Organization," *Grade Teacher* 68:164, January 1951.

Huffman, H., "Reconciling the Bond Statement," *Journal of Business Education* 26:71-72, October 1950.

Kinker, H. R., "Preparing and Using Lesson Plans," *Industrial Arts and Vocational Education* 41:209-14, September 1952.

Loughlin, R. L., "Master Lesson Plan for Teaching Poetry (Grades 8-12)," *High Points* 32:59-64, September 1950.

Michaelis, John U., and Paul R. Grim, *The Student Teacher in the Elementary School.* Englewood Cliffs, N.J.: Prentice-Hall, Inc., 1953.

Rivlin, Harry N., *Teaching Adolescents in Secondary Schools.* New York: Appleton-Century-Crofts, Inc., 1948. Chap. vi.

Spellman, C. L., "Lesson Plan Making," *National Association of Secondary School Principals Bulletin* 39:150-54, May 1955.

9

Unit planning as a significant approach

Because of certain problems encountered in attaining the goals of a growing concept of education, day-to-day and lesson-by-lesson teaching practices are gradually being replaced by unit teaching. In addition to increasing the scope of goals attainable, unit teaching has provided a way of organizing materials and methods in closer agreement with modern principles of learning. Unit teaching and the planning of units to be taught are highly desirable competences, and the growing teacher will find efforts expended in this area contributing significantly to his total insight into teaching.

Problems that have led to unit teaching. Among the problems of teaching to which the unit approach brings help are preservation of essential relationships among learning products and meeting the wide range of individual interests and abilities found in every class. In addition, unit teaching often incorporates essential factors of motivation found difficult in a day-to-day approach. Another point of significance relates to the complex and multiple outcomes of learning discussed earlier. The hope of education is to bring about new ways of responding to a situation or the improvement of responses already learned. Many desirable goals of education are really behavior patterns consisting of a combination of things learned. Examples were given in the earlier presentation. Unit teaching provides an opportunity to teach patterns of response more effectively than the day-to-day approach.

Unit teaching is carried out in such a manner as to contribute to the security of the learner. Pacing work to the rate of learning possible for each pupil relieves the frustration that often accompanies a steady day-to-day pace. For the slow learner the pace soon outreaches accomplishment; for the fast, the pace is likely to be too slow, leading to poor work habits, boredom, and waste of talent.

Unit teaching expedites curriculum reconstruction. The functional adjustment of the curriculum through the teacher's planning was pointed out in an earlier chapter. The development of unit teaching and unit planning has presented a new means whereby effective curriculum reconstruction can be effected. Adjustments in existing courses can be made as the need arises and new course structure can be developed one unit at a time. Curriculum construction is possible as a continuing process through units planned as educational problems arise.

Schools across the country do have many common characteristics; they also have many local differences. Within a given community, groups of children likewise vary. The unit as a method of organizing the educative experiences for a group of children provides a means of recognizing the special problems of a given group. Unit organization makes it possible to capitalize upon the interests and drives of the individuals in the group.

Unit teaching emphasizes life adaptation. The concept of unit teaching has, from the beginning, emphasized the improvement of response patterns of the individual in life situations. The idea of adaptation may be illustrated in the life of a young man who has recently established a home and finds a water faucet operating unsatisfactorily. At some point in his previous experience, he has learned how water faucets are constructed. He knows that he can quickly correct the situation with some very inexpensive repairs and simple tools and proceeds at once to do so. The product of the learning experience, whether formal or informal, has enabled him to make an effective adaptation to the situation. Not all learning products are as simple as this; nor are all life situations to be met readily by so simple an application of a specific bit of learning. However, the idea is the same.

Assuming that a school has a course in household mechanics, the single learning of the construction of a water faucet would not be conceived as a unit. However, all of the mechanics of household plumbing placed together would include not only faucets, but drains, cut-off valves, toilets, and shower heads, as well as joints, elbows and tees, copper tubing, and many other items and operations. A unit would consist of all the learning necessary to cope with plumbing problems that face the home owner. The householder who had successfully "mastered" the unit would proceed with confidence in those simple repairs which he could make. Likewise, he would have enough judgment to call upon an expert when the problem was beyond his ability.

The teaching of a unit takes on whatever form is best adapted to focusing the learning upon an improved response pattern. The relationship of unit teaching to effective transfer of learning thus becomes another important consideration. The teacher of household mechanics would arrange the unit on plumbing so that as much realism as possible would be involved. Job sheets involving problems with various common parts of the plumbing system and the actual handling of repairs from turning off the water supply to completion would be used to the maximum. All of the principles of teaching for transfer would be implemented.

Comparison of unit teaching and day-to-day teaching. The way in which a unit is taught is different from day-to-day teaching. In the first place, by some means, a long view is taken of a unit so that the learner sees what the end result of his work may be. This may take the form of an overview statement by the teacher, or it may result from cooperative effort by the teacher and pupils to find ways to solve a problem. That is, the pupil can sense in the beginning the direction in which his endeavors will lead him. This fact alone often makes the work seem worth while. Approached on a day-to-day basis, this important point may not be reached until the many daily segments of learning are near completion. It may never be realized by some pupils.

Self-sustained quality. With a goal established some time ahead, the activities leading up to it can be outlined by the teacher or in cooperation with the class. This feature is very important since, by the use of duplicated guide sheets or other means, the pupils can be made individually aware of the sequence of things to be done and responsible for their part in doing them. The development of the plan and the explanation of what is to be done will possibly take two or more days in opening a new unit. It should be carried far enough for the pupils to feel that they are ready and eager to go ahead.

The introductory phase of unit teaching is much like a good assignment described in the preceding chapter. It accomplishes the same purposes as the assignment, but is superior in that it makes clear in the beginning the interrelationships of the various subproblems. Supplemented with a pre-planned guide or notes made during the introductory planning stages, this unit introduction lays the pattern of activity for several days at a time. This fact produces the condition of self-sustained activity and flexibility which is so highly desirable.

Individual needs served. Once the unit is launched each pupil proceeds with his part, whatever it is. In certain specialized subjects—mathematics, science, language arts—the sequence of activity to be followed by each individual may be the same. In this case the first part of the guide sheet will usually consist of activities simple enough to be done by all pupils. These activities will at the same time provide complete coverage of the learning or adaptation upon which the unit is focused. Later sections will become more complex and will "lateral out" into more and more challenging operations. The more challenging activities are, of course, not required of all pupils but show the able pupil more about the topic under consideration. For example, an algebra class is solving problems that involve the solution of quadratic equations. A problem that leads to a third degree equation might be introduced. The initiative of the student would be challenged to resort to graphic methods. This kind of activity is related to the work at hand but is definitely more than busy work. It provides an educative experience of a higher order on the topic at hand.

As implied above, the first part of such a plan outline is relatively easy and when the pupils start on it, following the introduction of the unit, the average and good students will literally "whiz" through it. It helps them check their understanding of the unit as a whole, yet it seldom offers any difficulty. They come to know that better things lie ahead. The class begins to scatter out over the outline. The slower learners may have some trouble with the early problems. The teacher will check the progress of all individuals periodically to see how things are going. A quick check on a graphic chart will be helpful. Short tests to assure understanding may likewise be used from time to time. Sometimes poor quality of work is found with too rapid progress. This condition requires counselling of the pupils involved.

The teacher's part. The daily class period for a time after the introduction of a unit will be largely devoted to work. The teacher seeks to find out what kinds of problems the pupils are encountering and frequently stops the group for a short time for discussion and clarification. Sometimes the introduction has not been clearly understood and requires reteaching.

It is during this working period of self-sustained pupil activity that the teacher finds his opportunities to help individual learners. If the things that pupils are doing are skillfully developed, not only the slow learners but the fast ones as well will be seeking counsel. New problems often arise that deserve the consideration of the entire group. The teacher's time is given to advising, helping, and challenging pupils at their level. He does not use up all his energy starting and stopping as is often the case in day-to-day teaching.

Closing a unit. There comes a time when the maximum return has been achieved and the unit should be closed. This closing may be arbitrarily determined by exhausting the time allocated to the unit. It may be determined when the slow group has completed the coverage of the first section of the unit. Whatever the situation, the teacher assists the learners in bringing together in a systematic fashion whatever has been accomplished. A closing exercise may take the form of a demonstration of all the things learned during the unit. It is common practice to include a test or some other form of evaluation. The group may include an evaluation of the unit itself and their progress with it. When appropriate closing activities are completed the entire group starts together on a new undertaking.

Different procedures in different situations. The unit teaching procedure just described is most appropriate in a mathematics or science class or other situation where a list of exercises or activities can be laid out in sequential fashion. The procedure will vary somewhat in other types of classes that involve teacher-pupil planning to a greater degree. In the latter, the self-sustaining feature of the work will often consist of carrying out plans of committees. Such committees grow out of the introductory phase of the unit which is usually characterized by teacher-pupil planning. Through this planning activity the pupils comprehend the wholeness of the unit and make plans for carrying out their work. Plans worked out by each committee take the place of the uniform outline for individual direction described above. The effect upon the self-sustaining quality of the class is the same; the kind of activity will be different. There will be division of responsibility and sharing by the members of the committee as the work takes shape. Each member of the committee is expected to contribute as much as he can to the effort.

Project provides for individual differences. The manner in which individual differences are met in teaching this type of unit differs from the previously described conception. The group project may take on many forms. Its completion may involve planning and elementary research that will challenge the best pupils of the group. It may require construction of a map or mural to express some of the ideas. Sometimes ingenious construction, using lights and other materials, is involved. A child may be able to do some of these things very well and still be unable to do the more intellectual tasks of planning and research, yet he shares in and profits from the total group project. He learns both information and ways of cooperative endeavor. He achieves something of an all-important sense of success and belonging.

Unit planning needed. To accomplish unit teaching it becomes evident that planning must be adjusted accordingly. The next sections of the chapter will develop principles of unit planning. Suggested guides and outlines will be supplemented by descriptions of units that teachers have written. These examples are selected from units that are not too far removed from the teacher's usual initial thinking about planning. That is, the first example is a unit composed of a sequence of daily plans. Other examples will be largely concerned with subject matter of one kind or another and involve planning, for the most part, by the teacher. Much of the planning is done in advance of meeting the class. The concept of teacher-pupil planning is mentioned, but its complete presentation is postponed until Chapter 11.

The teacher's problem in learning to plan units. The easiest approach for most teachers is to plan units closely related to their subject-matter preparation. Both elementary and secondary teachers are directly concerned with subject matter. The skills of arithmetic, reading, algebra, spelling, cooking, and crafts comprise an important portion of the teacher's equipment and occupy an important place in his work with his pupils. The teacher's knowledge of science, literature, government, and history likewise constitutes an important resource. The majority of college students have come through subject-oriented programs in high school and have found an increasing amount of college work so organized.

Guides for making and evaluating unit plans. Teachers have often stated that it would be helpful if the guides to be used in evaluating unit plans were known to them before the units were written. Such a list of guides is given below. Further interpretation of what these guides mean is found in the various unit descriptions later in the chapter.

1. Is the form of the written unit plan acceptable in general?
2. Are the objectives clearly stated?
3. Is the approach interesting?
4. Are the learning activities pupil-centered?
5. Are the learning activities closely related to the objectives?
6. Are the learning activities varied?
7. Is evaluation given adequate attention?
8. Is evaluation planned in relation to the objectives and the learning activities?
9. Are references, teaching aids, and other helps listed?
10. Are the objectives and learning activities appropriate to the age and developmental status of the learners?
11. Do the learning activities provide a challenge to the fast learners and a chance of success to the slow ones?

A suggested outline for unit plans. The teacher will be assisted in the organization of materials and things for pupils to do in a teaching unit plan by using an outline. The following headings for an outline from Burton are suggested as satisfactory guides for constructing many units. The teacher will find a complete analysis of each of the parts in the Burton text and is strongly urged to use this important source of information. The several parts are illustrated in portions of this chapter also.

    I. Overview
    II. The Teacher's Objectives
    III. The Approach
    IV. The Pupil's Aim or Objective
    V. The Planning and Working Period
    VI. Evaluation Techniques
    VII. Bibliographies
    VIII. Audio-visual Materials, and other instructional aids with sources[1]

A unit composed of daily plans. In the discussion of lesson plans it was pointed out that a well planned series of such lessons could approximate the learnings to be derived from certain kinds of subject-oriented units. It is not uncommon for teachers to make this approach in their early efforts, understandably enough in view of the newness of the concept for many of them. The development of competence in this area of planning should not stop at this intermediate stage, however. An example of such a series of lessons is found in a unit plan on child care and baby-sitting.

This unit plan on child care and baby-sitting was developed by a teacher in home economics for a class of twenty-five or thirty pupils. It was thought that it would cover approximately four weeks. The teacher who developed the plan was in the very first quarter of laboratory experiences.

Objectives. The unit on child care and baby-sitting was designed to help pupils care for children with greater security and increased satisfaction to themselves and their charges. It was intended to help these pupils to feel the responsibility attached to baby-sitting. Some elemental child study was planned to help them understand that

[1] W. H. Burton, *The Guidance of Learning Activities*, 2nd ed. (New York: Appleton-Century-Crofts, Inc., 1952), pp. 451-53.

every action of a child has meaning. Specific helps in entertaining and controlling children were included among the things to be learned.

Approach. An effort to motivate the study was made through the medium of a bulletin board showing pictures of baby-sitters enjoying their work with children. Also exhibited were some books of stories and magazines that would be useful. In addition, the teacher pointed out that observation and actual work in the kindergarten with young children—reading stories for example—would be provided. A film was shown as a further interest-arousing device.

Working period. The body of the unit or the working period outline was composed of fourteen plans for daily activities. Following two days of general introduction, each lesson took up one of a series of predetermined problems. These problems follow:

> 1. Make out daily schedule of activities including sleep for the child of the age you are interested in. What variations will there be at the time when the child is not attending school (summer or vacation schedule)?
>
> 2. List some typical examples of the child's three meals—breakfast, lunch, and dinner. Should the child eat between meals? Give any suggestions. Should the child eat along with the family or alone?
>
> 3. (A) What is considered a good sleep program for the child at the age you are studying? (B) What are some good suggestions for helping the child get ready for bed so that he or she can enjoy a good night's rest?
>
> 4. Answer the questions below to learn the responsibility of the parents who are going to be away from their child for a few hours and are going to leave the child in the care of another person. This will help you find out the responsibilities of baby-sitters, too.
>
> > a. What duties should the parents have carried out with the child before leaving him or her?
> >
> > b. What can parents do to make the situation pleasant for the person who is to care for the child?
> >
> > c. What are the obligations of the child caretaker to the child? to herself and the family? to the home? to the parents of the child when they come home?
>
> 5. Behavior problems come up frequently when one cares for children of another family. You need not understand why children do the things they do. You need to know how you can help children. Select one of the problems listed below,

read about such a problem and what can be done about it. Make a brief report (A) describing or defining the particular problem of behavior (how it shows up), (B) telling what causes the child to act in this way, and (C) telling what can be done to help the child.

    a. Disobedience
    b. Destruction
    c. Dishonesty
    d. Good manners, or lack of good manners
    e. Temper
    f. Showing off
    g. Going to bed
    h. Eating
    i. Cleaning up

6. What kinds of stories seem best to suit the interest of the child you are studying? How can these stories be presented to the child so he will enjoy them? Prepare a story that you can present to a small group of children.

7. What kinds of games seem best for children of the given age?

8. What kinds of activities seem best for children of a particular age, to develop some skill or allow them to express an idea?

The plan includes a good bibliography and, of course, numerous suggestions along the way for carrying out the several projects. A day-to-day plan for observations is provided and a day of actual observations in kindergarten. There is also a day for introducing the summary of observations and a day to introduce story-telling and working on a baby-sitter's kit containing toys she can take along to help with the job.

Observations about this unit plan. An analysis of such a unit plan provides some interesting observations. This is essentially a subject-matter unit, because it undertakes to cover a series of predetermined points. In other words, it consists of ready-made learning largely determined by the teacher. The goals that are included are teacher-made goals which indicate something to be done *for* the student. The plan is arranged on a day-to-day basis, but does provide considerable flexibility and opportunity for discussion and raising questions. The plan has unity, since it does seek to bring about improved responses on the part of the learners in baby-sitting situations.

Setting up the things to be done on each successive day gives the teacher security founded upon his previous experience in his own school work and in much of the teaching which he has observed. There is even a possibility that additional questions may be studied as they arise, although the extent to which pupils will participate in determining what problems will be studied, how, and when, is not too clear. It is a matter of speculation, then, as to whether or not this was a part of the teacher's planning.

All in all, this teacher-developed plan can be said to incorporate some of the desirable characteristics of unit teaching. It does not deviate so far from familiar ground and familiar kinds of teaching as to bring about feelings of insecurity on the part of either the teacher or the pupils. At the same time it is clearly developed around a desirable learning product that is identified with improved performance in a life situation.

A subject-matter unit stressing inductive thinking. For many years a great deal of effort and controversy centered around whether or not the teaching of the liberal arts subjects improved abilities to do good reflective thinking. The research on transfer indicates that certain subjects—as a matter of fact, almost any subject—could improve problem-solving and reflective thinking, if taught in a manner designed specifically to accomplish that end. Perhaps no subject has enjoyed a greater reputation for teaching reasoning than the subject of geometry. An analysis of the work prescribed in high school geometry texts reveals that only the deductive portion of a total problem-solving procedure is emphasized.

A unit in geometry was planned to provide practice in the inductive phase of reflective thinking. The title of this unit was "What makes a four-sided figure a parallelogram?" In keeping with the organization of Euclidian geometry, this unit was placed at a point appropriate for developing those propositions by which a quadrilateral with certain known characteristics could be demonstrated to be a parallelogram.

Individual differences. A mimeographed guide was provided for the pupils which enabled them to work at different rates of speed. The guide sheet contained references to the textbook for certain materials, but it also raised questions at crucial points in each theorem, the answers to which required some degree of understanding. A supplemental list of exercises of increasing difficulty and complexity was provided for the fast learners who completed the required problems in the unit in time to engage in these more challenging pursuits.

Exploring possible happenings. The introductory sections of this unit plan, which was designed to bring out a clearer notion of inductive thinking, are quoted below.

What Makes a Four-Sided Figure a Parallelogram?

I. What experiments have we already made with lines in a plane?

From time to time we have explored the possibilities of simple chance arrangements of lines in a plane. Upon the basis of these experiments we have built up the facts of geometry little by little. What was the first and simplest thing which we did to begin our study of geometry?

(*This initial experiment was to drop two yardsticks upon the floor and speculate upon what could have happened. Of course, they might cross, or, once in many, many throws, they might have been parallel.*)

A. When did we discover a triangle from our experimentation?

(*When the third line was dropped into the picture.*)

B. After comparing two triangles that could be made to coincide, how did we find out the sets of facts that had to be known about them to make them congruent?

(*By trying various guesses about combinations of sides and angles, three principal methods were determined.*)

C. Later we went back to investigate a special case of two lines in a plane. What was this special case and what kind of lines did we define from it?

(*This special case occurred when the two would not intersect and we defined them as parallel.*)

D. To continue this study of lines that never meet, we again threw into the picture a third line. What was it called?

(*Transversal.*)

E. Thus, we see that the important kinds of things we have worked with so far have been the result of simple experiments. In each case we looked into the things that could be found out with two and three lines arranged in different ways in a plane.

II. What is the next thing you would naturally try?

    A. Of course you suggest immediately that you would try four lines in a plane and see how they can be arranged. This is just what you should do by drawing figures as suggested below, each representing four lines in a plane.
    (Demonstrating this portion of the unit, the teacher would actually drop four yardsticks upon the floor and speculate about possible ways in which the lines might fall if all the possibilities of chance arrangement were explored.)

       1. Represent any four line segments not forming a quadrilateral. *(This is to be shown in at least three ways.)*

       2. Represent any four lines that form a quadrilateral. *(Here extension of lines to indefinite lengths is implied.)*

       3. Represent four lines, two of which are parallel, the other two being non-parallel.

       4. Represent with four figures two pairs of parallel lines intersecting, forming *four* distinct types of quadrilaterals.

    B. If you do not know the names of the figures formed in numbers two, three, and four above, learn them from your textbook and write these names in the proper spaces below.

    C. Thus, we see that again we have evolved some new figures from the simple process of trying out all the possible ways of arranging four lines in a plane. The most important thing we shall learn in this unit is just what sets of facts have to be known about a four-sided figure to identify it as a parallelogram. *(A series of experiments and exercises in writing possible statements of conditions that would produce the parallelogram in all cases precedes the deductive proof. The four principal criteria result from testing the suggested hypotheses by the usual deductive procedures of geometry.)*

Advancing hypotheses. This example is chosen because of the relative simplicity of the materials used. The equipment needed consists only of four yardsticks and enough space to drop them upon the floor or table in random arrangements. The unique purpose here is to teach pupils how to search for all possible chance happenings in a situation and how to phrase their observations of these simple events. With the desired outcome in mind evolving the ways of identifying a parallelogram, various hypotheses were advanced. Some of these hypotheses proved erroneous. Others could be demonstrated to be consistent with the definition of a parallelogram. The scientific method includes systematic observations of events and statements of tentative truths. Thus, inductive procedure is a necessary first part of the total process of reflective thinking. If the teacher's purpose is to improve reflective thinking through the teaching of geometry, or any other subject, similar arrangements in the organization of the learning experiences must be devised.

A unit stressing personal adaptation through subject matter. This particular unit was developed for a twelfth-grade class in government. The subject of the unit is the Constitution. Many units planned on this topic become a rather lifeless analysis of the Constitution as a document. Undoubtedly, the purposes of all competent social science teachers reach far beyond the knowledge of the Constitution as such, and seek to bring about certain understandings of our form of government through the study of the basic document. The Constitution itself, then, becomes a means of bringing about important learnings which, it is confidently hoped, will result in better citizenship performance.

Overview. Perhaps the most revealing feature of the plan as written is found in the overview, in which it is pointed out that the scope of the unit will be determined by the problems that the teacher and class together decide are the most important ones in studying the Constitution. The further suggestion is made that the list of problems will grow as the unit progresses. Then follows a list of probable questions, which represents the teacher's effort to anticipate the turn which the class will take. This indicates the kind of teaching anticipated. It reveals that the teacher has in mind trying to follow through the real concerns felt by the class members.

Objectives. The general goals stated for the unit included bring-

ing about a feeling that the Constitution is important in the pupils'
lives today, and making them aware of some of the problems in
volved in the operation of our form of government and what is
necessary in order to solve them. These general objectives were
supplemented and made more specific in a list of special unit objectives. Included among the latter were: knowledge of the circumstances leading to the Constitutional Convention of 1787; the
organization of the Federal Government; and the functions of its
branches. There were certain understandings listed: that basic
principles of our government include such things as separation of
powers and that the Constitution has been expanded and strengthened
through the use of implied powers, legislation, amendment, and
custom.

Approach. In the approach were certain interest-arousing features.
Among those suggested were use of films about the Constitution, the
gathering of materials and sources of information including suitable
bulletin board displays, and the selection of current events having
a Constitutional background.

Planning and working period. The activities in which the class
engaged were selected to contribute to the kinds of learning products announced. One of these was a program developed using dialogue and costumes. This was to be a dramatization prepared and
enacted by the pupils around some related incident of their own
selection. There were debates, with the pupils using the arguments
of large and small state representatives presented at the Constitutional Convention. There were opportunities for the drawing of
diagrams and cartoons to show the mechanical features of gov-
ernmental structure such as checks and balances and separation of
powers. There was also the opportunity to develop important human
interest material about some of the outstanding characters of the
Convention.

It would be impractical to analyze further the teaching of this
unit unless one had at hand a log or a day-to-day report of the things
that actually happened and the problems which developed. Unfortunately, such a log is not available for this unit. The plan was
actually conceived as a subject-centered plan, but the way in
which the teaching was organized and the various activities and
methods used added greatly to its significance and the breadth of
the educational purposes it served.

Evaluation. Evaluations, in terms of the kinds of goals announced, certainly challenged the ingenuity of the teacher. While a certain amount of learning could be measured by ordinary pencil and paper means, it was obvious that much of the most important learning must be evaluated subjectively. The effect on the citizenship activities of later adult life could not be immediately observed. Therefore, subjective evaluations were made upon the basis of participation and interest in the activities of the class in lieu of more adequate evidence. The plan stated that the class would have its own evaluation sheet on the list of objectives that they chose at the beginning of the unit.

Observations about this unit plan. It might be helpful to consider a few of the points listed previously on the guides to evaluation. The objectives were stated well enough to give direction to the structure of the plan as a whole. While the description of the approach, or interest-arousing activities, was not very extensive, it did seem to offer possibilities. The participation of pupils in planning added to the motivation of the work. The learning activities were certainly pupil-centered. They were related to the objectives and they were varied. One has but to read a little about the great Constitutional Convention and the personalities involved there to see the possibilities for dialogue, costume, debate, and dramatization. Within the group activities listed, there would seem to be a place for almost any level of ability likely to be found in a high school senior class. While the plan does not specifically bring out how the problem of individual differences is to be met, the activities suggested would provide opportunities to care for these matters.

The evaluation section of the unit recognizes the problem of evaluation of learning of this kind; however, it neither lists in detail nor gives examples of evaluation devices and procedures. If test questions are to be used, examples, at least, of each type thought to be appropriate should be included. If observations of various kinds are to be used as a basis for evaluation, the growing teacher should constantly strive to put down guides for making these observations. The estimation of the degree of learning by subjective means is a respectable procedure. Its effectiveness and consistency can be improved, however, if an effort is made to put down guides for the observation of behavior that is thought to have a relationship to the desired learning product. If guides are developed and a little time is spent regularly in making estimates on observed behavior, progress can be made in this difficult teaching task.

SUMMARY

Unit teaching is a concept that incorporates improved methods of organizing teaching and learning experiences. A broad range of methods are actually included in the term. A unit can include any degree of emphasis among the broad types of educational goals. Response patterns involving the combination of different learning products are within the province of unit teaching.

Unit teaching presents a means of functional curriculum construction. Needed shifts in emphasis may be accomplished one unit at a time to bring about modernization. New courses can eventually be formulated in this manner if desired.

Numerous principles of learning and teaching are observed through unit teaching to a greater degree than otherwise. Pacing learning activities to the capability of the learner reduces tension and contributes to desirable feelings of security on his part. Individual differences are further met through adjustment of the complexity of contributions required. Motivation is advanced through the adjustment of units to the problems and concerns of young people at their level of maturity. This is achieved by involving pupils in planning to the degree that the learning goals and materials permit. Unit teaching is concerned with life adaptation of the learner. Therefore, teaching is organized to make the maximum use of principles of transfer.

Unit teaching differs from day-to-day teaching in numerous ways. The assignment involves a larger amount of work and greater variety of experiences. However, the introduction to the unit shows how all the activities contribute to the principal goals of the unit.

The self-sustaining characteristic of unit teaching makes it possible for the teacher to give more adequate attention to direction of individual learning. Individual differences are also cared for through possible variation in rate of progress, quantity of work, and difficulty of work relating to the principal goals of the unit. It is likewise possible to utilize group projects in certain types of units to which individuals of widely different ability levels may make appropriate contributions.

Unit teaching requires the teacher to do unit planning. Guides to the making and evaluation of unit plans are suggested to help the teacher comprehend the qualities of a satisfactory plan. In addition to the guides or criteria a suggested outline of the major parts of a unit plan is offered. These two items are intended to help the teacher comprehend the total involvement of unit planning. Three units are described with reference to certain guides and corresponding headings of the outline and observations relative to the adequacy of the parts are offered as further explanation.

Recognition is given to the teacher's probable subject-matter orientation and accommodation to day-to-day teaching in his own educational background. A unit is described which consisted of a series of daily plans. This type of unit plan is sometimes easier as a first step. It should be regarded as an intermediate point in the development of competence in unit planning.

A unit in formal subject-matter is described illustrating the way in which the inductive aspects of reflective thinking can be strengthened through planning. Another unit described shows the increased use of pupil participation in planning activities contributing to the goals sought.

The chapter has attempted to introduce the concepts of unit teaching and unit planning. The teacher should have as a result a feeling of increased competence in these areas:

1. Relating teaching plans to the improvement of complex patterns of behavior that lead to life adaptation.

2. Incorporating several methods of teaching into an integrated plan to achieve the multiple objectives of a unit.

3. Writing outlines for unit teaching that will facilitate self-sustained work by learners.

4. Envisioning a learning situation in which pupils are engaging in different activities while moving toward a common goal.

PROBLEMS

1. *Using the* Education Index, *turn to the section on "Units of Work." Select a unit which is in your field and grade level of interest. Make sure that this is a teaching unit that can be or has been carried out by a teacher with a class, and not a resource unit. Using the eleven guides for making and evaluating unit plans given in this chapter, write a critique of the unit.*

2. *Using the same unit or a different one attempt to trace the relationship of objectives, learning activities, and evaluation techniques. Be specific, quoting from the unit adequately to make the relationship clear.*

3. *Write an analysis of the objectives and determine as far as possible the extent of balance or imbalance between goals of personal growth and goals of specialization.*

4. *Hold a conference with your supervisor and select a problem or topic that your group of pupils will study within the next several weeks. Prepare title, overview, objectives, and approach for a unit for this class on this subject.*

5. *After conferring with your supervisor on the adequacy of the items in Problem 4, develop descriptions of learning activities in the form of instructions to pupils or plans for discussions with pupils leading to cooperatively planned activities. Can you show how each one relates to some of your objectives?*

6. *Develop a test that can be used to evaluate the extent of learning of the factual information and skills that were set forth as goals in the objectives.*

7. *Develop some guides to be used throughout the progress of the unit to direct your thinking and observation as you evaluate by subjective estimate, learning in those stated goals that cannot be measured by tests.*

BIBLIOGRAPHY

Association for Childhood Education, International, *Children Can Work Independently*, General Service Bulletin No. 90. Washington, D.C.: The Association, 1952.

Alberty, Harold, *Reorganizing the High School Curriculum*, rev. ed. New York: The Macmillan Company, 1953. Chap. xiii.

Association for Supervision and Curriculum Development, National Education Association, *Action for Curriculum Improvement* (1951 Yearbook). Washington, D.C.: The Association, 1951.

———, *Education for American Freedom* (1955 Yearbook). Washington, D.C.: The Association, 1955.

Burton, William H., *The Guidance of Learning Activities*, 2nd ed. New York: Appleton-Century-Crofts, Inc., 1952. Chaps. xii-xiv.

———, "Implications for Organization of Instruction and Instructional Adjuncts," in *Learning and Instruction*, Part I. Forty-ninth Yearbook of the National Society for the Study of Education. Chicago: The University of Chicago Press, 1950. Chap. ix.

Clarke, C. M., "Unit Theory in Teaching Practice," *High School Journal* 33:104-10, May 1950.

Garrison, Noble L., "Changing Concepts in Methods of Teaching," *Elementary School Journal* 52:197-206, December 1951.

Hanna, Lavone A., Gladys L. Potter, and Neva Hagaman, *Unit Teaching in the Elementary School*. New York: Rinehart and Company, Inc., 1955. Pp. 101-53, 533-60.

Hockett, J. A., "Planning the Unit of Work," in Paul R. Grim and John U. Michaelis, *The Student Teacher in the Elementary School*. Englewood Cliffs, N.J.: Prentice-Hall, Inc., 1953. Pp. 112-49.

Jenkins, David H., "Interdependence in the Classroom," *Journal of Educational Research* 45:137-44, October 1951.

Jones, Arthur J., E. D. Grizzell, and Wren J. Grinstead, *Principles of Unit Construction*. New York: McGraw-Hill Book Company, Inc., 1939.

Melvin, Gordon A., *General Methods of Teaching*. New York: McGraw-Hill Book Company, Inc., 1952. Chap. iii.

Morrison, Henry C., *The Practices of Teaching in the Secondary Schools*, rev. ed. Chicago: The University of Chicago Press, 1931. Chap. ii.

Rivlin, Harry N., *Teaching Adolescents in Secondary Schools*. New York: Appleton-Century-Crofts, Inc., 1948. Chap. v.

Simpson, Ray H., *Improving Teaching-Learning Processes*. Longmans, Green & Company, 1953. Chap. xiii.

Smith, B. O., W. O. Stanley, and J. H. Shores, *Fundamentals of Curriculum Improvement*. Yonkers, N.Y.: World Book Company, 1950. Chap. xxiii.

Spellman, C. L., "How to Prepare a Unit," *Grade Teacher* 71:62, September 1953.

Strickland, Ruth G., *How to Build a Unit of Work*, U.S. Office of Education, Federal Security Agency, Bulletin, 1946, No. 5. Washington, D.C.: Superintendent of Documents, U.S. Government Printing Office, 1946.

Walters, T. L., "The Unit Plan of Instruction," *Bulletin of the National Association of Secondary School Principals* 39:85-90, May 1950.

10

Pre-planning
in teaching

Because of his own dissatisfaction with his students' transference of learning to practical situations, the bookkeeping teacher mentioned earlier devised a way to improve transfer. He wanted to have his pupils see the bookkeeping cycle in real accounts in the community.

The urgency of the teacher's action stemmed from observations of pupils who had graduated the year before, his first year in the community. His former students had been dissatisfied with the bookkeeping course; most of them made up their minds during the course that they did not want to do that kind of work. The few who did enter office work seemed to comprehend what the businesses were doing, but could see little relationship between high school bookkeeping systems and those used in offices. The teacher realized that there were relationships, and deplored the fact that some students even had to attend business college to gain employment.

The real problem confronting this teacher was how to get businessmen in the community to cooperate with him in such a way that students could see bookkeeping systems actually in operation, while studying the high school course. The teacher personally called on a large number of businessmen to talk over his project and orient them to his purposes.

His proposition was received with enthusiasm when it was clear what he was trying to accomplish. Without this preliminary contact it might have seemed to some men, not understanding the reasons for their visit, that pupils were being sent out to find out something confidential, and they might not have been welcome. As it turned out, when the pupils did make their visits, there were very wholesome reactions. An entirely different attitude on the part of the class became apparent and, needless to say, the lives of teacher, students, and businessmen were greatly enriched by this interaction.

The community. In recent years travel has been planned by parents, pupils, and school officials to provide added experiences for young people in the growing-up process. Many details as to the types of experiences to be included in each tour need to be referred to parents and pupils for discussion, evaluation, and final determination. Whereas one group of pupils and parents might desire to emphasize theater, music, and other forms of entertainment, another group might feel that visits to literary shrines, historical landmarks, and seats of government are the more desirable kind of experiences. It is this problem that thoughtful teachers and administrators pose for the parents and pupils of high school classes for evaluation and decision. Such activities fall properly in the realm of pre-planning. Similar pre-planning with parents and community would be desirable regarding field trips, vocational advisement, or social activities that might conceivably come within the total curriculum experience offering of the school.

Similar reference by way of pre-planning should be made to the community when deviations from the usual pattern of attempting to develop leadership or citizenship responsibility are anticipated. Surprising and even violent reactions of communities have occurred when seemingly advantageous plans have been inaugurated by professional teachers. Giving necessary information and the accompanying opportunities for parental and community discussion and development are pre-planning activities that must not be overlooked.

Throughout this book there has been recurring emphasis upon the principle that the community determines what education shall be provided the young. For those established learnings contained in the curriculum this sanction by the community will be assumed. It is natural to expect, however, that if a new series of outcomes is sought, or new means of reaching old goals are developed, a fundamental, preliminary recognition of need by the community is necessary.

Previous work of the group. In order to teach a unit or lesson effectively it is necessary to know what previous experiences pupils have had. Many schools will have files of work units that have been carried on in different grade levels preceding the present situation. Therefore, as close a determination as possible of the previous experiences of a group is necessary as part of this activity. Further than this, some knowledge of the interests of the group and the individuals that compose it provides clues to the motivations that will be required. A survey of the abilities to be found in the class will often help in the determination of plans to take care of individual differences. All of these matters that can be included in pre-planning activity for any teaching-learning experience will add greatly to the accuracy of selecting the problems to be undertaken and the kind of work that can be expected.

Resources are surveyed. An important step in preparation is to survey resources in the way of supplies, teaching materials, general surroundings, and availability of help. It is obvious that the teacher who is new in a school situation will encounter great difficulties if he finds an unexpected lack of supplies and materials. It is wise, therefore, to investigate the extent to which the library, for example, can be used. Sometimes very desirable teaching and learning activities involve construction of objects which add greatly to the meaningfulness of teaching. Some of these objects can be constructed by pupils and teachers with simple tools. If more than the most ordinary skills of construction are involved, however, it is wise to see what resources are available in the school shop and how much help the shop and art teachers can provide.

The very fact that a library may not be complete or that a school shop may not be available does not necessarily mean that an activity must be abandoned. A careful check among the pupils themselves will reveal a surprising amount of material and tools and even parental help that can be brought to bear on such a situation. It may be possible to set up direct experiences such as visits to dairies, farms, stores, banks, radio stations, and industries in the community.

This review of resources, while it adds to the inconvenience of teaching, sometimes pays extra dividends. Such surveys of possibilities are a proper and continuing part of pre-planning activity.

The teacher does not overlook the fact that certain expendable supplies can be purchased through the school office if the need is anticipated far enough ahead for procurement to be possible. This is particularly true of art supplies and all kinds of craft materials, as well as scientific supplies used in laboratory classes of all kinds.

As a part of pre-planning a teacher will avail himself of opportunities to check research related to the teaching he expects to do. Access to reviews of educational research greatly facilitates such an activity. It is recognized that this resource will not be readily available in many localities, but it is a fact that many valuable findings in all areas of teaching have not been exploited.

Finally, and closely related to the above suggestion, the teacher will usually want to refresh his own knowledge on many subjects, to the extent that needs for information can be anticipated. Sources of such information to which the teacher and pupils alike can turn will frequently be reviewed.

In summary, then, it has been suggested that pre-planning of a general nature will include community acceptance, sequence of topics, selection of content, characteristics of pupils to be taught, a survey of resources, availability of materials, necessary help, procurement of supplies, research in teaching, and sources of information for the teacher. All of these considerations are proper preliminaries to the actual introduction of new learning experiences in a classroom.

Daily lesson pre-planning activities. The importance of determining the present status of learners has been emphasized earlier. The determination of the margin between what is known and what is to be learned is a difficult but necessary part of the pre-planning. The very determination of the manner in which one will proceed in attempting to find the status of a group of learners is in itself an act of pre-planning. Such an activity may characterize either daily lesson planning or unit planning.

As the teacher looks ahead to a day of work to be accomplished, he will try to devise ways of teaching particular points. For one teaching problem he may choose a film; for another he may draw diagrams upon the blackboard and explain their development. For still another, he may devise an experiment for the pupils to carry out. Not only do particular points to be taught require preliminary consideration; the procedures that will be most effective with particular pupils will also be a problem. For example, in teaching an arithmetical process a large segment of the class may respond in the way that the teacher anticipates; a minority for some reason or other may be unable to learn through the experiences provided. It becomes necessary to cast about for different approaches that, it is hoped, will get the job done.

One problem that confronts teachers of arts subjects in which pupils are working upon several different individual projects is to anticipate probable errors. The question then becomes one of whether to point out the error and thereby cause the pupil to avoid

The supervisor seeks opportunities to improve the lesson plans of the teacher through analysis and discussion.

Courtesy of *The Indiana Teacher*

it, or to let the pupil go ahead and encounter his own mistake in the hope that by so doing he will gain insight into the total procedure. There is no pat answer to this question. Economy in cases of expensive materials and the personality of the pupil will govern the teacher's decision. Such considerations very properly belong in pre-planning for each day of teaching.

Another general area of anticipatory planning on the part of the teacher is related to evaluation. Evaluation is an essential part of the total teaching-learning process. To be most effective it must be a part of the pupil's experience as well as a teacher activity. Many times in creative work the final product is not necessarily the most important thing to be evaluated. The predominant concern in planning for evaluation is always what the pupil has learned. Furthermore, it is essential to bring about an awareness on the part of the pupil that he has learned something. A significant question that must be considered is the manner in which evaluation will be approached, so that the emphasis will be upon the pupil's total learning rather than the visible product alone. It is true, of course, that in such areas as reading, arithmetic, spelling, or skills in chemistry, the product is the major consideration. However, in other areas such as art, industrial arts, or creative work in home economics, one does not expect professional skill to result. It is, rather, the growth that has taken place in skill and the efficiency with which the learner has developed his procedure that is important. It is desirable, therefore, to plan evaluation activities with the learner when possible. It is important that he help set up the procedure so that he may understand why it is used, and as a result will be aware of what he really has learned. The extent to which evaluation procedures will be designed by the teacher and the extent to which they will be cooperatively designed is clearly a matter for preliminary consideration by the teacher. If the pupil is to be involved, it is necessary that the teacher decide how this involvement will be brought about.

Other decisions related to evaluation have to do with the timing of such activities. It is also necessary to decide how much time will be devoted to evaluation procedures. If the evaluation nets a measure of accomplishment, it is also necessary to decide how this measure will be used to advance learning.

These are some of the more immediate problems of the daily lesson that require advance consideration. The teacher will recognize that not all of the preliminary activities listed above will be carried out entirely for every learning procedure that is planned. Much of what has been described is cumulative; a great deal of what has been learned in one situation will be applicable in later situations. An effort has been made, however, to point out that there are many possible aspects of the total pre-planning problem.

Teacher-planned units. One type of unit, sometimes called the subject-matter unit, consists largely of a pre-planned series of learning experiences directed at specialized goals. An example of such a unit was one prepared by an experienced teacher in a laboratory school. The topic under consideration was actually indirect measurement. It was designed for an eighth-grade class.

In his pre-planning activity, the teacher first developed a work sheet. The sections in the work sheet were headed: *Suggested Titles, Aims, and Subject Matter.* Under the heading of Subject Matter were listed specific understandings which it was hoped would result: mathematical relationships involved in carrying out the study of indirect measurement, attitudes, skills, and facts. The fourth section had to do with the problems. These were problems of mathematical understanding required for the unit on indirect measurement. Stated in question form the problems were: When are triangles similar? What relationships exist between similar triangles? What applications can we make of the principles of similar triangles? Creative work and free reading were listed as optional work. Actually, the problem section outlined the learning activities which were set up for the pupils. A further feature of the work sheet, accomplished after the pupils' instructions were designed, was that it related the learning exercises to the stated goals for the unit.

The next job, then, was to set up a guide for pupil use showing the things that the pupils would be expected to do, by means of which the teacher hoped his goals would be accomplished. A very definite effort was made to make this unit interesting. The very unusual title "How Do We Know It Is Two Hundred and Fifty Thousand Miles to the Moon?" was adopted from three or four possibilities listed on the work sheet. There was an introductory statement raising the question, "Can we measure the width of a stream without crossing it?" Such questions seldom fail to arouse the interest of junior high school boys and girls, and it was pointed out that it would be expected that such questions could be answered as a result of the activities in which they were about to engage.

The guide sheet for pupils outlined step-by-step observations and experiments with similar triangles from which intuitive conclusions were drawn. There was little effort to bring in any demonstrative proof; rather, the principles were derived from observations and drawings and experiments. The things that pupils were expected to do were outlined in the order in which the instructor expected them to proceed. Having intuitively derived the principles involved, numerous applications were carried out by the pupils individually. References, naturally, were made to the textbook, and in some cases to other books. A list of supplementary problems of somewhat greater complexity and difficulty was provided at the end of the outline, and finally some suggestions for optional work were included. The optional section involved readings and the construction of such things as a field protractor.

The teacher's plan, as it was actually carried out, provided each pupil with the outline. After being carefully introduced to the idea and the kinds of things they were to do, the pupils proceeded through the outline. It was immediately apparent that the brighter children would work through the prescribed activities at a rapid rate. As a matter of fact, they were encouraged in so doing by being told that the supplementary section contained problems that would be challenging to all who could do the basic work in time to undertake them. The supplementary section was of sufficient length and difficulty to absorb the productivity of the best pupils by the time the majority of the slower ones completed the basic activities. Thus, a profitable experience for strong pupils was integrated into the plan.

Such a unit plan, which is obviously designed to contribute heavily to specialized learning, has many advantages in a subject like mathematics. In the area of specialized learnings, pre-planning by the teacher is appropriate. It is obvious to the thoughtful teacher that there will be questions nearly every day that need to be clarified by the class as a whole. Once the unit was under way, the study period lasting possibly two or three weeks consisted largely of discussion of questions raised by pupils about their daily work, followed by study in the classroom under the teacher's direction. Short diagnostic tests revealed very quickly the extent to which quality of work and the pupil understanding were being maintained.

In the plan for this particular unit the evaluation devices did not appear. However, a unit test was a part of the pre-planning. As has been suggested earlier, consideration of the types of evaluation devices that will be used is a necessary part of pre-planning.

A great many of the general pre-planning activities listed earlier in the chapter were demonstrated by this teacher. It should be apparent, also, that not only were the materials and the exercises selected a part of pre-planning, but thought entered into this work on the manner in which the unit would be introduced and how the class periods would be managed for its duration.

The description and discussion of the above unit has shown pre-planning functions carried to great detail in determining just what the pupils would do in the classroom. It should be understood that the extent to which this is true in planning a particular unit is dependent upon the goals sought. It will be recalled that this unit was in mathematics, which in this situation was being taught for specialized purposes. The work was planned for individual pupil progress. There were no group or committee activities of the type that would be expected in a social studies unit, for example, where it would be the teacher's purpose to develop leadership training opportunities through cooperative projects a portion of the time.

Teacher-pupil planned units. All of the pre-planning activities mentioned above, except those having to do with final pupil guide sheets, are appropriate for teacher-pupil planning. However, one additional aspect should be noted: teachers give careful consideration to how they will go about the teacher-pupil planning process itself. If the teacher has had little experience, he cannot afford to enter into teacher-pupil planning without giving careful consideration to all possible angles that may develop. It requires a considerable amount of skill on the part of the teacher to bring about a democratic situation in which pupils will express their ideas and discuss them until some kind of consensus is reached.

In addition to having made a careful survey of the pre-planning activities outlined in this chapter, the teacher will need to decide how much responsibility his group is ready to take. He will be well advised to review the principles of group leadership and to recall all experiences that he has had in group planning. A group of pupils should be given opportunities to carry as much responsibility as their development and maturity will permit. However, the teacher is responsible for the ultimate outcome, and in pre-planning for teacher-pupil development of a unit he must be ready to pick up the process if the pupil group is unable to carry on.

Resource units. The pre-planning activities of the unit on indirect measurement described above were carried out by the teacher using his own knowledge of mathematical principles to a large extent. He had, of course, numerous textbooks and reference materials at hand that were suggestive of some of the things which he incorporated into the unit. Although activities went beyond the textbook the class was using, the textbook had its place in the total picture. The arrangement and selection of activities were designed to meet the needs and abilities of the group being taught as judged by the teacher in charge. The unit worked very well with that group of children. It is likely that if it had been tried the next year on a different group of children, modifications would have been necessary to make it work as well.

In the event that the teacher planned a unit in indirect measurement the following year, he would have found this unit plan a good resource to which to turn. It would then be used as a record of the activities that produced desirable results with a previous class. He would decide which ones would be likely to produce good results with the new class. The utilization of previous ideas and experiences in teaching is one desirable way for any teacher to improve his work. This suggests, therefore, the desirability of each teacher retaining files from year to year of what seem to be good teaching-learning activities.

As an outgrowth of this very simple, yet often overlooked, principle of developing resources, the practice has developed of forming planning aids known as resource units. For example, since work in indirect measurement is commonly incorporated in arithmetic classes, it is conceivable that a resource unit might be compiled around this topic. The teacher whose unit has been described might have carried on his study toward the development of such a resource in one of two general ways. He might have searched mathematical teaching magazines for articles written by other teachers about how they had developed learning experiences in indirect measurement, or if there were a curriculum committee working in the field of arithmetic, all of the teachers would have pooled their own experiences and information they had found in journals, courses of study, and other sources. This pooling of ideas about how one might proceed could produce a written compendium of suggestions that have worked well for different teachers in different situations. This collection, when refined and organized so as to be made most convenient for reference, becomes a resource unit on indirect measurement. If an individual were to develop a resource unit alone, it is obvious that it would require more time, and demand that the collector of the ideas have an open mind for suggestions. The advantage of the committee approach is that each person can share with the others such information on the circumstances in which his suggestions were carried out as to make what otherwise might seem an unworkable idea acceptable.

It is easy to see how a teacher would be greatly aided by having such ideas available. There are, at present, literally hundreds of such resource units available, collected from all parts of the country in libraries, curriculum laboratories, and teaching materials centers. The teacher who lives near a teachers college would be wise to check periodically to see what resources have been collected pertinent to his own program.

As a further illustration, some resource units designed by teachers working in cooperative committee situations will be described. Some of these resource units will be specialized, and some will be directed toward personal growth. It should be kept in mind in all pre-planning that the maturity and previous experience of the children will govern the activities selected and the manner in which they will be carried out. Children who have been trained to work on their own will be found more nearly ready to enter into self-sustained activities with the assistance of a guide sheet such as was described for the unit on indirect measurement. Younger children working in arithmetic could not be expected to carry on for the same length of time as eighth-grade children. It should be remembered also that the majority of units developed for the elementary school will be of a more integrated kind, having the characteristics of units for personal growth to a greater extent than the subject-matter units sometimes found in specialized subjects at a high school level. With these thoughts in mind, attention will now be turned to some examples of resource units through which essentials of organization and construction will be brought out.

A resource unit in safety for elementary grades. This first
example of a resource unit is one developed by a committee of seven
elementary teachers for grades three and four. The subject of the
unit was "Safety for the Primary Child in His Daily Life." The first
sections of the resource unit list objectives for teachers and pupils.
The second section lists some typical pupil questions, which follow:

1. What should you do when a light changes and you are in
the middle of a street?
2. What would you do if you were in the middle of the street
and a fire truck or ambulance were coming?
3. What does the yellow light mean?
4. What is the first thing you would do if your car caught
on fire in your own backyard?
5. What should you do if your clothes caught on fire?
6. What would you do if your boat upset?
7. What should you do with rubbish in a vacant lot?

Such questions are best determined with a particular class in
mind. However, for the teacher who is developing a technique of
planning, it is good to have samples of the questions that pupils will
ask included in the resource unit.

Focal points for the unit were listed as homes, streets, schools,
and playgrounds. That is, the intent of the unit is to develop attitudes and behavior related to safety in these points. This tends to
define the scope of the unit.

A third section had to do with the important matter of getting
started. This group of teachers suggested beginning with a bulletin
board, objects and displays of such things as first aid kits and fire
extinguishers, discussions having to do with potential danger spots,
careless behavior observed by pupils, and possibly a recent accident.

A list of topics and questions that might be used as centers around
which to organize activities and studies of safety was next offered.
These included bicycle safety, safe use of swings, safety around animals, the safest route to and from school, danger points, and how
children can help to make home a safer place in which to live. There
were others given, but these are typical of what one might call
groups of safety problems.

The introductory sections are followed by lists of possible activities. The use of films was suggested as one means of teaching proper safety practices. One film had to do with the safe use of tools designed for the primary level. Another was entitled "Home Safe Home" for upper primary and intermediate grade levels. An excellent feature of this resource unit was the fact that numerous possible activities connected with the use of the films were listed. These activities included vocabulary development and using the words found in the narration accompanying the film as points of study. Possibilities of further study of the film after one showing, prior to a second, were pointed out. Numerous reports on what the film showed with the later development of rules were also suggested.

In addition to the films, safety records were suggested, as well as activities designed as outgrowths of playing these recordings.

This group of teachers outlined field trips in considerable detail to remind the teacher using this resource unit in his specific job of planning not to overlook certain things. Field trips included a fire station, a police station, and other points of interest related to safety. Demonstrations were also recommended, with appropriate procedures, of fire alarms, fire drills, first aid kits, and fire fighting methods. A radio program on safety was formed and suggestions for developing such a program were included. Dramatization and pantomime were listed also in the activities recommended.

A bibliography listed a considerable number of books for children and some for the teacher—including appropriate plays, sources of free materials, magazines and pamphlets dealing with safety and records and films.

It is quite easy to see that an elementary teacher desirous of developing a teaching unit for his own class could find much help here in the field of safety. The unit was arranged conveniently for the teacher as a reference with various types of information listed in different sections of the outline.

This particular resource unit would have been strengthened greatly if the committee had followed through with suggested guides for evaluation to be used in determining the extent to which desired learning had actually occurred.

A resource unit on travel for high school. Another resource unit was prepared by a group of five teachers who were concerned with high school pupils. This resource unit was entitled "A Trip to the United Nations." Obviously, it is a type of thing that would be utilized by many high school classes planning travel tours to New York City. A wide variety of topics considered by this group would be helpful not only in understanding a pre-planning procedure, but also for many details in planning any important tour.

The group first listed a set of objectives appropriate to such a tour. There were those objectives having to do with an understanding of the participating nations and the relationship of the United Nations to the promotion of peace. There were also objectives having to do with reading of current events, the use of radio, and the library. There was also an objective of developing thrift, budgeting, and wise spending; likewise, personal responsibility when not under direct parental supervision. A brief overview listed the areas of information and personal growth that were to be enhanced by this experience.

The group next listed a number of interest-arousing devices or approaches. Among these were a film showing the workings of the United Nations and some of the social activities surrounding this organization. Displays of pictures were suggested for exhibit in the library and on bulletin boards. Arrangements for listening to the daily broadcasts of the United Nations were also recommended as preliminary to the more specific work on the unit.

Early consideration to evaluation was given in this unit. The scope of activities listed indicates both the wide variety of the learnings possible and the difficulty of the evaluation problem. It was expected that there would be written essays and oral reports, possibly poetry from some pupils, a special high school assembly with flags from the United Nations forming part of the decorations, reports on music of various nations, map construction, recordings, and reports on radio programs. The questions of evidence of increased tolerance as a result of the trip, more interest in current events, shifts in choice of radio programs, and increased awareness of world problems were raised. Unfortunately, the manner in which these evaluations are to be carried out is left to the resources of the reader in this unit. A resource unit should provide guides to be used in making subjective estimates of learning of personal growth nature.

The description of the working period for this unit was very enlightening. Major headings, under which there were many subheadings and subproblems, included planning the cost per pupil, group projects for earning the needed money, individual pupil methods of earning contributions, and other problems involved in acquiring finances. The next general item was transportation, which involved investigation of railway and bus transportation and costs and conveniences available under each one. Realizing the importance of personal appearance and personal relationships on an extensive trip, the committee included studies of meeting and choosing friends and personal grooming. Following this there were suggestions on keeping well, and a committee was recommended to study recreation en route. The itinerary was checked for important landmarks, and information was gathered so that as the group passed various landmarks an interesting and informative discussion could be provided.

The final consideration for planning had to do with the United Nations itself. Many questions could be discussed relative to the original planning and building of the new headquarters. Then, of course, communication with the United Nations about tours and opportunities for maximum learning while there rounded out the unit.

A rather extensive bibliography was prepared incorporating personal manners and behavior, places to eat in New York, how to make money at home, and other general suggested references.

This unit on a trip to the United Nations would be a valuable source of suggestions to the teacher planning any kind of a trip. It would be particularly useful to a group of teachers planning a class tour. It was obvious that the teachers who prepared this resource unit had considerable experience with this kind of thing and had pooled some of their best ideas in this outline.

SUMMARY

The teacher does pre-planning in some degree for every type of teaching in which he engages. The preliminary investigation of community acceptance for a new type of learning experience is the first phase of curriculum reconstruction.

The resources of any particular school in the way of materials and equipment will often require modification in teaching plans. The public library may be able to supplement the school's resources in some instances. The joint efforts of pupils, parents, and teacher often turn up an amazing array of materials and specialized help. Sufficiently advanced planning may make possible purchase of needed supplies from school funds. Sources of reference information for the teacher are investigated in pre-planning activities.

Evaluation has been emphasized as an essential part of the goal-objective-evaluation cycle of learning and teaching processes. Evaluation is as much a consideration for pre-planning as any other factor in learning.

The resource unit is a convenience that has grown out of the cumulative and cooperative efforts of teachers to make their most successful practices a matter of record. It is valuable to the teacher planning a unit whether he chooses to follow the subject-matter pattern or whether he is getting ready for a teacher-pupil planning session in which details of the unit will be worked out.

From the consideration of the various aspects of pre-planning outlined in this chapter the teacher should feel growing competence in these regards:

1. Ability to use a wider variety of teaching materials and learning activities in the classroom.

2. Increased confidence in ability to do effective planning inspired by the knowledge that many resources exist for his help.

3. Ability to organize and accumulate his own work into useful resource files for later reference.

4. Ability to use courses of study more effectively as resource materials.

5. Ability to construct better lesson plans and unit plans with the greatest economy of time.

6. Ability to make constructive preparation for co-operative planning of activities with pupils.

7. Understanding of the difference between teacher planning that helps pupil participation and teacher planning that thwarts it.

8. Ability to find an increasing number of materials through a wider acquaintance with sources listed in the references in the bibliography.

PROBLEMS

1. *Select from a course of study or other resource material a related group of learning activities which you think is more suited to the*

level of a class with which you might be working. Write why you think so.

2. *Make a list of places where you can find new materials in your field of interest.*
3. *Select, with the aid of your supervisor, a unit that will probably come up with a group of pupils. Carry on a program of pre-planning that would prepare you for a planning session with pupils.*
4. *Make a survey of a school with which you are familiar and find out what materials and equipment are available to help with a unit you have planned to teach.*
5. *Procure a cardboard box from a grocery store and design a file suitable for collecting teaching materials in your field. Show your collection to your supervisor at the end of the term.*
6. *Develop a plan to use persons in the community, in addition to printed materials, as resources for the unit you selected in problem 3.*
7. *Prepare an outline of the planning procedure you would carry out with a group of pupils preparatory to making a field trip in the community as a learning activity to be incorporated in your unit.*

BIBLIOGRAPHY

Alberty, Harold, *Reorganizing the High School Curriculum.* New York: The Macmillan Company, 1953. Chaps. xiv and xv.

Anderson, Vernon E., *Principles and Procedures of Curriculum Improvement.* New York: The Ronald Press Co., 1956. Chap. ix.

Association for Supervision and Curriculum Development, *Creating a Good Environment for Learning,* 1954 Yearbook. Washington, D.C.: National Education Association, 1954.

Burton, William H., *The Guidance of Learning Activities.* New York: Appleton-Century-Crofts, Inc., 1952. Chap. xvi.

Cook, Lloyd Allen, and Elaine Forsyth Cook, *A Sociological Approach to Education,* 2nd ed. New York: McGraw-Hill Book Co., Inc., 1950. Chaps. xvi and xvii.

Dale, Edgar, *Audio-Visual Methods in Teaching,* rev. ed. New York: The Dryden Press, Inc., 1954. Chap. xii.

Draper, E. M., and A. Gardner, "How to Construct a Resource Unit," *Clearing House* 26:267-70, January 1952.

Faunce, Roland C., and Nelson L. Bossing, *Developing the Core Curriculum*. Englewood Cliffs, N.J.: Prentice-Hall, Inc., 1951. Chaps. vii and viii.

Grambs, Jean D., and William J. Iverson, *Modern Methods in Secondary Education*. New York: The Dryden Press, Inc., 1952. Chaps. iv, v, and vi.

Hanna, Lavone A., Gladys L. Potter, and Neva Hagaman, *Unit Teaching in the Elementary School*. New York: Rinehart and Company, Inc., 1955. Part III, pp. 391-566.

Illinois Secondary School Curriculum Program, *Guides to Curriculum Building*, Bulletin No. 8. Springfield, Ill.: The Department of Public Instruction, 1950.

Johnson, Earl, "Field Study: An Experience in Getting Meaning," *Educational Leadership*, 10: 229-33, January 1953.

Klohr, P. R., "Resource Unit in Curriculum Reorganization," *National Association of Secondary School Principals Bulletin* 34:74-77, May 1950.

Meil, Alice, and associates, *Cooperative Procedures in Learning*. New York: Teachers College, Columbia University, 1952. Chap. xi.

Saylor, J. Galen, and William M. Alexander, *Curriculum Planning for Better Teaching and Learning*. New York: Rinehart and Co., Inc., 1954. Chap. 12.

Simpson, Ray H., *Improving Teaching-Learning Processes*. New York: Longmans, Green & Company, 1953. Chap. x.

Toops, Myrtle Dewey, *Problems of Growing Up, a Resource Unit*. Muncie, Indiana: Child Development Service, Ball State Teachers College, 1948.

Wiles, Kimball, *Teaching for Better Schools*. Englewood Cliffs, N.J.: Prentice-Hall, Inc., 1952. Chap. xiii.

Part Four

Development
through
assuming
responsibility

Introduction

As children develop they learn to be responsible for their
actions and increasingly self-directive. It is a part of the
function of the school to aid and nurture this aspect of development. To do so most effectively, teachers and schools
provide opportunities for children to share in planning various aspects of school activity and to participate in a responsible fashion in carrying out the plans. It is through such
participation, at a level commensurate with the developmental status of the child, that he learns to handle himself
in an increasingly mature manner. It should be understood
that the school contributes to the total process in a supplementary relationship to the many other community influences that impinge upon the growing child.

A satisfying school experience has much to do with the
behavior of children. Many pupils are agreeable to work
with, and learn satisfactorily in a situation of shared responsibility; the same children would be difficult in a situation
lacking this characteristic. To bring school into harmony
with the needs and interests of children is a means of solving many of the problems of discipline that might arise in
an authoritarian situation.

In order that classroom experiences may provide the pupil

255

with satisfactions arising from sharing in setting goals and selecting ways of reaching them, teacher-pupil planning is used in many classes. Some of the evolution of this practice has come about through teachers' observations of the favorable climate for learning found in informal extra-class activities.

Extra-class activities have served as a leaven in the whole loaf of school experiences of children for many years. Even the old-fashioned country school used the hike to gather nuts on a Friday afternoon, the spelling bee, and games and contests to maintain pupil interest and provide a thread of pleasure and satisfying activity that held the school together.

Properly conceived, extra-class activities provide for the expression of many interests that are adjuncts to school life and the purposes of the school but are not easily incorporated into the formal program. The extra-class program has been a testing laboratory for practices that increase pupil participation in the planning of regular class work. Pupil leadership and freedom of choice first found expression in the extra-class programs. The practice of democratic processes likewise found a place in these activities. With the exercise of freedom, pupils also found it necessary to assume responsibility. The social aspects of the extra-class activities were observed as fertile soil for the development of desirable qualities of personality. Class work designed for the purposes of personal growth now incorporates many features of the extra-class program.

While seeking the worthy goals implied above, the teacher does not leave his post of leadership. Children can be given freedom only so far as they are able to use it. They learn the values of freedom by experiencing it. Some children and some groups of children require almost constant external control. Therefore, the teacher must possess sufficient knowledge and skill in control measures to step in when the situation requires him to do so.

11

Sharing plans
with learners

The high degree of motivation observed in activities planned by pupils in extra-class activities is often the envy of the teacher of classroom subjects. The degree of responsibility exhibited in carrying out such programs is a revelation in contrast to the indifference sometimes exhibited in carrying out teacher-assigned tasks. The control that groups exercise upon members who do not contribute to the common goals seems to bring about quick modification of individual performance. Personal experience in experimental behavior brings about self-control efficiently and quickly under the searchlight of group evaluation, acceptance, or rejection.

Teachers have ventured to bring into their classroom teaching some of the characteristics of the out-of-class situations which seemed to contribute to the results obtained. They have found that some of the work that they want to do in school can be done better by giving pupils a share in setting goals, setting up ways to achieve them, and evaluating progress toward reaching them. Pupils will exhibit much the same degree of motivation for class work as for extra-class work when the situation is right. If pupils can express their own concerns by setting up problems for study, they attack the problems with vigor. When school time is spent in attempts to solve problems that are real to pupils by methods that make sense to them, work takes on a new complexion. Pupils carry out responsible assignments because these assignments are about problems they understand.

Teacher-pupil planning is a procedure that sets the stage for improved motivation, problem-solving activity, desirable interpersonal relationships, and opportunities for growth in self-control and ability to assume responsibility. The manner in which the teacher approaches the work with the group establishes the climate for utilization of cooperative group processes, use of a wide range of materials for learning, and identification of the things learned in out-of-school living.

The process of teacher-pupil planning is an important phase of teaching when the goals of personal growth are predominant. Unit teaching featuring teacher-pupil planning as its initial stage is increasing in acceptance as a means of accomplishing many outcomes desired in this aspect of education. Units that provide for such teaching are planned by pupils with teacher leadership and assistance. Such units cannot be planned in detail in advance of meeting pupils. The teacher finds much help in pre-planning activities described in the previous chapter. However, he must be careful that his "idea-gathering" does not close his mind to pupil suggestions.

In the sections which follow examples of units developed with pupils are described and discussed. The teacher should direct his attention to the kinds of activities that followed the planning of the units. Use of committees to make cooperative studies, sharing work among various individuals and groups, research and resources used, and evaluation problems in this kind of teaching are important considerations. The need for a growing understanding of group processes on the teacher's part soon becomes apparent.

How teacher-pupil planning originates. Children will reveal their interests and concerns in many ways. Such interests and concerns often provide leads for teacher-pupil planned units. A teacher constantly makes note of suggestions and questions that might provide opportunities for beginning a new teacher-pupil planning process. Sometimes textbooks provide the cue, as was the case with a first grade class that developed a unit about animals. It was only natural for this group of children, while reading about animals in their books, to suggest things about their own pets or farm animals or animals they had seen in various places. A second grade class became garden-conscious when bugs began to appear and the birds started coming back in the spring. Some of their parents had started gardening activities and the children were anxious to learn something about seeds and plants as well as flowers. The teacher reporting this center of interest stated that he had no need to worry about motivation because children were constantly coming in to report plants that were sprouting and growing. As an outgrowth of this interest and due to the fact that one day a child brought in a small paper cup in which he had planted seeds, the group planned a room project in which every child planted a cup of seeds if he wished. It was obvious that this study was off to a good start because it originated in their own wishes.

A third grade unit was developed around the home because this was one of the major interests of the children and most of them wanted to study more about the home and get more information on it. The unit involved the family as a group, the materials that houses are built of, furnishings, trees, lawns, and flowers. The study expanded into food and materials from which clothing is made. Silk, linen, cotton, wool, and rubber were involved. Care of clothing led to development of personal cleanliness. Relationships with other people and community social activities were finally drawn into the picture as a result of this start.

A good illustration of what can happen unexpectedly is found in a published report of a fifth grade science unit.[1] The teacher reported that a group of excited children followed a boy carrying a glass jar containing a mass of crawling bees into the classroom. The teacher capitalized upon this lead and developed with the children a very profitable science unit, using bees as the center of interest.

A graduate teacher on a master teacher's program reports the manner in which a weather unit was developed in cooperation with the supervising teacher in a campus laboratory school. In this case the interest grew out of deliberate manipulation of the environment by the teacher. For a few days particular attention was paid to the current weather conditions by the pupils. An aneroid barometer was placed on the desk for students to observe. Some newspaper and magazine articles on weather were passed around the class for

[1] Anna Fagerlie, "Honeybees for a Science Unit," *The Instructor*, June 1955, p. 57.

the pupils to read. This teacher then took occasion to discuss some experiences he had had in Florida, Washington, and England with different kinds of weather. The importance of weather conditions to the pupils' parents in their respective occupations was discussed. The pupils then began to tell about their own experiences with weather. Several possible areas of study were listed in terms of the groups of people who were concerned. This list finally was placed on the blackboard and included the farmer, the housewife, the aviator, the outdoor worker, the sportsman, and the school teacher.

One junior high school teacher, having spent a considerable amount of time in China, had become very much interested in the geography and culture of that country. He felt that a unit on China would be an appropriate area for study during the year. Accord-

A rich source for units of work is to be found in the natural interests that children have in other countries.

Courtesy of *The Indiana Teacher*

ingly, he put numerous interesting objects about the room which he had picked up in his travels. He gradually shifted his bulletin board display to include a map of China and other things having to do with China as preliminary interest-arousing devices. The children did exhibit interest in these things and he anticipated that they would choose China as their next unit. For some unknown reason, however, the children became interested in the culture of India, and when the time came to make a choice they requested a study of India instead of China. The teacher, being perfectly honest intellectually and desirous of playing fair regardless of his own personal inclinations, could think of no reason why a study of India would not serve their purposes quite well. Therefore, he found himself hurrying off to the curriculum laboratory seeking resource materials and resource units in this area. This incident illustrates the necessity of a democratic spirit and willingness to go along with pupils on the part of the teacher who enters into teacher-pupil planning activities.

Sometimes it is necessary for the teacher to inform a group of pupils about a new topic or present a new slant on an old one in order to arouse interest. One graduate teacher in a laboratory school felt that a class of high school juniors would profit from some experience in propaganda analysis. The first problem confronting him was to find suitable materials for his own pre-planning. At that time very little in the collections to which he had access had a direct bearing on propaganda. After spending a great deal of time and energy in college and city libraries searching for usable material he believed he was ready to propose the idea. It was necessary, however, for him to develop, through illustrations from current newspapers, magazines, radio and television programs, and motion pictures, an understanding of the impact of propaganda on all citizens.

Through combination of lecture and discussion classes, with maximum pupil involvement, the teacher and the class developed the propaganda picture. Having helped them understand the general problem, the teacher assisted the class members in identifying their own problems of propaganda influence. In the words of the graduate teacher, "Once the objectives were made clear the class became alert and activities worked out in a natural process." Further along in the report the teacher says, "The class cooperated in such an amazing way it was a joy to teach them. It was not long before

each student became a separate individual to think of and arrange
for." Teacher-pupil planning does not mean leaving the initiation of
units entirely up to spontaneous interest of pupils. The above illustration shows how new and desirable interests may be developed
under skillful leadership by the teacher. The motivation to study
the problem of propaganda was very high once the pupils had a
clear understanding of the nature of the problem itself. The teacher's
function in this case was to bring the problem into clear perspective.

Teacher-pupil planning can be utilized in a situation cutting
across classroom and department lines. A very interesting illustration of this fact is the log of a unit on a Christmas program. Late in
November during a music appreciation class, the question was
raised by a student as to whether there would be a school Christmas
program. The teacher encouraged the class to discuss the pros and
cons of a Christmas program. What such a program should mean
to the pupils and their suggestions on the type of program it should
be were brought out. As the discussion progressed it became more
and more apparent that it should be planned by pupils. Preliminary
exploration of necessary committees followed. About this same time
the general topic of Christmas was brought up in the English class.
Someone mentioned the school programs that are so common in the
Christmas season. As an outgrowth of the discussion and after considerable evaluation of previous programs, the group agreed that
the more serious type of program to bring out the underlying meaning of Christmas was the most appropriate thing to be done. The
group then began studying Christmas plays that would be appropriate. The problem of designing the front page of the Christmas issue
of the school paper arose in the journalism class. One of the pupils
in the journalism class had been elected chairman of the publicity
committee for the program as it was developing in the music department. He also knew about the plays that were being read and
that might be selected. By this time a stage committee that had
been designated by the music class had made preliminary contact
with the industrial arts department and had searched the school
premises for possible materials to use in building the sets. This contact with the industrial arts department in turn gave this teacher the
cue that he wanted so that the program now involved four areas of
the school. Each department was contributing in a cooperative
fashion toward the program taking shape under student initiative

and with teacher-pupil planning in process in all areas. This group of teachers had, of course, been in communication, but the developments were quite spontaneous, growing out of the Christmas season. Needless to say, the planning went forward in all areas with vigorous application. The pupils were sharing on a broad base of participation in an activity which contributed much to the joy and understanding of the Christmas season for the entire school and community. The program eventually was taped and broadcast over the local FM radio station, a recognition which added greatly to the satisfaction already derived by the pupils, teachers, and parents. The possibilities of various seasons and holidays as means of starting teacher-pupil planning activities are very great.

Current activities of the community furnish stimuli that can be

The preparation of major events requires wholehearted cooperation and hard work from the persons involved.

Courtesy of *The Muncie Star*

capitalized upon in some cases for the development of desirable teacher-pupil planned units. The teacher does not have to look far in the journals to find illustrations of such initiatory activities. One example of such a unit started with a county contour-plowing contest on a farm near a small rural school.[2] The children were so interested in what was going on that the teacher took the entire group to see the operations. As a result, a large number of questions were raised by the pupils upon their return to the classroom. Since a unit on conservation seemed timely, the teacher helped the pupils formulate their questions into a study that continued for some time after the demonstration. The unit brought out the origin of soil, how it is wasted through careless cultivation practices, and how it may be conserved. Such a study is obviously a desirable part of the school curriculum.

Another very fruitful source of teacher-pupil planned units is found in studies of problems which junior and senior high school youths face. In recent years problem inventories have revealed the extent and type of concern among young people of upper elementary, junior, and senior high school years. Excellent examples of such problem inventories are the Mooney Problems Check List and SRA Youth Inventory. According to one study using an inventory developed by Remmers and Shimberg, problems expressed by high school students were identified in the following areas:

1. problems having to do with the school and subjects taught;
2. problems about what they would do after graduation;
3. the "about-myself" area;
4. the "getting-along-with-others" area;
5. the home-parent area;
6. the boy-girl area;
7. the health area;
8. a miscellaneous area including such things as the possibility of another war, making the world a better place, race prejudice, and religion.[3]

An increasing number of schools are finding ways to reorganize their programs to permit the incorporation of studies built around

[2] Lillian Hethershaw Darnell, "A Unit on Soil Conservation," NEA Journal, September 1949, p. 446.

[3] H. H. Remmers and Lyle M. Spencer, "All Young People Have Problems," NEA Journal, March 1950, pp. 182-83.

selected problems determined in this manner. Such units are highly motivated and are found to provide learning experiences of a wide variety. Since these problems are not confined to subject-matter lines but often draw information from several fields, valuable experience in research activities and in oral and written expression are possible. Problem-centered units provide excellent opportunities to learn discussion techniques. Units of this kind form the nucleus for much of the work of core programs at the secondary level.

The problems approach is widely used in social science classes where a concerted effort is being made to develop personal growth for citizenship. When a group undertakes study of a problem of wide general interest to its members, opportunities are opened for developing leadership through wide participation. These opportunities become clear as leadership is defined in terms of doing the things that advance the group toward its own goals. Under such a conception of leadership many individuals share in it.

Summary of ways in which units for teacher-pupil planning are initiated. In the foregoing section the origin of selected units from a wide variety of recorded teacher experiences has been described. An effort has been made to show how teachers have watched for cues to the development of units based upon expected spontaneous interest of children. In the one instance the interest generated by reading about animals was expanded into a much wider learning experience. Seasonal interests in gardening for the second grade and in the Christmas unit at the high school level were anticipated by the teacher at appropriate times of the year. When the cue came, as the teachers knew it would, they were prepared to capitalize upon expressed interest.

The unit on the home was planned by the teacher because of known feelings of third grade children about their homes. In this case there was some manipulation by the teacher to bring out expressions of interest. In the case of the weather unit in the eighth grade, the teacher actually manipulated the environment. The unit on propaganda required definite leadership and teaching to inform the class sufficiently about the problem, to bring out the pupils' latent interest.

Other examples were cited to show how current activities in the community could result in teacher-pupil planned units. The unit on soil conservation was the result of such alertness. Finally, it was pointed out that local surveys of problems of children and youth using carefully developed techniques also provide valuable starting points for initiating such studies. From the consideration of these examples it is hoped that the teacher will be able to see how to use the interests, needs, and concerns of children to produce a highly motivated set of learning experiences. These experiences will be found to have taken on increased value because of the way they were organized. In the next section an attempt will be made to show how the next steps were accomplished.

Content and distribution of work. After the central theme of a unit has been determined, the next step in planning with learners is to establish clearly what is to be included. Teachers will meet with varying degrees of success in this aspect of their work, depending upon their own expertness in drawing out questions from children and upon the extent of the group's planning experience in previous situations. Teachers and pupils alike continuously learn how to work together in a cooperative fashion. The first time a teacher undertakes teacher-pupil planning he will lack confidence in his own ability to bring about a satisfactory outcome of the procedure. The technique required on the part of the teacher can be developed only through practice. A certain amount of courage is required to start. Pupils who have been accustomed to being told what to do by the teacher will have to learn that they are expected to and can take initiative. Some of the steps used by teachers in setting up the content of units with pupils are illustrated by reference to the same units described above.

The first grade unit on animal life proceeded from the teacher's suggestion that there seemed to be so many things about animals that could be learned that perhaps they could divide the class and find out different things about different animals, and share what they had learned. In this case the teacher hoped that suggestions for dividing up the kinds of animals, coping with different tasks, and planning activities would be forthcoming. One little girl suggested that she would like to make a scrapbook of all the animals that would make good pets; a boy thought he would like to work on one about wild animals. Committees were formed of several children who wanted to work on these two projects. While this was going on the children wrote stories describing their activities and the kinds of animals they were studying and read them to their classmates. Some of the children had an opportunity to attend the circus while the unit was in progress. This added to the study a considerable number of animals that otherwise might have been left out.

Certain problems began to arise. One little girl said that her mother wouldn't let her have a dog for a pet because she didn't know how to take care of it. She suggested she would like to know more about caring for pets so maybe she could have a dog. Another child said that her mother thought she fed her kitten too many times a day; she wondered how it really should be fed. Thus, a group became interested in learning more about caring for pets. By this time the teacher had listed on the blackboard their suggestions of

A reading corner with books and magazines gives each child a chance to find materials appropriate to his interest.

Courtesy of *The Indiana Teacher*

things to be learned: the names of the pets, how mother animals take care of their babies, what to feed each animal, where each animal likes to live, how each pet keeps clean, and what each animal is good for besides being a pet.

Next followed the process of deciding how they would go about learning these things. One of the children knew of some books at the library that he thought would be helpful. Another thought she would like to bring a mother hen and her little chicks from home and watch them. Under the guidance of the teacher, the children selected ways of keeping records of the things they were learning. Booklets on the care of pets were developed and attractive covers were designed for these booklets. Along with all of this they listed spelling words involving the names of the animals and the things they would need to feed and care for them.

Children learn from numerous sources as their alert and inquiring minds seek answers to their many questions.

Courtesy of *The Indiana Teacher*

The above suggestions do not by any means exhaust the possibilities, but they do show how a teacher working with this immature group first found out what they wanted to know about animals and then selected ways of learning those things. The teacher is at all times a positive force in this development. Indeed, he is very much in the picture, assisting the immature pupils as they work out their own problems. However, there is a sharing of leadership so that many pupils have a part in selecting and promoting the things which the group wants.

It is not necessary to discuss in detail the development that took place in each of the elementary grade units. As the maturity level of the children increases it may be expected that the extent to which they can share in planning and accept responsibility will grow. A further desirable feature of the activities developed is the extent to which they become self-sustaining. With older children certain projects that require a longer period of time can be planned and carried out with much less direction. Younger children tend to move from one activity to another more frequently; the attention of older children is sustained for a greater length of time. Projects that require too much time for completion are not selected for the younger groups.

A slightly different procedure was recorded by the teacher of the eighth grade weather unit. A discussion, led by the teacher, centered around problems such as: *Has there ever been a serious storm in this city? If not, why not? How is the weather important to your parents? How is weather important to the rural community around the city? How is weather important to the businessman? What would be the effects of extreme weather conditions of various types in the city? What are the sources for weather information? What effects of weather in other parts of the country are felt in this city?* In this way the pupils were drawn into a discussion, and their questions were listed on the blackboard as the discussion progressed. The teacher then summarized the questions on the importance of weather under the following topics: *the farmer cares, the housewife cares, the aviator cares, the outdoor worker cares, the sportsman cares, the pupil cares, and the schoolteacher cares about weather.*

The next step was to let each pupil choose from these areas the one in which he felt he was most interested. Those individuals who were interested in each topic gathered in groups in different sections of the room and talked over what they thought they wanted to do with their respective problems. Thus, through their planning, the content of the unit was determined. From this point on the teacher's activity consisted mainly of checking with the different groups to help them round out their programs and decide upon ways of reaching their objectives.

The cooperative unit on a Christmas program shows that following the initial discussion in the music appreciation class the pupils brought in materials for a program that was interesting to them. Materials collected at home and from two small city libraries included plays, Christmas stories, pictures from newspapers and magazine articles, poems, stage sets, picture books, and other things out of which ideas might be gleaned. During the third day of planning, after different ideas had been suggested, some committees were set up to facilitate the entire project. These included publicity, stage and properties, script, make-up, costumes, and music. The pupils were permitted to join the committees in which they were most interested. The next day the committees chose their chairmen, and each made an outline of what they were expected to accomplish and how they were to go about it. The script committee began to put together the program that would as nearly as possible fit the ideas that the pupils had previously expressed. The stage committee listed the materials required for any stage set and communicated that information to the industrial arts teacher. The next day the script committee made its report. A great deal of interest was indicated in the discussion that followed this report. The costume committee then asked the script committee what costumes would be needed and proceeded to work on that problem. Once the script had been pretty well determined the stage committee was able to make more detailed plans. The teachers reported, in the log they kept of the developments, that interest continued to grow as the program took shape. It was noted in the early portions of the log that each committee did a certain amount of floundering as it attempted to find its direction. Once sufficient time had elapsed for ideas to begin to take shape, each group picked up momentum. This condition is usually experienced in this kind of work.

The other teachers cooperating in the program reported similar procedures and developments. The English class, which carried a great deal of the development in the selection of the play and the purposes to be served, reported discussion of various problems which led up to final selection of the program's content.

The journalism class carried the responsibility for getting the story out to the students and the community. Pupils themselves suggested an educational campaign through the school newspaper to convey to the student body the purposes of such a program and the appropriate behavior on their part. There was a division of labor in the journalism class, one group taking responsibility for publicity itself, and the other for the development of the programs. Here again there was the opportunity for choice.

The industrial arts department, cooperating in the development of the stage settings, worked out their plans in a similar fashion and came up with crews working on sets and properties, lighting effects, and painting. Four of the boys who were members of the stage committee set up originally by the music class were also members of the industrial arts class. One of these boys was chairman of the stage committee and provided liaison between the industrial arts class and the music class where the original suggestion was made. Since there were two different scenes required on the stage, the stage committee had to work closely with all the other committees involved.

The stage committee found it necessary first to check what could be found out about stage settings and arrangements in general. Second, through reading the play they determined just what would be needed and the proper sizes and shapes in relation to the whole setup. It was also necessary to draw to scale plans for the arrangement of all properties. An inventory of supplies on hand and the new supplies needed was also required. Then the matters of actual construction, using the various materials, painting the sets, and wiring for lights had to be cared for.

Summary on content and distribution of work. From this description of procedures in different grade levels, it is seen that teacher-pupil planning involves a great deal of tact and skill in bringing out the exact concerns that children feel about the selected unit. When the teacher and pupils together have listed the appropriate areas for study, ways and means of carrying on the learning activities likewise must be devised. The principle observed in most of the plans described was seen to be a division of labor on the basis of committees of persons having similar interests. In setting up committees to accomplish different tasks, it is of course possible that a bad distribution may be experienced. In this case, after talking over the needs and the problem of poor distribution, it is quite likely that the children will realign themselves to bring about the desired result. This redistribution itself becomes an added problem of cooperative planning.

If the committee plan is used, as it frequently is, the teacher is careful to do two things. In the first place he will maintain communication with the groups by meeting with them periodically to see how well they are keeping their activities in balance. Another means frequently used is to have each committee report its plan to the whole class so that it may be evaluated and so that suggestions may be offered by other members of the class as well as the teacher. The second thing the teacher does is to arrange from the beginning for the results of each committee's work to be shared by the whole group. This matter of sharing is taken care of as the work progresses and at the termination of the unit.

Progress is maintained and evaluation accomplished. Some teachers have expressed the fear that some of the enthusiasm might wear off once the excitement of initiating the unit is over and the hard work begins. There is some validity in this apprehension, although few teachers report that it actually turns out that way. An observant attitude on the part of the teacher will quickly reveal those pupils who are, for one reason or another, slipping into habits of inattention or indifference. Sometimes a committee chairman is dominating the situation, causing others to feel that their contributions will not be received with proper consideration. Occasionally a pupil chooses the wrong committee. If these conditions become apparent the teacher will explore the whole problem with the group and, if possible, bring about an adjustment that will enable it to go ahead with its former enthusiasm.

Interest is maintained also through the progress reports that various committees are called upon to make. If things are not going very well with the group it will show up very quickly, either by direct reference or by the lack of accomplishment. Since the pupils have shared in the planning that has been done and have had an opportunity to select the aspects of the unit upon which they will work, there is every reason to believe that they will feel a greater sense of responsibility for carrying on. This is generally the case.

Periodic evaluation sessions in which the group discusses the extent to which their needs are being met are also helpful in maintaining the initial enthusiasm and effort. Even the first grade teacher, whose unit on pets has been referred to from time to time, used this procedure. As various committees moved toward completion of their work, he would sit down with them and inquire whether they were finding the answers to the questions they had asked. The little girl who wanted to learn how to take care of a dog thought she had learned enough to go home and ask her mother if she might have one. The teacher carried it a bit further by asking what she had learned. This led to contributions from the little girl herself and from several other pupils. The child who wanted to find out how to feed her cat pointed out that she had not learned much about her question. She persisted in raising questions until she had exhausted the possibilities of the discussion for her purposes. The committee that had been caring for the hen and chicks had kept a diary, which the teacher used as another device for reviewing the work of the unit.

As would be expected with children of first grade level, frequent periods of rest and relaxation from serious study were necessary. It was possible to use songs about pets for some of these relaxation periods, and some of the children wrote poems and read them for fun.

Often as a group works toward completion of a project it will want to develop some kind of summary or concluding activity. In the case of the pet unit the group planned to have an "animal party" for their mothers. They planned to exhibit the pictures and booklets they had made and read their favorite story about pets to the class and to their visitors. Variety in the program included plays or songs; for refreshment, animal crackers and cocoa would be served. Such a program offers splendid opportunity for mothers to be fêted by their young sons and daughters as hosts and hostesses.

The second grade unit on gardening developed along somewhat different lines. The group carried on as a whole with individual planting providing the center of interest for each child. There was a great deal of sharing of these individual interests in various ways. A number of learning activities such as writing stories and word study were worked into the room's current activity. Of course these activities related to gardening did not constitute the whole program for a day, but rather provided a thread of interest carrying over a period of time. Things the pupils did in relation to planting seeds and growing plants included learning to spell the names of plants, putting labels on the cups, and learning the numerous terms about gardening found on the seed packages. Such words as grow, plant, seed, vegetables, flower, water, dirt, and dig were common ones that occurred.

After the actual planting was completed, some of the children suggested that they would like to write stories about the seeds they had planted. Others joined in on this idea and the teacher then proceeded to brief them on some of the words they thought they might need in their stories. These words were written on the blackboard before the writing began. When the stories were finished they were read to the class. A great deal of pleasure was derived from this experience of sharing one another's work.

Several problems arose that necessitated further organization of the room. The matter of watering and taking care of the plants led to setting up a committee each week to take care of this function. One pupil brought in a book that told about plants needing light and sunshine if they were to have a good green color and sturdy stems, and that led to a further lesson about gardening. As a result, a committee was chosen to take the pots out of doors when the sun was shining in order to help with the germination of the seeds and the growth of the plants. This was necessitated by the fact that the school room was in a basement where the windows were very short, so that not much direct sunlight came in.

Through a bit of teacher suggestion, a diary on the plants was worked into the total plan. Details as to what would be included in the diary were worked out with the pupils. Included in the booklet were pictures of the plants drawn and colored as the pupils imagined they would be. The booklets were made more attractive by the addition of covers made from colored paper.

After the plants had attained some size the children decided it would be good to invite the other second grade room to see them. This led to the planning and writing of invitations which, of course, were quickly accepted. While the visitors were in the room the children volunteered to tell them all about planting the seeds and what was growing in each of the cups. The diaries were displayed on the desks so that the other children might see them.

A serious problem developed one week end when, because of too much heat or lack of water, some of the plants started dying. Some of the mothers gave the children new plants or seeds and they started over. The thread of interest in gardening carried through very successfully until Easter vacation. Because of the problem of keeping the plants alive during the prolonged period of absence from school, it was decided that they should be taken home and cared for from that time on. The interest continued, however, as was evidenced by the fact that some of the children wrote stories about what was happening to the plants after they were taken home. Some repotted their plants and brought them back from time to time to show how much they had grown.

The science unit about honeybees stimulated a large number of observational activities as the work progressed. These activities varied from observing various parts of dead bees under a microscope to finding egg, larva, and pupa stages in the comb that had been brought to school with the bees. Numerous drawings illustrating different parts of the bee were made by the children as their knowledge developed.

This unit was closed by developing a program about honeybees for the other fifth grade in the building. A play was written and staged by one group of children, a quiz program by another, and some of the better reports that had been written during the progress of the unit were read. Some word puzzles that had been developed as a part of the vocabulary study related to bees also provided a source of entertainment.

An evaluation of the unit itself revealed several kinds of learning that had resulted from this study of bees. Some of the children no longer feared the bee as a stinging insect, but appreciated it as a useful worker. Other children had never eaten honey until a "tasting party" was arranged in class. The evaluation of individual learning was not described, although it was assumed that the reports written by the pupils and the progress they had made on the several activities provided opportunities for such evaluation.

It will be recalled that the eighth grade unit on weather provided for study groups to investigate the effect of weather on certain types of workers. In addition to group studies on how the weather affects farmers, housewives, aviators, outdoor workers, sportsmen, pupils, and schoolteachers, some of the time was spent following a teacher-prepared study guide covering related information about weather needed by all groups.

Pupil learning in the weather unit was evaluated very largely on the basis of a written test. Notebooks developed while studying the general weather outline were also available for evaluation. However, there are no guides which would indicate the qualities of the note-book, to be considered in evaluating them. It may be assumed that these standards had been set up earlier in the year. Although mention is made of various types of personal growth associated with the unit and the numerous project activities, there is no indication of the manner in which such items as work habits or ability to work with other people might be evaluated.

Children can gain greatly increased understandings and pleasures from dramatizing familiar or original stories.

Courtesy of *The Indiana Teacher*

The high school class studying the unit on propaganda developed a wide variety of group activities. The class was divided into four committees, each of which was to work on one type of propaganda peculiar to a historical period. This assignment was pointed up by naming a person associated with each period who was either directly affected by, or used, propaganda. Films on the subject were used and a very interesting trip to the newspaper office and printing plant was developed.

A panel discussion was set up around the question of propaganda in textbooks, and pupils listened to complete radio broadcasts and analyzed the propaganda contained in them. Since this unit was developed early in an election year, many opportunities were present to observe use of propaganda by politicians.

Evaluation of pupil learning in the unit was accomplished in part through a written examination on the subject. Further evaluation was based upon principles of critical thinking that had been developed. Students were directed to take some problem like a political issue and carry through the process of analysis based upon these principles. This is undoubtedly a more valid procedure than merely asking questions about the process of analysis. Other areas of personal growth were largely overlooked, however, in the evaluation process in this unit.

Summary of maintaining progress and evaluation. From the description of these examples of teacher-pupil planned units, some of the things that are done to maintain a high level of activity become apparent. One observation made is that rather continuous replanning takes place. If the plan of dividing the class into committees is followed, certain decisions have to be made as to how the groups are to work and what kind of reports they will make. As they begin work new problems arise. Ways to solve these problems then have to be determined. From time to time each committee asks itself whether it is accomplishing what it has set out to accomplish. Individual pupils likewise raise this question about their own progress. Sometimes they find, as did the little girl who wanted to learn how to take care of a cat, that at a given point they are falling short of their objectives.

As the class gets deeper into the study of its problems in a unit of this type, desirable activities appear which were not considered in the beginning. This development occurred in the propaganda unit when it was decided to make a trip to the newspaper office to learn as much as possible about that medium of mass communication. Similar trips could be devised to advertising agencies, political headquarters, and other groups that originate programs designed to influence the thinking of large numbers of people. As a matter of fact it is in such agencies as these that propaganda really originates. As a part of its editorial policy a newspaper sometimes develops its own propaganda, but more often the origin is in such agencies as those mentioned.

Frequently the culminating activities of the unit are not chosen until the group is well along in its progress. It is not uncommon to find suggestions made toward the close of a unit that other rooms or parents be invited to share what the class has done. Under some circumstances the work of the class may be of sufficient general interest to a community to have an open house for the purpose of putting the various projects on display. To have some kind of culminating activity often helps to bring focus to the job and to bring the unit to a more orderly and systematic completion. In a great many cases this is one function of the examination.

Two types of evaluation are extremely important in a teacher-pupil planned unit. In the first place, each committee and each pupil evaluates periodically the progress being made toward the goals that have been set up. This kind of evaluation is a process of determining the extent to which the unit, through the experiences it is providing, is serving as a means of accomplishing the desired learning. This evaluation includes the group's evaluation of its own procedure—how well members are cooperating with one another in an effort to accomplish their original goals. At the close of the unit, the experiences they have shared are reviewed and suggestions are developed for a more effective operation the next time such a unit is undertaken.

In the second place, evaluation is concerned with growth of the individual learner, not only in terms of increased information and skill, but also in terms of general behavior. In the fifth grade unit on honeybees it was pointed out that certain children had lost their fear of bees because they understood them as useful workers and not merely stinging insects. The development of such appreciations is undoubtedly an important aspect of the unit's total function. It should be considered at least as important as the fact that the stinger of the worker bee has barbs on it. Because evaluations of growth in terms of behavior are quite often difficult to obtain, evaluation based on factual knowledge or skills may receive an unwarranted emphasis.

In the case of the propaganda unit, some of the pupils remarked at its close that they did not accept without good reason anything they now read. To the extent that their behavior bore out this attitude of mind with regard to information by word of mouth, from newspapers, radio, and television, the unit would seem to have been successful. There is no way of knowing how long such an impact will last. However, a comprehensive guide to the evaluation of this unit on propaganda would include observations of the extent to which pupils demonstrate a questioning frame of mind with regard to any alleged facts.

Evaluation of personal growth is based upon subjective estimates, since there is no known way of accomplishing this by pencil and paper means. Such estimates, however, can be improved and proper emphasis obtained through the preparation of various kinds of check lists, rating devices, and other guides that call attention to behavior related to desired growth areas. The goals of a unit for which teacher-pupil planning is developed are heavily loaded with personal-growth factors. In such units, then, evaluation by subjective estimates becomes of utmost importance.

Teacher-pupil planning is related to the principles of learning. One of the procedures common to many of the examples that have been used is to obtain from the pupils questions that indicate their concern about the problem that has been selected. Pupils' questions, obtained under the best possible conditions for a free give-and-take between the class and the teacher, are among the best guides to the status of the learners at a particular time. Through these questions the level of maturity becomes apparent and clearer indications of readiness are obtained.

Teacher-pupil planned units also rate high in motivation. It is a well established quality of human behavior that an individual will assume more responsibility for carrying out those activities that he has helped plan. Having had a part in deciding what is to be done and how it is to be done, pupils in teacher-pupil planned activities are in a better position to understand how they will be helped by them.

Teacher-pupil planned units generally contain a wider variety of learning experiences, providing not only more activity than many teacher-planned units, but also utilizing more direct experiences and more sensory avenues to learning.

In a classroom situation where teacher-pupil planning is carried on effectively there is a rapport among teachers and pupils that reduces tension and provides a maximum sense of security and belonging. The intelligent use of teacher-pupil planning also recognizes that the pupils may learn more than one desirable type of thing at once. Because of the cooperative nature of the learning activities used, important human relations are promoted.

Teacher-pupil planned units develop leadership. The conception of leadership is gradually shifting from thinking of one individual as the leader to a recognition that a number of individuals in a group share responsibility at different times in advancing a group toward its goals. Research in the area of leadership that has been concentrated on the individual has been generally disappointing. One research approach that studied the behavior of a leader and its effect upon the attitudes of group members has important implications for teachers, however. The advantages of a democratic attitude on the part of the status leader as opposed to an attitude of either autocracy or laissez-faire were demonstrated. Thus, the behavior of the democratic leader was shown to have very significant positive effects upon the group climate in which he worked.[4]

More fruitful approaches to leadership development, however, seem to be in the offing, as it is increasingly recognized that many individuals in the group contribute leadership functions. There are two broad classes of group functions. One type of group function consists of activities designed to advance the group toward the goals it is seeking. An illustration of such an activity would be the search for necessary information or the sharing of such information as has been obtained. The other type of group function consists of activities designed to maintain the group as an operating unit. For ex-

[4] Ronald Lippitt, "An Experimental Study of the Effect of Democratic and Authoritarian Group Atmospheres," Part II, *Studies in Topological and Vector Psychology,* Vol. I, University of Iowa's Studies in Child Welfare, Vol. 16, No. 3, 1940.

ample, the members of a class need to know one another well enough to communicate without undue reticence and without creating antagonism. If for any reason they do not have this extent of acquaintance, some kind of get-acquainted activity is used to improve the situation.

Under the concept of group functions, it is seen that numerous individuals within the group might make leadership contributions. Each person who, through his behavior, causes the group to move closer to its objective is making a leadership contribution. In cooperatively planned units pupils are brought into a sharing of responsibility for such progress. Through such participation the pupil is undergoing the most realistic form of leadership training.

Some special problems of the teacher. The teacher's role in planning process or experience units is obviously a very sensitive one. It has been pointed out that the chances for success in this kind of adventure are increased in proportion to the teacher's preplanning. However, this necessary function of pre-planning can lead to unfavorable consequences if the teacher allows himself to become so enthusiastic as a result of his own preparation that in reality he gives the class a ready-made unit. There is no limit to the good that may come from extensive pre-planning if this pitfall is noted and avoided.

The fundamental attitude of the teacher toward children and learning and the degree to which he can control his behavior in the planning process are at the very heart of the situation. Results are greatly improved if the teacher really feels children grow most when they share the maximum amount of responsibility for their own development at any maturity level. He gets his greatest satisfactions from the response of the pupils and gives them a maximum opportunity to respond. He restrains his own inclinations to move rapidly ahead with the class in terms of his own thinking in order to provide the pupils with an opportunity to develop their own thoughts at their own rate of speed. Finally, it is necessary that the teacher have a firm belief in the principle that many kinds of learning do take place simultaneously and that more kinds of learning will result when teacher-pupil planning is utilized in circumstances appropriate for its use.

SUMMARY

The use of teaching procedures that permit pupil participation in planning and that utilize methods of group
dynamics is becoming an increasingly important part of
teaching practice. Desirable features of the less formal
extra-class activity program have been added to many
classroom learning situations. Units of work designed to
foster personal growth will include a larger share of
pupil-planned learning activities that incorporate group
procedures.

The primary steps in planning units of this type are
significant. Numerous ways in which teacher-pupil planning situations are initiated have been illustrated and
include the following:

1. Watching for cues to spontaneous interest.

2. Use of subjects with a close emotional involvement
for children.

3. Seasonal interests.

4. Manipulation of objects and experiences.

5. Current activities in the community.

6. Problem inventories and surveys.

Maintaining satisfactory progress and providing for
adequate evaluation constitutes another area of concern
for the teacher. Some suggestions for satisfactory operations in this area follow:

1. As problems are undertaken it often happens that
new and unexpected conditions require replanning.

2. Progress in solving a problem often suggests desirable new activities that were not anticipated.

3. Desirable culminating activities for a unit often suggest themselves after work is well along.

4. Provision for periodic evaluation of progress of each
group and the class as a whole is a desirable part of the
over-all plan.

5. The individual learner is a subject for recurring
self-evaluation and evaluation by the teacher. These matters are more effectively cared for as the unit progresses.

6. The preparation of guides to help the teacher make

the subjective type of estimates required in evaluating personal growth is a necessary consideration.

Development of leadership is accomplished through experiences of contributing to group progress. In cooperative planning and accomplishment of units of work, pupils of all levels of ability make some contributions. Thus, each person grows in leadership ability in keeping with his potential.

As a result of reading this chapter the teacher may feel that he has grown in competence in these regards:

1. Use of pre-planning in more effective work with children.

2. Expanded repertoire and knowledge of use of acceptable learning activities of an informal nature.

3. Alertness to the indications of pupil interest and concern that lead to units of cooperative learning.

4. Ability to make initial efforts in teacher-pupil planning with a group of children.

5. Added insight into the use of cooperative projects to accommodate different levels of ability.

6. Understanding of the principle that many learnings occur simultaneously as viewed in cooperative activities of pupils.

7. Skill in adjusting conditions and pupils for most effective progress.

8. The ability to utilize subjective means of evaluating personal growth of pupils.

In the remaining chapters of this part other procedures that help pupils in growing into useful, responsible citizens are described. To be most effective, the school and the teacher utilize all opportunities in class and outside class to engage pupils in responsible self-direction.

PROBLEMS

1. Read the references at the end of this chapter and write a description of activities in which your pupils would be participants in democratic group procedures.

2. Keep a record for several days of the spontaneous questions and other indications of pupil interest you see. Select one or two

which might serve as a point of departure for a unit-planning activity.

3. *Visit a good elementary teacher or core teacher when a planning period is in progress. Write an analysis of what you see.*

4. *Observe an elementary classroom and write descriptions of one or two group projects in progress. Try an analysis of the learning you think is in progress.*

5. *Ask your supervisor to assist you in a planning period on some short lesson with a group of pupils. Write an analysis of your results.*

6. *Search the files and periodicals to find one or two group activities that seem especially good for giving individuals of widely different abilities a share of success. Why do you think the ones you selected are good?*

7. *Acquaint yourself with a cooperative learning project in progress. Develop some guides that will assist you in evaluating the progress of individuals in the several kinds of learning that are in progress.*

8. *Write a paper that sets forth the obligations and principles for action of the teacher who would engage in cooperative teaching-learning activities.*

BIBLIOGRAPHY

Association for Supervision and Curriculum Development, *Toward Better Teaching* (1949 Yearbook). Washington, D.C.: The Association, 1949.

Benne, Kenneth D., "Theory of Cooperative Planning in Education," *Teachers College Record* 53:429-35, May 1951.

Deer, George H., "Social Studies for What?" *Elementary School Journal* 52:511-17, May 1952.

Department of Supervision and Curriculum Development, *Group Planning in Education* (1945 Yearbook). Washington, D.C.: National Education Association, 1945.

Grambs, Jean D., and William J. Iverson, *Modern Methods of Teaching in Secondary Education.* New York: The Dryden Press, Inc., 1952. Chap. viii.

Hanna, Lavone A., Gladys L. Potter, and Neva Hagaman, *Unit Teaching in the Elementary School.* New York: Rinehart and Company, Inc., 1955.

Klee, L. E., "How to Do Cooperative Planning," *Social Education* 15: 121-26, March 1951.

Lane, Howard, and Mary Beauchamp, *Human Relations in Teaching.* Englewood Cliffs, N.J.: Prentice-Hall, Inc., 1955.

McCowen, E. J., "Rich Learning Experiences in the Third Grade," *Elementary English* 30:343-51, October 1953.

Miel, Alice, and associates, *Cooperative Procedures in Learning.* New York: Teachers College, Columbia University, 1952.

Noar, Gertrude, *Freedom to Live and Learn.* Philadelphia: Franklin Publishing and Supply Company, 1948.

———, *The Junior High School.* Englewood Cliffs, N.J.: Prentice-Hall, Inc., 1953. Chap. xii.

Punke, H. H., "On the Division of Responsibility Between Teacher and Learner," *Clearing House* 30:437-38, March 1956.

Richey, Robert W., "Using Group-Process Techniques in Your Student Teaching," in Grim and Michaelis, *The Student Teacher in the Secondary School.* Englewood Cliffs, N.J.: Prentice-Hall, Inc., 1953. Chap. v.

Simpson, Ray H., *Improving Teaching-Learning Processes.* New York: Longmans, Green & Company, 1953. Chap. xii.

Symonds, Percival, ed., "Classroom Dynamics," *Journal of Educational Research,* October, 1951.

Thelen, Herbert A., "Group Dynamics in Instruction: Principle of Least Group Size," *School Review* 57:139-48, March 1949.

Toops, Myrtle Dewey, *Working in the Core Program in Burris Laboratory School.* Muncie, Indiana: Ball State Teachers College, 1955.

Trow, William Clark, Alvin E. Zander, William C. Morse, and David H. Jenkins, "Psychology of Group Behavior," *Journal of Educational Psychology* 41:322-38, October 1950.

Wiles, Kimball, *Teaching for Better Schools.* Englewood Cliffs, N.J.: Prentice-Hall, Inc., 1952. Chaps. v-viii.

12

Teaching through extra-class activities

Extra-class activities include all those activities in which pupils engage that are not specifically covered by regularly scheduled class situations. Enthusiastic proponents of school activities find fault, and perhaps justly so, with the term "extra." Activities have gone by many different names —co-curricular, extracurricular, intra-curricular, extra-class, and a host of others. Names do not change them, and neither add nor detract from their significance. Anyone actively engaged in working with youth needs to know and appreciate the full value of all activities in which boys and girls participate to give expression to their energies. The difficulty encountered in naming these activities indicates to some extent their wide and varied coverage and gives significance to the fact that the educational values of those experiences not listed in a formal or even an informal schedule are just as essential as any other phase of the school program. They are just another way of indicating that school people see the broad implications of meeting the needs of all pupils by recognizing all the things that pupils do and in which they have a chance to take part.

The range of activities is almost as wide as one's imagination. Any activity involving moral, spiritual, ethical, social, intellectual, physical, or civic development meets the specifications for approval as an activity that the school may utilize for pupil growth. These activities may grow out of regular classroom experiences, or be so organized as to have no connection with formal scheduled class activities. As an illustration of the former situation, the school newspaper might grow out of classroom work but be assembled and prepared by a staff that is much broader than the classroom group. An example of the latter could be a Boy Scout troop that has no relation to classroom activity but is sponsored by the school. The former might carry credit that could be counted toward graduation for some of the staff members, but the Boy Scout activities would not.

The accumulation of credit has been used as a method for the determination of the fulfilment of academic requirements for graduation for so long, and is so universally accepted and understood, that it will likely be the pattern for many more years to come. Some experimentation has taken place to find a better way to indicate the academic accumulation of experiences leading to completion of the program required for graduation from secondary school, but no really satisfactory solution has been devised. The Carnegie unit of class work—meeting five days per week, with comparable time spent in preparation for two semesters, and with laboratory work recognized as half the value of class work—is the generally accepted unit. There are variations, but in general this is the pattern for determining credit. The number of units required for graduation from a four-year secondary program varies from fifteen to eighteen, depending on the individual school. Classes meeting less than five days per week carry proportional credit.

The entire rationale of curricular thinking stems largely from the practice of granting credit for scheduled class work where it is relatively easy to assign credit, and where sound defense can be given to accrediting associations for approval of credit. Schools gain status by conforming to those standards they agreed to uphold when they were accepted for accreditation. Accrediting associations are voluntary, and the school agrees to abide by the regulations when it joins. The teacher needs to know what these commitments are, and should strive to help live within their limits and work to uphold the regulations and their spirit. The United States is divided into six regional associations for accreditation of secondary schools and colleges. The stronger schools across the nation belong to one of these regional associations. Those who do not meet these standards are accredited by the State Department of Education in the state where they are located.

So the school itself makes the decision of how much credit to grant for a particular course, but it is generally quite closely governed by the practice approved by the agency accrediting the school. Any tendency toward liberal allowance of credit for work done in a school system is accompanied by the extension of the number of credits required for graduation. Pupils do have a tendency to become credit conscious and many schools classify courses into those which are called "solid" and those thought of as "nonsolid." The traditional courses meeting five times per week and requiring preparation either within the period or outside the scheduled period are known as solids. Such courses as English, social studies, physics, and algebra are, of course, called solids. The nonsolids are such courses as physical education, chorus, or recreation. There is a definite trend to get away from such classification, and it will be a welcome move. But many teachers will find themselves faced with the problem of working in areas where the stigma of "nonsolid" is still quite common in the minds of pupils. Both the so-called solids and nonsolids carry credit toward graduation.

Extra-class activities usually do not carry credit, and this is probably an advantage. As long as no credit is granted the activity is not under artificial pressure to meet a certain number of times per semester and for a specified length of time. The quantitative scale is not applied and that in itself is wholesome. The pressure of quantitative requirements has a tendency to detract from the informal nature of an activity that arises from the sincere interest of the boys and girls and their sponsor, all working together with no intention of earning formal credit. There is something wholesome about activity that contains its own rewards. You don't earn or expect credit, which is perhaps one of the good reasons the activity became extra-class.

Extra-class activities are all those things done by pupils that are not included in the scheduled work leading to credit required for graduation. However, the records of extra-class experiences do become a very real part of the pupil's profile of school activities when the pupil leaves school. They are just as important a factor in the pupil's set of recommendations as any other part. They give balance to the record; a record made up of all credit and no activities would not be considered favorably. On the other hand, a student could not graduate with all activities and little or no credit. It is the school's best evidence that it has considered the "whole" development of the pupil if his record contains a balance between credits for graduation and activities as a participating member of the school society.

Pupil activities may be classified into (1) semicurricular activities that grow out of regular class work and supplement the objectives of the courses that are taught; (2) those activities that are completely social or recreational and have little or no connection with formal course objectives; (3) athletic and nonathletic activities that are heavily pitched toward competitive contests; (4) civic and student council organizations that enable pupils to share in demo-

Club activities enrich school experiences and give pupils opportunity to explore and develop special interests.

Courtesy of *The Indiana Teacher*

cratically operated school functions to give pupils real-life experiences in being active school citizens; and (5) activities that are merely attached to an institution of some kind to give them status. Others might classify all these activities differently, and just as correctly.

Semicurricular activities include all those activities that grow out of and supplement the experiences of the classes that ordinarily carry credit. Examples of such activities are the Latin Club, Science Club, Music Club, Art Club, French Club, Commerce Club, Bird Club, Dramatics Club, and Camera Club. The school newspaper, magazine, senior yearbook, hobby clubs, Thespian society, the handbook, the honor society, and scholarship society are organizations that are somewhat more general in membership. Class plays, operettas, festivals, and debating clubs are still another type and offer an opportunity for specialized expression that is valuable to the pupils in a school. The foregoing list is limited, but still is sufficient to illustrate this particular group. Teachers find it difficult at times to keep some of these groups from going entirely social, and thus losing the purpose for which they were organized.

The activities that are largely or completely social or recreational include dancing, fun nights, parties, carnivals, circuses, swimming, intramurals, and field days. These activities have great value for developing wholesome attitudes and social graces as well as being physical outlets. Teachers need to recognize that the work will be strenuous, but that rewards in appreciation by the students will more than repay the teacher who takes the time to work in these activities. They are a part of the developmental program without which the school program would be bleak indeed. The good teacher wants to help with them.

Athletic and competitive activities are almost entirely interschool contests. All of the school sports such as basketball, football, baseball, wrestling, track, soccer, hockey, swimming, and tennis are included in this group. State athletic associations control the activities and go a long way toward eliminating many of the evils that would otherwise grow out of misdirected fan enthusiasm. Some elementary school coaches and administrators let their better judgment get out of control and permit elementary children to engage in interschool athletics. Practically all the literature on sound developmental programs for pupils in the elementary school question severely the wisdom of permitting children in the elementary grades to participate in interschool athletic contests. In school systems where the "feeder system" is in practice this is one of the questionable practices that is certain to be found. The "feeder system" is the practice of having junior teams especially coached to become senior or varsity teams.

There are all types of nonathletic contests carried on in schools with the approval (1956) of the National Association of Secondary School Principals. These include agricultural contests, art contests, essay contests, examinations, forensic contests, examinations leading to scholarships on a nation-wide selection, talent search programs that are competitive, and home economics and industrial arts contests. The approved list is almost endless, and there are frequent changes and additions. The state and regional accrediting associations have standards for approving such contests as are sound and for the best interests of youth. The classroom teacher should always check with his principal for approval before making commitments about entering pupils in contests of any kind.

Activities that have as their objectives the development of civic practice and understanding include student council activities and allied committee groups, youth forums, assembly programs (pupil-sponsored), school service organizations such as Junior Red Cross, Community Fund, bicycle or safety councils, school store, and school bank. This is only a small list, but the opportunity for pupil participation in school activities that provide for civic training and civic pride are as broad as the imagination of the pupils, teachers, school administration, and community leaders. The field has unlimited possibilities and furnishes excellent opportunity for immediate participation in civic enterprises.

The last category of activities includes quite largely those that are community-centered and community-directed but need a meeting place and special institutional sponsorship. They include Boy Scouts, Girl Scouts, Brownies (Girl Scout), Hi-Y, Y-Teens, and other similar community organizations that team up with the local school. Such organizations use the civic-minded leaders in the community as boards of directors and for leadership, but work closely with the school personnel to carry out the objectives of the several organizations. The school and the community share a much-needed service to boys and girls.

The groups just listed and suggested do not have hard and fast limits, and there is much sharing and inter-directorship and sponsorship practiced. The school and the teacher work closely with all of the organizations and with public-spirited community personnel.

Responsibility for extra-class activities. The school organization, including teachers and other personnel, is one of the best known promoters of activities that seek to further the wholesome development of boys and girls. Schools can be counted upon to avoid exploitation of children, and the teacher has the specific challenge of guarding the rights of youth against over-enthusiastic but well meaning groups when such exploitation is attempted. Children are susceptible, and the school provides easy access into all the homes where children live.

Teachers are expected to know what activities have the specifica-

The teacher seeks unusual opportunities to relate the activities of the Girl Scouts to school experiences.

Courtesy of *The Indiana Teacher*

tions for meeting the educational needs of youth. Activities should be promoted that give pupils the greatest opportunity to actually participate in the administration and promotion of the activity. They should be activities in which boys and girls have a natural interest. Activities that drag because of lack of interest have no justification for continuance. Some that prosper in one community don't seem to go in others. The school has to make the decision based on natural interest and community concern for the activity, and qualified leadership.

The school administrative personnel needs to be constantly alert to the number and kinds of activities that serve the needs of the pupils in the local school. These needs sometimes stem from the interests of pupils and their parents in the community, and sometimes the interests spring from the concerns and energies of the teacher. Again, the activity may start from some well meaning person or group outside the school or the home, or it may have been going on so long that everyone just takes it for granted. Regardless of where it originates, the school is obligated to weigh the merits of the activity and assign leadership to it to give status and direction to the program.

Interestingly enough, activities give greater opportunity for pupil leadership and participation than anything that goes on around the school. Activities come nearer to being pupil-centered and pupil-energized than any educational activity. If pupils are not permitted to share in leadership, the activity soon withers and disappears. It is one of the tests of the kind of sponsorship that is afforded the activity. A teacher who is quite formal in the classroom must become a different sort of person as an activity sponsor. If he doesn't, he either kills the activity or loses his chance to act as sponsor.

Young teachers get their chance to build status in the area of activities. Pupils like to have the younger teachers with them in activities, and the older ones, sometimes to the dismay of the younger teachers, want to give way to youth. This is a compliment to the young teacher and he should be ready to accept the challenge of the experience. It need not be looked upon as drudgery, nor does the young teacher need to find himself in a situation where his authority is challenged. Instead he gains prestige and respect from working among and close to his pupils in this situation that he does not attain in more formal class experiences.

The school does have the burden of determining load for both teachers and pupils. The student council can serve an effective purpose in setting up limitations on pupil participation. Boys and girls have a tendency to want to get into more things than they can do justice. Balance is essential, and neither too many activites nor too few are healthful to physical and mental development. Unhappiness results when someone tries to be in too many activities just as it occurs when pupils are left out. Activities serve as opportunities, and in order to serve that purpose, controls either from within or without are set in motion. It is far better to guide pupils to see their own limitations than to lay down rules and regulations for them from an authoritative source. They feel happier and cooperate more enthusiastically when they can be helped to make their own decisions.

The school, represented by the administration with the help of staff council, is responsible for the determination of teacher load. The wise administrator knows the strengths and interests of each of his teachers, and seeks to utilize these to the best interests of the greatest number of pupils. He sees the futility of overburdening the teacher and spreading the teacher's energy too thinly. He also knows that teachers do have special capacities that can be used to advantage. The teacher should see that his interests are recognized, and should, in protection to his principal, not permit himself to be loaded with extras so that he can't be at his best at everything. His professional responsibility calls for him to do those things for which he is well fitted. However, he must carry his fair share of these responsibilities, and not try to hide behind a cloak of incompetence and disinterest. He soon loses his prestige, and even his position, when he can't do anything well. He does have the responsibility to volunteer and let it be known what he can do best.

Extra-class activities must be recognized. Extra-class activities should grow out of need felt by pupils, faculty, or community. But if they are to flourish and be of any lasting help to boys and girls they must soon be felt as a need by boys and girls. The beginning can be touched off by the more experienced leadership in the school or the community, but if it is not geared to the interests of those whom it would help the activity is of little value. Illustrations of failure in pitching to the interests of youth can be gathered from club activities growing out of class situations where the teacher hopes to supplement the class work by club activities. Quite frequently the pupils hope to make the activity more social than the teacher can approve. It may end in disappointment for both pupils and sponsor, and yet both may have equally worthy ideas of what the club should contribute. Pupils feel they do not want some more of what they have had during the day, while the teacher is not anxious to use his time on heavy social activities.

But extra-class activities must start with an idea. Someone's idea has to appeal to a group of pupils who have an interest in putting the idea into action. A perfectly good idea may in one school be taken up by a group that has vigorous leadership and organization and have great value to those who participate; the same idea in another school where pupils with other interests or less initiative or with a teacher who does not have the time or the interest as sponsor fails to sparkle. The idea was good, but the action did not take anyone anywhere.

Someone in a position to look beyond the present has to have a keen insight into not only the needs but the interests of boys and girls. There must be considerable permissiveness on the part of adults. An attitude of "Let's see" or "Let's try it" can go a long way toward encouraging boys and girls to throw themselves into helping move ideas into action. Insight on the part of leadership is of great help. Studying the size of the student body to determine how many activities can be supported effectively and keeping the number down so that pupils can use their energy on fewer activites is essential.

The teacher has the responsibility of knowing those activities that grow out of his own specialization. The art teacher can be expected to know what kinds of extra activities have a good chance of succeeding with pupils. The same would be true of the English teacher, the mathematics teacher, and all the others. If an idea comes from the pupils the teacher should be able to determine whether the idea would catch fire or not. The principal in turn would be able to point out strengths or flaws in the movement. Parents also can be expected to detect merits and faults in an activity proposal. Then there are those activities that are time-tested and have been going for years. All the trials and tribulations have been met and conquered. A background of experience has been built up so that the newness of the adventure is only a local matter. It is merely a matter of adapting it to the local situation. Such activities as the student council are no longer experimental. The student council is only new in a local situation, and there is enough material on the student council that no school needs to make gross mistakes even in the initial steps of the program.

In all of these situations the staff and the administration assume responsibility, but that implies responsibility for using every opportunity available to utilize to the fullest the ideas, energies, and leadership in the student body so that the activities will be of the greatest value to the students themselves. If it is otherwise the activity fails of its function and consequently soon passes from the picture—and often the principal and teachers wonder why!

How extra-class activities get recognition. Extra-class activities really get recognition by doing something worth while. But it is not as simple as it sounds. In the first place, the teachers are the key persons to show either a willingness to do hard work in the initial stages or be so sympathetic to the interests and concerns of boys and girls that they make sure that no stumbling blocks or serious discouragements are encountered. This is where the young teacher makes a powerful contribution to youth activities. Boys and girls go to the young teacher and can be made to feel at ease as they talk about their problems. They have confidences which they share with the young teacher because there are no great age barriers. The young teacher has had recent experiences in similar problems. His sympathies and concerns are easily awakened. All of these factors give impetus to the activity and make it more effective for students themselves.

The problem involves doing something that interests boys and girls, and for which they find themselves able to carry most of the responsibility. In doing so they reconfirm that time-tested principle of learning by doing. Teachers who find it difficult to put this principle into practice in their classrooms often are able to utilize it in extra-class activities.

Those things that involve utilizing pupil initiative show up well. Parents know when their children are in activities. They are able to see the roles that they play. Local newspapers give ample space to activities which feature roles of pupils in the activity. Good examples, of course, are class plays, athletic contests, student council activities, discussion forums, and musical programs. But publicity is not restricted to these traditionally recognized activities. Any activity that features boys and girls doing things makes news that the local paper is glad to have. The school publications also find such items widely interesting to their readers. School columns in local newspapers are almost entirely devoted to what boys and girls are doing; this is another way of recognizing what activities are currently featured in the school. Bulletin boards carry clippings of the activities featured in newspapers, school paper, magazine, and school bulletins.

All of this points up the fact that when pupils do things it makes news. The school's best public relations come out of the publicity that pupils are doing things, are being responsible persons, are making noteworthy accomplishments. Parents develop confidence in the school, the pupils take pride in it, and the teachers reap rewards in the increased esteem that the community holds for them because they put boys and girls in positions where they could be important.

Teachers' attitudes toward the extra load. This problem is one of extreme concern for school boards and administrators. Three ways of handling the situation may be cited: The first and probably most common way is that of dividing all of the extra-class duties among the staff. The principal and faculty recognize that the activity program is essential, but there are not funds to employ more staff members and thus lighten the teaching load. So each teacher carries the work above and beyond his teaching load without extra remuneration. It is one of those things that thousands of teachers do because they feel the call of teaching and recognize the needs of boys and girls. This is so frequent because there are so many small schools where the needs of youth are great but the funds to take care of this need are limited, or the communities have not been sufficiently aroused to provide more funds. The teacher in such a community should accept the position realizing that he will be expected to share this responsibility, and should accept it cheerfully and willingly.

The second approach to the problem is that of recognizing that activities do represent a real part of the service that teachers render in a community, and the actual teaching load is lightened in proportion to the work that is devoted to activities. Thus if some teacher works with the school newspaper, directs the play, coaches an athletic team, or supervises intramural activities, the number of classes taught is reduced. This is a sound approach because it reflects an appraisal of the worth of all a teacher's effort at school and makes the extra-class work as worth while and important as all other work that the teacher does. It tends to remove the stigma of "extra" on some activities and puts all school work on an equal footing. Teachers should welcome this approach in thinking, and would do well to encourage their superior officials to consider this way of solving the problem.

The third approach is much like the first, only salary schedules are set up to recognize the work of activities as extras. Salary schedules are drawn up so that definite amounts are paid, presumably on the basis of the extra time spent and the extra responsibility that is assumed by the person who supervises the activity. For example, the social chairman may receive $50 per year extra, elementary track coach $75, tennis coach $100, senior high drama coach $100, debate coach $100, sponsor of yearbook $150, wrestling coach $200, sponsor of weekly publications $250, head football or basketball coach $800, and track coach $300. In some instances in addition to the extra remuneration the teaching load is lightened also. This indicates that recognition is given to the extra work that goes into activities, and is an effort to reward the teacher who carries the added burden. There are possibilities that morale among staff members may be disturbed because of the salary differential for various types of responsibility. However, a policy of allowing faculty members to share in these decisions would tend to minimize the ill feelings that could be generated.

The problem of extra-class activities is so significant and offers such gateways to the pupils' interests that the teacher can ill afford to be handicapped in his teaching efforts because he feels unappreciated in that he receives no extra remuneration or lightening of teaching load. Teachers have an abounding faith that their services do not carry a price tag but that the task of teaching is one of looking at the job as a whole. Seeing the *whole* child also involves *wholeness* in seeing the problem of teaching. It means giving totally of one's self to his professional task. Activities are a part of the total school assignment. Plenty of signs are on the horizon that those who are responsible for promotions, salaries, and any other recognitions notice the teacher who accepts the assignment in teaching and carries all of the tasks that make his work more fruitful.

Extra-class activities are coordinate with other teaching activities. It is difficult to differentiate between teaching in scheduled class activities and teaching in extra-class activities. Teaching takes place where teacher and pupil work together. However, the school is so organized that there are courses organized into curricula any one of which not only leads to completion of the school program but is basic to what comes later, either in college or in the pupil's occupational career. These curricula are set up without very much formal recognition being given to allied noncredit activities, but grant them great significance and influence in an evaluation of the pupil's total school record. This significance is important to the pupil, and the school that enriches the total experience of the pupil gives much more than the school with a limited extra-activity program. It is this enrichment in experience that the activity adds to the classroom situation.

Extra-class activities need not be appendant; an integrated whole is more meaningful. However, many schools are not organized to differentiate within the curriculum or deal with the program through some variation of the core program. Under a differentiated program there are certain courses that contain a much heavier enrichment of activities. For example, courses in English within a given grade in the large school can feature newswriting, creative writing, dramatics, and drama, and meet the English requirements as well as the traditional English class in American literature, world literature, or English literature. It would be strictly a matter of emphasis. Another school could combine courses and block the time into longer periods, and have a correlated program meeting the requirements of social studies and English or any other combination of courses that fit. Science and English work well as a correlated unit if the teachers see it that way.

There are many ways of looking at the core program, but it more nearly conforms to the thinking of the supporters of the core program if it stems from a problem that has interest for the learners. It should tap as many resources as are within the range of the learners' experiences. It may take the form of correlation, integration, or unification. The one requirement that seems important for our purposes here is that it should be pupil-teacher-planned and have its setting in a problem that is basic to the needs and interests of the pupils. Such an approach to teaching offers excellent opportunity to utilize the activity approach to learning, both curricular and extra-curricular. Here the terms curricular and extracurricular are used loosely to emphasize the total activity interest of boys and girls. Informal and formal learning situations are involved, and many ways of presenting material to and sharing with the group involves group activity that is well adapted to the needs of the pupils, the nature of the material, and the methods used.

Another situation involves a group of courses in an area such as business education. A commerce club draws pupils from all back-grounds, the only requirement being that the pupil has taken or is currently taking a course in business education. This same situation applies to clubs in mathematics, science, social studies, and others. The activity is not too closely related to the course, but the pupil derives his interest from the fact that the club activity is supported by pupils with similar background and concerns.

Still another activity has its origin in a class group simply because by assignment or by election the members happen to be in school together. The teacher, sensing the natural desire of boys and girls to share club activity, encourages these natural interests. An activity of this sort common in the elementary grades is a bird club or a book club. It may be quite temporary, and replaced by another that proves equally temporary. A group of pupils have a common interest, do things together, work in school together, enjoy sharing each others' company. It can be a study group, it can drift toward greater social emphasis. It does serve a natural urge and it springs from a school interest. A camera club, stamp club, or hobby group can spring from just such a situation. The teacher finds himself called upon to serve as an adult sponsor. He finds still another way to help boys and girls, and perhaps a way to spend one more session at not too infrequent intervals.

Thus we see numerous ways for the teacher to get involved in natural activity interests, whether those interests stem from the classroom, merge back into the classroom, or just grow like Topsy. Because the teacher has interests in boys and girls and *their* interests, he takes on the task of working and playing with them. It is an avenue that leads very close to the hearts of vigorous boys and girls.

Activities affect the pupil in various ways. The teacher is impressed constantly with the differences in pupils. Although the school classifies pupils into semihomogeneous groups, the teacher is always amazed at how *different* pupils are. He is likewise challenged constantly with the problem of reaching each pupil in the most effective way. Extra-class activities are another avenue to meet individual needs. The teacher, often hard pressed to find something that the child can do that will give him self-respect, status, and importance and add zest to his interest, finds ample opportunity in extra-class activities. Even the chance to count votes in a pupil "election" is a minor role, but at least means participation. Even the chance to vote is important. The young teacher will come to see that the faintest kind of participation is worth while because it is a start.

In extra-class activities pressure is lower because no mark or evaluation is involved. Restrictions are removed, the pupil is freed from the compulsion of doing well. Pupils themselves by their very natures tend to give importance to everything. This possibility of attaching importance to all efforts, or perhaps leveling all efforts to equal importance, is greatest in activities. The substitute on an intramural squad can convince his mother that he must be there to sit on the bench in case he is called upon to play a few minutes by his friend, the captain. Watch the sandlot ball game and see how important everyone feels, even the bat boy. This holds for almost all extra activities.

Another result affecting the boys and girls is that of civic responsibility. Participation and status lead directly into responsibility as a school and community citizen. Pupils need to attain, or at least attempt, all of the academic goals that the school requires of them. This is fundamental. But just as important is the opportunity to put into practice these basic learnings. Not being able to do so would be like passing six days of the week with no opportunity to put into practice the moral admonitions heard in church on Sunday. The situation is equally true in the economics class. Much might be *said* about factors that influence the selling price of stocks, but if there is a school bookstore, with capital stock owned by the pupils, the stockholders soon find out how the demand for stock is affected by the size of the dividends that were declared for the last dividend period. Such an activity can attract the attention of the entire student body and teach them the trials and problems of buying and selling stock and the relationship between dividends and reserves. There

are unlimited possibilities in such an activity. As school citizens they
soon come to see the relationship of service to the group and how
one's true worth in a society is tied up with services that he may
either donate or sell. Some services, he finds, he always gives, and
some have a price tag. This is only one example, but the chance to
put civic principles into practice is best found in extra-class activities where teacher and pupils have real experience in sharing.

In addition, there is another consideration that teachers quite
often overlook: What does the pupil really think about the teacher
as a person? We read a great deal about professional status and how
teachers need to keep themselves from being too informal with
their pupils, but the teacher who would do most for his pupils must
work with them in a sharing relationship, close to their joys, fears,
sorrows, and fun. Working with them adds an intangible quality that
makes him, in the language of the pupils, a real guy, a real pal, a
real friend. The teacher's contribution is stored in the memories of
boys and girls; here is where the teacher becomes really effective
for most boys and girls.

So the teacher seeks that way of adapting work to the pupil's
needs. It gives the pupil a chance to achieve status, meet his civic
responsibilities, and get confidentially close to the teacher. All of
these things are good for boys and girls.

When should an extra-class activity be dropped? Teachers may have so much confidence in the value of an activity that
they are loath to let it pass. A young teacher will be apprehensive
about letting something drop, because he feels that it could be interpreted as a reflection on his leadership or his effectiveness as a
teacher. This could of course be true, but it is a well known fact that
activities do ebb and flow and are quite dependent upon pupil leadership and interest. What thrives for several years as an activity of
great importance ceases to have its holding power because something else has more appeal. When strong personalities get into an
activity and the effect of that interest spreads among a student
body it thrives. Strong leadership arouses strong followers and more
strong leaders are created. This cycle may continue for several years.
Not to be overlooked, of course, is the element of strong faculty
sponsorship. The young teacher has the chance of letting his talents
show too, and it may be the new, young teacher in some other ac-

tivity that attracts pupils out of a dying activity and hastens its demise.

There is nothing wrong with this process. Many good activities serve their purpose with a particular group at a particular time and then give way to new activities, new personalities, and new ideas. The teacher should keep alert to adjustment and community change and growth. These changes are perfectly normal. If the teacher is not sensitive to changes that are going on all around him or becomes lethargic to the needs of the boys and girls themselves, he loses the spark of leadership or the power to harness leadership, and fails in his service. This alertness to need and adaptation to change is a challenge to the teacher who decides to sponsor an activity that is losing its vitality.

When should an activity be added? The problem of adding activities may grow out of the problem of dropping activities. Either problem may arise first. A school can only support a certain number of activities, and both pupils' and teachers' time is limited. Activities cannot be permitted to exist without adult leadership, nor can the school afford to risk sponsoring any activity without utilizing its very best leadership in each case. It is the responsibility of the school to see that this leadership is fitted to the activity that most nearly suits the talents and background of the leader. There is nothing gained in trying to set square pegs in round holes.

If the school is operating on peak activity load—that is, if all the teachers are carrying capacity activity load and all the pupils are in as many activities as seems reasonable—the situation is relatively simple. That being the case, nothing is added unless something is dropped.

The vigorous young teacher in his first position can very easily let his enthusiasm overcome his judgment. On being approached by a group of pupils who want to start a new club or activity, he may feel so honored and excited by the prospect that he forgets himself. In a situation of this kind his professional duty is the same as if he had gotten the idea himself. His first step is to talk his idea over with his principal, then, if given any encouragement, with his colleagues. The new activity may start another activity on its downfall; it is sure to draw leadership and personnel from other existing activities. If the way seems clear he still has the problem of determining the value of the activity.

Some of the criteria of value are found in the answers to these questions. Is there a real need that appears to indicate considerable permanency? Is there an existing activity that can readily meet this need? Is the demand supported by a relatively large cross section of the school society? Can it be absorbed by a scheduled class program and hence not require extra-class activity? Would it be in harmony with the ideals and customs of the community? Would it be within the reach of the majority of the pupils financially? Could membership be open to all who wish to enter? Would it be free of all restrictions of caste or class? Would it promote the strongest ideals of a democratic society? Would it contribute to the general welfare of the school, or at least rest in harmony with the generally accepted purposes of the school? If the activity meets the majority of these standards or a set of standards which the school may already have in existence, the teacher should feel relatively confident in starting the new activity.

Finally, the teacher does well to remain open-minded toward evaluation of any activity he is sponsoring. Periodic evaluation of all activities is healthful, and keeps pupils and sponsors on their toes to see that the activity is meeting its avowed purpose. Many activities started with high motives and excellent purposes can degenerate and stray from their original purposes. The sponsor and the pupils should realize that an evaluation is periodically made and that those who make the evaluation will expect high standards to be met. Evaluation of extra-class activities is regarded as a wholesome and profitable measure both for the school and the pupils served by the activities.

SUMMARY

Extra-class activities are a vital part in the school's effort to meet the needs of boys and girls. Any teacher may see this as a chance to enrich the lives of the pupils and give an opportunity for participation in worth-while experiences that otherwise might not be tapped. The teacher who is alert to differences in individuals and their interests sees immediately the great possibility of reaching all pupils through this widened point of view. The pupil who seems difficult to interest in regular school activities quite frequently is reached fully in some extra-class activity. The person who would do most as a teacher becomes vitally interested in one or more extra-class activities, and knows full well that he has enlarged his potential to be a good teacher to the extent that he becomes a skilled person in this enlarged area of work and interest.

Extra-class activities are both school supervised and sponsored. However, the widest value of pupil activities comes from those in which community resources are utilized as fully as possible in carrying out the objectives. The effective teacher will use his energy to help with some activities that are run quite largely by parent and adult community leadership, while he selects those activities where his own energies and talents are going to be used more generously. He cannot spread his energies so widely that his effectiveness is lost.

The teacher will keep in mind that many well meaning organizations tend in their enthusiasm to exploit the interests of young people. He must be ever alert to these possibilities, and seek the advice and counsel of his principal at all times to see that proper approval is given to the activity. He should be mindful of the fact that even his own enthusiasm can lead him beyond the realm of prudence. This necessitates a check on his own enthusiasm against the judgment of his colleagues, and especially with his supervisor or principal.

Extra-class activities are needed, but at the same time it becomes necessary to discontinue those that have no further value to pupils. All things are measured in terms of value to pupils. When the usefulness of an activity seems to have been spent, the teacher must be willing to discontinue the activity and give his support to some other activity that has more value. The teacher must be relied upon to keep the best interests of pupils in mind and be alert to ways in which he can be most effective as a teacher.

Some competences that must be acquired if the teacher is to be effective in the area of extra-class activities are:

1. The ability to appreciate all the elements that make up the total picture of a pupil's school growth, including all curricular experiences.

2. The ability to assume a leadership role in some of

the extra-class activities that the school supports, in order to meet the needs of its pupils more effectively.

3. The ability to appreciate the work of colleagues in the activities that they are sponsoring, to the end that there is full coordination among all the activities that the school maintains.

4. The ability to utilize the help of parents and lay people of the community in rallying support for activities that are most needed in the school.

5. The ability to help students and others who may be involved in extra-class activities to share in determining those that are most likely to succeed and prove valuable.

6. The ability to determine when the time is right to discontinue an activity that is no longer of service, or to start a new one that bids well to succeed.

7. The ability to appreciate the many problems that necessitate administrative consideration, and the necessity for referring such problems to those who must share responsibility before making commitments.

8. The ability to integrate many of the activities into the regular school program so that a minimum of extra-class activities will be necessary.

PROBLEMS

1. *Make a survey of three of the extra-class activities in your school, and attempt to determine the special purposes they purport to serve.*

2. *Select an activity that seems to be weak and determine the factors that tend to make it weak. Try to extend your thinking into ways of strengthening the activity. Take another approach and determine how you would satisfactorily discontinue it.*

3. *If a new extra-class activity is getting under way or has been newly organized in the school where you are working, follow the progress of the activity and determine to your own satisfaction whether the activity is serving a function that is helping to meet pupil needs. Extend your investigation somewhat further, to determine whether there is possible overlapping of function with an already established extra-class activity.*

4. *Determine your own strengths in at least two extra-class activities of differing purposes, and discuss with your supervisor your capabilities in each of the activities. After this has been done, through the help of your supervisor go to the principal, and with his approval go to the leader of one of the activities and volunteer your services. Then see what the results are.*

5. *If you happen to be teaching in an area to which an extra-class activity is attached, work as closely as possible with your supervisor in order that you may get first-hand experience. In this capacity analyze the problems that arise in carrying out the activity and give special attention to how the extra-class activity supplements and reinforces the class situation to which it is attached.*

6. *Analyze an activity named by your supervisor that has little or no connection with the school other than being school-approved. Determine how it adds to the program of development within the framework of the school's purposes.*

7. *Secure the most recent list of approved activities of the National Association of Secondary School Principals and, in addition to acquainting yourself with the list, determine whether all the activities in the school in which you are working are approved or are on the approved list.*

BIBLIOGRAPHY

Benerd, G., "How Can We Evaluate the Co-Curricular Program?" *National Association of Secondary School Principals Bulletin* 37: 61-62, November 1953.

Bowden, E. L., "Current Trends in Administration of Student Activities," *School Activities* 25:27-30, September 1953.

Fedder, Ruth, *Guiding Homeroom and Club Activities.* New York: McGraw-Hill Book Company, Inc., 1949.

Foster, M. R., "Social Organizations in the Elementary School," *School Activities* 25:27-28, October 1953.

Fretwell, Elbert K., *Extra Curricular Activities in Secondary Schools.* Boston: Houghton Mifflin Company, 1931.

Grubes, Frederick C., and Thomas Boyard Beatty, *Secondary School Activities.* New York: McGraw-Hill Book Company, Inc., 1954.

Hearn, A. C., and D. Reuwichn, "Some Basic Trends in School Activities," *School Activities* 26:147-48, January 1955.

Kelley, Janet A., *Guidance and Curriculum*. Englewood Cliffs, N.J.:
    Prentice-Hall, Inc., 1955.
McKown, Harry C., *Extra Curricular Activities*. New York: The Macmillan Company, 1952.
Moyer, J. H., "Pupil Participation in the Organization and Control of Co-
    Curricular Activities, Fact or Fancy," *National Association of
    Secondary School Principals Bulletin* 38:98-101, March 1954.
Steeves, F. L., "Student Teaching in Extra-Curricular Activities," *School
    Activities* 25:187-89, February 1954.

13

Responsibility for
self-discipline and control

The teacher's highest achievement in the development of a well organized learning environment will take on real meaning as pupils are helped to be responsible persons as they work and grow. The climate for learning will be good insofar as pupils operate as responsible school citizens. The ultimate, of course, is reached when citizenship of the positive type is practiced both in and out of school throughout the year. Such citizenship doesn't just happen. The best answer to delinquency is a united effort on the part of school, home, and community working toward the fulfillment of the goal where all boys and girls are helped to be self-directing and purposeful individuals. The school must take the lead in uniting these social forces.

Setting the stage for good learning through the physical environment. Ideal conditions for learning depend largely upon the attitude of the learner, environmental conditions conducive to learning, and the skill of the teacher in setting the stage for learning, which includes teaching skill itself. Inasmuch as this chapter deals directly with developing responsibility, the problem of teacher-pupil responsibility for conditions favorable to learning will be considered first. This will involve classroom management, taking care of housekeeping details, and organizing materials for teaching. Pupils will gain much from assuming a heavy share in this problem and will be strengthened in their attitude toward school by this participation.

First, how do you feel toward housekeeping? Is it a chore that is pleasant and do you look upon it as important work? Do you have a sense of well being when the place where you work is tidy? Have those around you complained about your housekeeping? Have you been accused by your parents or your peers of trying to get out of housekeeping details, or has housekeeping been a source of pleasure to you? Do you often say, "Come on, let's get things cleaned up"? These are good questions that the teacher must ask himself early in his experience in the classroom. A woman usually isn't as bothered by this problem as a man. However, the woman teacher usually is working with that age level where more materials are on the floor and more things are to be got out and put away. A man can and should be just as meticulous and have just as high standards for good housekeeping as a woman teacher. But the real center of the problem rests with one's ability to get all the pupils to participate happily and cooperatively in sharing the job of keeping the work space usable and at the same time orderly. This problem is present whether the teacher be man or woman, and the details are dependent on the type of work, the kind of laboratory, or the age and interest of the pupils.

Much of the detail of providing a good work space can be routine. There should be a place to put things out of the way, and everyone in the room should know where things go. It isn't the teacher's work to put things away, nor is it a pupil's job; it is everyone's job. When things have been used, if they are put in their place anyone will know where to find them. This is time and nerve saving, and it is also good education. The teacher may need to be patient but firm, and insist that the practice be followed. It does not need to be his rule. Pupils can be led to participate in plans that are for the common good. Many pupils come from well ordered homes where all help to keep things back in their place. This should not in any way be read to mean that the pressure to have things in their place must be so great that they aren't used. It really can mean they will be used more, for they can be found and they will be kept in good condition. Pupils will like it, the teacher will like it, all can be happy in the situation.

Some of the difficulty of having a good working environment stems from the problems in heating, lighting, and ventilation. There is a condition in which optimum work can be done. If the temperature is about 70° and the relative humidity is about 50 per cent, the room will be in almost as good condition as possible. Most teachers will know the thermometer reading, but few will know about the humidity unless it gets so extreme that it causes one to feel it. The administration of the school will try to be responsible for such matters and the wise teacher will depend on his principal to see that these conditions are satisfactory for good work.

The modern schoolroom is well provided with proper temperature, and modern lighting is answering the need for effectively lighted classrooms. Ventilation is made satisfactory by forced air; if the system is not modern, window boards are used to prevent direct drafts. The good teacher will come to know the general problems of his room heating and ventilation so that he will not tamper with mechanical features such as thermostats and thus disturb conditions in his own room as well as other rooms on the same system. The custodian or principal will be able to direct him wisely about these features.

The teacher who finds himself in a classroom that is not modern may have to resort to the same practices that the good teacher used a generation ago. Such devices as an open pan of water where it will evaporate most rapidly, opening windows at the top, adjusting shades to prevent glare, locating pupils who are doing close, detailed work in the spots where light is most favorable, and closing or opening hot air ducts or radiators when the temperature varies from 70° are matters that need attention now the same as they did when our forefathers were in school. The teacher today can be more alert to the problems and careful to permit or encourage pupils to share in these details. The understanding can be fully worked out that the pupil has freedom to move where light is most favorable or let his discomfort be known when he is uncomfortably hot or cold. Any of these conditions in extreme create disciplinary situations that can easily be avoided.

The lighting in the classroom will be good if the building is modern and if lighting engineers recommended the lighting that has been installed. Otherwise the room lighting may be inadequate. Not only are lights poor in many classrooms, but the walls, floors, and equipment are not of a color that makes the most of what is available. Standards for lighting have been set up, but it takes different degrees of brightness for different types of work. Here again the teacher should be aware of the lighting conditions and discuss poor conditions with those in a position to improve them. Many conditions are beyond his control. He can be careful of his own position in the classroom, and that of his pupils, so that they are not forced to look toward intense glare. His chief responsibility lies in making the best of his conditions and utilizing what good features are at his disposal. Wall colors and location of equipment can do much to overcome conditions that otherwise are not good. Those in position to remedy conditions will want to do so if conditions and suggestions are brought to their attention. The alert teacher will be ready with these suggestions.

Making the room a cheerful place to work. Fortunately the majority of teachers have a room that is considered their headquarters for teaching. Departmentalization and crowded conditions force use of rooms by more than one teacher on many occasions. But administrators recognize that there is much to be gained by assigning teachers to rooms and permitting them to get the feeling of belonging. It is good for the teacher, and it is good for the children to develop the feeling of unity in a certain room with a particular teacher. Some administrators avoid leaving a teacher in a room so long that he seems to feel ownership for the room. The teacher can help in such cases by avoiding the appearance of possessiveness. The teacher will be more likely to take a vigorous interest in bringing things into the room and fixing it up if he does have a feeling of permanency. What harm can come if the room is made attractive through the efforts of the teacher by many items that the teacher owns but probably could not acquire for his class through public money? Teachers are collectors of teaching materials, pictures, and auxiliary items that make rooms more attractive and teaching more effective. The teacher should possess the feeling that it is his responsibility to make the room in which he teaches as attractive as possible through every means at his command. This will include what he owns and what he can suggest to his administrative officer to purchase from appropriated funds. All good administrators want teachers to have more ideas than they can use where purchases are involved and the teacher cannot afford to be disappointed if he doesn't get all for which he asked. However, a good teacher is always on the lookout for new materials and new ways of using what he already has on hand.

Some teachers have the particular ability to make a room attractive through the use of plants, pictures, children's work, posters, vases, appropriate books, and interesting objects. The teacher is particularly alert when he puts on bulletin boards, window ledges, or shelves things that pupils have contributed. Enthusiastic appreciation for things brought in serves as encouragement to others. Posted materials and work of pupils serve as standards for good work. How happy is the teacher if some pupil has done something worthy of putting up for all to see and the parent drops by! The object can serve as the basis for a parent-teacher discussion and may send the parent on her way happy that she put forth the effort to pay a visit.

Library corners, special interest areas, bulletin boards, and just plain "doodads" can all be skillfully arranged to make the room a place where pupils like to be. Shelves, ledges, hanging vases, and flower pots can help make a room attractive and add to a teacher's general effectiveness. The use of all available items is a skill that the teacher has to acquire. But fortunate indeed is the teacher who uses the skill of his pupils as well in setting the room arrangement. Many pupils excel the teacher in such matters and if the pupils have had a share in this responsibility it not only adds to their contribution to learning, but makes them true partners in the whole adventure of doing things together.

Teachers, administrators, custodians, and building superintendents can make a team for keeping the educational plant attractive and in good condition. Many teachers like some colors and dislike others greatly. Modern decorating of classrooms has indicated a general understanding of the value of using colors that are attractive to children. Many administrators have found that it is highly practical and good judgment to secure the opinion of teachers and pupils regarding colors with the necessary appeal. It is another way of developing teamwork and is productive of good outcomes and results. Even rose or pink walls in classrooms are appealing to some teachers, and almost all pupils would approve of colors that add zest and vitality. So if you have ideas or a chance to express opinions be ready and eager to give them. It is your opportunity and your challenge to make a worth-while contribution. Do not be afraid to go on an adventure in this area. The time of school gray and classroom ivory has passed. Blues, pinks, greens, aquas, and even lavenders are pleasing and make classrooms desirably homelike.

Total physical environment involving heating, lighting, decoration, and orderliness has direct bearing on the way pupils work with each other and the attitudes they take toward the teacher and the school. Much could be said about the general opinion of parents toward school. Pride in a new building or pride in keeping an older building in top condition affects the way the members of a total community feel toward the school and education itself. Cooperation and wholesome relations stem from working together for observable effects. The teacher can work for these things and give credit to those about him for his accomplishments. Everyone can feel happy about it. The whole area of developing responsible pupils has its setting in this kind of environment.

Noise as a factor in the classroom. The teacher is likely to discover that noise does not seem to bother children as much as it does him. Consequently noise may not be too disturbing unless the children themselves object. It is worth the effort to work for standards of quietness established by general discussions with the group. Many ideas can be provided by the pupils themselves regarding what is legitimate noise and what is a disturbing racket. If children can be helped to study their own reaction to disturbance it will help to establish awareness of the individual's responsibility for the group, and at the same time help in the over-all attitude toward disturbances. If standards have been approved, and distractions identified, the group is in a good position to keep work conditions favorable for those who find it hard to work with noise. When group approval has been established the deviate is brought back in line by his own peers. Some children are disturbed more easily than others. It is a child's right to have conditions favorable and it is well for all children to recognize the right of a minority to have conditions favorable for good work.

But noise, like material removed from shelves and bookcases, is often a good sign of activity. The teacher and children, for that matter, must recognize noise that is good as well as bothersome and unnecessary noise. Busy children with minds on their work and high interest can create much noise, and if the sound comes from honest work where progress is being advanced, it is not distracting. Pupils recognize that talking across the room about something of concern to only a minority is impolite. Likewise, children recognize that something of concern to the total group merits the attention of all pupils. When such is the case all will want to listen. Children are intelligent, courteous, and concerned about the welfare of their peers. The teacher needs to recognize this fact and use it to good advantage.

The teacher who is constantly calling for silence becomes quite frustrated and irritable simply because he is unable to gain the condition he seeks. He could secure it if he became drastic enough, but drastic measures are undesirable. Teachers of a generation or so ago attained their goal by bringing a bundle of switches in on the first day of the school year and standing them in the corner of the room. Not much more needed saying, unless a general demonstration from time to time of the use of the switches became necessary in his judgment. Control through fear or autocratic measures has been discontinued, except in places where the teacher or the community or both do not use intelligence and ingenuity to solve problems of control with the learners themselves.

Some teachers of course are more disturbed by noise than others. It is hardly wise for the teacher to be the judge of what is too much noise, although the teacher's point of view and feelings must certainly be respected. On the other hand, the teacher will do well to be a student of this problem and of himself and observe the actions of his group, and if good work can be done under conditions that severely try his patience it should be a reminder to him that perhaps he is oversensitive. Under such conditions his time can be spent better than by fighting noise that bothers only him. In any case, the teacher should bear in mind the standards of quiet of the principal or supervisor with whom he works. The teacher may insist that all is well and still lose his position if the principal believes that what is going on is detrimental to learning or the best interest of children. This factor cannot be overlooked, and must be thought through by all persons who share in the responsibility for learning. If there are differences of opinion they can be talked out and agreements, adjustments, and understandings reached.

The positive approach to classroom management and control. Control will be of two general types: (1) the teacher on his own authority sets the pattern for the general behavioral conduct of children or, (2) the teacher through his knowledge of the effectiveness and long-range desirability of self-direction leads the pupils to set up goals for themselves of patterns of conduct and behavior that will give them stability, insight, and courage to follow the socially acceptable ways of living. In the first the teacher calls the strikes, and in the second the pupils effectively share in all the activity that makes up living together in a classroom. Both may be positive in a way, but the first will be charged with so much negativism that much of its effect will be neutralized.

A young student teacher was heard to complain that when his supervisor was in charge everything was in good order, but if the supervisor left the room the roof fell in. Here it was obvious that the control resided firmly in the supervisor and his presence was necessary to have things going on in an orderly and meaningful fashion. When the leader left, no one was in control and no one practiced self-control, so the result was bedlam. Has this ever happened to you? Of course it has. All of us have been in places where no leadership was recognized or where no one present felt any sense of responsibility.

The classroom is a place where many kinds of learning take place. Neither the parents nor the children nor even the teacher desire that all of it be academic. The social and civic behavior of learners is basic to all other learning. Citizenship is fundamental wherever one goes, and involves relationships, responsibility, concern for others, and civic thoughtfulness. It goes with the pupil as a social being, throughout his entire life. His ultimate goal is membership in a society of his choosing, and this goal is present in his classroom.

Do we obey laws because of fear or because an urge within us impels us to do so? If it is from fear, when the cause of fear is absent we run through stop-lights. We become hit-and-run drivers. Only the policeman keeps us orderly if this is the way we think and act. On the other hand if the urge for civic responsibility is within us, we need no one to force us to do the things that reason and wisdom would dictate. We do those things that are best because we want to do them. If we practice letting our wiser selves rule us, we need no help from without. The strong teacher gives pupils the opportunity to make decisions, practice self-motivation, and enjoy authority to guide themselves. Help and advice? Of course that is his responsibility. But the responsibility for one's action must be to one's self. When we realize that, we judge, evaluate, reject, and accept. We do all those things that the worth-while and active citizen is compelled by his inner self to do. We become mature and dependable by sharing in decision making.

A positive approach really means looking for favorable, constructive conduct and commending pupils for it, and on most occasions ignoring conduct that is not acceptable or commendable. This is very difficult for the adult unless he practices great restraint. Adults feel responsible for the behavior of juveniles and usually want to step in and put a stop to the things to which they object. Each generation in general is fearful of the final moral and social outcome of the generations that are following. The foolish things we did as we grew up stalk our memories and remind us, when we permit them, that we too were a lost race in the minds of our elders. You are a youth one year and a teacher the next. When you become a teacher, if you don't practice many self-restraints and use your best judgment, you are likely to see situations in such a vastly different light that you feel compelled to put a stop to things and fast. Then is when you start saying "don't" and "stop." Merely telling a child not to do something does not mean that conduct will be altered; it may even mean that the child will be more likely to do what the teacher prefers him not to do. On the other hand, if you fail to take a more reflective point of view and join in behavior that is acceptable for adolescents but questionable for teachers, then you are likely to be more severely criticized than you really deserve. It is healthful to be appreciative of the antics of pupils, but one cannot afford as a teacher to be one of the clowns.

Again, the positive approach to altering questionable conduct means rational analysis with the pupil to make him see the situation from a constructive point of view. In this way his actions will be altered not because the teacher or someone else has demanded that he change but because he sees that, in the light of possible consequences to his present behavior, he will not only add to the discomfort and dissatisfaction of others but to his own as well. Pupils usually elect to act for the good of the total group when they stop to contemplate. Many offenses of children are thoughtless little things that are disturbing but should be ignored because there is no wrong intended. The teacher's reaction under such circumstances should never be more than a fleeting look or a halt in proceedings to indicate disapproval, but without punishment or even unpleasantness.

A practice that should be carefully avoided is that of directing the pupils' attention to bad behavior by scolding the offender in their presence. To call out to a pupil who may be doing something unacceptable simply brings to the attention of all the offense that is being committed. This has two bad features: first, making an example of poor behavior, and second, soliciting the sympathy of members of the group who may disagree with the teacher's point of view. Either is detrimental to the total welfare as well as to the individual. We hold up good things for all to see, and maintain pupils' respect through a pattern of justice and fair play; we emphasize, point out and commend all things that are wholly acceptable and avoid as long as possible any reference to what is not good. We all fail to do this at times, but it is a good principle to observe.

Kinds of misbehavior that disturb teachers and pupils. This problem is a rather difficult one, but perhaps each of us needs to take a thought about what bothers other people and then take a searching look at ourselves to see if we know what bothers us. Do the same things bother us each day, or are we bothered by the way we feel? The story is told of the widow with ten children who, when she found one being so troublesome that neither she nor any of the nine could get along with him, gave him a big dose of castor oil. But when all of the children were worrying her and she seemed not to be able to get along with any of them—she took the castor oil herself! Now that is an excellent story for any teacher to remember. There will be many days when it is not the children who need treatment but the teacher himself. When everything is wrong it doubtless will be someone other than the pupils.

There is little need to list here all the things that bother teachers.

Many quite complete lists can be found. Furthermore, you will find out soon enough what bothers you most. It would be interesting and valuable for each teacher to make a list of the things that really annoy him, and then check off those that, on careful thought, are really quite superficial and inconsequential. The smaller the list the more satisfied one should be with himself, and the greater his ability to avoid being too fussy about the natural antics of growing boys and girls. On the other hand, many things pupils do that disturb others the school could prevent by more attention to such factors as lighting, heating, overcrowding, curriculum, and such physical needs of children as rest periods and lunch hours.

The problems that confront a teacher have been put in five classifications by Burton, as follows:

1. Incidents due to surplus energy.
2. Incidents due to physical discomfort.
3. Incidents due to poor curriculum and methods, poor classroom management.
4. Incidents due to simple, uncomplicated desire to be noticed, to attract attention.
5. Incidents which may be due to subtle and hidden causes.[1]

Under these headings rather detailed, down-to-earth illustrations of types of problems are given. These are interesting and helpful and are worth scanning.

Each group of pupils and their teacher should list the kinds of conduct that are generally agreed to be unfavorable for best work, because there are wide differences from one group to another. What really matters is behavior that is so disturbing as to prevent someone from accomplishing what he is supposed to do. Excellent opportunities for tolerance appear when we are in situations that involve sharing or being sympathetic toward the other person's sensitivity. What disturbs one person may not disturb another. But if what one person does bothers another the situation needs study. No one person should practice selfishness to the extent of causing others discomfort or waste of time. Pupils can be guided to see that they have responsibility toward everyone, even the one who has difficulties in concentration with only minor disturbances going on.

[1] William H. Burton, *The Guidance of Learning Activities*, 2nd ed. (New York: Appleton-Century-Crofts, Inc., 1952), pp. 713-15.

Certainly the kind of conduct that needs the teacher's attention is represented by those incidents Burton and others attribute to "subtle and hidden causes." Those symptoms of deep-seated troubles that affect personality and attitude may have consequences that are of great importance to both the individual and the society in which he lives. Most good teachers today would not even list gum chewing, writing notes, throwing chalk, giggling, walking about, teasing, and a host of such minor incidents that are inconsequential except at the moment. Even fighting, though annoying at the time, is really just one poor way of settling conflicts and can be used by the wise teacher as a springboard for good lessons. Many a bright teacher also sees incidents in fighting only from the corner of his eye. Children's tempers are not as stable as adults', and fisticuffs usually are followed by a renewal of friendship. Too much concern about a passing incident is just wasted time. So it is with many other adolescent pranks that should be taken in stride. Even language that isn't acceptable is often an attempt on the part of a youthful aspirant trying to appear grown-up. Simply ignoring many incidents that "try teachers' souls" is a pattern that the inexperienced teacher can well afford to follow.

Young teachers are probably aware of the many weaknesses that prevent adults from dealing patiently with youth. Teachers have brought a great deal of ridicule upon themselves by the unrealistic attitude they take on the immorality they read into normal behavior of vigorous, growing boys and girls. Many adults never learn that a suggestive note, more often than not never delivered, is merely a compensating type of sex outlet for both boys and girls. The adult who goes prowling about searching for these adolescent incidents will likely do nothing more than cause the pupils to become more secretive and evasive. It is a truism that one usually finds what he is looking for, especially when it comes to observing youth. This type of characteristic is mentioned because it represents very well the attitude of the adult when his sense of morality is being disturbed. Fortunately more emphasis is being placed on mental hygiene today and a much more generous attitude toward child behavior and causes of deviant behavior is being taken. It is difficult to determine the cause of teacher concern over pupil behavior, in that one does not know whether the behavior really was actually as reported by the teacher or whether the teacher's background or attitude caused him to react to what he thought he saw. His punitive measures against pupil behavior will be tempered accordingly.

Wickman's study of a quarter century ago, reviewed but recently, still stands as one of the really good studies on children's behavior and teacher attitudes.[2] As he points out, behavior that disturbs teachers most is that which violates the teacher's principles of morality, his authority, order in the classroom, or his standards for study, or that makes it difficult to work with other children in the group. This study becomes impractical for use today only to the extent that the impact of better methods for preparing teachers has been put into practice in the last decade or so.

Dr. George A. W. Stouffer, Jr., made a study in 1952 following Wickman's pattern.[3] In Dr. Stouffer's study there is rather conclusive evidence that teachers still place emphasis on the annoying, disobedient, disorderly, irresponsible, and untruthful child, but are now more concerned with behavior that indicates social and emotional maladjustment. Mental hygienists recognized this problem as the more serious one 25 years ago.

However, it is pointed out that the teacher is the one upon whom society places the responsibility for educating the child. The teacher knows and feels this, and any behavior that tends to diminish his teaching progress is disturbing to him. It is pointed out that in reality these social pressures work to the detriment rather than to the total welfare of the child.

If we consider Dr. Stouffer's results as conclusive enough to indicate a change in teacher attitude, they provide a hopeful sign. They indicate that teachers are being led by their reading and by the teacher education programs to see that behavior problems indicating shyness, sensitivity, unsociability, and other recessive traits are more serious than those that have traditionally disturbed the teacher. The helpfulness of mental hygienists in leading the way to sane attitudes toward pupil behavior is most encouraging.

The Wickman and Stouffer studies are both highly revealing and contain such vital material for our thinking that Table 3 of Dr. Stouffer's report is given below.

[2] E. K. Wickman, *Children's Behavior and Teachers' Attitudes* (New York: The Commonwealth Fund, 1928).

[3] George A. W. Stouffer, Jr., "Behavior Problems of Children as Viewed by Teachers and Mental Hygienists," *Mental Hygiene* 36:271-85, April 1952.

A COMPARISON OF THE RANK-ORDER ARRANGEMENT OF 50 BEHAVIOR
PROBLEMS OF CHILDREN AS RATED BY 481 OF TODAY'S TEACHERS
(FORM A) AND 511 TEACHERS IN E. K. WICKMAN'S STUDY

Wickman's Study (1928)	Stouffer's Study (1952)
1. Heterosexual activity	Stealing
2. Stealing	Cruelty, bullying
3. Masturbation	Heterosexual activity
4. Obscene notes, talk	Truancy
5. Untruthfulness	Unhappy, depressed
6. Truancy	Impertinence, defiance
7. Impertinence, defiance	Destroying school material
8. Cruelty, bullying	Unreliableness
9. Cheating	Untruthfulness
10. Destroying school property	Disobedience
11. Disobedience	Resentfulness
12. Unreliableness	Temper tantrums
13. Temper tantrums	Unsocial, withdrawing
14. Lack of interest in work	Obscene notes, talk
15. Profanity	Nervousness
16. Impudence, rudeness	Cheating
17. Laziness	Selfishness
18. Smoking	Quarrelsomeness
19. Enuresis	Domineering
20. Nervousness	Lack of interest in work
21. Disorderliness in class	Impudence, rudeness
22. Unhappy, depressed	Easily discouraged
23. Easily discouraged	Suggestible
24. Selfishness	Fearfulness
25. Carelessness in work	Enuresis
26. Inattention	Masturbation
27. Quarrelsomeness	Laziness
28. Suggestible	Inattention
29. Resentfulness	Disorderliness in class
30. Tardiness	Sullenness
31. Physical coward	Physical coward
32. Stubbornness	Overcritical of others
33. Domineering	Sensitiveness
34. Slovenly in personal appearance	Carelessness in work
35. Sullenness	Shyness
36. Fearfulness	Suspiciousness
37. Suspiciousness	Smoking
38. Thoughtlessness	Stubbornness
39. Attracting attention	Dreaminess
40. Unsocial, withdrawing	Profanity
41. Dreaminess	Attracting attention
42. Imaginative lying	Slovenly in personal appearance
43. Interrupting	Restlessness
44. Inquisitiveness	Tardiness
45. Overcritical of others	Thoughtlessness
46. Tattling	Tattling

47. Whispering   Inquisitiveness
48. Sensitiveness   Interrupting
49. Restlessness   Imaginative lying
50. Shyness   Whispering

The young teacher is quite concerned about his status or his authority being challenged. In a way this is what one would expect, but the teacher should realize that this is important largely only to him at the present, and he will do well to discard such trivia. Some of the things children do and say that loom so large at the moment should be ignored if at all possible. The child who says, "I don't like you," or "You're not as good a teacher as Miss Sunshine," or "I don't have to do what you ask me to do," might tell any other person the same things under similar circumstances. The adult who is told by a child, "I don't like you," should reply, "Well, I do like you." But vindictive behavior in such circumstances is too often the practice.

The young teacher needs to recognize that the pupil quite often feels much the same toward him as toward his peers. The language that the child uses will be quite as frank and bold to the teacher as toward another child. In fact, the teacher finds it quite difficult to be Mr. Bright in the classroom and just plain "Jim" everywhere else. The pupils get a real lift out of being "palsy-walsy" with him and have truly, almost without exception, a feeling of kind affection and respect in their hearts for this young person. Yet the things they do and say disturb the peace of mind and feeling of importance that the young teacher is so anxious to establish.

Another problem that faces the young teacher is much akin to the feeling that mothers have when company comes. The calmness and sereneness of mother can be quite shaken when company is around. Her children's behavior is not nearly so acceptable when company is present. So it is with the young teacher when someone comes to visit; he becomes apprehensive about child conduct that he was approving cheerfully before the arrival of the visitor. We often hear teachers say that children acted up so badly when company was around. We have no good way of determining whether the conduct really changed, or the teacher's anxiety increased because of the visitor's presence. It is a real problem for the young teacher either to realize that the visitor is not coming to be critical or to develop confidence and poise in the presence of everyone. At any rate, the pupils will fare far better if he can maintain his balance and sustain his faith in his pupils to help. If pupils are not at their best it is probably because they recognize that the teacher is not at his best either. However, this is one of the very difficult problems that many teachers never really overcome.

Conduct that hinders study is a more serious problem to the young teacher. However, moving about in the room, whispering or talking in subdued tones, pinching or tickling, passing notes, and similar types of conduct are really quite inconsequential except in situations where extreme quiet is demanded. An examination period, for example, rules out almost any type of disturbance if each pupil is to do his best. The pupils themselves, by the very nature of the situation, will cooperate, especially if discussions involving both teachers and pupils have lead to understandings and agreements. Agreements that are self-imposed are to be desired. The young teacher should recognize early the kind of activity that is really attributable to energy and bright spirits, and realize that it is a "bubbling over" type of game shared by everyone. His tolerance will increase *esprit de corps* and develop pupil appreciation for his attitude. A kindly understanding is back of the remark when pupils say about their teacher, "He's a good sport," or "She's our friend." The squelcher makes it hard in the long run for himself.

Let us turn to the more serious type of conduct that may do real harm to another pupil's personality. Pupils can ridicule the efforts of an already timid, shy child and make it next to impossible to get any valuable responses from him. The bitter, sullen, sensitive, or shy child becomes more so under the pressure of adverse behavior. His unhappiness becomes more pronounced and it becomes more difficult to secure a favorable response even under the best conditions. Some class groups drop into the practice of giggling at answers or remarks by their peers, which cuts down greatly on the normal, informal flow of discussion so desirable for successful group work. It can become so bad that only the most bold or those most sure of themselves dare to open their mouths to make a statement or to answer a question.

Another kind of pupil conduct, closely related to the one just mentioned but more sutble, is the kind that the pupil brings to the classroom with him and restricts very largely to himself. It is the secretive, shy, frightened reaction to the school environment, which has its setting in deep-seated feelings so hard to overcome and to deal with in a constructive, developmental manner that they pose serious problems to the discerning and conscientious teacher. Symptoms are observable, but causes are elusive and difficult to discover. In many instances the things that concern the teacher are characteristics involving the entire family pattern. Parents themselves are not even aware of the problem and have no sympathy with an outsider who would change it. This type of pupil is the one who refuses to be drawn out, says nothing, is quiet and retiring, and often is so unobtrusive as to be liked by the unsuspecting teacher who likes children who don't bother him by extroverted conduct.

The problems of dishonesty—taking things that belong to some one else, cheating, and untruthfulness—bother many teachers and a great number of pupils within a group. In some instances the pupils themselves are in the process of building standards in these areas. The problem of respect for ownership is in formative stages, and the borderline between borrowing and taking things is not too well established. Also the distinction between serious untruths and fanciful imagination is not clear in the minds of young pupils. Again, the problem of what is wrong with giving and receiving help gets all tangled up with teacher pressure on grades and praise given for good marks. All of these things create a confusing state of values for the immature mind, and the young teacher who has not met all the problems created by such situations has difficulty in knowing just how he should feel toward an offender and how he should deal with him.

The problem of "tattling" and how to react when a pupil reports deviant behavior becomes a problem. The young teacher has a set of values on loyalty to one's friends that involves protecting the offender. The obligations and moral codes involving one's peers, especially from the young teacher's point of view, are quite similar to those of his pupils.

All of these problems are difficult indeed for even the mature, experienced teacher. What the teacher really hopes will come from the many situations where the pupils are involved are standards of conduct and personal values of the pupils' own making that will evolve and serve them in times of temptation when opportunities for theft, cheating, dishonesty, and untruthfulness present themselves. These are great challenges to the child who is setting his own behavior patterns in situations involving frequent temptations.

One other problem that the teacher dares not ignore involves situations where physical pain and injury are inflicted upon other pupils by a few of the more energetic, rough-and-tumble persons or the bully who inflicts both fear and injury upon the others in his group. Parents get even more alarmed when their children suffer physical pain than when mental pain is inflicted. The teacher cannot afford the appearance of condoning such conduct; he maintains his status in the community only by taking a fair, concerned, and positive position on matters of this kind. He is an impartial, honest person in whom reside both kindness and firmness, from whom the weak receive courage and those in the wrong receive justice.

The parent must rely on the teacher to protect the child, and the confidence and faith that the child builds up toward the teacher give him springboards for helping the child in matters of social and civic adjustment. The teacher also needs to find ways to demonstrate kindness and consideration. No other opportunity is so observable and so readily felt as when the child suffers pain, either physical, mental, or emotional. Mothers demonstrate how effectively therapeutic a pat or a kiss may be. Even the stray dog in the street responds to a pat on the head and offers his affection in return. Thus we are impressed with the importance of the teacher in all situations where trouble and inadequacies abound and some pupils need encouragement and others need restrictions. The teacher is sought after to settle disputes and administer punishment that will leave the weak stronger and the strong more compassionate.

Some guiding principles that seem developmentally sound. What shall I do? This is the big question of the teacher. It is even more loudly sounded by the young teacher. To answer in a sentence would be like prescribing a patent medicine for any disease under the sun. However, it can be answered with some feeling of assurance by pointing out alternatives and warning against things that are universally undesirable. It is also possible to direct the young person toward practices that have considerable merit and advise against thoughtless methods that may have rather serious consequences. Each person needs to tailor his ways of dealing with problems to fit his own temperament and personality. Also each person ought to be thoroughly sold on the idea that the ultimate goal in discipline is self-control. Control from outside is only valuable until the one who cannot take care of himself is ready to take command. Jails are full of those who have never been able to make this second step consistently or successfully.

Some underlying principles are worthy of consideration before anything is done relating offense and punishment or punishment and the individual child.

1. *Punishment should be constructive in nature.* It is very easy to retaliate in kind. "You hit me, I strike back." "Eye for eye and tooth for tooth" prescriptions are quite common to our behavior. Children are taught by parents to accept the idea. Many a father feels happy about teaching his child to take care of himself. Translated into action it means, "You hurt me, I return the hurt with interest." This idea is so completely accepted by so many people that it is retained from one generation to another and becomes another way of expressing fairness. Parents accept and even condone it; nevertheless it is to be avoided. A teacher should scrutinize his own motives to make sure that he is rising above this thoughtless tendency on the part of adults to trample feelings of children just to prove "who is running things." This is usually done in the spirit of vindictiveness, but who really wants to be vindictive in dealing with children? Put this way it is pretty ugly. Teachers should avoid it always. The child will feel better after a situation has been settled with kindness and consideration. Better ways for doing things can then be pointed out and agreed upon.

2. *Avoid emotion or anger in dealing with children's problems.* Anger is a sign of weakness that children detect and fear. Some teachers use anger as a means of control; "Try to keep me in a good humor" seems to be the pattern. The teacher should not expect pupils to be stronger and more patient than himself. If anyone is to be an example of faith, patience, and endurance it is the teacher. Anger causes people to do things for which they are ashamed after tempers cool off. The angry person shakes his victims, he strikes them, he cries, he says unkind things, and worst of all he thinks at the moment he doesn't care. If the teacher is to do justice and work skillfully with children, he will avoid anger with all the strength he possesses. The more tense a situation becomes the more need there is for calmness on the part of the teacher.

3. *Be deliberate, searching, and slow to act.* The teacher who works carefully in his relationships with pupils will first of all avoid punishing so quickly that he hurts the innocent. If the wheels of justice run deliberately, mistakes will be few. There is something to be said for punishment closely following the offense, but this smacks of retaliation and the idea of retaliation is not good. We make much of the child's learning that the stove is hot by getting burned, and this follows closely enough to suit even the most exacting. Few would prescribe haste to the exclusion of reason or discussion. It is imperative that reasoning, talking things through, understanding why, all become part of the process in dealing with children's problems. These all take time and patience.

4. *Talk with a kind, soft, understanding voice.* Children often are emotionally disturbed when in difficulty with those who represent authority. Unfortunately the problem is complicated by the same type of parental threat about teachers that is commonly made about policemen. Many a parent controls his children by suggesting that the teacher will not like the pupil or the principal of the school will punish him. This is of course sheer nonsense, but goes on in homes that are considered good. The teacher gets a more cooperative response and is in a better position to deal effectively with a situation when he appears calm, unperturbed, and casual, with a kind voice that draws children to him. Yell at a child and he yells back. Many an adult punishes a child for impoliteness when in reality the adult was impolite in the beginning. How often a pupil gets into trouble because he yells back! A good soft voice can be cultivated and as children's voices get higher the teacher will be wise indeed who knows what a soft voice does for a stormy one. Teaching means developing pleasing temperaments in children, too. In this situation teaching by example is the best plan.

5. *Keep the situation within your own control.* Many a young teacher wants to hand his most difficult problems to someone else. The principal's office or a chair in the principal's office is a favorite place to send the boy who is troublesome. It is comforting to have the feeling that there is someone to whom to turn if situations get rugged, but the wise teacher will get his moral support from this feeling without asking for help. The teacher needs to utilize every situation that arises to strengthen his relationship with the learner.

Confidences are built up and faiths are established by the teacher-pupil relationships necessary to solve difficult problems. The teacher who sends his problem to the principal's office admits his own inadequacy and builds up no reserve or resource with which to deal with possible future difficulties. Furthermore, the principal often enters the situation uninformed and with insufficient time to treat the situation effectively. Then he too often lays down the law and behaves in such a way that his office gets a bad reputation with children. The principal's office should be a place where children want to go. It rapidly becomes just the opposite if the teachers use the principal as their strong-armed disciplinarian for bad boys and girls. The good principal will prove to his teachers that strength comes to both them and him when problems are settled in the classroom where they originated. The teacher will help his principal to be stronger by keeping his problems in his own control.

6. *Know the physical condition of each of the pupils.* Much difficulty in working with children comes from those who are not well. In fact healthy, clean, vigorous, well fed children offer a minimum of difficulty in the classroom. The physically ill child is cross and impatient and needs all the kindness and consideration that those about him can give. Children may see no need for humoring him but the alert teacher will understand that there are physical factors operating and will be guided accordingly. Bad teeth, poor eyesight, deafness, aches, and pains complicate the teacher's problem. If he knows these, he can be skillful and increasingly thoughtful of the handicaps under which his pupil is working. One of the first places to look for cause of difficulty in the child is in his physical condition.

7. *Know the social and economic status of the pupils.* Many a child is difficult because he is just plain hungry. Even in a community of plenty, there are children who do not have enough to eat. Cross dispositions and fussy temperaments often can be traced to undernourishment or inadequate clothing. The pupil who is always in want finds it difficult to understand why he can't have what he needs, when he associates with so many who have no wants unfulfilled. Theft often begins when wants are so strong as to overcome any moral standards that the child may possess. The case is quite different when a child steals because of extreme want and when one steals for the fun of it. It might be well to remind the

young teacher that the latter may, in the long run, be far more difficult to handle.

Children who feel inadequate economically very often feel inadequate socially and do not want to associate with other children. When left to themselves, for example, trouble flares and fists fly. Unacceptable vocabularies are put to work and lead to misunderstandings. Even parents of economically secure children find it difficult to understand the problems of children from less economically secure homes. The answer is not for the *haves* to give to the *have nots*. That may even further complicate things. The alert teacher will be on his toes to approach the problem better. He will be kind to the hungry and try to help the parents of the economically insecure prepare better menus and use their clothes more carefully. He can find little ways of helping that will do good in times of extreme pinch.

8. *Respect the pupils' rights when you investigate.* The pupil's desk, his locker, and his pockets are his own and are inviolate. What better way can a teacher lose the respect of a pupil than to go through his desk or locker, especially if he is not around? The teacher would not think of going to the pupil's home and ransacking the place, but many feel no guilt at all about doing just that to his locker or desk. Furthermore, the finger of suspicion is pointing at the pupil if the teacher insists on his proving his innocence by turning his pockets wrong side out. The innocent are terribly offended and the guilty are absurdly embarrassed. Pupils resent being treated like common thieves, and shake-down tactics have no place in the classroom. The courteous, thoughtful, self-respecting teacher retains his dignity as he conducts an investigation. He talks to the pupils in such a way that their dignity is respected even when admitting their weakness. After guilt has been established the guilty are treated respectfully and positive consideration shown.

9. *Avoid sarcasm in talking to pupils.* Of all the unkind manners adults use in dealing with children, sarcasm is the most ruthless and unforgivable of all. It is cheap, bitter, and cutting, and no self-respecting adult will resort to its use. In the first place, it is punitive in nature and develops the worst in those upon whom it is used. It does not produce decency in a reply and if the child replies in kind he will be severely treated. If he replies kindly to words of sar-

casm, he really is being master of the situation, which no teacher wishes to admit either. No good at all comes out of sarcasm; it should be avoided as one would avoid poison. Strangely enough, many adults resort to its use because it is so powerful.

10. *Plan a vigorous curriculum for vigorous boys and girls.* The teacher who has his work organized with his pupils so that he and they know cooperatively all the outcomes, purposes, and goals has gone a long way toward preventing many of the troubles that beset the teacher. The inadequate, poorly prepared, poorly organized teacher creates his own troubles. Busy, purposeful pupils don't have time to get into trouble. Activities that appeal to the interests and age of those in the group keep children alert and on their toes. What teacher would sit still and listen if he were bored? He would get up and walk out. Yet he demands that the child sit and be quiet while he makes a miserable bore of himself. Be prepared to utilize those activities that are known to be of interest to boys and girls and that are vital in their lives.

11. *Talk the situation through with the pupil.* The pupil's point of view is most important. The teacher will do well to encourage the pupil to do as much of the talking as possible. Pent-up feelings are bad for children and the listening teacher learns much. Teachers cannot learn when they are talking. After the pupil has told everything and been encouraged by the patient, kindly listener to unburden his heart, the teacher then is in a position to act wisely. The teacher who talks too much too soon shuts off the source that he wants to tap, and quite frequently engages in differences of points of view that can easily lead to harsh relations. The alert teacher will direct the discussion about a situation rather than engage in personalities. If the child becomes angered at the personal behavior of the teacher he is likely to insult him, and it may be the teacher's fault. The pupil likewise gets angry and insulted if the teacher gets personal. This may lead to a situation in which the pupil loses the argument and the teacher loses face.

12. *Avoid authoritarian behavior.* The teacher is in a position to be quite "bossy." Children expect it and parents encourage children to respect the teacher's point of view. There is nothing wrong with respecting the teacher's point of view, but the trouble arises in what it does to the person in the role of authority. The teacher must be-

ware lest he fail to respect the child's point of view. Teaching means drawing out, encouraging, sympathizing. Speaking with finality and authority closes up the affair and leaves the child overwhelmed. Insofar as possible doors must be left open, voices heard, opinions given. Relations between teacher and pupil are best when ideas travel two-way streets. The authoritarian point of view makes one-way streets on which pupils' ideas cannot travel.

13. *Let the pupil know that you remain his friend even when you have to punish.* Adults feel that punishment, to be effective, must leave the pupil defeated. Children, like adults, need to save face. The adult wants the child to show that he is hurt. Many an adult harangues, scolds, threatens until the child begins to cry. Then he feels that he has been effective. The pupil who resists and steels himself against a show of remorse or offering regrets is looked upon as stubborn and tough. It may not be that way at all, but the pupil does have self-respect at stake and he resists greatly a show of weakness. Teachers send their pupils out of the room to the principal, then complain that the pupil comes back smiling. Certainly he smiles —his face is at stake before his peers. Why should he appear defeated before them? None of us would want to do that.

As soon as an issue is settled the teacher should be the first to reinstate the pupil to good standing. Give him something to do. Make him feel worth while. Meet him in the corridor and greet him in a friendly manner. He is at a loss to know what attitude to take. He doesn't know whether the teacher would speak if spoken to, and the teacher does well to set him at ease and put him back in full standing. No real good can come from keeping the child ill at ease, and much good can come from clearing the decks of doubt, apprehension, and worry. The pupil will admire the teacher for being generous and kind. Conditions are completely restored for good work.

Some do's regarding punishment. Frankly, the good that punishment does children by the time they are of school age is quite debatable. The adult too frequently thinks that he cleared the air by punishing the child when in reality he only released his own emotional self by using disciplinary tactics. The child did not become a different person, but the adult did. It does not seem right that the teacher must take measures against the pupil in order to cleanse his own soul.

There are no prescriptive measures that fit all situations. The three factors—the teacher, the pupil, and the offense—determine what may be done; even then there are unpredictable variables that limit the procedure. For example, in the offense itself there is the problem of whether an offense has actually been committed or whether circumstances just looked that way. As to the pupil, there are all kinds of varying implications and even doubt as to guilt. The teacher's judgment is not infallible and his feelings are quite variable, depending on how he feels or how it happened to look to him at the time.

Peter Howard, in his book *Ideas Have Legs,* illustrates quite well how adults in general act toward children while illustrating his own behavior toward his own.

> My technique of correction was to bribe them with promises of treats, and to bully them by threats of penalties. "Now, Anne, I was going to give you a chocolate. But I shan't be able to do it until you stop that awful howling noise." "Anthony, run and get my slippers. There's a good boy. I'll be so grateful and I'll have a surprise for you when you have done it." "Phillip, I'm not going to have you banging the floor with that hammer. It's absolutely intolerable and will give your mother a headache—if you do it once more you go straight to bed."
>
> In fact, my efforts to induce children to conform their conduct to my desires varied between a whack and a wheedle. Whether the whack or the wheedle was employed depended entirely on the mood of the billy goat, not the conduct of the kids.[4]

Each of us needs to give careful consideration to how we work with pupils. We would probably discover that we are most inconsistent and leave our pupils not knowing what to expect from us. A bad night, a hurried breakfast, worry over bills, a misunderstanding in the family—all create behavior that makes us do things that seem so unlike us.

Some guiding principles seem important and may be helpful:

1. *Be sure that your measures are constructively sensible.* Isola-

[4] Peter Howard, *Ideas Have Legs* (New York: Coward-McCann, Inc., 1946), p. 107.

tion from a group is frequently quite valuable. But it should be done to remove the pupil from the stimulus of members of his group who are a detrimental influence. Simply to sit in solitude with nothing to do but think gives the pupil just as good an opportunity to think bad things as good things. Time to think about perplexing problems would be helpful. If isolation is prescribed see that wholesome things can be done. Sitting away from a group but still close enough to hear and see is good. This still makes learning possible and avoids depriving the pupil of his right to learn. Do things that keep the child in school. If busy work is a prescription make it effective, instructive, challenging work.

2. *Make sure that punishment is reasonable.* It is most questionable whether any form of corporal punishment is justifiable. However, if after careful consideration and deliberation it is prescribed, the teacher should administer the punishment and it should be spanking with the hand on the part of the anatomy built for spanking. The teacher should bend the child over his lap just like a mother, and it should be a private affair. If witnesses are present it will be too severe. With all these restrictions most honest teachers will likely decide to use some other punishment, which would probably be wiser. Anyone too large to spank should not be given corporal punishment.

Reasonableness is related to all forms of punishment. No one really wants to be charged with being unreasonable. The word unreasonable is a harsh word. Courts decide cases on the basis of things being reasonable. Reasonable implies the use of good judgment, matching consequences with an offense, harmonizing cause and effect. The very artificiality of punishment makes it easy to make an unwise prescription. Any person can pass judgment on the reasonableness of the other person's acts and stands a better chance of being right than the person who is trying to pass judgment on himself.

There is considerable evidence that the effects of punishment are largely negative. In the first place those teachers who apply punishment almost invariably do it when they are not at their emotional best. It is done as a last resort, when a teacher is angered or nerves are tattered. Under such conditions judgment about reasonableness is not at its best. It is even felt that the teacher who cannot resist punishing pupils is neurotic himself. Pupils themselves feel truly sorry for the teacher who finds it necessary to discipline. Thus it is worth repeating again—make all punishment truly reasonable from every point of view.

3. *Discuss your views on discipline with those whom you respect.* Every teacher needs to work out a decent, forward-looking point of view about discipline. He needs to see discipline through the other person's eyes. He must believe in the probable futility of punishment as well as its possible benefits, and realize that each time he disciplines he stands a good chance of losing status and prestige. He must see that there are vast differences of opinion about imposed discipline. He must learn what works in a progressive, wholesome, developmental way for him, remember that the things he does will be copied by others, even his pupils. It isn't a topic to be avoided; it is a topic to be much discussed so that one gets a well organized point of view of his own.

4. *Study your own community.* The teacher may have a "forward-looking" and well thought out point of view about control, but he cannot be too far removed from the generally accepted points of view of his clientele. If he is too patient parents will conclude that he is too easy, and will predict his complete downfall. He will need to discuss the problem with parents if he differs greatly with their point of view. He must listen to the things they say and observe the things they do, but he must in turn give them a chance to know his point of view. He need not engage in arguments or magnify points of difference, but he may be positive in his views and give the parents a chance to see the good results he gets. It should be understood that the teacher is limited in what he can get done if his relationships are widely different from parental relationships with pupils. Here again teamwork is needed.

5. *Put reliance in sound, modern developmental methods.* There is ample evidence that pupil conduct is almost never willfully bad. Children are not inherently stubborn, but they are more likely to resist commands after you put a tag of "stubborn" on them. Children are active, noisy, carefree, thoughtless, restless, talkative, and a host of other things that adults are as well. Adults want to dictate children's behavior and children may disagree or simply not know when they need to be quiet or thoughtful or polite. This is the teacher's task, and the parent's too; it is everyone's job. We don't beat

politeness into children or crack their heads to get them to be still. We teach correct behavior the same way we teach reading or anything else. We use patience, we reason with them, we talk things through, we direct, we point out, we use examples, we practice, we teach them the things to do, we teach them the things to avoid. The whole situation involves learning, the teacher teaching the things children should learn. It is all done through a positive experience that leaves children stable and sure of themselves.

Self-discipline is our ultimate goal. Eventually the pupil must discover that he is not surrounded by policemen who will protect him and constantly discipline him as well. He comes to know that control is ever present—we all have many controls set for us, many of them social—but attitude toward control is a matter of one's own choosing. One can choose to control himself or he can so mismanage his life that someone else must step in to control him. This may be his parents, his teachers, his neighbors, his peers, or his enemies. Let it be fully understood that control of some sort puts its limitations on whoever is being controlled.

Obviously a person who would be mature, self-respecting, respectable, courageous, dependable, admired, useful, honest, interesting, constructive, intelligent, and powerful must acquire the ability to control himself. Self-control is taught by parents and teachers, and practiced by the child who would acquire it. It is like learning to swim. The child who is not able to swim is given the chance to swim, and he is carefully guided so that he succeeds. So it is with self-control. Pupils must be given opportunity to practice self-control. They must be given the chance to make mistakes. They must see that self-reliance and decision-making are important learning activities from which strength is derived. They come to be bold and strong in making decisions that affect their lives. They become masters of themselves—this is their ultimate test.

SUMMARY

Much of the problem of management and control stems from our concerns for having the environmental conditions favorable to learning. Teaching materials must be readily available; all members of the learning group will feel happy and work more cooperatively if they not only have a share in arranging the total learning layout, but also share the responsibility for putting materials away. The same principle is involved in decorations, color combinations, and room arrangement. The teacher who is given a responsibility by the administration and then shares this responsibility with his pupils goes a long way toward setting a climate for cooperative work and behavioral attitudes that keep work moving smoothly and minimize the need for disciplinary action. Having an opportunity to share in all that goes on causes the participating member to feel responsible also.

With the teacher working closely and sympathetically with children, at things they like to do and in which they have interest, control is a natural outcome of the activity and work situation itself. Many of the problems that teachers worry most about arise from idleness and lack of purpose. If the learner has purpose things fall into line.

The behavioral problems that concern teachers are those that prevent the teacher from getting the work done. Teachers have a feeling of pressure that society expects the school to get certain schoolwork taught, as it does. But this does not mean that parents and the school community want the teacher to overlook and ignore the emotional and social problems of children that eventually become matters of major general concern. A pervading atmosphere of sympathy, kindness, and willingness to make the other person's concerns our own, and a positive effort on the part of teacher and pupils alike to live with each other in a respectful, courteous, considerate spirit is extremely "catching" to every member of the group.

People who disregard the feelings and rights of others must be punished, but the punishment must leave the offender with a feeling of good will, determination to do better, desire to be liked, and a general over-all spirit of well-being and forgiveness. These are the feelings that help the offender improve and practice control when the opportunity to do so presents itself.

Some competences that each teacher must develop and strengthen are:

1. Working with learners in such a way that all have something to do compatible with their interests and abilities.

2. Encouraging pupils to take responsibility for doing things and causing them to feel proud of what they have done.

3. Sharing everything with the learners that goes on, to the end that they know they have rights, responsibilities, and interesting duties. The capacity to say "Let's all do this together" should predominate.

4. Increasing dedication to the idea that all effort is worth commending and so encouraging pupils, by approval and commendation, that it becomes common practice on the part of all in the group to commend those who practice the art of wholesome living and good relations.

5. Developing an enlarging concern about recessive and unsocial behavior and ignoring behavior that gives concern largely to the teacher only.

6. Knowing the relative significance of the major behavioral problems that confront teachers.

7. Acquiring and working within the framework of some guiding principles that fit one's own particular personality in establishing good working conditions and control.

8. Working at all times on the basic understanding that the pupil with purposeful things to do will be helped most and in turn will help most.

PROBLEMS

1. *Secure permission from your supervisor to be responsible for the housekeeping details for a period of time and determine for yourself how well you get cooperation in keeping things in agreed-upon places.*

2. *Discuss with the building custodian the kind of heating that is provided in the building. Find out from him what problems are encountered when a window is open, when the thermostat control is changed, or when a corridor door is left open. Determine whether this is a problem that pupils can solve for you.*

3. *When you find yourself unusually disturbed by noise ask several of your pupils of both sexes whether it seems noisy to them. See if the girls are disturbed more or less than boys by noise.*

4. *Try several ways of obtaining quiet such as standing quietly and waiting, striking a pleasant chord on the piano, tapping on a desk, turning off the lights, commending the good workers, or merely asking for quiet. Determine what works best for you. Find out for yourself whether any one seems to work most of the time.*

5. *Take Wickman's list of behavior problems of children and list them in the order of seriousness according to your own opinion. Determine how you feel about these behavior problems.*

6. *Select the pupil who seems to disturb you most. Make an analysis of the problem and determine how serious it is by Wickman's scale.*

7. *Select the pupil who disturbs you least and make an analysis of why he is not disturbing you. Could it be because he is so quiet?*

BIBLIOGRAPHY

Alexander, William M., and Paul M. Halverson, *Effective Teaching in the Secondary Schools*. New York: Rinehart and Company, 1956.

Burton, William H., *The Guidance of Learning Activities*, 2nd ed. New York: Appleton-Century-Crofts, Inc., 1952.

DuBois, Dr. Franklin S., "The Security of Discipline," *Mental Hygiene* 36:353-72, July 1952.

Grambs, Jean D., and William J. Iverson, *Modern Methods in Secondary Education*. New York: The Dryden Press, 1952. Pp.248-59.

Grim, Paul, and John U. Michaelis, *The Student Teacher in the Secondary School*. Englewood Cliffs, N.J.: Prentice-Hall, Inc., 1953.

Howard, Peter, *Ideas Have Legs*. New York: Coward-McCann, Inc., 1946.

Hymes, James L., Jr., *Behavior and Misbehavior*. Englewood Cliffs, N.J.: Prentice-Hall, Inc., 1955.

Klausmeir, Herbert J., Katharine Dresden, Helen C. Davis, and Walter Wittick, *Teaching in the Elementary Schools*. New York: Harper & Brothers, 1956. Pp. 507-34.

Michaelis, John U., and Paul R. Grim, *The Student Teacher in the Elementary School*. Englewood Cliffs, N.J.: Prentice-Hall, Inc., 1953. Pp. 150-70.

Stouffer, George A. W., Jr., "Behavior Problems of Children as Viewed by Teachers and Mental Hygienists," *Mental Hygiene* 36:279-85, April 1952.

Wickman, E. K., *Children's Behavior and Teachers' Attitudes*. New York: The Commonwealth Fund, 1928.

Wiles, Kimball, *Teaching for Better Schools*. Englewood Cliffs, N.J.: Prentice-Hall, Inc., 1952.

Part Five

Evaluation and reports

as part of

the teaching process

Introduction

The teacher is responsible for carrying out the curricular program that the school, in cooperation with the community, agrees should be provided to meet the needs of the youth of the school unit. How well he is achieving the goals must be determined by measurement instruments that are available or can be constructed locally by him.

The school may be quite concerned about using instruments of measurement that have been quite widely used, and adopting standards or norms that will enable the school to make comparisons with what other schools expect. Of course the school will understand that only if tests are strictly relevant to the subject matter taught will the instrument have value. Nevertheless the school will likely wish to use some standard achievement tests and the teacher should be fully aware of the strengths and limitations of such tests. He should be in a position to take real leadership in helping to select the tests, and if called upon to do so, he must be able to take an objective, professional attitude in administering and scoring them, and interpreting the results.

In like manner, the school will be concerned about measuring the intellectual power of the pupils and will be searching for good tests to determine mental ability. The school will understand that the teacher must know all he can about the potential of each individual as well as the general intellectual profile of each group of pupils. The teacher will be called upon to take an active part in such a testing program and can ill afford to be unprepared to give vigorous professional advice on not only the test to be given but also uses that are to be made of the results of a testing program. The effectiveness of any testing program is limited only by the professional boundaries of the teacher himself as he gives the test or applies the results in his teaching.

Another rich area of evaluation, probably the most fertile in the results to be obtained, rests in the teacher's facility for devising instruments of evaluation that are within his own professional skill. The objective tests that he may construct, the essay test, the conference, or the observation are all excellent ways to determine pupil growth. The skilled teacher who constructs such tests with care and professional ingenuity has within himself the ability to make effective and meaningful evaluation that serves his purposes admirably. Such a teacher can be relied upon to be a master teacher, highly respected by his co-workers.

If we assume that measurement has been sufficient and careful, the results can be used as background for transmitting to parents and other concerned personnel the interpretation of the results. This may take the form of reports to parents or the establishing of results in the records of the school, by marks or by letter in which the teacher goes into whatever detail necessary to make a lucid and satisfactory report. It can serve as a basis for conferences with parents or professional discussions where the needs of the particular individual are involved.

Finally, conferences, reports, tests, and evaluations have value only insofar as they enable the teacher to help the pupil develop as effectively and as efficiently as possible. The only good reason for anything a teacher does is the eventual goal of effective teaching and satisfying pupil growth. To these ends all teacher efforts are dedicated.

14

Techniques of evaluation
and measurement

The function of the school in our society is to assure youth of the chance to grow. The teacher's major concern is that this growth be commensurate with the pupil's potential for growth. In order to work with any degree of assurance, the teacher must use instruments of measurement that enable him to determine the power for growth within each individual. Then he must use another entirely different type of measurement to determine whether this growth is actually taking place. The first type of test is called the mental or intelligence test. The test ordinarily used is a standardized or formal test. The second type is the achievement test, which may be either a formal, standardized test or an informal, teacher-prepared test. *Growth,* as the term is used here, refers to educational growth, with social, civic, and physical growth being essential ingredients of that educational growth.

The meaning of standardized intelligence and achievement tests. Standardization of tests includes uniformity in testing and in scoring. In order to secure this uniformity, directions are provided with the test so that the one who gives it will know the time limits, instructions, and preliminary demonstrations, and how to deal with questions

343

that arise. The one giving the test follows all instructions implicitly. Any variation from them tends to destroy the effectiveness of the test. The same is true of scoring. An answer or scoring card is provided with the test and is expected to be used without sympathy or variation. If at any time the one who is scoring the test allows his own personal ideas to affect the scoring, the test is made useless to that extent. It should be clearly understood that the value of the test is dependent upon the integrity and objectivity of the person giving the test, and in similar fashion the one scoring and recording the results.

Another step in the standardization of a test is that of setting up norms. Norms are average scores for a large random group of pupils on a given test for a given age or grade. The test has maximum value as an instrument for measurement only if the test material covers a wide sampling in the particular field it proposes to measure and has been given to a wide sampling of pupils with a great variety of experiences and native intelligence. With the scores derived from such a program of testing, norms are set up. Two technical terms that usually accompany a test and are derived from the standardization process are *reliability* and *validity*. *Reliability* means consistency in measuring what it does measure. *Validity* means how well it measures what it is intended to measure. The teacher should study carefully these two qualities in any test he uses.

Such tests have more value to the teacher if there are at least two equivalent forms. This enables him to use the tests on the same group of pupils or the same individual pupil without the factor of memory or practice affecting its value. It should be clearly understood that these tests do have great value as scientific instruments of measure. The teacher who uses them should do so with a completely open, professional mind. They should be given with the greatest care possible under strictest compliance with the accompanying instructions. This attitude is one of the earmarks of a professional person. It is a part of his search for information that will help him to do the most for each of his pupils.

Some of the more widely used intelligence tests. Any tests that are specifically mentioned here are listed because they are either quite generally known or have stood the test of time supporting the claims that have been made for them.

Individual tests. The best known individual test is the Stanford Revision of the Binet test, first offered in its present form in 1937. It is in two forms—Form L and Form M. Each of the two forms contains 129 items. They are quite different in content but are equivalent or nearly so in difficulty, reliability, and validity. A test kit with instructions for administering and scoring the test may be secured from Houghton Mifflin Company in Boston. Any person giving the test should be a skilled person, so that it will be given properly and the interpretation of the results may have significance and value.

Two other individual intelligence tests that are widely used are the Wechsler-Bellevue Intelligence Scale and the Wechsler Intelligence Scale for children. The Wechsler-Bellevue Intelligence Scale, in two forms, is suitable for adults.

The Wechsler Intelligence Scale for children is at present only in one form—Form II. It is in reality an adaptation of certain elements of Form II of the Wechsler-Bellevue Intelligence Scale. It has twelve subtests, six in the Verbal scale and six in the Performance scale. The reported reliability for the scale is quite satisfactory but the validity still may seem inadequately reported. A test kit and manual of instructions for giving and scoring are available through the Psychological Corporation, New York. Again, the person giving the test must be skilled in administering the test. In fact only qualified personnel can secure the test.

Group tests. Group tests are more generally used in schools than are individual tests. Two reasons for this are (1) the group test is more readily available, and (2) the test may be given to a group in about the same time as is needed to give the individual test. Only the clinician skilled in giving the test ordinarily should give the individual test. The group test requires careful, skillful administration but the professionally competent teacher can follow the directions and get quite accurate results. All testing requires accurate, ethical, and professional behavior on the part of the tester.

The following group tests are widely used in elementary and secondary schools:

> American Council on Education Psychological Examinations
>   (High School Students)
> California Test of Mental Maturity
> Kuhlman-Anderson Intelligence Tests
> Otis Alpha, Beta, and Gamma Tests
> Pintner General Ability Test

The above list is only a very limited sampling of the many tests that are available. It does represent the field of group tests at the present time. The Pintner-Cunningham is an example of the non-verbal or picture test for children too young to read. The Otis Alpha and the Kuhlman-Anderson are used for the lower primary grades as is the California Test of Mental Maturity, Pre-primary and Primary. The Otis Beta is used in the intermediate grades; the California Test of Mental Maturity, Elementary Level, for grades 4-8, the Pintner Intermediate Test for grades 4-8, and the Kuhlman-Anderson Intelligence Tests for grades 1-6 and 7-8. In the upper grades the American Council on Education Psychological Examination (High School) is widely used, as are the Otis Gamma, Pintner Advanced, Kuhlman-Anderson (grades 9-12) and the California Test of Mental Maturity (grades 7-10, and Advanced). There is no attempt made here to evaluate any of the above mentioned tests. All certainly have been acclaimed by users as satisfactory for the purpose for which they are used. Buros' *Mental Measurements Yearbook,* containing valuable sources for reviews of tests that any teacher may consider using, is available in any good college library.

It is the teacher's responsibility to secure every bit of information that he can about the pupil he teaches so that he can make the necessary curricular prescriptions more accurately and more advantageously for the pupil, and so that he will not expect accomplishments beyond him. He cannot have all the technical knowledge that is necessary for clinical testing, but he can be open minded about useful services and alert to the applications of available information.

Mental testing is professionally confidential. The term intelligence quotient (I.Q.) is a professional term growing out of the intelligence testing program. It refers to the relationship between chronological age and mental age, determined by means of the psychological test constructed for that purpose. The I.Q. is found by dividing the mental age by the chronological age and multiplying the quotient by 100. If one could determine mental age with the same finality that chronological age is known there would be less need for caution. But even after years of experimentation and research it is well known that mental age is dependent on so many factors that it cannot be looked upon with any degree of absolute certainty. So when one of the factors is not absolute in determining a quotient the quotient itself is correct only within the limits of accuracy of the factors from which the quotient is derived. After several tests given over a period of years, an individual's mental age may be fairly accurately known and his I.Q. established within reasonable limits.

Most parents' background for understanding the meaning of mental age and intelligence quotient is very limited. Many parents have heard or read enough popular material to know that the 100 I.Q. represents something near normal; that is, the mental age and chronological age are about equal. They also know that an I.Q. of 125 represents a rather high intelligence and 80 a significantly low one. The general public is inclined to look upon the I.Q. as something as real as brown eyes or big feet. The professional worker knows better but cannot give the time even if he had the words to get the information across to the parent. Furthermore, no good can come from bandying such information around among neighbors, as parents too often would do.

Only those who know how to use such technical knowledge for the welfare and advantage of the learner have need for it. The teacher and the school do need all the information that they can accumulate. Much of the information is only relatively factual. The parent needs to understand that there are limits to his child's abilities that cannot be unreasonably pushed about. He needs to respect the interests and abilities of his child within those limits that are readily observable. But the school has no professional responsibility to get into the realm of professional techniques that are reserved for skilled personnel and deal with such intangible measurement. The wise teacher will stay on ground that both he and the parents can tread safely.

The teacher has problems with retardation and acceleration. The beginning teacher will perceive standards in children's behavior from his teacher-education experiences and as he goes into his actual teaching situations. Even though he may not have tests to give him more exact data on which to base his judgments, he comes to look upon some behavior as mature for the chronological age of the pupil, while other is immature. Thus he arrives at the ideas of slow and fast learners without having much real basis for the estimates he makes of various pupils. If he has no basis for his evaluations other than the experiences he has with the pupils he teaches, his base can be in error, depending on the kinds of pupils that are in his classes. If they represent a normal distribution he may not be badly in error, providing he has the capacity to analyze broadly enough to get a true picture. But he cannot depend upon so unreliable a basis for decisions.

A teacher has a pupil repeat a year of school if he thinks the pupil is a year or more behind the standard for the group in which he is located. But even granting that repeating a year might be helpful—and there is plenty of evidence that repeating a grade is seldom beneficial—the teacher has very little evidence unless he resorts to the use of measurements that are standardized on many kinds of groups. These norms may be state, regional, or national in scope, depending upon the sampling of the cases. The alert teacher will soon see that he cannot rely on his own background to give him evidence for making decisions about promotion, non-promotion, and acceleration. He might be tempted to rely on such vague ideas if no one challenged his judgment. But if he is questioned, he soon finds himself without resources to back up his action. He wants growth to result from his efforts at teaching and he needs to use all the evidence he can command to find out the results of his efforts. Tests are part of this evidence.

Part of the picture that must be taken into consideration is the mental potential of the pupil. By means of tests mental age can be determined accurately enough for the professional purposes of the teacher. If the teacher is professionally alert he will use the results of the psychological test from which he derives the mental age and, supplementing this with observations, conferences, data involving health and physical development, and any other evidence available to him, will arrive at a mental age that has significance. With this as his revised profile the teacher may reasonably expect that the pupil's school performance should be compatible with his potential.

If the teacher regards progress in terms of working to capacity, teaching becomes much more nearly a professional art, and the child is led to set up goals that are within his ability. When looked upon in this way the matter of retardation or repeating becomes a rather unnecessary practice. The teacher should not expect the pupil to repeat an effort in which he has no real expectation of succeeding, regardless of how many times he tries; the work must be beyond his capacity in the first place. The teacher must guide the pupil into situations where success is possible. This means adapting the work to the pupil's ability. Barring absence, illness, and other similar factors the child need not fail; hence, he need not repeat. The teacher can make no mistake in determining the pupil's potential and the work in school must be geared to that power. This is not new. Teachers have been charged with work being too hard or too easy for pupils for years. Each teacher's challenge is to have the lowest possible number of frustrated pupils.

Acceleration means progressing more rapidly than is ordinarily expected. Schools are set up to move the pupil along one grade each year. Ordinarily the pupil of six enters the first grade; the pupil of eighteen graduates from secondary school; the college freshman class is ordinarily made up of eighteen-year-olds. These are standard age-grade locations. The skillful teacher anywhere from beginning to end is impressed by differences in pupils in any of these groupings, and no one is more aware of these widening differences than the secondary principal as he hands the pupils the diplomas at high school commencement time. The range of differences may seem slight at age six, but the relative potential is just as great at six as eighteen.

The school has three choices: The pupils can move along at the rate of one grade per year without much concern for challenging the stronger or helping the weaker find things they can do with success; all are moved ahead. The curriculum and educational experiences are focused on the ability somewhere near the middle of the group. This attitude tends to make mediocrity popular. The strong coast; the slow are pulled along. No one is badly inconvenienced, including the teacher. The general philosophy embodies a curriculum-centered program. No one is retarded; no one is accelerated.

Another choice is to pitch the focus of attention toward the upper half of the group. Here the situation becomes somewhat more unpleasant for the majority of the group. The pupils in the upper group are happiest because they are being challenged most in experiences where they meet with rather consistent success. The lower group finds very little to be pleased with themselves about and the teacher becomes convinced that it is useless to try to do much about it. The pupils either become convinced that he is right and proceed to make the situation even more futile for themselves and the teacher, or they decide that if they are docile and pleasant the teacher will be charmed into passing them along. The others in the lower group who may not be so cooperative simply "flunk." The school eventually becomes a place where they cannot succeed and they drop out, to the pleasure of the teacher who didn't have the time or the patience to make the work fit the pupil.

The other general choice lies in the area mentioned earlier, where the teacher focuses his attention on individual pupils. Here each pupil is recognized, with the teacher making every effort to know his potential for growth and having him work within the limits of that potential. He is challenged, but neither confused and frustrated because it is too difficult nor bored because it is too easy or a review for him. Here the teacher again has a choice with the stronger. He can advance him to another group where there are more of his developmental maturity, where he may be the youngest chronologically but older mentally. This involves reclassification and regrouping in the elementary school and moving to a more challenging situation in the secondary school. The other choice, of course, is a strong enrichment program with the pupil continuing with his own school group. There are arguments for both sides, but with large class groups the problem of enrichment may become increasingly difficult and regrouping may be the more satisfactory method. The social problem with the younger pupil in an older group is not as acute as often declared because the younger pupil is able to hold his own scholastically and finds plenty of opportunity for leadership. In this situation, as stated earlier, the teacher does not require pupils to repeat a course or a grade. He will guide pupils around courses for which they have no aptitude and direct them into those situations where they can succeed. In the required courses in the secondary school adaptations will by necessity be made so as to enable the pupil to move along with the group.

Each teacher has to work out his own way of thinking. The practice here proposed involves advancing a strong pupil to a group that has a greater number of the same mental age and development, for both expediency and challenge to the learner. It denies the value of retaining the pupil in a grade or course, with the exception of those who by reason of health or absence have not been in the group sufficiently long to succeed. This position is taken on the premise that the embarrassment of the pupil who is over-age and over-size, combined with the futility of doing work that is obviously too difficult, is more than he can endure. The standard for that pupil must be within his range, and his growth is to be measured in terms of the things he can do instead of the things he cannot grasp. Every person entering the profession must determine his own philosophy of what to do with the fast and the slow learner. The suggestions given above may enable the reader to evolve his own way of looking at this most difficult problem. He must work it out in terms of his group, his community, his facilities, and last but certainly not least the attitude of the administration in the school. Some administrators are adamant in their positions regarding both acceleration and retardation, which sometimes go by another name, double promotion and failure—it all means the same. However, under a system of adaptation of school to the individual pupil, failure is blamed on the teacher. The teacher is the one who eventually gets the criticism for the failure.

Standardized achievement tests and teaching. It is highly necessary to differentiate clearly in our thinking about achievement testing between standardized tests and teacher-constructed tests. Achievement tests are available that are purported to measure general achievement, while others are built to measure achievement in a special subject. The person selecting the test must first decide what he wishes to measure and then select a test that seems most nearly capable of measuring what the teacher or school wishes to measure. It must be kept in mind that whereas the general intelligence test draws on all that the testee has ever learned, the achievement test more nearly tests what has been taught in a given period of time under controlled conditions.

It should be kept in mind that there are definite limitations to standardized achievement tests as well as other kinds of tests. It is easiest to select a sampling of factual material or to test to find out how well a pupil has mastered a basic skill as in reading, spelling, or arithmetic. It is far more difficult to test for creativity, understanding, evaluation, critical thinking, or application of principles. It is easier to teach certain skills and then test to find out how well the skill has been mastered than to teach for interpretation or critical analysis and then test to find out how well the pupil can apply the principles involved.

One of the dangerous pitfalls in the use of standardized achievement tests lies in the selection and administration of the test. It is useless to select an achievement test that contains a predominance of test items that have not been included in the instructional program and hence are foreign to the pupil being tested. It is unwise to select tests that have a predominance of items that are foreign to the curricular program of the school. Quite often the teacher's academic concern to teach so that the pupils will show up better on the test than they might otherwise, or his feeling that the administration expects the pupils to show up more favorably, causes him to teach for the test. This defeats the purpose of the testing program and is really unethical.

General achievement tests (battery) are built to cover a wide general area of academic learnings and have been standardized on a wide sampling of all types of schools as well as all types of pupils at various grade levels and ages. Insofar as these samplings have been wide enough, they are adequate in covering each of the fields that make up the battery. The fact that these batteries are derived from courses of study, textbooks, curriculum experts, and all kinds of instructional materials tends to assure the school system or the teacher that rather complete coverage has been accomplished. The teacher who uses these tests is able to determine with considerable accuracy how well his group performs on the test as compared with norms provided by the publishers of the test.

In the special areas, standardized achievement tests have been built in almost every area common to the elementary or secondary school. As in the general batteries mentioned in the preceding paragraph, the test items are selected from all available sources covering the particular area and standardized by giving the test to as wide a group of pupils as possible in a wide area of schools. Comparison with the norms, so prepared for the test, enables the teacher to arrive at some conclusions about his own effectiveness in teaching his own group. This is contingent on the extent to which the test covers the area that the teacher himself has been teaching. This is the crucial point both for the teacher and the school.

The teacher should recognize that the standardized achievement test has even further limitations in that his particular group may not be a typical one from the standpoint of socio-economic background or from the standpoint of age-grade distribution. He may have been attempting to teach the same things for which the test was built but local factors may have prevented him from being able to do what he might have under normal circumstances. In other words, he may have been working hard with a seventh grade group with an intellectual level so low that he was really making good progress to achieve the results he did. Just as troublesome from the standpoint of interpretation is the fifth grade pupil who by superior work in the fifth grade achieves the level of the seventh grade norm. It does not mean that he has mastered seventh grade work; it means that he has done excellent work at the fifth grade level. The teacher must recognize all the limitations of achievement tests, but at the same time keep a fertile mind to all the service that the achievement test can render in helping him learn more about the members of his group and determining his own effectiveness.

Some of the available achievement tests: General achievement (battery) tests. Three quite well known and widely used general achievement tests are the California, Metropolitan, and Stanford Achievement Tests.

The California Achievement Tests cover grades 1-13 and are built to cover reading vocabulary, reading comprehension, language, arithmetic fundamentals, and arithmetic reasoning. There are three forms for each battery of tests and there is a wide distribution of data from which norms have been prepared. The tests are constructed only in the skill areas listed above. In some ways this is an advantage since there is fairly universal agreement in schools as to the content in these particular areas.

The Metropolitan Achievement Tests include five batteries of tests from first grade through grade 9. Each battery is available in five equivalent forms. The primary test has three reading tests and one arithmetic test. The junior high school test contains tests on reading, literature, English, vocabulary, spelling, arithmetic fundamentals, arithmetic problems, history, geography, and science. The test requires a long time to take and consequently is what is commonly called a power test.

The Stanford Achievement Test is made up of four batteries: primary, elementary, intermediate, and advanced, covering grades 2-9.

There are four equivalent forms at present available. The test is very much like the Metropolitan Achievement Tests. The tests are widely used, are revised often enough to keep them reliable and in conformity with curricular developments.

Achievement tests in special areas. Achievement tests in special areas include reading, mathematics, English, social science, spelling, and science. These tests, like battery tests, are based on curriculum materials, texts, and courses of study. Together with these bases, reference is made to aims and objectives common to the particular area. To the extent to which the person who builds the test is able to construct it in terms of tapping all of these elements in an area, the test has merit.

The following tests are given as examples of tests which are available in the special areas and for special purposes:

Reading—readiness: Betts Ready to Read Battery, Gates Reading Readiness Tests, Metropolitan Reading Readiness Tests, and Monroe Reading Aptitude Tests are good examples.

Such tests are designed for what the name implies. Is the pupil ready to learn to read? The tests are given at the end of the kindergarten period or the beginning of the first grade to determine whether or not the child has acquired the facility necessary for learning to read and has sufficient background information. The material covered includes general information, motor coordination, vocabulary range, visual and auditory perception, and intelligence. The items on the test are quite similar to those found in intelligence tests.

Reading—diagnosis: Monroe Diagnostic Reading Examination, Gates Diagnostic Tests in Reading, and Durrell Analysis of Reading Difficulty are examples of diagnostic tests in reading.

These tests are intended to analyze difficulties that the individual pupil encounters in reading. They list the specific errors that are common in reading. The errors and observations made by the tester form the basis for analysis of reading difficulties. Such tests seem to have value only insofar as the one doing the testing is highly skilled in giving them and in analyzing the test results.

Reading—survey: The better known survey type of tests are Iowa Silent Reading, Gates Basic Reading Test, and the Cooperative English Test.

These tests cover a variety of aspects of the general phases of reading. The Cooperative English Test makes possible separate scores in speech and level of comprehension and vocabulary. The Iowa and Gates Tests are often listed as diagnostic tests, but appear to meet the pattern of the so-called survey tests and hence are listed under this heading.

Mathematics—prognostic: Tests of this particular function are Lee Test of Algebraic Ability and the Iowa Plane Geometry Aptitude Test.

The purpose of these tests is to predict the probable success of pupils who might enter these special areas. The Lee Test consists of subtests in arithmetic problems, number series, number analogies, and formulas. The Iowa Test has four parts also, covering reading for content in geometry, algebraic computation and reasoning, arithmetical reasoning, and visualization. The mathematics teacher specifically interested in this phase of teaching will find this type of test stimulating and helpful.

Mathematics—survey: Some tests that can be classed in this category are the Iowa Every-Pupil Tests of Basic Skills in Arithmetic, the Cooperative Mathematics Tests for grades 7, 8, and 9, the Cooperative Tests in algebra and geometry, and the California Achievement Test.

The purpose of these tests is to cover such elements in mathematics as basic skills, solutions of problems, mathematics vocabulary, quantitative knowledge, mathematics concepts, and application of mathematics and appreciation. No one test is devised for all of these abilities, so anyone desiring to use the test must examine it to determine what the test purports to do.

Mathematics—diagnosis: Tests commonly considered diagnostic in purpose are Compass Diagnostic Tests in Arithmetic, and Diagnostic Test for Fundamental Processes in Arithmetic by Buswell and John.

These tests are devised to give the teacher a chance to determine the errors in arithmetic operations and difficulties that the pupil encounters. The test by Buswell and John is an individual test and naturally will require more time, but probably enables the teacher to discover more difficulties.

English: There are many tests available in the field of English. The field is commonly broken down into many specific areas such as vocabulary, language, grammar, literature, composition, and rhetoric. Some of the tests purport to be diagnostic and prognostic in function, while others are of a general survey type covering the basic skills in the areas of language.

Some of the tests that are representative of the field are: Clapp-Young Self-marking Test, Iowa Every-Pupil Test of Basic Skills in Language, Metropolitan Achievement Test in Language Arts, Hudelson Typical Composition Ability Scale, Pressey Diagnostic Tests in English Composition, Cooperative English Test, California Achievement Tests, Purdue Placement Test in English, Iowa Language Abilities Test, and Michigan Vocabulary Profile Test.

Social science: Standardized tests in the field of social science are numerous, but each teacher must decide for himself whether a particular test has value as a device for testing the subject matter that he has taught and that he considers most important. There are wide areas of material, and the points of emphasis and importance attached vary greatly among teachers. Too many of the tests seem to be built to test factual material. This tends to affect both the teacher and the pupil in attaching more emphasis to what may have relatively less importance.

Tests that appear to be more widely used are: Cooperative American History Test, Wrightstone Critical Thinking in the Social Studies, Wrightstone Scale for Civic Beliefs, Stanford Social Studies Tests, and Metropolitan Achievement Test in Social Studies.

Spelling: Although spelling is generally agreed to be quite important in our written communication, there is wide disagreement as to what words are of such universal usage as to be important for all pupils. Somewhere around five thousand words seem to be necessary for a basic spelling list. Such well known lists as the Iowa Spelling Scales, Horn Basic Writing Vocabulary, the Thorndike Teacher Word Book, and the Ayres Spelling Scale have been used as the base for most lists that have been selected. The tests that require that the word be written appear to be more effective than those that merely require the recognition of the correct word. Standardized tests seem to be quite inadequate in the field of spelling, but those that are built to require the pupil to write and pronounce the word seem more valuable. The Guy Spelling Scale is an example of such a test. Both the Metropolitan and the Stanford Achievement Tests contain spelling sections.

Science: Tests in various areas of science have been constructed from tests and curriculum materials in the particular area. As in social science, emphasis is quite largely on factual material instead of understanding and applying principles. Teachers wishing to use the tests would do well to acquire specimen samples first. Illustrations of tests that have been built are: The Anderson Chemistry Test, the Dunning Physics Test, Nelson Biology Test, Cooperative General Science Test, and Stanford Science Test.

It should be kept in mind that standardized achievement tests have definite limitations in measuring the effectiveness of teaching. They, however, do have their place in the field of measurement, and the teacher should be constantly alert to the developments in his particular area.

Other standardized instruments for measurement used in meeting the needs of pupils. Many of the measurements discussed in the following paragraphs are extremely valuable when used by specialists in the areas of guidance and counselling or as part of the clinical services of special divisions in larger school systems, colleges, or universities. The classroom teacher has neither the time nor the ability to make interpretations and evaluations that would be highly worth while. He does need to be aware of the kinds of instruments that have been constructed, and he should be aware that clinical services are available.

Character, attitude and personality tests: It is important that teachers tap every known source to learn more about their pupils. Juvenile delinquency in each generation gets front page attention, and strong social demands are made to do something about it. Most of the adult population that speaks so alarmingly about the problem seldom goes further than to point out the acts of delinquency, without attempting to go into the possible underlying factors within the individual that affect his behavior in various social situations. It is fairly well agreed that personality does affect the total behavior of the individual. However, it is not too widely agreed just what "personality" really means.

Efforts are made to get at the problem by interest inventories, adjustment inventories, and attitude scales. Interest inventories try to determine kinds of reading, kinds of recreation, types of occupations, and kinds of behavior that have an attraction for the individual. The Pressey Interest-Attitude Test is an illustration of such a test. Adjustment inventories attempt to get at the problems of personality measurement by asking the pupil about his likes and dislikes, and his reactions to certain environments such as home, community, and school. The Bell Adjustment Inventory and the Detroit Adjustment Inventory are examples of this type of measurement. Attitude scales are devised to determine how strongly the pupil agrees or disagrees with statements involving controversial issues or issues on which opinions may differ quite widely. Remmers' Scales illustrate this type of scale.

The measurement of personality is not far advanced. These tests, of course, are not intelligence tests in the strictest sense, unless the designer of the test has the total individual in mind. This is an important area and any teacher will do well to keep informed about the development in this area.

Performance or situational tests were first constructed by Hartshorne and May about 1930. These tests were designed to determine the strength or weakness of the child in such behavior areas as lying, cheating, cooperation, stealing, deceit, and persistence. In any of these tests the subject's reactions in certain situations are observed insofar as possible without his being aware of it.

Another approach to the problem of testing personality is that of projective techniques. In tests of this kind the testee is given tasks to do without much direction so that he may do them his own way; the idea is that in so doing he will reveal his own mode of response. The purpose of the test is concealed as much as possible so that the person being tested will give a typical performance. Tasks commonly used in projective techniques include drawing, play acting, arranging toys so as to produce a particular scene, selecting objects or pictures in order of preference, and interpreting a series of pictures or inkblots. Probably the best known projective technique is that of the Rorschach Ink Blot Test. In this test the subject reports his reactions to each one of the ten designs. Such tests are not yet fully utilized or widely understood.

The use of such tests is largely limited to counselling and guidance workers in the school. Personal adjustments are most essential to many pupils, and those who work closest with the pupils turn to those sources that enable them to help the pupil make adaptations to his social and environmental situations.

Another test of a different approach is the Kuder Preference

Record. This test is widely used in high schools. It includes ten scales: outdoor, mechanical, computational, scientific, persuasive, artistic, literary, musical, social service, and clerical. It is apparent that classifying according to wide interest groups achieves relatively higher reliability than testing in specific occupations. For example, a person might show a strong interest in social service and go any of a dozen or more separate ways—physician, teacher, social worker, minister, nurse, etc. This is the vocational interest test.

Aptitude tests: Aptitude tests attempt to measure the pupil's capacity for a particular occupation. By means of the aptitude test it is possible to determine the extent to which a pupil possesses the specific qualities and abilities essential for success in a particular trade or occupation.

Examples of such tests are Psychological Corporation Engineering Test and Physical Science Aptitude Test for the field of engineering, Psychological Corporation General Clerical Test for Business and Clerical Occupations, and Minnesota Spatial Relations Test for mechanical occupations.

There are many other kinds of tests, and the field of testing is wide open in experimentation and research. There are thousands of tests on the market. In closing the section on standardized tests it bears repeating that tests should be skillfully selected and expertly administered. Only those who have highly specialized backgrounds will be able to utilize the results of instruments scientifically constructed to measure human intelligence and behavior.

The functions of teacher-constructed tests and examinations. The teacher who is with the pupils all the time while they are in school has the most advantageous position to make appraisals. He sees them as individuals, and as members of a group. He sees them with their problems and in the process of solving them. He sees their interests and knows about the stability of these interests. He sees the pupil in situations that test his character and honesty, and he sees him struggle with forces that tax the best there is in him. He talks with him, laughs with him, has ample opportunity to make judgments about him. He knows the strengths and the weaknesses as no other person. It is his privilege and his most serious challenge.

The standardized test impersonalizes the evaluations he wishes to make of the pupil. It widens his horizon and strengthens his confidence in his ability to make appraisals. It helps him to confirm judgments he has made or stimulates him to revise the estimates he may have about his pupils. It may help him to revise and adapt the material he has been using. Above all, it gives him a chance to know how the results of his work compare and contrast with the norms. This is advantageous. It prevents complacency and stimulates open-mindedness, and should result in better teaching.

But none of this takes the place of the teacher's own appraisal of the pupil's work. He knows that he has at least attempted to teach. He knows better than any other person the limitations of each pupil, and his own limitations. Because of this he should be in position to make appraisals that have meaning and value for him as the teacher. Furthermore, he can make these appraisals in terms of the individual and the group. It is the teacher's desire to know how much growth the pupils have made and also how much he has contributed to this growth. Whereas standardized tests were largely subject-matter tests, the achievement and growth that the teacher will endeavor to evaluate will be reflected in attitudes, appreciations, and adjustments as well as facts.

The teacher has the responsibility for building his tests in accordance with the objectives in the learning situation where he has been the teacher. The pupils, by necessity, should know these objectives. He should make the test as free from ambiguity and trickery as possible. It is a test not of wit, but of growth. After building the test he should edit it carefully and make sure it covers what he thinks he has worked through with his learners. It should be a credit to his teaching and be done with the expertness expected of him as a teacher.

The measurements that the teacher devises himself may be classified as essay examinations, objective tests, and quizzes.

The essay examination: Inasmuch as practically all teachers other than those teaching in the lower primary grades use the essay examination, it appears valuable to consider the advantages and disadvantages of this approach to measurement. The essay examination gets its name from the fact that it gives the pupil the opportunity to write about a topic or answer a question in his own way, with or without delimiting prescriptions from the teacher. It is intended that the test be of sufficient sampling to give the teacher a basis for making a satisfactory appraisal of the pupil.

Many advantages are ascribed to the essay type of examination. It is the best method yet known to secure the qualitative aspects of a written piece of work. It gives the pupil an opportunity to be original in style and creative in content, an exercise that is of vast importance to the master teacher. It gives the pupil more latitude than do many other types of written tests to demonstrate his ability to think and to organize answers. There is more likelihood that the results of essay examinations are the pupil's own work. Preparation for essay examinations can in itself be more valuable than preparation for other types, because it requires more ability to organize and think through the material covered. This is as true for the teacher as for the pupil.

The disadvantages are numerous also, but many of them can be neutralized by the skillful teacher. The essay examination is quite subjective and the grade can be determined by the mood the teacher is in at the time he grades the papers. They can be haphazardly prepared and consequently quicker to construct and score, but the sincere teacher knows when he has prepared a poor examination and should be guided by this knowledge when he evaluates it. Pupils may have difficulty in adjusting to the unfairness that may result from poor examination practices. Teachers are conditioned to react adversely to poor writing and poor appearance. The sampling is so small that the validity is limited. Pupils have a tendency to bluff by writing long answers containing much irrelevant material. Teachers have a weakness of falling for volume, and pupils know this. This list of disadvantages should serve as a challenge to the teacher to reduce the objections to a minimum. Grading is difficult and the teacher should avoid that type of work when he is under stress or over-tired.

The objective type examination: This category of examinations includes the true-false test, the multiple-choice form, completion test, and matching test. In preparing a test the teacher again needs to keep in mind the material he wishes to cover. An outline of the material and any text references will be sufficient to enable him to know exactly what samplings he desires. The samplings will be much broader and much more complete than the essay test. This is a decided advantage of the objective tests. He should avoid trick and catch questions and exercises that confuse the pupil and make him feel that the test is not fair. Pupils should like to take tests, and they do when teacher and pupils recognize a good purpose and wholesome outcomes of the results. Tests should be easy enough that no one completely fails. They should be so organized that the first exercises are the easiest. The pupil needs to get the feeling of success in the early part of the test. It should be difficult enough that practically no one gets a perfect score.

The true-false test is made up of a number of separate statements that are clearly false or clearly true. There should be no ambiguous statements where the interpretation of the statement is not certain. Statements should be short with a minimum of qualifying clauses. The test should be devoid of characteristics that make it easy to determine that the statement is false, and free from copied statements that necessitate only a good memory. It should make applications of principles or generalizations that are new to the pupil. The true-false statements should number at least 100 and be in no particular order. There should be approximately as many true as false. The score should be number right minus the number wrong, not counting omissions. The pupil should always know the rules for scoring and the instructions should be unmistakably clear.

The multiple-choice test is made up of statements having a principal or introductory part and a subordinate or concluding part. In the concluding part there are several choices, preferably four or five, that may be used. Of the four or five only one is correct. The others do not fit the introductory part. This choice of one of four or five concluding statements reduces, to a great extent, the factor of guessing. The test should contain a minimum of 50 statements, which should be sensible and instructive. There should be no absurdities or ambiguous statements. Each should be stated positively and should require thoughtful weighing of the various choices. The correct answers should form no pattern in the test. The material should require the pupil to apply what he has learned.

The completion test is composed of an incomplete statement which can be completed by some important word, phrase, or clause. The omitted part is the clue to the correctness of the statement. It requires recalling information and for that reason is preferred by some people over the recognition factor in most of the other objective type tests. It should be well written and make sense to the pupil. In scoring, the teacher should recognize equivalent answers even though it may make the process more difficult.

The matching test is made up of two columns of words or phrases that are related or complementary to each other. In one column the pupil will find a word or phrase that matches a word or phrase in the other. There should be more items in the answer column, so as to reduce possibility of answering by the process of elimination. The number of matching items should not exceed ten or twelve, as any greater number involves too much time in scanning the list and makes the test too difficult for its value. The items in each column are numbered and the numbering should be completely random, not in ascending or descending order. This test is best for measuring, identifying, and classifying factual material. Any honest and straightforward technique to reduce guessing is commendable. The test should be built around items that make sense, and absurdities should be avoided.

The oral and written quiz: Many teachers rely on little oral and written quizzes for spot checks on their pupils. These quizzes are short, often given at the beginning of a period, and take only five or ten minutes. They serve the purpose of keeping pupils on their toes and give the teacher a chance to determine how much preparation has been made on assignments. If given under wholesome conditions where the pupil feels that the exercise is fair, they serve a useful purpose for both teacher and pupil. It may be either written or oral. In a music class, orchestra, or band it may take the form of a spot performance check. These quizzes serve a purpose and open up new ways of evaluation both by the teacher and even the pupil himself. The pupil knows how well he has done.

Other ways of making pupil appraisals. Probably the most satisfying methods to the teacher himself, who sees beneath and beyond the more academic phases of growth, are yet to be discussed. What children do in day-to-day situations reveals much to the alert teacher. The young teacher through experience will come to see the many things children will do that indicate growth. He will keep notes on their behavior or work samples. Informal situations where pupils are talking and working with each other will be highly valuable to him for appraisals. All of these will have real merit and provide the discerning teacher with bases for judgment about the progress of his pupils.

Samples of the pupil's work, both the best and poorest, systematically taken from time to time, provide an excellent profile of the student. The material may be dated and put in a manila folder. Some pertinent facts, such as testing conditions, comments made both by the pupil and teacher, and any other expressions that might be forgotten, should be jotted down on the material. This should be kept throughout the year. Original stories, spelling lists, samples of art, original poems, pictures, examples of exercises in arithmetic— anything representative of the pupil makes excellent material for such a file. It serves as a reference for the teacher and can be used as illustrative material for a conference with the parent or the pupil. The pupil himself is quite capable of making comparisons within his own work.

Observations are another important source of information. The teacher and the pupil are together throughout the school year. The

The discerning supervisor soon learns, through observation, how teacher and children feel about each other.

Courtesy of *The Indiana Teacher*

teacher sees the pupil in almost every conceivable situation. He sees him alert and tired, prepared and blank, happy and unhappy, eager and lethargic. All of these situations come and go. The composite of all that the pupil is, was, and will be must be part of the total picture that the teacher finally constructs. All of the things he sees and jots down in his notes help him to make his evaluations and, finally, the decisions he as a teacher is professionally responsible for making.

Conferences too are useful—particularly those that the teacher has with the pupil whenever there is time and whenever needed. The exchanges of ideas with the student or little discussions when the pupil comes to ask for help are golden opportunities for the teacher to make appraisals. The kinds of questions that are asked, the kinds of attitudes that are shown, and the kinds and levels of ideas expressed are some of the teacher's best cues to what the pupil is and what he is becoming. In addition, the teacher has excellent chances to build up pupil-teacher relations.

In this last group of appraisal methods there are no standards other than those built up in the teacher from the first day he steps into the classroom as an observer or student teacher. He begins to see the work, answers, questions, reactions, and behavior of the pupil that he appraises. How apt and how skillful the teacher becomes depends upon his way of looking at himself, as well as his constant alertness to be continually a student of teaching. This serves as a check against either standardized tests or more formal examinations that he constructs. It takes the total appraisal to do justice to the pupil.

The teacher utilizes all the kinds of measurements at his command; some he will administer himself, but for others he needs to call on outside resources, even skilled, clinical services. Intelligence test, achievement test, informal test, observation, anecdotal record, sample of work—whatever it may be, all must be included to make the picture complete and completely useful.

SUMMARY

Intelligence tests are devised to determine intellectual power, while achievement tests are used to find out how much growth has been attained. Intelligence tests are always standardized, while achievement tests may be standardized or made up by the teacher himself to find out whether he has accomplished what he set out to do. Intelligence tests are used to show the teacher more about the pupil's potential so that work can be assigned commensurate with his strength, and to minimize the chance of expecting too much from the weaker pupil or pitching the work below the attainment power of the stronger pupil.

Achievement tests are built in many areas of the school's curricular program to enable the school and the teacher to determine the growths that are taking place. Tests have been devised in almost every imaginable phase of pupil accomplishment but there are definite limitations on one's being able to measure all of them. The intangibles in learning such as understanding, evaluation, judgment, creativity, thinking, and analysis are quite difficult to determine, and certainly teachers who have not specialized in clinical service would find themselves inadequate. Nevertheless, it is the responsibility of the classroom teacher to equip himself with as much background as possible in testing and to know where to turn when his own training is inadequate.

The classroom teacher will strengthen himself by keeping abreast of the current development of tests in areas such as character, attitude, personality, aptitude, and interests. Developments are being made all the time and the teacher needs to be fully aware of the possible new avenues to knowing more about his pupils and how he can do more for them.

Poor thinking and poor use of teacher time is all too frequent in the area of tests and quizzes that teachers themselves make. These examinations, while relatively crude, do form the bulk of the testing that takes place in the American classroom. The teacher can ill afford to do shoddy work in building his test, and surely needs to realize that there is a vast difference between the test that he deliberately sets up to measure the pupil's application of what he has learned and a test that at the most determines the pupil's ability to remember facts. Many quizzes will do only that, and the teacher should be warned against writing tests that go no deeper.

It is worth repeating that all informal, incidental conferences and conversations provide rich opportunity for the skilled teacher to gather valuable information about the strength, interests, and growth of his pupils, and that this forms a solid base of material upon which the teacher makes important judgments, not only of what has been accomplished, but what the next steps are to be as he continues to work with his learners.

Some competences that each teacher will need to develop in order to serve his pupils adequately in the area of measurement and evaluation are:

1. The ability to look objectively at the whole field of testing and measurement so that any prejudices can be removed from the way one approaches the task.

2. The attainment of necessary skill in giving and scoring tests so that a true measure can be secured of their validity and reliability.

3. The knowledge of what one wants to measure and the ability to select an adequate instrument.

4. The acquisition of enough background to know the general field of tests common to the ordinary school curriculum or, failing in that, knowledge of where to turn to secure that background.

5. Similarly, the same kind of background in the area of intelligence testing and special tests needed to know more about one's pupils.

6. A sound attitude toward the values and limitations of tests, so that a teacher will not only know how and when to use them but also how to discuss their value with the parents of the pupils.

7. The ability to transmit to pupils a feeling of security when taking a test, so that the pupil will understand that the test is a measure of his own strength and will avoid those tendencies often found in pupils to be unduly concerned about test results, even to the extent of seeking help by illegal means.

8. The ability to build a good test in any of the objective type forms.

9. The ability to build a strong essay type examination.

10. The ability to make strong analysis of conversations, conferences, and observations while working with pupils.

PROBLEMS

1. *Obtain samples of some of the more common achievement tests in your field and make a careful study of the content as it relates to what you and your supervisor are doing.*

2. *Obtain at least two well known group intelligence tests and make a careful analysis of the directions and the manual for interpretation of test results so that you will have some acquaintance with manuals.*

3. *In an area that lends itself well to an essay type test, build what seems to you to be a good essay test and get the permission of your supervisor to use it. In the light of the results determine the strengths and weaknesses of your test.*

4. *Build a completion test, a true-false test, a multiple-choice test, and a completion test. Determine their strengths and weaknesses.*

5. *Secure O. K. Buros' The Fourth Mental Measurements Yearbook (Highland Park, N.J.: Gryphon Press, 1953) and make a careful study of how this yearbook can be of help to you in your work as a professional person. Discuss your analysis with your college supervisor.*

6. *Get samples of tests of aptitude, character, personality, and attitude and build up your background of information about their function and reliability.*

7. *Talk with your supervisor about the clinical services that are available in your community for going beyond the testing that you yourself can do.*

BIBLIOGRAPHY

Anastasi, Anne, *Psychological Testing*. New York: The Macmillan Company, 1954.

Bean, K. L., *Construction of Educational Tests*. New York: McGraw-Hill Book Company, 1953.

Buros, O. K., ed., *The Fourth Mental Measurements Yearbook*. New Brunswick, N.J.: Rutgers University Press, 1953.

Cronbach, Lee J., *Essentials of Psychological Testing*. New York: Henry Holt and Company, Inc., 1950.

———, "Test 'Reliability': Its Meaning and Determination," *Psychometrika* 12:1-16, 1947.

Goodenough, Florence L., *Mental Testing, Its History, Principles and Applications*. New York: Rinehart and Company, 1949.

Greene, E. B., *Measurement of Human Behavior*. New York: Odyssey Press, 1952.

Greene, H. A., A. N. Jorgenson, and J. R. Gerberich, *Measurement and Evaluation in the Elementary School*. New York: Longmans, Green & Company, 1953.

———, *Measurement and Evaluation in the Secondary School*. New York: Longmans, Green & Company, 1954.

Otis, A. S., *Otis Quick-Scoring Mental Ability Tests: Manual of Directions for Alpha Test*. Yonkers-on-Hudson, N.Y.: World Book Company, 1939.

———, *Otis Quick-Scoring Mental Ability Tests: Manual of Directions for Beta Test*. Yonkers-on-Hudson, N.Y.: World Book Company, 1939.

Remmers, H. H., and N. L. Gage, *Educational Measurement and Evaluation*. New York: Harper & Brothers, 1955.

Ross, C. C., and Julian C. Stanley, *Measurements in Today's Schools*, 3rd ed. Englewood Cliffs, N.J.: Prentice-Hall, Inc., 1954.

Terman, L. M., and Maud A. Merrill, *Directions for Administering Forms L and M Revision of Stanford-Binet Tests of Intelligence*. Boston: Houghton Mifflin Company, 1937.

———, *Measuring Intelligence*. Boston: Houghton Mifflin Company, 1937.

Travers, Robert M. W., *How to Make Achievement Tests*. New York: The Odyssey Press, 1950.

15

Responsibility for reporting to parents

One of the major considerations of the school is that of the school report to parents about their children. There is nothing compulsory about the school reporting to parents, other than the ethical responsibility and the fact that the school needs to build up good relationships in order to be in a position to do more for the child. Parents are legally responsible for their children. The state assumes the responsibility for public education and demands that parents send their children to school. The compulsory attendance age limit varies from state to state, but is usually between the ages of seven and sixteen. Compulsory responsibility for children, however, is most difficult to establish in the mind of the parent who does not choose to assume it. However, the filial obligation is naturally strong, and parents by nature are generally strongly concerned about their children. On the other hand, this concern is often misdirected or erratic. The school too often seems to take the attitude that all parents are assuming responsibility when in reality many are not, and only through social and legal pressure do some parents assume even a token portion of the responsibility that is necessarily theirs.

The problems of reporting. Problems often arise because not all parents possess background and intelligence to understand what comes to them by way of a report, and not all teachers possess sufficient background and ability to report lucidly. The general deficiency here is not so much an inability to understand as a mere lack of information. Often neither has the teacher the facility to report nor the parent the facility to understand, and when both factors are operating together it is indeed difficult. In between reside all the emotional complications resulting from an unfavorable report card together with the teacher's tendency to add personal conduct to the report, thus seeming unfair to the child and parents who dislike evaluations of conduct as part of the report.

In almost all cases the report is written about the pupil and addressed to the parents. This is in itself a rather unfortunate circumstance. If the report is unfavorable the pupil finds himself carrying his own indictment home. Often by its very nature the report card carries implications of carelessness, laziness, bad attitude, and a host of similar bad attributes against which the child must defend himself. The teacher is the accuser, and the parent is the judge, who becomes all too often quite impatient with the accused. What a predicament for the child! Much of the difficulty would be completely eliminated if the teacher faithfully avoided any written report that involved conduct, and left this for personal conferences.

The school too often brings another difficulty upon itself by giving the impression that the report card is a report of progress or growth. Growth in children is often very slow and the period between reports is usually too short to reflect growth. Because teachers are hard pressed to detect growth in such short periods, reports should not declare that no progress or growth has been observable. Reports in such negative terms are in themselves discouraging and damaging to the child. Such expressions as "shows no interest," "disturbs others," "not cooperative," and "does not use his time to advantage" all may be true, but are symptoms of problems that are far more difficult of solution. The expert clinician can well afford to be reserved about mentioning symptoms to his lay clientele or to those who would be involved so closely as to become emotionally upset about his hypotheses.

The report card does need to give information about the child, in a language that the one who receives it understands. Just as we find individual differences in learners, there are individual differences in their parents. Yet the school puts out uniform reports and assumes that all parents have equal facility in interpreting the message they impart. Unfortunately parents are not equally able to understand because they have such wide variations of backgrounds. In addition to these variations are the many attitudes that they carry into adulthood from their own experiences in carrying home the school report to their own parents. Not all parents had pleasant experiences with report cards, nor were the reports themselves always favorably received.

A great deal has been written about the report card carrying a message consistent with the philosophy of the school. If the teacher is to report in the light of the school's philosophy, it is highly important that both the teacher and the parent understand fully what the philosophy of the school is and, better still, that they share in determining that philosophy. This introduces a difficult problem for the teacher. He not only must know thoroughly the philosophy of the school and the pupil, but he must understand the attitudes of the parents to whom he sends the report.

The teacher will have a most difficult time informing parents of the school's purposes and the direction in learning that is being promoted. On the other hand, the parent too has responsibilities for knowing the school and coming to grips with its problems. But here again it seems that the school carries the heavier burden of education on the subject of parental responsibilities. Vast numbers of parents are exceptionally active in their efforts to know all they can about their children and are unusually helpful in cooperating with the school in coming to understand what the school's purposes are, and in sharing with the school its educational activities. However, since the school exists for all children, the teacher cannot be led to complacency by the success he enjoys with the more cooperative and intelligently active parents. The greatest difficulty lies with those parents who either do not have the time or do not see the values in taking time to work closely with the school. Unfortunately, the children of these parents often encounter the most difficulty in school. They are entitled to all the help that the teacher can give.

The young teacher will soon realize that one of his most difficult problems lies in the area of communication with the home. If he assumes that all parents are equally proficient in reading the written report his thinking is unrealistic. He can expect his parents to be eager to read what he writes and hopeful that the report will be favorable. The favorable report will likely be easier to write, but not necessarily more understandable. So many of the expressions that are more or less standard on reports are quite meaningless when looked at with scrutiny. Take for example the expressions, "Is a good group worker," "Does excellent work," or "Gets along well in the group." All appear favorable and are meant that way. But the parents may wonder by what standards the teacher arrived at the decision. Even an "A" may be most satisfying to the parents and pupils, but represent quite mediocre performance by the standards of many teachers. These are representative of the problems the teacher faces when he attempts to send a message home about a pupil's work.

It is extremely important for the teacher to analyze how he feels about the report, and also how he feels about the person to whom he is sending it. Perhaps the teacher can sympathize with the position of the parents and direct the message to their level of comprehension. If he can take an attitude of kindness toward the parents and toward the task of reporting, the report will carry a spirit of good will, kindness, and gentleness that is essential. It is one task that should not be put off until haste, fatigue, and irritation are likely to show. Too often just because the task is hard and other things have pushed the work aside, the report to parents is written late at night under circumstances that are not favorable for good messages. A kindly spirit reflected in the report can set the stage for wholesome relations between the home and the school that will bring great rewards in teamwork later. Just a note of a few words on an otherwise formal report can soften the impact of a harsh report. Like a tender smile, a kindly tone to a note carries its message to the parent. It is worth trying.

Characteristics of a good report card. A good report card should be in language that is familiar to as many parents as possible. The teacher should avoid words that are familiar only to the profession. Words that may be easily misinterpreted should be omitted. Simplicity of terms will add greatly to its effectiveness.

As stated earlier, a form of report that has been worked out cooperatively between the school and parents is quite likely to meet with far more favor from the home. This matter of having shared in the construction of the report increases the likelihood of its bearing many points about which parents have considerable interest. Likewise, in the process parents and teachers come to understand each other better.

Here again the philosophy of the school can and should be reflected in the report. Take, for example, something as simple as the matter of promotion and retention, especially in the elementary school: If the report goes out from a school system where there is rather general agreement that retention in a grade is quite useless, both from the point of view of the teacher and from the standpoint of natural growth of the learner, the report should carefully avoid language that reflects failure or futility. Instead the emphasis should be placed on those areas where growth has taken place and where encouragement will result in an effective effort.

The report will describe the child as an individual and stress his progress in terms of his own capacity and in relation to his own personality. It will not be couched in terms that give the parents any reference to a standard or norm, and will emphasize those things that parents want to know. The school and the home will have agreed on those points. They will be accurate, fair, and thoughtfully stated so that both child and parents will respect the report.

It will not be enough to point out what the weakness may be. The report will go further and point out reasons, so that if at all possible the child will understand and agree with the teacher on why the problems are encountered. If the child knows *why*, a better contact with the home will have been made, because the child can aid in the explanation to the parents.

The report should be so structured as to lend itself to efficient use by the teacher. The clerical work necessary for its use should be at a minimum. The teacher should encounter no difficulty in its use due to complexity; simplicity in form will lend simplicity in understanding. This may be resolved by the use of symbols and phrases that are easily inserted or checked. However, there should be space where added statements can be written to clarify matters that are not routine. Likewise, there should be space for the parent to write a simple return message or comment that will add to the teamwork of communication.

Insofar as records are essential, the report should provide necessary data for cumulative reports on the developmental aspects of the child. Such considerations will keep to a minimum the clerical services that are needed, many of which fall on the teaching personnel in small schools.

Lastly, the report should be of such content, form, and style as to enable the teacher to feel kindly about it because it requires a minimum of his time to write. It should reflect a teacher attitude that will solicit teamwork on the part of the parents and the child and thus add to the over-all effectiveness of the school in the development of the pupil as a learner.

Some types of written reports. There have been many types of report cards. The very fact that so many schools are engaged in revising them indicates that the schools are not satisfied. The prevalence of faculty and parents' committees giving time and thought to the problem is indeed encouraging. While they may conclude that there is no best way, the process of joint thinking goes a long way toward clarifying purposes and resolving misunderstandings. The school administrator and teacher are wise indeed who think through the matter together with representative parents. The teacher should always be ready to work in such a venture. It will be time well spent.

Many schools use letter or number grades to report the work of the pupil to the parent. It makes very little difference whether letters or numbers are used. Any grade that is symbolic of a quality of work done has the same type of message. The per cent mark does the same, but the gradations are even more finite. Teachers find themselves doing the same thing to letter marks when they use a plus or a minus sign after the mark. Schools have complicated the problem even further by suggesting that each group or class in some manner approaches a normal curve. This forces the teacher to mark about as many with low marks as with high marks, and spread the remainder in between.

Per cent and letter grades are used in as many schools as any other form of report—even today. They are used by people who think they serve the purpose as well as any other, and by those who take neither the time nor the initiative to change the report. Many teachers and administrative personnel think that the mark or percentage grade reports a degree of skill or knowledge that is necessary for competence in a course, and find it quite satisfactory for providing an incentive for more diligent application or a reproof for loafing on the

job. They also say that it is more generally understood than anything else and takes less of the teacher's time. Employers and college
admissions officers quite often appear to think that they understand
the significance of the mark, especially when coupled with a candidate's specific rank in his class.

This opens up the most disturbing factor about marks. Rank in
class denotes a competitive climate and creates many frustrations
and disappointments, which are likely to be quite harmful to the
growing boy or girl, and to create at the same time many problems
for those responsible for the situation. Grades are closely related to
special intelligence or special aptitude. The school tends to put a
premium on school-brightness and a stigma on school-dullness. No
child is really dull until he goes to school, and usually is never dull
after he leaves its doors. Grades and marks are the school's best devices for showing up the dull and the bright—and incidentally for
producing inferiority in the minds of those who are not able to do
what the school expects.

Pupils work for grades, but such an incentive for learning is
scarcely to be defended. In the first place, marks have no real meaning. How different are the marks of the teacher who gives every
child the benefit of the doubt from the one who is by nature somewhat skeptical! Academic progress is emphasized out of proportion
to the more important elements of social and emotional development that the school should be emphasizing. Furthermore, it is far
too discouraging to the slow child who is not school-bright but for
whom society has an important place, and gives false complacency
to the bright child who by virtue of his native intelligence has *accomplished* comparatively little. Teachers will continue to use
grades and marks, but they should recognize the limitations of the
method and examine themselves often lest they create worse results
than are actually necessary. A grade or mark tailored to the individual's own ability will lessen the evils of the system, but may complicate the problems for the teacher when he is asked to explain how
he arrived at a grade. Moreover, directors of admission at colleges
would tend to lose faith in the transcripts they receive. On the other
hand, grades and marks do lend themselves to cumulative academic records, even though the reliability of such a profile may be
questionable.

A variation of the grade is the check sheet where characteristics as well as area analyses are featured. Such phrases as, "Gets along well with others," "Uses his time well," and "Industrious" attempt to point out behavior characteristics that the school considers important, whereas phrases such as, "Speaks clearly," "Uses punctuation marks correctly," or "Reads with understanding" attempt to point up area analyses that are considered worth while. These lists give the parent a descriptive report that will carry more meaning to the discerning parent with well formulated opinions of what growths he feels are important. Some schools vary this type of report by using two symbols in the place of a check mark. One denotes satisfactory progress (S), the other unsatisfactory progress (U). In either case the task of checking is heavy unless the school follows the practice of marking only a part of the characteristics or reports at longer intervals. Really the teacher who reports at longer intervals is in a more defensible position, because growth or change can be better determined if longer periods of time have elapsed.

Such a plan, if used carefully and thoughtfully, will do justice to the pupil, because it speaks in terms of the ability of the individual and avoids comparisons with others who may have different academic capacities. It could well be used to encourage both the rapid and slow learners to do their best. Competition for marks can be largely eliminated and the scope of the report can be as broad as the school's area of concern. It will not be narrowed by academic boundaries that apply too frequently to the "school-bright" pupils.

One limitation of this system is that in eliminating the factor of competition incentive will be lost for a great number of pupils. The strong and slow student alike will be satisfied with mediocrity. A cumulative report will be difficult to transmit to another school, college, or employment office. The marks may be more subjective in their origin than academic grades. The task of recording and reporting will likely be infinitely more involved and time consuming for the teacher.

The letter. The practice of reporting to the parent by letter is limited only by the time or analytical ability of the one who is writing. It can go into all phases of the development of the learner and be as meaningful as the descriptive vocabulary of the teacher permits; it can carry almost any message that the teacher wishes to convey to the parent. However, the limitations on the letter are much the same as with the personal conference. How the teacher feels toward the child, or toward the parent for that matter, will be reflected heavily in the letter. To convey a maximum amount of information the teacher should be at his very best when he writes a letter, so that the things he says will be in terms totally acceptable to the parent. Negativism and destructive criticism should be avoided completely. A letter written when the teacher is annoyed by the conduct of a child is quite likely to reflect the feelings of the teacher at the time. If a teacher should write a letter while under stress, he should put it aside and re-read it to see if what he has said will prove constructive, or at least has portrayed his message in his most effective language. No teacher who professes skill in understanding children can afford to be incapable of analyzing himself. He should know quite well when he is capable of communicating with the parents in language that carries dignity, professional enthusiasm, and encouragement. The pupil about whom he writes should be portrayed at his best. The letter should strengthen the teamwork between home and school and nurture the bonds of cooperation necessary for the child to progress at his best.

Even at his best, the teacher will face real difficulty. It is not easy to say unfavorable things in a favorable way. The teacher has the opportunity to strengthen the confidence parents have in him and in the profession each time contact is made with the home. To be able to relay difficult messages favorably is an art that the teacher should develop, because the dividends in cooperation and appreciation are well worth his consideration. The one who possesses such a skill makes a notable contribution to the total profession in the good will he helps to generate toward all teachers.

Each letter can be personalized so that no reference need be made to others in the group by way of comparison and contrast. It can be specific in that it may set forth what the teacher wishes the child to be able to do and state in simple language what the child now seems able or unable to accomplish. It can give the reasons why the child does or does not do what is required, and how the teacher proposes to go about getting results. It can make suggestions to the parents, although unless the teacher knows the parents quite well this is perhaps best omitted in a letter and postponed to a personal conference. The stigma of low marks can be omitted because the teacher need not write in terms of grades at all. If the teacher can write letters in such a way that he elicits a reply, so much the better. From the reply he can learn much, even though it may not be written with as much tact and good judgment as he, himself, tried to use. The burden of good relations will reside in the teacher. He should take full re- sponsibility for whatever good he is able to create. The emphasis should be on positive relationships throughout the report.

The difficulty that arises in reporting by letter is that it is very time consuming. It is also quite true that a teacher would much pre- fer to say nice things in a personal letter, and consequently makes the report even more favorable than is justifiable. Every teacher must learn that a false report eventually catches up with the writer. Then the problem of explaining his way out becomes quite humiliat- ing to him. It should be fully understood that letters that cannot be misinterpreted are hard to write. If the teacher is not alert he will find himself stereotyping his letters in much the same manner as a formal report. The good effect is totally lost when such a condition occurs.

The conference. Still another way of reporting to parents is through the conference, which in many ways is superior to any other method. It takes time, in fact much time, but there are many who assert that it is so worth while that the time is well spent. In fact, more and more schools are allotting regular school hours to conferences with parents. In the conference method, understand- ings should be so established that both the parents and the teacher feel free to ask for a conference; in fact, the school is in a more favorable position when the parent has asked for a conference. The more nearly that full mutual confidence is felt, the more likely the conference is to be helpful to the child. Benefit to the child should be uppermost in the minds of both the parents and the teacher. The teacher, however, carries the professional responsibility for seeing that it reaches that high purpose.

The best result of a conference is the friendly relationship that can be developed. This relationship is the potential for a partner- ship in which the child gains. Conferences are in this way creative: where understandings did not exist before, after a conference, con- fidences, strengths, and teamwork can be developed. Where the parent and the teacher had previously gone each his own way in working with the child, after a good conference they have the feeling of mutual effort. They come to accept each other's point of view, and differences are smoothed out.

Naturally all of these benefits depend upon the attitudes of the participants. The only one that can be actually controlled is that of the teacher himself. He can be master of the situation. If his attitude is one of kindliness toward the conference, the parent, and the child, the chance for success is practically assured. In fact, that sort of attitude can extend to the parent himself. It is most difficult to be against someone who is demonstrating an attitude of cooperation. If the teacher has the time and the desire, the possibilities within the conference are limited only by the potential of the other party for an effective contribution to the conference.

One limitation to conferences worth noting is that mothers carry

The good teacher welcomes the opportunity to sit down with a pupil's parent to discuss their mutual problems.

Courtesy of *The Indiana Teacher*

too much of the responsibility that fathers should share. If the conference is during the day the mother is almost sure to have to carry the burden. Another limitation is that it is difficult to keep a record of understandings and agreements. If too much is made of keeping a record the informality is partially destroyed, and faith created may be shaken. The teacher may be obligated to file some form of report on the conference and this will add to the time factor and make the conference method less attractive.

Still another problem arising from the conference is the emotional disturbance with the parent. The parent will be more likely to ask for a conference when he is emotionally disturbed, while the teacher will seldom ask for a conference when he is emotionally disturbed if he is using his best judgment. The conference that grows out of an emotional upset could hardly be classified as the ordinary "reporting about Tommy" variety but it is a real part of the picture, and conditions the situation and possible success for any future relations.

Experienced teachers have found that the best way to conduct a conference with a parent when the parent has come in disturbed is to sit quietly and listen. Even if the parent is making statements that are untrue and even unfair, such an occasion is no time to engage in argument. A kindly, sympathetic attitude encourages the parent to talk himself out and then be in a frame of mind to discuss the problem objectively. The burden of setting up a climate for a conference is always on the school, and a failure in a conference rests squarely on the individual representing the school. No teacher or administrator can reap any satisfaction from a poor conference or for "getting a parent told." The child alone suffers from a poor conference and the function of the conference is destroyed. A poor conference may make it impractical if not impossible to have another in the future. An ambassador in a community declaring that conferences with Mr. Sour are useless helps neither the teacher nor the school. So the pattern for a conference when the parent asks for one is to encourage the parent to talk. After all, he asked for the conference and has something to say to the teacher.

On the other hand, if the teacher asks for the conference the problem is entirely different. The teacher should ask for a conference only when he is at his best. After all, his professional poise and dignity should be utilized, and by the very nature of the situation he is involved in talking about a technical, professional problem to a lay person who may not be as well informed about it as he. It is his responsibility to set the parent at ease. This can be done by chatting about something in which the two have mutual interest. Something as simple as the weather may be discussed—or civic affairs or entertainment. People have many things in common that eliminate barriers. The opening remarks about the problem at hand should be such as to put the parent at ease. The parent will quite often say "I hope something has not happened." The teacher should be relaxed and start his conference on a cheerful note. If the conference is about a difficult conduct problem the good things can be said first, because every child does have good points if we take the trouble to see them. The parent most assuredly knows some good points about the child in question, and the teacher is under a handicap if he hasn't discovered them also.

The teacher should speak sincerely and straightforwardly after the real problem is introduced, but his use of words should be carefully thought out. He should give his point of view based on facts that he can rely upon. He should always have the child's welfare in mind and discuss the case with such clarity and simplicity that the parent will be able to see that the teacher is working for the best interests of the child. If the problem is an academic one he should have samples of the child's work to support his case. He should be well informed about ways of working with such situations as the one in question. He must remember that he is expected to be the authority in matters of this kind. On the other hand, if he is in a system that has specialists in reading, speech, or arithmetic he can call upon them.

The principal and teacher should work as a team and decide together whether the conference will be helped if the principal is present. There are many situations where just teacher and parent, who are close to the problem, can do more than when others are added who are not intimately acquainted with all of the facts. Principal and teacher should work so cooperatively that mutual understandings are operating to determine who shall make up the participants in the conference. The teacher should use the child's first name and should avoid use of a nickname, even if it is prevalently used by other children or even by the parent.

Here might be a good place to advise young teachers that nicknames should be avoided at all times when teaching. Many children dislike their nicknames very much, and teachers endanger their good relations with the child when they use them. The possible exception would be when the teacher is asked by the child to use a name other than his given name—although even under these conditions it remains questionable.

After the teacher has presented his facts he should solicit the parent's suggestions. The parent cannot be expected to give ideas of a technical nature but he may be able to uncover emotional, physical, or social factors that have a direct relation to the problem, even if it is an academic one. It will help greatly to avoid any reference to nonpromotion or failure. Some schools place great emphasis on having made parents aware of an impending failure, but such practice is questionable because of the strained relations and pressure created by such implied threats. Even if the parent inquires whether failure is imminent, the teacher should look hopefully for improvement instead of taking a defeatist attitude that will probably increase the problem. Suggestions to the parent for outside professional help of a medical nature are always possible, and often worth while. Tutorial service is questionable, especially if the parent suggests that the teacher be the tutor. If the teacher does give help as a tutor no charge should be made. The teacher should carefully avoid anything that sounds as if the school is accusing the parent of being short of responsibility. The teacher may quite accurately think such is the case, but no real good can come of saying so and it would only widen the differences between school and home. When the parent himself suggests that he may be derelict in his responsibility, the teacher need not contradict, if he thinks the parent is really making a factual statement. In other words, if the parent convicts himself correctly let it stand. If the parent proposes helping the child it is probably best to encourage him. No great harm can be done, and the parent may come to see the problem more clearly. The teacher may even offer suggestions if the parent seems eager to help and capable of doing so. Conferences offer every possibility for strengthening teamwork; the whole relationship can be entirely transformed after a good conference.

The other kind of conference, involving discipline and conduct, is something entirely different and merits some thought. Almost always the school asks for the conference when the problem is conduct, unless some disciplinary action has been taken to which the parent takes exception or about which the parent may have a question. The teacher should bear in mind that disciplinary measures quite often bring questions and concern from the parents. This is the way it should be. Parents should be concerned when matters reach the point where disciplinary action is necessary. The teacher should be prepared to explain why he proposes to take the action he does, or to defend if necessary the action he has already taken. The teacher should use those methods that he is sure are approved by parents and that he is confident are therapeutic in nature. He should also always know that what he does meets the complete approval of his principal. This is very important, because the principal, while professionally obligated to support his teacher even when he may be making mistakes, loses faith in the judgment of the teacher. This is quite detrimental to the school staff morale. Faith is a reciprocal situation for which all parties have direct responsibility. Probably the best that can come from conferences of this kind are mutual understandings, clearings of points of view, and teamwork that will be helpful to the child. Here again out of the conferences comes a relationship that did not previously exist. That relationship can bring home and school closer together. If the school is determined to practice understanding, good can result. It is when both parties are obstinate that no good results are produced.

One other approach to the conference is worthy of note. This is the conference that supplements some form of written report. The two methods make a worth-while combination, when written statements of the more formal type or of the letter form set the stage for a conference either at home or at school. Here the teacher will probably be the one who proposes a conference, unless the home writes back a note requesting further clarification. In any case, the basis is set for the conference. It can then be directed to the child and the problem in question and misunderstandings can be resolved. It has great possibilities for both the teacher and the parent and for the ultimate good of the child.

The child can become a party to the report or conference. In all situations the child is the focal point in any discussion between parent and teacher. The teacher has the responsibility for demonstrating the greatest of respect for and faith in the child's parent. This should be so obvious that the child can under no circumstances point out instances or quote the teacher in a way that will be derogatory to the parent. This will be difficult at times, because some parents do conduct themselves badly and are surely unworthy of the trust that they hold. The teacher, however, has an ideal toward which he is working that is embodied in home strengthening. This cannot be accomplished by criticism that can be misinterpreted. Therefore the often-quoted statement that the teacher is always right can be rewritten that father and mother are always right, too. This sets the stage for the ambassadorship of the pupil, who is part of both the home and the school.

The pupil and teacher can talk through their problem and, as stated earlier, lasting improvement only comes when the pupil assumes the responsibility for change. This assumption of responsibility comes about because of the pupil's voluntary or involuntary action. It is largely voluntary when through interest, challenge, or encouragement the pupil sets up new and better goals for himself. It is involuntary when through certain choices of action there are coercive elements involved. This can happen when the purposes and goals of the pupil are not totally accepted or understood, or are more acceptable to the teacher and parent than to the pupil. The goal of the teacher is to help the pupil build purposes and goals that he feels a share in and takes pride in claiming as his own. These can range all the way from being able to know how to read a sentence to having reasons for being proud of the government in his city.

If it has been established that it is fundamentally important for teacher and pupil to have mutual purposes and goals, it is only one step further to have the parent share in this responsibility also. If the parent does not know what these purposes are, the pupil and school alike can make them known. In fact, it is better still if the parent has had a share in their formulation. But if this is not the case, then the pupil is a front line contact into the home. To the extent that he is enlightened and informed, the parent can be made aware of the problem also.

Inasmuch as the pupil carries the written report and even oral messages to the home, there is nothing wrong with his knowing what is contained in the report, and it is really imperative that he understand why it is the kind of report it is, and if possible he should share in its making. How far better if the child says that he agrees with the report than that he doesn't see how he ever received that

grade or check mark! Some teachers find it advantageous to have the
pupil write a report also, and then after making the reports as compatible as possible put both reports in the envelope, thus sharing
the message in the simple act of inserting it in the envelope. Shared
feelings about the report that goes home make the pupil and teacher
a team, and they too become different persons because of this sharing. Lastly, the teacher can reap great rewards from diligently striving to send the child home from school in a happy frame of mind.
Extra work after school hours under duress is likely to be wasted. It
probably has very little effect and may modify the attitude toward
school to a great extent. A happy ambassador leaving school results
in a happy ambassador reaching home.

The report or conference affects public relations.   In the
first place the report stems from all the purposes for which the
school exists. The report can be a substantiation that the purposes
and the results are in a state of compatibility and that the goals are
being met in a satisfactory manner. If the report performs its function as efficiently as possible in bringing about mutual understandings, it will indicate that school and community have worked so
closely that all the goals set for the school have been mutually derived from the thinking of all persons with a stake in the program.
With this as an optimum situation, the degree to which these understandings have been achieved determines the strength of the report.

Assuming that the school and community have cooperatively determined the program of education for the youth of the community
under consideration, the report is the school's guarantee that the relationships are operative and that the understandings are at least attainable. Communications are the avenues through which relationships are developed. The degree to which these communications get
through and parents see accepted goals being reached will determine the extent of approval or disapproval of those who support the
educational program. The school leadership recognizes that this approval is basic to the very existence of the school, and the extent to
which this support is maintained determines the ultimate level of
provision for schools in the community.

When one looks at the report as a part of good honest salesman-
ship of the schools to the community it appears vitally important.
The teacher needs to recognize that he holds the master key to the

home of every child he teaches, and with this in mind he must make the report in all honesty but make it in a constructive manner—even to the extent of saying unfavorable things favorably.

The spirit of experimentation in the area of reporting. In no place in the field of education is there less agreement on method than in the field of reports to parents. Teachers may agree on the merit of conferences as a method, but the element of time bears so heavily that many will give up in despair, and judge the results as good but deplore the fact that they just can't take the time from a busy day. And really it is not only teachers who complain about the time consumed. The parent as well is too busy to give the time.

Watching the cycle in a community where teachers honestly attack the problem of improving reports, and seeing how they go from letter grades to marks of satisfactory and unsatisfactory, then to check lists, then perhaps to an informal letter or to the conference and then, if the cycle is complete, back to letter grades or some one of the forms already used, one recognizes the general concern and the general dissatisfaction with any one method used. With the search generally on, the teacher will do well to keep his mind wide open for better ways of communicating to his clientele.

Maybe the most he can do is to search for what fits his own personality, his busy schedule, or the levels of understanding of those with whom he would communicate. The search will go on, and through the professional improvement of each new generation of teachers and the equally strong advancement in the concern for children in each succeeding generation of parents the picture will not continue to be dark. Either of the two factors in the school-community partnership will strongly influence the other.

In the meantime the teacher, recognizing that he has an important public relations opportunity, will search for better ways to say the things that have to be said if the parents are to know the facts. No other area needs so much thought, and in no other area will rewards for improvement be so satisfying as in the area of communication between teacher and parent. Bear in mind that each good communication affects both parties to the communication and may improve the welfare of the pupil about whom the report is made.

SUMMARY

The school has a clear responsibility for keeping parents informed about the development and growth of their children. The teacher is the one person best qualified to report intelligently to the parents. The parents can be expected to make a reasonable effort to understand the message or report that comes from the school. However, there are great differences in background and concern on the part of parents, and the school must take this fact into consideration. The teacher will recognize that letters or even telephone conversations to some parents must be much more simply worded than to others. The parent with a meager education will not understand information given in a vocabulary that only the more intelligent or more highly educated would understand readily. The wise teacher will use simple words, and language that is common to the great mass of the population, so that he will not be misunderstood.

The report should be direct and so stated that it relates to the person about whom the report is given. Possibly the most effective report is the conference with the parent. But this takes much time and in many instances is impractical or almost impossible. However, the parent who is hard to reach through conferences is likewise quite often difficult to reach through written messages. Nevertheless the good teacher sets as his goal to reach all parents, regardless of apparent difficulty in communication.

Teachers will find all kinds of techniques used for reporting, and the intervals will range from once each month or six weeks to once each semester or to any time when it seems that a report would be helpful or necessary. Ideally, this is the best approach to reporting, since need for reports arises at irregular intervals. Practically, though, the school cannot afford to be placed in the position of apparent neglect in reporting, and many teachers get busy at other more pressing problems and neglect to report when it really is urgent. Reports, in addition to the two forms just mentioned, are made by check sheets, formal grades, and standardized statements of progress or failure to progress. Any report takes time and the good teacher will set aside time for this important function.

The teacher should always be straightforward and careful to say or write just what he means. Many times the teacher is obliged to say unpleasant things in a way that is not offensive or that may not alienate the cooperation of the parents. Much experience will be needed in developing this particular skill. The teacher must be sincere and honest, but he needn't offend the pride of the parent. A spirit of mutual confidence must be maintained and the teacher can take the lead in working in such a way as to develop faith and confidence. Only rarely will a parent so treated fail to return the same kind of working attitude.

The pupil can aid in this all-important problem. The teacher-pupil relationship can be such that the pupil will understand what he does well and where he is making little or no growth. Pupil purposes and teacher purposes can be compatible and mutually set up. The pupil can be an important factor in keeping his parents informed or in a frame of mind to be sympathetic toward the efforts of the school and his own progress. The teacher can ill afford to work with the pupil in such a way that the pupil feels inclined to blame his teacher for his lack of growth or progress. The teacher should always be right and in the minds of parent and pupil be doing everything possible for the pupil, but such confidence must be merited. Only the teacher can make it that way.

Competences that are essential in the field of reporting to parents are herewith suggested:

1. The ability to set up timetables for work so that making reports is done when the teacher is at his best both physically and mentally.

2. The ability to write or speak in language that conveys readily to the parent the ideas that the teacher wishes him to receive.

3. The ability to say unfavorable things in such a manner that the parent remains loyal to and sympathetic toward the efforts of the child, teacher, and school.

4. The ability to be versatile in language usage so that varied ways of wording messages can be put into use. Stereotyped reports lack color and become ineffective.

5. The ability to listen to the parent during a conference and then make a kindly but straightforward answer based on facts that are available to the teacher and can be interpreted to the parent through the teacher's use of effective words.

6. The ability to work with pupils in setting up mutual purposes so that the pupil feels a responsibility for sharing reports to parents based upon his success in carrying out those purposes.

7. Similarly, the ability to work with parents so as to engage them in sharing purposes that are for the successful development of the pupil, and that pupil and teacher have agreed upon to carry through.

8. The ability to utilize the kind of report that is best adapted to the pupil, the parents, and the situation, material, or condition that the teacher is reporting.

9. The creative ability to see new ways of making contacts with parents regarding the educational experiences of their children, together with the continuous desire to retain best ways of reporting but willingness to discontinue those ways that do not prove effective.

PROBLEMS

1. Ask your supervisor to permit you to sit in on some of his conferences with parents in which your presence will not be detrimental. Analyze the role of each of the parties in the conference, drawing your own conclusions as to their respective ability to convey ideas to each other.

2. Secure samples of report forms in school with which you are familiar. Determine what problems you would encounter in reporting the progress of a few selected pupils with the report forms that are used in the school.

3. Select a pupil in your group about whom it will be difficult to report favorably. Write a letter to the parents of this pupil, writing frankly your analysis of the pupil's problems, but do this in such a way that you are confident of retaining the good will of the parents or even strengthening their faith in the school.

4. *Your supervisor permitting, discuss the progress of one of your better pupils with his parents. Determine how you can best present the report to the parents, and assess how well you permit the parents to present their views and how well you lead them to present their problems.*

5. *Since you will find it helpful to keep your mind open to new ways of communicating with parents, try devising your own form for reporting that seems to meet the needs as you see the problem.*

6. *Visit at least three homes and under the direction of your supervisor discuss the progress of the pupils concerned. Determine the problems that the teacher faces when he goes into the home for a home visit.*

BIBLIOGRAPHY

Adams, Harold P., and Frank G. Dickey, *Basic Principles of Student Teaching*. New York: American Book Company, 1956.

Curtis, Dwight K., and Leonard O. Andrews, *Guiding Your Student Teacher*. Englewood Cliffs, N.J.: Prentice-Hall, Inc., 1954.

Freeland, A. M., "Helping Parents Understand," *National Elementary Principal* 35:236-44, September 1955.

Garrison, Noble Lee, *The Improving of Teaching*. New York: The Dryden Press, 1955.

Grim, Paul R., and John U. Michaelis, *The Student Teacher in the Secondary School*. Englewood Cliffs, N.J.: Prentice-Hall, Inc., 1953.

Grinnell, J. R., and Raymond J. Young, *The School and the Community*. New York: The Ronald Press Company, 1955.

Huggut, Albert J., and T. M. Stinnett, *Professional Problems of Teachers*. New York: The Macmillan Company, 1956.

Hymes, James L., *Effective Home-School Relations*. Englewood Cliffs, N.J.: Prentice-Hall, Inc., 1953.

Klausmeier, Herbert J., *et al.*, *Teaching in the Elementary School*. New York: Harper & Brothers, 1956.

Langdon, Grace, and Irving W. Stout, *Teacher-Parent Interviews*. Englewood Cliffs, N.J.: Prentice-Hall, Inc., 1954.

Michaelis, John U., and Paul R. Grim, *The Student Teacher in the Elementary School*. Englewood Cliffs, N.J.: Prentice-Hall, Inc., 1953.

Passon, A. H., and M. L. Goldberg, "Overcoming Blocks in Communication," *Childhood Education* 32:60-63, October 1955.

Reeder, Ward G., *An Introduction to Public School Relations*. New York: The Macmillan Company, 1953.

Schorling, Raleigh, and Howard T. Batchelder, *Student Teaching in the Secondary Schools*. New York: McGraw-Hill Book Company, Inc., 1956.

Simpson, Ray H., *Improving Teaching-Learning Processes*. New York: Longmans, Green & Company, 1953.

Taylor, E. R., "Conferences or Report Cards," *American Childhood* 41: 29, March 1956.

Thomas, R. Murray, *Judging Student Progress*. New York: Longmans, Green & Company, 1954.

Wiles, Kimball, *Teaching for Better Schools*. Englewood Cliffs, N.J.: Prentice-Hall, Inc., 1952.

Part Six

The continuing
development
of the teacher

Introduction

In this part a fresh point of view will guide the student to look ahead into the experiences that are to be encountered as he becomes a teacher in our American school system. It is said that each person is constantly in the state of becoming. In the program of education under study, the person is in the state of becoming a fully qualified teacher, with professional organizations eager to bring the new teacher into the group. This is a desirable state of affairs, and the young person is anxious to be a qualified, professional member of organizations that will increase his competence and improve education for those for whom the school exists and whom the teacher would serve.

The student in teacher education, who has been called "the teacher" throughout this volume, has the problem of becoming a better teacher and will be challenged constantly by the problem of self-improvement. Chapter 16 is devoted entirely to the topic of self-evaluation and improvement, with the idea uppermost that only those improve themselves who have an honest professional desire to improve, and that those who would help them most are those who work closest with them, together with the supervisory staff whose principal function is to improve teaching.

Professional organizations are established to promote the welfare of the membership and to enable the members to render their services more efficiently. Organization is not anything strange to American society; quite the opposite is the case. Almost every person finds himself a member of some group organized to improve the members and to contribute to their mutual welfare.

So it is with teachers who join their own professional organizations. They have common interests and they subscribe to the lofty purposes of improving themselves both educationally and economically. They serve as a great bloc of professional workers seeking to improve the educational services for those whom they wish to serve—the youth of America. The greatest unifying force in the profession is the code of ethics that each person worthy of being called "teacher" comes to know and work by.

In Chapter 18 an attempt is made to draw back the curtain from what inevitably lies ahead for the teacher as he takes up his life's work. He either enters the teaching profession on a career basis or he uses the education he acquired to become a teacher in being a better, more worth-while citizen. Society does not lose by the expenditure it has made in preparing the teacher. The teacher is a dedicated person interested in youth and schools. He goes through life actively working at educating youth or serving in a supporting position to see that schools are maintained at a continuing higher level as civilization advances. He is proud to be a teacher. He is just as proud to have been a teacher.

16

Practicing
self-appraisal

Probably one of the most common characteristics of man's behavior involves what he thinks and does about his environment. He can react favorably and approve it, he can react unfavorably and disapprove. He may simply ignore it. He is more likely to ignore it if he feels a futility of being able to alter or change it. Then is when he says, "What's the use?" Man as far back as records go has constantly attempted to change and improve both his environment and himself. He has probably been far more concerned about changing his environment than he has about changing himself. However, the teacher is one of society's key persons in affecting the development of its members and the teacher's role in evaluation has many implications. He not only has a major role in evaluating the social, intellectual, and civic behavior of youth, but in helping youth develop attitudes toward these important forces. He is also able to help youth form attitudes about evaluation and, even more important, self-evaluation. At the same time, he is broadening and developing his own attitude toward evaluation and sharpening his ability to help himself grow through self-evaluation. This is extremely important because his whole professional development hinges on the way he deals with the problems of self-evaluation and self-improvement.

The teacher practices self-evaluation. One of the most difficult tasks any person faces is that of honestly passing judgment on his own strengths and weaknesses. It is a well-known fact that most people face a difficult task when put in positions in which they meet criticism. This is not entirely the fault of the one being criticized. The ability to criticize another person helpfully is not strong in many people. Constructive criticism is valuable to the person being criticized, but to be constructive is not always easy. The general supervisor in the school, whose real reason for existence is for the improvement of teaching, finds one of his most difficult tasks to be that of developing the right climate for those whom he is expected to help. The responsibility for favorable climate is just as great for the teacher as for the supervisor, and improvement is proportionate to the extent to which both are cooperative in establishing favorable relations.

The real path to growth and improvement lies in the zeal of the teacher to improve himself. The teacher must get his standards for determining his success as a teacher from many sources. The simplest source, but often the most satisfying, is the children themselves. When a child says without solicitation, "I like you," "Thank you, I understand now," or "Now, I see how to go ahead," the teacher has real reason for appraising himself favorably. On the other hand, if the children are uninhibitedly frank in telling the teacher his weaknesses and he finds himself able to take the criticism by his pupils in his stride and without rancor, he is also on the high road to improvement. Too few teachers are able to take criticism from those whom they teach.

Similarly, the teacher who can visit another teacher's class, or receive visits, and later sit down and talk through with him the things he observed, is fortunate indeed, for he too is getting a base for establishing standards for his own teaching. Another source for the teacher who is striving diligently to discover good teaching practices is the principal or supervisor. If he shows by his attitude that he welcomes visits by his supervisor, the supervisor will take an added enthusiasm for being helpful to him.

Certainly not the least important is the parent who drops by to visit and stays to talk about his children. Here the teacher tests his ability to discuss professional problems with one who shares his anxiety for doing what is best for the child. His ability to use meaningful language and give insights that enable the parent to be more helpful and understanding will get a real test in such a conference. Throughout, the teacher can help himself by thoughtfully analyzing his reaction to the parent's contribution to the discussion. He can learn much even from the remarks that may not sound kind. After all, the parent may be very apprehensive and not in the mood to be tactful.

The real meaning of self-evaluation. Every time a teacher and pupil work together, the teacher has the obligation of doing something with and for the pupil. Too often the teacher thinks in terms of the pupil's success or failure without much thought about his own success or failure. Teaching would be greatly improved if each time a poor mark is given, the teacher admitted to himself that he was awarding himself a poor mark—that he too, in a way, was failing. Teachers view with pride the successes of pupils whom they have taught, but shrug off as impossible the cases where the pupil has not turned out well. It is well for the profession to see both the good and the bad, so that the good may be increased and the failures decreased. If such recognition is made, the first step is taken toward doing something for self-improvement, and this is extremely necessary.

All this means a process of self-improvement having its origin in self-analysis. The teacher in his work with children tries diligently to plan specifically for the pupils in his group. The organization is in terms of the material and the activities which he uses. There are several ways in which he may succeed or fail. He may overestimate the ability or the maturity of the pupils. He may not take the time to organize his activity or present the material in a way that is meaningful, thus bearing the full burden of ineffectiveness. He may schedule the activity at a time not conducive to optimum growth. A good illustration of this is placing a quiet work period immediately following a vigorous activity; for example, music after physical education without an intervening relaxation period. One may decide that a situation of this kind does not involve self-analysis, but the climate for learning is unfavorable and is unfavorable because of the teacher's error. He may experiment with the situation and discover that the conditions do not improve with a simple change in schedule. Then he will look further, and in his analysis may discover that his difficulty lies outside of himself and what he is doing. This willingness to try to find out why is very important.

A healthful practice for the young teacher is to sincerely think through at the close of each day all the activities that he felt were successful and why, and similarly, all that did not go well and why. During this procedure he might quite advantageously alter the entire procedure, even to the kinds of questions he asks or his own reactions to the replies. The next day he should make a second analysis, to see whether the results show improvement. This may be called crude experimentation, but the teacher is forced to experiment both with himself and with his pupils. The human factor is most unpredictable and uncertain. Children do not react as the teacher had anticipated and he finds that he must make necessary adjustments. Even one's facility for making adjustments needs appraisal.

The beginning teacher will do well to avoid getting emotionally upset about his deficiencies. In the process of self-evaluation he may be helped by a discerning supervisor or principal who will point out his weaknesses. This is the supervisor's responsibility, and it is possible that the supervisor will not use as much tact and patience as the teacher might desire. He should remember that supervision too is responsible for setting up the best possible learning situation for pupils, and that the principal is making suggestions for his improvement. Each suggestion should be highly appreciated and applied in the program of self-improvement. It is hoped that the supervisor will be tactful, but that is of less concern than the teacher's improvement. The supervisor may not be in the mood to be tactful by the teacher's measuring stick.

What should the young teacher expect? The beginning teacher probably gets one of his greatest joys when a child calls him "teacher." On the other hand he may get his severest setback when some pupil asks him a question that he finds himself totally helpless to answer. One of the first lessons he will learn is that the pupil can ask many questions that he cannot answer. In his zeal to be helpful and in his anxiety to win status, he may feel that much has been lost when he displays ignorance. However, his ultimate goal will be to develop an atmosphere where pupil and teacher recognize mutually that they are all learners and that all must search for answers to questions and solutions to problems. The teacher may well learn a good lesson in tolerance when he finds that he cannot answer questions. He may expect to meet many situations where his authority seems in jeopardy. However, in thinking about himself or the climate he desires he must see signs of improvement in himself, and realize that he can learn from his bad experiences if he attempts to discover why his errors occurred.

Another area in which the young teacher will attempt to discover his strength will be that of parent relations. He will want very much to give only favorable reports about the pupil when talking to the parent, because he will be afraid of hurting the parent or of stirring up a situation with which he will be unable to cope. In either situation he will feel inadequate. He may simply be unable to analyze the pupil's difficulties in terms that can be understood by the parent. This need not be discouraging, because many mature teachers never acquire ability to use language that parents understand. Furthermore, ability to say unpleasant things is not easy. It is most difficult to say unfavorable things in a favorable way. Each conference should cause the teacher to reflect on the conversation and through this set up ways of discussing problems with parents that appear to be mutually satisfying and helpful.

Still another area of concern is that of being able to talk to the pupil himself. How does one get the pupil to alter his ways of doing things, or cope with the more difficult aspects, especially attitude, of pupil behavior? Certainly the teacher can expect to be faced with all sorts of variations of these problems. He will have a pronounced concern for acceptable behavior. However, he must constantly check his own standards. He cannot be far behind the times or he will lose his effectiveness. Adults have a tendency to lag in accepting what youth does, and youth then accuses its teachers of being behind the times. The teacher who has a vivid memory of his own youth tends to be more patient and understanding, and this is what is meant by "staying young." How young can you stay? The teacher is expected to stay young in point of view and in ability to feel kindly toward youth.

There are pitfalls in self-evaluation. The most prominent pitfall, of course, is one's own inability to look at one's self. Excuses, self-pity, and flattery by those close friends who really know

better but cannot be helpfully frank, all tend to give us false notions about ourselves. They blind us so that we cannot make effective
self-appraisals. Sometimes we cannot objectively study ourselves
apart from a situation. In working with a group of children we
realize that the success or failure of the children in the particular
situation rests quite largely on us. But there are many other factors
involved that do have considerable bearing on one's success or failure. Some of the pupils on whom we can usually depend for major
contributions may be absent, or they may simply not be interested
in this particular activity. Other adverse factors are unpredictable
interference by a visiting parent, a special assignment that proves
to be a distraction, or a change in the day's activities that may alter
the entire timing for the teacher. All of these, and a host of other
quite obvious reasons for lack of success, make us minimize our real
obligation to be prepared for any eventuality and to make adaptations to unpredictable interference. We make excuses when this
happens. What really becomes our problem in evaluation, then, is
not specifically how well we accomplished a certain goal, but how
well we made necessary adaptations in the light of unforeseeable
and unpreventable circumstances. Or, put another way, how flexible
were we so that even the learners themselves were able to make
adaptations and adjustments?

Another problem that the teacher faces lies in the difficulty of
actually putting his finger on his good and poor qualities. The
teacher may have a sincere desire to improve himself, but he is
either unable to isolate the factors that need consideration or incapable of altering his behavior once he has determined what the
weaknesses are. This may be thought of as stubborn persistence,
but the one who is inflexible may not realize he is that way. It is a
rather rare ability for one to recognize his own weaknesses and
establish a systematic program of self-improvement.

Another annoying pitfall is that our own close friends bolster us
up and give us a false sense of security. We like to hear pleasant
things, and tend to discount the validity of unfavorable criticisms.
This fact puts a rather odd responsibility on us in the screening of
our critics. Those that would have us think we are better than we
are must be appreciated for their kindness but not taken too seriously. They fall in three categories: First, those who love us too
much to hurt us; second, those who want to trade compliments; and

third, those who are too shallow or stupid to make a valid analysis, and have no real contribution to make. We face the real problem of improving ourselves by getting good evaluations of our efforts by persons who are analytically keen, patiently sincere, and courageously honest. Our pitfall is in our fear of the truth—either what we discover ourselves or what is revealed to us by those about us.

How the supervisor looks at the teacher. *In the teacher-supervisor relationship:* Not many teachers go on an assignment now without someone who has a rather intimate responsibility for supervising them. There are all kinds of supervisors. There is the good supervisor who sees his responsibility of working with his teachers for their improvement. He feels responsible for the improvement of teaching by effective and helpful methods that produce not only better techniques in teaching but a greater zeal and a warmer spirit for using those techniques. Many supervisors have that worthy quality of causing each teacher to discover his own worth and feel so enthusiastically about himself that he works continually at his optimum level. In order to do this he leads his teachers to examine themselves, and through skillful and sympathetic suggestions constantly keeps them improving themselves. He knows that supervision goes much further than pointing out weaknesses; in fact, he knows that the teacher must be helped to discover his weaknesses himself, because then he will be most likely to do something about it. It cannot be pointed out too often that we tend to correct those deficiencies within ourselves that we discover ourselves. The good supervisor helps us make these discoveries. In this case our whole mental attitude toward improvement and seeking help in ways for improvement is vastly better.

At the other end of the scale is the supervisor who is just as sincere and worthy, but does not have the vehicle for transmitting his help to the teacher. If the teacher himself does not have the ability or the desire to make the necessary adjustments, the situation becomes quite unfavorable for improvement. Under these conditions the teacher would do well to seek a position elsewhere in the hope that conditions would be improved. After all, children are entitled to work in learning situations that are favorable for optimum growth.

In order to make the most of a situation of this kind, the responsibility rests squarely on the teacher. The supervisor may see his responsibility as one of inspection, out of which may come straight criticism. It may not be clothed in tact or sympathy. The supervisor may be honest and correct in his appraisal. He may not have the temperament for tact, or the time that a person of a more kindly disposition would spend. In such conditions of evaluation it is highly improbable that excellent results or strongly favorable change will occur in the teacher. On the other hand, the teacher can rise to the occasion and not only seek to make the desired change, but by skillful behavior on his own part help the supervisor improve his own methods. This would be a delightful experience and well worth the teacher's efforts. In the final analysis the children would profit by so noble an effort by the teacher.

Between these two extremes are those teacher-supervisor relationships where improvement of teaching is taking place in varying amounts. The supervisor overlooks many opportunities to help, either because he feels the effort would be futile or because he knows his own limitations in transmitting helpful suggestions and therefore refrains from making the teacher unhappy. Similarly, the teacher fails to seek help because he either lacks drive or does not know how to go about getting helpful suggestions. The burden rests with the supervisor in this situation; however, if the supervisor does not take the initiative it would be extremely helpful if the teacher pressed the request for help. Supervision's only function is to improve teaching, and even the teacher's highest goal is to make supervision attain its function. Teachers can make supervisors good!

In the "participating teacher"-supervisor relationship: In this situation several factors assure the student teacher or participating teacher of a relationship that is favorable for growth. The teacher-education institution, by its selective process in assigning students into the classrooms, selects supervisors who have the necessary qualifications for carrying out supervision at its best. One of these qualifications, of course, is that the supervisor is a mature master teacher highly skilled in working with people. He endeavors to direct the student teacher into many types of learning situations in which the two may share in appraising the student's work in teacher education with boys and girls.

Since the burden of the problem of improvement rests heavily on the supervisor and he has been selected to give valuable help to the participating teacher, the participant cannot be negative to the

supervisor's efforts. The supervisor realizes that the student is immature and in need of help, and that he will be in position in many
situations both to commend the student and suggest ways of improvement. He will lead the student into those situations in which
both supervisor and student recognize the weakness of the student,
in an effort to develop strength and a feeling of security.

The supervisor has a major responsibility that the student should
recognize and share—the responsibility to his group of children.
However, the supervisor knows that in most situations the student
teacher helps him to do more for those children, and that it really
makes the supervisor a better teacher. Parents recognize that a
participating teacher–supervisor combination usually strengthens the
learning opportunity for their children. The supervisor, however,
carries much of the burden to insure that such is the case, so the
student teacher may expect to present lesson plans when he takes
over the teaching. Lesson plans not only assure the supervisor of the
teacher's aims and methods, but they also give the student teacher
an assurance and security that he might not otherwise possess, and
serve as a basis for communication. In addition, lesson plans give
focus to evaluation on the part of both the one supervising and the
one being supervised. They can also help to impersonalize the evaluation itself, by focusing attention on a situation or plan instead of
the one who is teaching.

Thus the student teacher can see that he will find himself in a
program where supervision is heavily focused on his work. All efforts
to develop a good teacher, both in the school where he is doing his
student teaching and in the teacher-education institution that is responsible for developing teachers, will be centered on him. Theirs is
the task of doing a masterpiece of work in supervision, and although
they will be sympathetic and kindly they will not let up on their
energetic approach to their duty in the preparation of teachers.

How the teacher feels toward the supervisor. *In the
teacher-supervisor relationship:* The teacher will almost always find
himself working with or for someone who has a measure of supervisory responsibility. It is a far more favorable situation if it is *with*
someone. This situation implies a cooperative relationship in which
both the supervisor and the teacher have mutual responsibilities and
understandings. It also implies the authority of both parties in the

relationship. The teacher should use his every power to avoid any development of a feeling of inferiority or insecurity. The supervisor will share this concern, but he will be relatively helpless to do much about it unless the teacher sets about to improve and strengthen himself. The burden of responsibility may even rest with the supervisor to enable the teacher to feel secure, but the teacher's own attitude toward supervision will be a powerful factor in determining how he works with other people. The teacher will likely help himself most by remembering that supervision enables him to do his most effective teaching. He can strengthen his position by actually inviting the supervisor to visit him while he is teaching and then cordially insisting on a conference for frank discussion of his own weaknesses and how best to improve them. The teacher who demonstrates an eagerness for honest appraisal sets the stage for wholesome relationships.

One problem in teacher attitude toward supervision lies in the teacher's imagination that the supervisor is *picking* on him. He reads into the supervisor's behavior all kinds of distressing elements that are not really present at all. The teacher has dignity and need not be afraid to express ideas that he is prepared to defend intelligently and honestly. The supervisor will respect him for it and will welcome the opportunity to tackle problems of mutual concern. Problem situations are the center of concern and will help the supervisor avoid dealing with the teacher as a personality. Thus the teacher can give the supervisor valuable aid in his work as a supervisor. The teacher can assume just as much responsibility for appraisal as the supervisor; in fact, it will be the keystone for improvement if the teacher sees his own weaknesses instead of having them pointed out.

The teacher thus will find himself either in the position of seeking or of resisting supervision. If he seeks supervision, recognizing that his future in the profession lies on his self-improvement and supervision is his richest source for this improvement, he will open wide the doors for a successful future as a teacher. The supervisor will accept the challenge of his own position of being helpful and improving the teacher.

In the "participating teacher"-supervisor relationship: Improvement and growth are dependent on one's own desire to improve himself. It is impossible to point out too often that only when the student teacher practices self-appraisal, or at least only when he opens his mind to the suggestions of those whose sole motive for working with him is that of improvement, that change really takes place. Self-appraisal, in fact, is the master key to all his attitudes and receptiveness to the help that those who work with him might be able to give.

The student teacher or participating teacher is inexperienced in the position of teacher. Although he may have been around children and perhaps have come from a large family, he is still a novice in the skill of teaching. He has been taught by teachers and as so often is said, "may teach as he has been taught." However, those who are in position to help him recognize that he is beginning and try sincerely to let him know that they expect no more of him than he is capable of doing. The teacher-education institution usually has a selective process that operates in determining the more able students. It likewise has a retention process that helps to keep the more able and get rid of those who are less able. This in itself is an evaluation process that should enable the prospective teacher to know his own limitations and see the places where improvements are relatively imperative. His success in his various courses should give him ideas about himself.

If the student as he progresses through his basic years in his teacher-education program finds that his mechanics in the communications area are weak, or even if he frequently discovers that such an ability as penmanship is poor, he can set about to improve it. If he has not taken the necessary steps, he need not be surprised if his supervisor questions his ability to write legibly or write correct sentences, speak fluently and coherently, or even spell words without error. The teacher communicates in the written and spoken word. How well he has mastered these arts of communication determines very definitely his eventual skill as a teacher. When those who would teach him point out these deficiencies he will do well to set about then to take steps for improvement. To resist such improvement will only add to the complexity of his own development and his own insecurity.

The student teacher can take the initiative in many situations and demonstrate to his supervisor that his attitude is sincere and that his concern for his own improvement is genuine. One of the first steps for the student teacher is to approach his supervisor and open a discussion about lesson planning. He can find out early in his association with those who seek to help him what ideas they have about lesson planning or planning in general. He can discover what kind of teacher-pupil relations the supervising teacher feels is most favorable for his classroom. If he discovers that his supervisor has a more authoritarian approach than he would like, there is no need for conflict. The supervising teacher feels his responsibility to the children and to the parents of these children. The student teacher is only assigned for a short period—probably not to exceed one semester or quarter. The supervising teacher carries the burden for the whole year and is committed by a contract, with all its professional implications, to serve the school district capably. He must do it his own way, and the adjustment in such a situation is strictly up to the student teacher.

His role as an observer as well as a participant carries him into many situations where he sees how the supervising teacher handles a situation. He can discover how the supervising teacher speaks to children and how they address him in return. He can discover the kinds of disciplinary measures that seem to work best for the supervising teacher. Similarly, he begins to discover what teaching methods seem to work best. Temperaments and manners of the supervising teacher differ from the student teacher's, and what works for one may not work for the other. This is very important for the student teacher to recognize early, lest he try to adopt the "tricks" of his supervisor and find them, to his sorrow, not workable for himself. Voice, manner, movement, and even smile, must fit the individual teacher, and none of these can be captured from the supervisor. Better still, he has his own capabilities and teaching manner that he only can develop and put to work.

Finally, the student naturally will hold his supervisor in the highest regard, and in so doing will be able to do the most for himself. It is a professional trademark to focus the attention on those things that appear good. The other person has his weaknesses, but we do neither ourselves nor the one whom we depreciate any good by dwelling on weaknesses. We grow by our own strengths and the strengths we see in others. We can make the most of supervision when we pursue this professional policy of looking for strengths.

Other sources that can help the teacher in his self-evaluation. *The children whom he teaches.* Children are quite frank. In fact, they are at times too frank for the teacher's comfort. The young teacher would do well to try to direct his improvement in light of the criticisms that his pupils make. Children usually temper their strongly critical remarks with warm compliments that help soften the sting. However, if the teacher realizes that they only express their unsheathed feelings, he can see how those he teaches look at him—and this can be a source of real help.

Such common remarks as "teacher's pet," "Tommy can get by with anything," "Teacher never catches Helen," "You wear the same thing every day," "Your shirt is dirty," "Why don't you shine your shoes?" "Your breath is bad," "Why don't you get wise?" and a host of others are all straws in the wind that indicate that a good look at one's self might be helpful. Even though the teacher may be quite sure that a criticism has no foundation, if he looks that way to his children he has to deal with the impression he has given. How the teacher looks to the children is a factor that he cannot overlook if he would do the most for them.

On the other hand, from the same source the teacher gets his assurances that he is doing well—little signs and tokens of appreciation that make teaching more attractive. Quite often the teacher gets strength and courage to go ahead in a direction where before the pupil had spoken he was unsure of himself. Quite often one feels that what works is good. In this situation the teacher must depend upon the learner to help make a venture work. Without the willingness, the helpfulness, and the cooperation of the pupils the teacher would be doomed to failure in many efforts. Pupils are discerning and analytical and make many helpful suggestions, and when the teamwork of teacher and pupils is at work learning at its best takes place. Wisdom comes from such a wholesome situation and the teacher can get a good look at himself through the eyes of his pupils.

The parents of the children. The teacher does not work long before he is confronted with a questioning parent. A mother asking "Why doesn't my child read?" or "Why did my child fail in algebra?" gives the teacher a difficult question to answer. The diagnosis may be extremely difficult, and putting it in language understandable to the mother is even harder. Nevertheless it is good for the teacher, and keeps him on his toes, to study each child thoughtfully and effectively and be ready to explain or defend his action to those who might question him.

The parent, above all others, has a major stake in the child's welfare and the teacher is obliged to ask himself, "How do I feel about

a parent asking me questions or causing me to defend my methods?"
If he must answer that he is irritated by parent concern then he
needs to analyze his feelings very thoughtfully, because the parent
cannot be expected to depend on faith, but has a right to ask questions. One takes a child to a physician and is expected to trust the
professional intelligence of the physician without question; in fact
he takes only the information his physician chooses to give out. Not
so with the teacher, who may be called upon to account for his actions by the least intelligent parent in the community and is professionally obligated to keep his poise and good grace.

One of the first lessons to be learned by the young teacher is that
of keeping quiet and gracious when confronted by an irritated, emotional parent. The teacher who keeps his peace and returns sweet-
ness for ugliness finds himself in a position to deliver good advice
and helpful suggestions after a mother has unburdened her mind of
her worries. One of the young teacher's first questions for himself
could well be, "How well can I 'just listen'?" or "How much poise do
I really have at my command when I need it most?" or "In times of
emotional stress do I demonstrate that I am master of the situation?"
After all, the teacher is educated, competent, and qualified. He is
expected to be a professional person.

It would not be right to discuss parent-teacher relations without
giving some description of the more pleasant side. Truthfully, almost
all parents have unlimited faith in the skill of their child's teacher.
Whatever the teacher does is right and best. Mothers go to school
and work with and for the teacher and show him all the consideration and appreciation that anyone could hope to receive. Teachers
are defended "over bridge tables" far more often than they are criticized, and the skillful efforts that teachers are making to help children are passed on from one parent to another and good explanations made of the work the teacher is doing. Here the teacher may
take occasion to ask himself whether or not he is accepting every
opportunity to utilize the helpful hands and voices that are offered
to him. How well does he keep those that would help him informed
so that they can join in keeping the public informed? How often
does he even show that he appreciates the faith put in him? How
often does he take time to thank these kind mothers?

The community where the children live. The teacher has a real
opportunity to test himself as a community member by the way he

is sought to take part in community affairs. For instance, no person in the community may be better qualified to teach in a local Sunday school than a teacher. A high school teacher may be eminently qualified to teach the young peoples' class, a junior high school teacher may be most skillful at working with adolescents, and the primary teacher may be ideal to work with the young children in the church school. To be asked to serve in any of those positions could be considered a mark of trust and respect. The church is an essential factor in the community and the spiritual lives of its members are nurtured by its activities. The teacher who sees himself as an active member in his community may find that he can get real satisfaction in sharing his talents in a church school, choir, or service unit. It may prove to be a real test of his general value to the community, and he can get a good measure of his worth by the demands that are made of him. Civic clubs, either for men or women, are dedicated to the general improvement of the community. Such organizations make an effort to select men and women as members who by their activities demonstrate civic leadership in the community. To be asked to join, gives the teacher a chance to investigate his worthiness of the distinction, and if he accepts the challenge he can then test himself as a member making his contribution in service along with the other members. Such a challenge is helpful to the teacher, and gives him an opportunity to be accepted as one of the civic workers of his neighborhood.

The teacher is a voter. Each time there is an election, whether it be primary or general, the teacher will distinguish himself by going to the polls as a free citizen and casting his vote. He helps the citizenry of the community look upon him as a member if he conducts himself as a normal citizen. There is no surer way of being deprived of one's rights than to fail to exercise them. The confidence, sincerity, and honesty he demonstrates are the teacher's best assurances that the community will expect him to participate in civic activities. This in itself is an acid test of how he regards himself in the community.

These and other community affairs are his keys to becoming a vigorous, vital factor in the welfare of his community. How well he exercises his rights as a citizen may, in large measure, determine how well he serves as a teacher. The teacher need not have any fears of being a member of the church of his faith, the political party of his choice, or the civic club where his help is needed. Choice is the right of every American. People expect teachers to be good and able citizens who can do most for the pupils in the classroom when they are exercising their rights as citizens.

We set up standards for evaluating ourselves. There is nothing mysterious about the source of standards for measuring ourselves. From the first day that the student steps into the classroom where learning is taking place under the direction of an experienced teacher, he observes the teacher at work and has some reaction to what he sees. The reaction may be negligible even to him, but if he has a sincere desire to become a teacher what is going on will interest him. It is highly probable that the first reaction will be one of comparison or contrast to the way he has been taught. Pupil conduct itself is quite observable and the deviate in behavior will attract his attention, perhaps quite violently. The first reaction may be, "Is this what teaching is?"—especially if his experience has been quite formal and he finds himself in an informal classroom where children are permitted more freedom than he has been accustomed to seeing.

A young teacher should avoid making up his mind too soon about anything, whether the problem is one of classroom control, noise in the classroom, politeness or impoliteness, dullness and brightness in learners, or any other of the host of problems arising from presenting material or working with curricular problems. If one can approach the situation with an open mind he is spared the burden of shock and even apprehension about things misunderstood.

Standards are derived from all of one's experiences in teaching. In early experiences they do not necessarily need to be one's own. In fact, one may be strictly in the role of an observer and feel no urgent responsibility either for success or failure. One can be very impersonal in his relationship, and stand apart and look on. Nevertheless the observer will make his first small beginning in appraisal, not of himself, but of the situation he has under observation. This is constructive, because the observer can detach himself from any emotional, sentimental, or aspirational feeling and see cause and effect, effort and result, without feeling any particular responsibility.

As the responsibilities increase in any teacher-learner situation, the potential teacher begins to formulate notions of his own effectiveness. He begins to analyze a situation where results were not as he anticipated. He studies his own approach, his timing, even his own preparation and plans. It is essential that he appraise his own methods, techniques, and purposes first, lest he do an injustice to others. If there are adjustments and revisions within his own immediate control he can probably be more effective immediately, and furthermore grow in the process. If in his analysis he decides that the failure lies outside himself, he still has the burden of skillfully diagnosing the situation and then taking remedial steps that improve those with whom he works yet leave them with increasingly favorable attitudes.

What, then, are the standards? They are personal measuring sticks that are quite likely to be far more subjective than objective, since we are obligated to measure ourselves with them. They measure how we feel toward our work, how well we are personally prepared to work with learners, the interrelations between teacher and pupil, our own personal characteristics, and how well we get the particular work done. Their effectiveness depends on how clearly we can appraise a situation honestly and correctly, so that we really feel satisfied if it is good, or improvement measures are set up if it is considered unsatisfactory.

In the area of our feeling toward our work there are several observable elements. Do you get up rested each morning in time to bathe, dress attractively, and get to work in ample time to be completely relaxed and in control of yourself and the situation where you are expected to be the leader? If so, did it just happen, or was it due to careful, skilled planning? If not, what were the reasons for your delinquency in personal responsibilities? Are all factors under your control or do they involve others whose influence you have to change or eliminate altogether? Are you fully aware when you are appropriately groomed and attractive, or have you built up little idiosyncrasies that prevent you from seeing yourself as others see you? Do you have little beliefs tied up with your upbringing, related to your religion or your parents' prejudices, that would handicap your success in some communities? Are you drab and colorless, or so odd that you are happy about it? If you have formed the habit of coming to work at the last minute, is it because you miscalculate time or are you so slow-moving that you just don't get things done? In either case, can you remedy the situation? If you have not sold yourself on the necessity for punctuality and promptness, are you aware that there is great likelihood that those with whom you work will disapprove of your tardiness, and may find it advantageous to replace you with someone who can be punctual and prompt? This is a good barrage of questions with which to test your conscientiousness. You will think of many others.

In the area of preparation one has had ample chance to get some notions of his intellectual and educational capacity. We hear quite often the remark, "Those who can, do—those who can't, teach." This is an unfair statement in view of the many capable classroom teachers at work everywhere. But the person who struggles through college making barely passing marks, going on probation and then off, and finally being graduated near the bottom of his class, is not prepared to be a self-respecting, successful teacher. Teaching is an art, and being a learner is an artistic endeavor. Intelligent, successful learners are needed for the teaching profession. Have you discovered the area where you can be successful in school and happy and potentially successful as a teacher? Have you broadened and enriched your educational resources so that you have not only been considered good by instructors but also have the capacity for impartially passing judgment on your own strengths and weaknesses? Have you been carefully collecting material and educational resources in your specialty so that you have a storehouse of interesting things to bring to those you teach? Do you have an eye for discovering valuable material, and have you developed an ability to present it in an interesting manner? Do pupils come to you and treat you in such a way as to show anticipation of your being able to work helpfully with them? In brief, are you an excellent resource person and do the pupils show by their behavior that you have demonstrated it? Honest answers to such questions as these will help you to analyze your strength or weakness in preparation and thoroughness.

In the field of classroom relations, the climate is set for successful work by the teacher and pupils. Do you really like children as learners? In answering this question one must be discriminating enough in his analysis to distinguish between professional appreciation and maternal or paternal love. We want love in the home, but in the classroom we want appreciation, respect, and consideration. Children should not be cute little fellows to the teacher; they should be respected learners. They deserve tenderness and kindness, but only if it is seated in educational admiration. Questions such as the following will point up your reactions and capabilities in this important area: Do you speak with a calm and soothing voice, yet command respect? Do the pupils "catch" your manner and address you in such a way as to engender mutual respect? Is there a work atmosphere that gets things done without pushing people around? Is there steady progress without the spirit of hurry? Are the purposes of both teacher and pupils harmonized so that all are involved in a mutually acceptable learning activity?

How do you know that children respect and like you? Do you care whether or not they do? Is it important to successful learning that they like you? If children speak impolitely to the teacher, does that mean that they do not like him? Do you either scold, punish, or demand apologies, or ignore rude behavior so that eventually the supervisor says your control is weak? Do you use inward resources such as personality, charm, and enthusiasm so as to be attractive to young people and thus gain their sincere admiration for you as a person?

Finally, the true test for success in the classroom is whether or not learning takes place. Parents have a real concern for the development and progress of children. The teacher who takes pride in his work has an equal desire to discern growth. Out of this desire comes the setting for making the educational experience so meaningful that the interest of the learner is centered on purposeful work. Do you see that the purposes of the learner, the aspirations and hopes of the parent, and your own purposes are harmonized? Do you know the learner's capacity, so that you do not expect more than is possible? Do you have a clear insight into the learner's background, so that you neither baffle him with what is too difficult nor bore him with what is too easy? Are you so in tune with the learner's capacity to learn, his interest in intellectual activity, and his social concerns that you attain an optimum reward for your mutual efforts? These are the final tests of our adventure in learning.

We must apply our own standards. In our early stages during participation, student teaching, and our early years of teaching we will find many situations where our facilities are limited to accomplish what we know is best. There is considerable trial and error. The nearness of a supervisor will be both felt and needed. The teacher-education institution and the laboratory for teaching are both greatly concerned for developing a strong teacher. Experienced practitioners are professionally concerned for the development of more and better teachers. All that is known in the preparation of teachers is brought to bear on the process for this development.

Among the techniques for helping the student become a good teacher are scales of evaluation, comprehensive formal and informal reports by supervising teachers, and log books, diaries, and all types of written reports by the teacher in which he analyzes his own experiences. These in turn are used as a basis for conferences and prescribed activities that, it is hoped, will bring about improvement.

The log book may be one of the best instruments for evaluation, because it contains a record covering a period of time. An important warning must be given against merely making a series of descriptive reports without much reference to appraisal or analysis. It then becomes a simple diary that makes very little contribution other than as a record. Situations in which teaching and learning are taking place form the best source for material for a log book. In the first place, these tend to impersonalize the report, and secondly they are the most vital classroom situations on which to focus attention. Pupil-conduct description should be held to a minimum lest one fail to see beyond the troubles that are encountered in the deviates in the group who are making little or no contribution to the learning situation. Similarly, mere description of what happens without reference to causal factors makes no worth-while contribution and furnishes very little opportunity to determine the teacher's power of analysis.

Each activity or exercise in the child's day should grow out of a plan or purpose. Everything the teacher does should have a reason back of it. The inexperienced observer or participant may have considerable difficulty in determining the sequence of learning situations, but even to set up a proposed program is a valuable step and provides foundation for speculation and thought.

As an illustration of an effective report, one could give an account of planning an excursion to the fire station. In the preliminary plans the teacher and pupils have carried on a full discussion of the duties of firemen and how they are trained to protect life and provide a minimum of loss from fire. Considerable time might be spent in describing all of the skills that the fireman possesses, such as giving artificial respiration, carrying injured or frightened people from a burning building, knowing how to approach a building to avoid danger to one's self, and what kind of materials to use in putting out different types of fires. The critical part of such an account would not be the mere reporting of *what* was done in preparation, but *why* the time was spent as it was. The teacher in training would bring out the point that by so doing the learners were led into areas of research regarding the duties of the fireman; that all the pupils had a common store of information to which they could add the information gained at the fire station; that they could pool the questions they wished to ask the firemen and thus experience sharing in planning their discussion; and even above all this would be the opportunity to talk with each other, to write their plans and questions, and even to correlate art and music with the experience. Why do all of this? To give meaning to the experience and to demonstrate purpose in the things that the learner did. "Why," "because," and "in order that" are valuable words in the log book. This report could go on into the trip itself and all the things that took place at the fire station: If restrictions were placed on the activities of the boys and girls, reasons for doing so and how they affected the learning that took place should be pointed out. From here could follow an account of the post-excursion discussion and why it was held. What came out of the discussion and how it contributed to the total learning experience would wind up a satisfactory report.

The basis for evaluating the teacher's interpretation of the experience would be centered on his effectiveness at analysis and in giving reasons for the entire series of experiences. Lack of such analysis would denote weakness and need for improvement, and completeness of analysis would indicate strength and reason for encouragement and approval.

The log book, of course, can serve as a complete record of the student's teaching experience and need not be confined to situations where an analysis has been made. It can provide a means of keeping a record of the ideas garnered as well, and really is one of the best devices for self-evaluation. It enables the writer to describe the setting for a learning situation, his own part in the situation, and his own interpretation of his effectiveness as a leader.

A second method is an evaluation scale, which can either be used by the student teacher himself or jointly with his supervisor. On such a scale those factors that seem important in the development of a teacher can be evaluated. Some of these, of course, are:

1. Is the teacher punctual in arriving for his work and is he ready to contribute to the group when he arrives?

2. How well does the teacher use the ordinary channels of communication of writing and speaking when working with the learners?

3. Does the teacher dress attractively and use good taste in the auxiliary devices for making his appearance suitable for the classroom?

4. Is the teacher a good resource leader and do the children show indications of being aware that he is dependable as a resource person?

5. How obvious are the indications that the teacher really likes to work with children?

6. How obvious are the signs that the children are sincerely attracted to the teacher?

7. How well qualified in general is the teacher to carry on work with the learners in his group or how well adapted is he for the age-grade level of his group?

The above list can be expanded, but these general areas are revealing enough to indicate to the teacher his strengths and weaknesses and to point out areas for improvement.

Growing professionally through self-evaluation and self-improvement. The teacher never stops growing. He learns right along with his children and he is continually casting about to see how he can become a better teacher. Like the good physician who is alert to all the new discoveries and practices in his field, the teacher subscribes to the leading professional magazines and keeps himself abreast of the advancement in the field of teaching. He attends workshops, conventions, and seminars. He selects a college or university that has specialists in his field and continues his graduate work in the light of his known needs and interests.

He finds himself in need of a widened background and travels to interesting places where he can gather information to take back to his classroom. He talks to people wherever he goes, becoming an interesting conversationalist and at the same time enriching his own life so that he can give to his pupils the things that he has learned.

Above and beyond this, he is a frequent visitor to the library, the storehouse of all that is good in print. He visits the theatre, recitals, and concerts; where good things to enrich his life are to be found, there one will find the good teacher. He knows that his future and that of the boys and girls who work in his classroom are dependent on his constant vigil to learn all he can of the past and of his enlightened age. From his torch of wisdom all the youth he touches may light their torches and move on. This is the privilege of the good teacher. The teacher will have to be constantly improving to reach this high goal.

SUMMARY

The teacher, by the very fact that an increasing number remain in school, must be a better teacher in order to cope with his present-day teaching problems and the vast differences between the strong and the weak that he finds in his classroom. The present day finds the school system providing more supervision than formerly. The supervisor aims at the lofty purpose of improving instruction by improving the teacher, and by seeing that better supplies and equipment are provided. The teacher who goes about accepting all the help provided and assumes an attitude that he is obligated to be a better teacher utilizes all the forces that work with and for him toward his improvement.

Open-mindedness toward criticism and an earnest desire to use his pupils, fellow teachers, the parents, and even the lay public to discover his strengths and weaknesses will go a long way toward helping the growing teacher to improve. He must assume that all these forces want to help him and that their motives are worthy and their suggestions valuable.

In addition to these are the organized forces within the school system—supervisors and administrators, whose only reasons for existence are to help him. Given these helps both organized and unorganized, the teacher continues to improve himself by wholeheartedly accepting every means at his command to find ways for growth. These stimuli to growth are constantly about him and he has no trouble through in-service training, travel, research, conferences, and workshops to find other ways for improvement.

Competences that the teacher needs to develop and establish are:

1. The ability to recognize his weaknesses as a teacher and the earnest desire to seek improvement.

2. The ability to utilize all the facilities that surround him for his own self-improvement.

3. The acquisition of a sincere and cooperative attitude toward all supervisory and administrative personnel, to the end that their functions may be facilitated.

4. The ability to turn the criticisms and suggestions of the pupils toward improving one's self.

5. A facility for seeking suggestions from fellow teachers or observing the techniques of their fellow teachers and making the necessary adaptations for improving one's self in their light.

6. The capacity to encourage those who would be helpful so that they feel free to make suggestions for improvement.

7. The ability to make suggestions to others for ways of improvement in a constructive manner, so that one demonstrates practices that are highly acceptable in achieving improvement.

8. The ability to apply standards to one's own situation so that total improvement can be accomplished.

PROBLEMS

1. *Ask your supervisor to take time to give you a straightforward appraisal of your strengths and weaknesses. In the light of these, determine how you can go about making improvement in yourself.*

2. *In the light of the above conference, discuss the conference with a close professional friend, asking him to help you analyze your behavior toward the suggestions of the supervisor.*

3. *Ask the members of the class or group you are teaching to write how they feel toward you and your teaching, without having them sign their names. Take the papers, sit down by yourself, and see if you can determine just how you feel toward these frank and unsheathed suggestions.*

4. *Ask another student teacher in your building to visit your room for a half-day. Then discuss the visit with him, attempting to determine what really constructive gains you can secure from the visit and conference.*

5. *Reciprocate in the visit suggested above. Analyze the situation from this different point of view.*

6. *Make a careful self-analysis of your teaching power in such a way that you can make reference to it at a later date. Two months later make a similar self-analysis. Seek out points of improvement that have been achieved.*

BIBLIOGRAPHY

Barr, A. S., *An Introduction to the Scientific Study of Supervision.* New York: Appleton-Century-Crofts, Inc., 1931.

Boardman, Charles, Harl R. Douglass, and Rudyard B. Bent, *Democratic Supervision in Secondary Schools.* Boston: Houghton Mifflin Company, 1953.

Burton, William H., and Leo J. Brueckner, *Supervision, a Social Process,* 3rd ed. New York: Appleton-Century-Crofts, Inc., 1955.

Grim, Paul R., and John U. Michaelis, *The Student Teacher in the Secondary School.* Englewood Cliffs, N.J.: Prentice-Hall, Inc., 1953.

Hymes, James L., *Effective Home-School Relations.* Englewood Cliffs, N.J.: Prentice-Hall, Inc., 1953.

Lee, Irving J., *How to Talk with People.* New York: Harper & Brothers, 1952.

McKenzie, Gordon N., Stephen M. Corey, and associates, *Instructional Leadership.* New York: Bureau of Publications, Teachers College, Columbia University, 1954.

Melchior, W. T., *Instructional Supervision.* Boston: D. C. Heath & Company, 1950.

Shane, Harold G., and Wilbur A. Yauch, *Creative School Administration.* New York: Henry Holt & Company, Inc., 1954.

Spears, Harold, *Improving the Supervision of Instruction.* Englewood Cliffs, N.J.: Prentice-Hall, Inc., 1953.

Wiles, Kimball, *Supervision for Better Schools,* 2nd ed. Englewood Cliffs, N.J.: Prentice-Hall, Inc., 1955.

17

Importance of
professional organizations

One seldom stops to define the term "profession," but when one does he soon becomes aware that even though he has used it for as long as he can remember he finds it hard to define precisely. Is it based on a background of both general and technical training? Is it based on the uniqueness of the service involved? Is it based on the social service performed? Is teaching a profession? There are decided differences in incomes of members of different professions; need there be such differences? Is medical service more valuable to society than education and therefore more expensive to the individual? What factors determine the value of any kind of service in terms of price? Who determines the price? Is it determined by the person rendering the service or by the one receiving the service? Or is it determined by a board or committee that in a way represents the interests of both? These are all vital questions that eventually enter into one's thinking.

A dictionary definition of the term "profession" will usually be somewhat as follows: "An occupation that requires a liberal education and involves intellectual rather than manual skill."

A more descriptive approach utilizing some of the dictionary definition and yet going beyond and attempting to

422

describe, in general, the educational background involved might be somewhat as follows: "An occupation that requires a specialized education based upon a general education, and involving a highly technical skill requiring a predominance of intellectual power.

Teaching as a profession. It is easy to see that all persons working in an area that requires similar training and intellectual skill could very readily have common interests and concerns. These persons would find it easy to discuss common problems and work together for their mutual benefit. These mutual benefits might be in the form of sharing what they had learned, or might be for the establishment of standards or codes that would be beneficial to the members of the group. When the group becomes identified by virtue of similarity of training, kind of work, and similarity of interests, it is accepted as a professional unit including the members who profess to have attained the intellectual skill ascribed to that occupation. The teaching profession proposes to be one of these specialized, learned groups. One should keep in mind the factors of skill, intellectual power, and kind of service involved.

One can approach the topic of a profession from the viewpoint of one within the group, one contemplating entering the group, or one outside the group who has no intention of becoming a member. One's point of view will greatly alter his definition and how he really feels about the person within the group. It will influence his behavior toward the member quite perceptibly. Let us take a look from the various angles.

If one looks at a profession from within the group, he will probably think in terms of similarity of the members' work and educational background for doing that kind of work. He will recognize that the remuneration for the service will be based upon the length of time spent in preparation for the work and the number of years that have been spent actually working in the field. It will not be difficult to accept the principle that training and service are factors that contribute to making teaching a profession.

He will know all the effort, sacrifice, joys, friendships, and decisions that made up his total experiences leading to the day when he became a teacher. Also, he will know all the satisfactions that come to the person after he becomes a teacher—personal and professional satisfactions of seeing children develop power through the things taught, the satisfaction of seeing the fruits of his efforts in the form of successful citizens whom he once had as boys and girls in the classroom. Similarly he will know all the sacrifice he has made financially. There is no need to evade the issue; many ways of earning a living pay more in dollars in proportion to the time spent in developing that earning power. He will substitute other values and rewards for a larger pay check.

What these substitutes are will vary greatly with individuals. Some of them may be simply personal satisfactions of a professional nature that come to the person dedicated to a life of service to his fellow man. Some are found in cultural values that are obtained through an environment that has many intellectual and aesthetic elements.

Others of a more monetary nature come from security benefits that are set up to compensate teachers for their lower pay, such as a retirement system that is ample to provide for them in their old age. Teachers' retirement programs are becoming much more attractive and will be a factor in inducing people to enter teaching as a life vocation. All of the above factors certainly enter into one's thinking as he looks at teaching from within the profession.

If one looks at teaching from the viewpoint of the person not yet a teacher but contemplating entering the field, many of the same factors are operative but not so strongly felt. The person contemplating becoming a teacher will be motivated in his thinking by a desire to help people, especially youth or at least those who desire to learn. An impelling force from within will focus his attention more upon his satisfaction in helping society than upon the remuneration he will receive. These are the dedicated persons to whom the pay check is actually secondary. This awareness of dedicating one's self to a life of working with youth comes to the person who has not yet become a teacher but is seriously contemplating the profession.

It is important that these considerations become a part of the prospective teacher's thinking. It is essential to think of all the unfavorable factors as well as the favorable ones. How have you felt toward teachers and teaching in general? Do most of the teachers that you know lead lives that would make you happy? If they are married and have children, have you admired the way they are rearing their children? Do they seem to be able to apply the same principles of education that they use in their classroom to the situations they face as parents? Have you observed and admired the sort of life single teachers choose to lead? Do they seem to participate in and share the finer things in the community? Are they respected as community members in the church, in social organizations, and civic affairs? Are they the kind of person you wish to be, and do you feel that you could be happy doing the things that you see them enjoying?

Would you be able to select a chosen area within the teaching field and make that your area of specialization? It might be necessary to take additional work in graduate school, either in summer sessions or on leaves of absence. This involves additional expense and use of savings that one may hope to use in some other manner. However, one will soon discover that continued study is satisfying and valuable to the superior teacher. In order to be self-respecting one must feel competent and skilled in work in which one takes pride. This is important to the teacher who wants to make it his life's work because success, promotion, advancement, and happiness are dependent on competency.

The person who is not a teacher and who has no intention of becoming one looks upon teaching from an entirely different point of view. Many persons in this group are parents of children whom the teacher has in his classroom. The mother probably looks upon the teacher as the person on whom she can rely to give her excellent help and advice in the problems she has with her children. The father may have identical feelings, or he may be somewhat more remote in his feelings toward the teacher. Both, however, see the teacher as a skilled practitioner working with their children. The degree to which they appreciate the teacher as a professional person depends very largely on the cooperative attitude they have toward the teacher, which has significant bearing on the teacher's success with their children. There will be persons who in a general way have very little regard for the teacher and do not look upon him as a skilled professional. Some of these will be parents, some will be adults with no personal connection with youth. This can happen to any of the professions and may have its origin in unethical or unprofessional behavior by those in a particular profession. Here the profession itself should be constantly aware of the need for good public relations, because a favorable attitude of society is essential to the profession. In general, a group of citizens will look upon the work as a skilled profession if the membership assumes a responsibility for operating at a high level both in practical and in personal behavior. Good work results in high esteem. Service is a good salesman to those outside of the profession whose support and respect is necessary. The code of the profession helps the outsider to have more respect for it.

Thus we see that being a member of the teaching profession puts heavy responsibilities on an individual. It is a commitment to render service. To the teacher the commitment has been made and teaching becomes a challenge to render service. To the prospective teacher the challenge has not yet been met but the romance of opportunity to serve is apparent. To the person outside the field, teaching may have little romance, but anyone who is aware of the dependence of all society upon the service of the classroom teacher cannot fail to recognize the great contribution the teaching profession is rendering, and will rally to support the strength of the profession.

The professional organizations of the teacher. There is a wide variety of professional organizations to which a teacher may belong. These extend from the local organization that may include only those teachers in the immediate community to the nation-wide organization that includes teachers of every specialization throughout our country. One should not look upon one organization as being necessarily more important than another. Each renders an inestimable service to its members.

The local organization may make personal contributions to the welfare and happiness of the members that are not easily possible at any other level. The members of the local group have an intimate concern for each other. If death or sorrow strikes a member, the professional associates are concerned and take steps to be helpful. Social get-togethers, picnics, parties, and coffee hours are helpful and most worth while, and are held often by members of a local group. In addition, through committees at the local level, instructional materials, report cards, salary schedules, and teacher tenure problems are developed, and matters of concern to the local community as well as the teacher are considered. The local group also joins with other community organizations for the solution of problems that are broader than the particular problems of the individual teachers.

The state teachers' association is somewhat removed from the local picture, but here those matters related to salary, retirement programs, certification standards, school facilities, child welfare, and general improvement of schools are matters of foremost concern. A code of ethics patterned after that of the National Education Association is quite common among state associations. Research departments, public relations services, and even placement services are common concerns in most states. Legislative programs for general improvement of education for children and general upgrading of the membership are of utmost importance to the state association.

The National Education Association stands out as the singly most important association for the improvement and welfare of the teaching profession. In significance and strength it stands alongside such professional organizations as the American Medical Association, the American Bar Association, and the American Dental Association. All are important organizations that have as their outstanding function the improvement of the profession they represent and serve. The National Education Association has stood for better schools for all children and better teachers for those schools throughout its long existence. It is interesting to recognize and remember that the National Education Association, organized in 1857, is not as old as state and local associations. It was created out of a necessity for sharing ideas that were broader than those of local or state groups, and for helping promote programs at the national level that are of concern to all people throughout the country who are interested in schools. People who are sincerely interested in educating children regardless of race, creed, color, or where they happened to be born know that the problem crosses state lines everywhere. The National Education Association is the child's most powerful assurance that democratic principles will be upheld.

Another organization that merits consideration at this point is the American Federation of Teachers. The Federation of Teachers was first organized in Chicago in 1897. Between 1897 and 1916, numerous instances of labor's support in teachers' struggles for better salaries, better taxation programs for school support, and better conditions under which to work is a matter of record. The American Federation of Teachers, chartered in 1916, is an affiliate of organized labor, and has had as its motivating purpose the expansion of the principles of democratic living for teachers and all other people. The organization has been most vigorous in seeking higher salaries, better working conditions, more adequate jobs, and social security for teachers. The Federation is on record as standing for and vigorously demanding recognition of the right of all men to participate in a free society. It has joined forces with all organized middle-class groups to protect this right.

The contributions of these organizations to the teacher.   Perhaps it is best to examine in considerable detail the work of the National Education Association, which is really the umbrella, so to speak, of all the state and local associations. The value that it has for the individual teacher comes usually through the local and state organizations, and the national leaders have a record of strong and useful activity in their local and state association. It is highly improbable that a leader in the national organization could have achieved his recognition save through faithful and dedicated service at home or in his own state. One need not feel critical of this point of view, because it is the case in almost any organization, whether it be professional, civic, or political. One's first good work starts at home and in one's own community.

The following pages are quite largely taken from reports of the Research Division of the National Education Association. It is not a complete picture, but it will give enough to permit a prospective teacher to know more about an organization he will be called upon to join, and in which he will no doubt become a devoted, faithful, and hard-working member.

Probably one of the outstanding contributions of the National Education Association to the profession of teaching has its beginning from its expressed statement of purpose when it was organized on August 26, 1857. It reads: "Purpose—To elevate the character and advance the interests of the profession of teaching and to promote the cause of popular education in the United States."

Its long record of action recorded in the publications of the Association and its affiliated departments bear testimony to the fact that it has been guided by this original purpose.

Each person entering the profession of teaching needs to work by his own ethical code, but he must derive it from somewhere. He will find the Code of Ethics of the National Education Association of inestimable value in the formulation of his own way of working as a professional person. It follows:

Code of Ethics for the Teaching Profession[1]

We, the members of the National Education Association of the United States, hold these truths to be self-evident—that the primary purpose of education in the United States is to develop citizens who will safeguard, strengthen, and improve the democracy obtained through a representative government;—that the achievement of effective democracy in all aspects of American life and the maintenance of our national ideals depend upon making acceptable educational opportunities available to all;—that the quality of education reflects the ideals, motives, preparation, and conduct of the members of the teaching profession;—that whosoever chooses teaching as a career assumes the obligation to conduct himself in accordance with the ideals of the profession.

As a guide for the teaching profession, the members of the National Education Association have adopted this code of professional ethics. Since all teachers should be members of a united profession, the basic principles herein enumerated shall apply to all persons engaged in the professional aspects of education—elementary, secondary, and collegiate.

FIRST PRINCIPLE: The primary obligation of the teaching profession is to guide children, youth, and adults in the pursuit of knowledge, and skills, to prepare them in the ways of democracy, and to help them to become happy, useful, self-supporting citizens. The ultimate strength of the nation lies in the social responsibility, economic competence, and moral strength of the individual American.

In fulfilling the obligations of this first principle the teacher will:

(1) Deal justly and impartially with students regardless of their physical, mental, emotional, political, economic, social, racial, or religious characteristics.

(2) Recognize the differences among students and seek to meet their individual needs.

(3) Encourage students to formulate and work for high

[1] *NEA Handbook for Local, State and National Associations, 1956-57* (Washington, D.C.: National Education Association, 1956); pp. 111-13.

individual goals in the development of their physical, intellectual, creative, and spiritual endowments.

(4) Aid students to develop an understanding and appreciation not only of the opportunities and benefits of American democracy but also of their obligations to it.

(5) Respect the right of every student to have confidential information about himself withheld except when its release is to authorized agents or is required by law.

(6) Accept no remuneration for tutoring except in accordance with approved policies of the governing board.

SECOND PRINCIPLE: The members of the teaching profession share with parents the task of shaping each student's purposes and acts toward socially acceptable ends. The effectiveness of many methods of teaching is dependent upon cooperative relationships with the home.

In fulfilling the obligations of this second principle the teacher will:

(1) Respect the basic responsibility of parents for their children.

(2) Seek to establish friendly and cooperative relationships with the home.

(3) Help to increase the student's confidence in his own home and avoid disparaging remarks which might undermine that confidence.

(4) Provide parents with information that will serve the best interests of their children, and be discreet with information received from parents.

(5) Keep parents informed about the progress of their children as interpreted in terms of the purposes of the school.

THIRD PRINCIPLE: The teaching profession occupies a position of public trust involving not only the individual teacher's personal conduct, but also the interaction of the school and the community. Education is most effective when these many relationships operate in a friendly, cooperative, and constructive manner.

In fulfilling the obligations of this third principle the teacher will:

(1) Adhere to any reasonable pattern of behavior accepted by the community for professional persons.

(2) Perform the duties of citizenship, and participate in community activities with due consideration for his obligations to his students, his family, and himself.

(3) Discuss controversial issues from an objective point of view, thereby keeping his class free from partisan opinions.

(4) Recognize that the public schools belong to the people of the community, encourage lay participation in shaping the purposes of the school, and strive to keep the public informed of the educational program which is being provided.

(5) Respect the community in which he is employed and be loyal to the school system, community, state, and nation.

(6) Work to improve education in the community and strengthen the community's moral, spiritual, and intellectual life.

FOURTH PRINCIPLE: The members of the teaching profession have inescapable obligations with respect to employment. The obligations are nearly always shared employer-employee responsibilities based upon mutual respect and good faith.

In fulfilling the obligations of this fourth principle the teacher will:

(1) Conduct professional business through proper channels.

(2) Refrain from discussing confidential information with unauthorized persons.

(3) Apply for employment on the basis of competence only, and avoid asking for a specific position known to be filled by another teacher.

(4) Seek employment in a professional manner, avoiding such practices as the indiscriminate distribution of applications.

(5) Refuse to accept a position when the vacancy has been created through unprofessional activity or pending controversy over professional policy or the application of unjust personnel practices and procedures.

(6) Adhere to the conditions of a contract until services thereunder have been performed, the contract has been terminated by mutual consent, or the contract has otherwise been legally terminated.

(7) Give and expect due notice before a change of position is to be made.

(8) Be fair in all recommendations that are given concerning work of other teachers.

(9) Accept no compensation from producers of instructional supplies when one's recommendations affect the local purchase or use of such teaching aids.

(10) Engage in no gainful employment, outside of his contract, where the employment affects adversely his professional status or impairs his standing with students, associates, and the community.

(11) Cooperate in the development of school policies and assume one's professional obligations thereby incurred.

(12) Accept one's obligation to the employing board for maintaining a professional level of service.

FIFTH PRINCIPLE: The teaching profession is distinguished from many other occupations by the uniqueness and quality of the professional relationships among all teachers. Community support and respect are influenced by the standards of teachers and their attitudes toward teaching and other teachers.

In fulfilling the obligations of this fifth principle the teacher will:

(1) Deal with other members of the profession in the same manner as he himself wishes to be treated.

(2) Stand by other teachers who have acted on his behalf and at his request.

(3) Speak constructively of other teachers, but report honestly to the responsible persons in matters involving the welfare of students, the school system, and the profession.

(4) Maintain active membership in professional organizations, and, through participation, strive to attain the objectives that justify such organized groups.

(5) Seek to make professional growth continuous by such procedures as study, research, travel, conferences, and attendance at professional meetings.

(6) Make the teaching profession so attractive in ideals and practices that sincere and able young people will want to enter it.

Purpose in joining the National Education Association. Every teacher has two or three organizations in which he finds professional help and stimulation. This number is a minimum, as there are likely to be more. The teacher is first of all an elementary, secondary, or college teacher. There are divisions in the National Education Association in which the teacher will find association both satisfying and professionally helpful. The Handbook of the National Education Association, published annually, can be found in any college or university library and will give valuable information about each department or special division.

Some of the services that the National Education Association provides for the schools and that the prospective teacher should know about are contained in the following paragraphs. It should be fully understood that the teacher is free to join what he chooses and that his real obligation to himself is to be an informed person about all professional organizations.

The public relations problem for the school is of major importance. Only an informed public is willing to pay the cost of supporting the schools. The Division of Press and Radio Relations of the NEA is an important factor in getting facts to daily and weekly newspapers, magazine writers, editorial services, radio commentators, and television specialists. These are the channels through which the lay public can be kept informed. In addition to these media of communication, moving pictures, filmstrips, and news releases are constantly available and are being used by those who wish to make sure that information reaches the public. All of this is in addition to the releases about research studies through regular publications, yearbooks, and articles put out by the NEA and its departments.

The teacher by his very function in society must be free to teach the truth without fear, and the learner must share that same freedom to learn without harassment. The NEA has taken an intelligent position on freedom to teach and learn. The Platform of the National Education Association, published in the 1955 Proceedings, expressed clearly the rights and responsibilities of the teacher:

> To freedom of speech, worship, press, assembly, and thought, subject only to such controls as those of other responsible citizens. Freedom to present all points of view without danger of reprisal, intimidation, loss of position, reduction of salary, loss of opportunities for advancement, or deprivation of their usual assignments and authorities. The right to organize and support organizations they consider in their own and the public interest.

This is the teacher's assurance of moral backing by the strongest professional organization in existence today—backing that it is hoped will enable him to exercise his initiative and independence in the preparation of pupils for freedom in our democracy. However, one must be realistic and be aware that weak administrators, poorly selected school board members, uninformed and ungrateful patrons and lay people resort to unethical practices that violate the statement by the NEA.

The NEA has been active for almost a century in legislation that has affected favorably the welfare of the schools. The Association, with its headquarters in the national capital, is close to where legislation is proposed and passed; it takes vigorous part in promoting the passage of legislation favorable to education, and is equally ready to oppose what is not considered good for the schools. One must have faith that the association, dedicated to promote the welfare of children, uses the best minds in the profession to determine what to support and what to oppose.

The dedicated teacher knows that life membership in the NEA is the best way to make the profession strong.

Courtesy of *The Indiana Teacher*

As shown earlier in its stated purpose, the Association's foremost reason for existence is the strengthening and improvement of the profession of teaching. It has steadfastly worked for improving schools, raising salaries and retirement programs, and increasing the public's esteem for teachers. The raising of certification standards has provided better prepared teachers for the children and at the same time has caused teachers to command better salaries. Interestingly enough, those states that have the highest standards for teachers pay the best salaries and have the greatest supply of competent teachers. It is a well established fact that lowering standards does not increase the supply of teachers.

The foregoing paragraphs, along with the Code of Ethics, are only a limited account of what the NEA stands for or does, but it is enough to let the young teacher know something about the profession as an organization. It permits him to know the support he may have as a member and the code that 700,000 of his fellow workers are committed to live and work by.

It bears repeating that only the teacher who works with his group in the local community can make very much of a contribution at any higher level. Also, any proposals that are made at the highest level have their fruition and application at the local level. The teacher who would gain most from his profession must put his beliefs into practice as he works with the teacher across the hall, with the mother in her doorway, with the principal who works with him, and with the boy who would rather be somewhere else. These are his challenges but, at the same time, his opportunities.

All of these organizations to which he is eligible as a teacher to belong merit his honest consideration. The teacher must be careful lest he be a joiner but not a worker. The organizations are made stronger and consequently of more help if they are made up of workers with convictions. Every teacher owes it to himself and to the organization he seeks to enter to find out whether his beliefs and the organization's purposes are compatible. He needs to find out the dues and expenses he will be expected to pay, and convince himself that the benefits will be worth that cost. He will need to see where the organization has held its meetings, and whether at rather frequent intervals the meeting has been held close enough to him for him to attend. All of these factors are essential in his final decision in joining an organization.

The departments of the National Education Association. The National Education Association now has thirty departments, organized to meet the special needs of the teaching profession. NEA membership is required before one can join one of the departments; the Association as a whole meets the general needs of the professional person.

The thirty departments of the National Education Association are as follows:

> Administrative Women
> Art Education
> Audio-Visual Instruction
> Business Education
> Classroom Teachers
> Deans of Women
> Educational Research
> Elementary School Principals
> Exceptional Children
> Health, Physical Education, Recreation
> Higher Education
> Home Economics
> Industrial Arts
> Journalism Directors
> Kindergarten-Primary Education
> Mathematics Teachers
> Music Educators
> Public School Adult Educators
> Retired Teachers
> Rural Education
> School Administrators
> School Public Relations
> School Secretaries
> Science Teachers
> Secondary School Principals
> Social Studies
> Speech
> Supervision and Curriculum Development
> Teacher Education
> Vocational Education

It is obvious that the departments have wide coverage, yet are specialized enough for almost any teacher to find a department where his special interests can be met and where he can make a contribution to the organization because of his special interest.

One of the very vital programs for the young person wishing to become a teacher is the Future Teachers of America. The FTA includes two organizations: the high school organization is a high school club made up students who plan to be teachers. It really is a recruitment program for getting young people to go into teaching. The college unit is a student association of the National Education Association, called the Student National Education Association. This enables the local, state, and national associations of teachers to take students in as associate members before they actually become teachers. The goal of the FTA movement is to have an SNEA chapter in every teacher-education institution in America.

Teachers' unions. The teacher may work in a community where the American Federation of Teachers is strong and he has not only a considerable urge from his associates but an urge within himself to join. He will be fully aware that many of the personal benefits that have come to teachers are due to the efforts of the Federation. There will be many well-meaning associates urging him to join, and many just as well-meaning urging against it. The following paragraphs are given presenting both sides and quoting from some well-known sources. It would be well for the prospective teacher to read the references in their entirety in order that no meaning will be lost, because the quotations are lifted out of context from longer articles.

In Favor of Joining a Teachers' Union[2]

> The truly successful teacher is the thoroughly alive teacher. She teaches from her experience. The knowledge she has accumulated from classroom and textbook has been mellowed by life. Life to her is more than the routine of home and school—it is contact with the struggle of mankind for a better tomorrow. The really superior teacher knows her boys and girls as part of a family, part of a community, part of a state. She is interested in the welfare of society as it affects her students. She knows, if she is at all alert, that it is not enough to talk about health and housing and nutrition, that concrete things must be done to make medical service, good food, and adequate homes available for all. She understands that she can neither live in a vacuum, nor teach in one. She is a part of life!

---

[2] Kermit Eby, "Teachers' Unions?—Yes!" *Progressive Education* 20: pp. 260, 262, and 301, October 1943.

The ideal teacher has convictions. She is not one who believes that it is possible to be neutral on controversial issues. Democracy, to her, is something to be preserved, nothing to be neutral about. And in adding two and two, she insists it's important whether the answer equals four bombs or four homes. Airplanes to her are a boon to mankind if they carry serum, a curse when they destroy cities. Boys and girls are not means to ends. They are the ends for which we strive to build a better world. This teacher loves them all—black or white, rich or poor, Protestant or Catholic or Jew. Otherwise, she could not really influence them.

Believing as she does, she seeks to identify herself with groups of like minded people, in an effort to take her part in the march of progress. Her seeking must inevitably lead her to the labor movement, to the teachers' union—not because the labor movement is perfect, or the teachers' union without its faults, but because in these organizations she finds people with interests and beliefs common to hers and because organized labor in America from its very beginning fought for the free public education. In our modern world, education is essential to democracy, labor leaders have always believed. That democratic institutions cannot survive among illiterate citizens is labor's conviction.

The creative teacher with the attitude I have described needs the teachers' union to protect her tenure and security. It has fought innumerable battles in the interest of academic freedom, over the years. It has protected the fearless teacher who refuses to permit a threat to her job to keep her from teaching the truth as she sees it.

Against Joining a Teachers' Union[3]

The relation of education to the public welfare stands, in general, fairly clear. The child is born immature; he must in our complex society be guided to grow up into effective membership in the social group. The conscious effort to provide this guidance we call education. As the medical profession has been set apart by society to be its responsible agency to care for the element of health in the public welfare, so is the profession of education responsibly set apart to care for the public welfare in the matter of education.

As we consider education in our modern world, we see the two factors of democracy and rapid social change making peculiar demands on it, demands which taken together both

[3] William Heard Kilpatrick, "Teachers' Unions?—No!" *Progressive Education* 20: pp. 261, 263, and 301, October 1943.

set the problem here under consideration and determine its solution. Modern social change, to consider that first, has under the impact of modern science and technology become so different from what had previously prevailed that we have not yet digested it. Specifically, there remain with us many cultural lags, both in the commonly received thought and in our institutional arrangements, which severally thwart social progress; and new lags must be expected as far as we can see into the future. Society must then accept the abiding task of a continued attack upon these cultural lags. So far as we can now tell, change may come at any point, and no social doctrine or policy can in advance claim exemption from critical scrutiny and possible revision. Education must accordingly accept the duty of building in youth the attitudes and techniques necessary for the more adequate and wise revision of the culture. At the growing edge of the culture, controversy often arises as to which proffered path promises best. It is these controversial problems and the democratic way of treating them that set the problem before us.

In respect of these controversial problems, as in all other matters, the democratic school, looking forward to effective democratic citizenship, must help each pupil as in him lies to develop the ability and disposition to think and conclude for himself. And "conclude" here means to reach a conclusion which not simply or primarily pleases the holder; but such a conclusion that on it all concerned may reasonably rely. The controversial problems present here peculiar difficulties. The purpose the school has in studying these problems is not that the teacher (or the school or society) may tell the pupils what conclusions to reach, nor even to guide the pupils to the answers the teacher deems right (however superior the teacher may be to the pupils in judging such matters). The proper purpose of the school, in dealing with the controversial aspect as such, is that the pupils may in studying first become intelligent in the area studied, and, second and primarily, that they may by actual study of live unsolved problems learn to deal effectively with as yet unsettled problems. To study a live problem is a very different matter from holding an inquest over a dead problem; it calls for its peculiar kind of study, and it entails its peculiar dangers: danger lest complexity prove insuperable, danger lest essential points be overlooked, danger lest partisan advocacy confuse and deceive.

Amid these difficulties and dangers the teacher is there to help the pupils learn the necessary techniques of honest, open-minded, penetrating and constructive study.

The teacher also faces dangers. Possibly the chief of these

is that he may allow his personal convictions to interfere with the independent and adequate personal study of pupils. The NEA Committee on Academic Freedom thus stated (in 1941) its principle on this point:

"If any teacher, by the way in which he teaches, either willfully or carelessly permits some bias or prejudice of his own, or even the inappropriate expression of his reasoned convictions, persistently to mar the process of fair-minded study on the part of those studying under him, he is to that extent damaging these students and in the same degree is manifesting his unfitness to teach."

This does not mean that the teacher is not to have convictions, nor that he is never to say outright what he believes. But it does mean that the teacher's task and duty is to develop his pupils—develop them into as adequately self-directing personalities as he possibly can—and not to make converts to his particular cause. In the words of Bronson Alcott, "The true teacher defends his pupils against his own personal influence."

The teacher must then come to each succeeding year's study of any controversial problem with a mind as considerate as he can compass, for his pupils as they face an area relatively new to them. He must keep his previously formed opinions in the background and he must be willing himself to seek and find new aspects of the problem; and, if significantly new data appear, to re-think his previously formed opinions. And—what is here crucial—he must so reflect these open-minded attitudes on his own part that, as he joins this year's pupils for study, they can and do see and feel his honest willingness to consider afresh with them the unfolding merits of the problem as the matter itself unfolds in their shared study. In the degree that the teacher cannot honestly so impress his students, by so much does he fail of good teaching. In particular, any public commitment on his part, if known to his pupils, carries the risk of hurt to his teaching. In this respect the personal duties of aggressive citizenship may have to yield to the higher duty of fair-minded, effective teaching.

It is at this point that we reach the crux of our problem. The proper place of "labor" within our industrial society is today highly controversial and promises so to remain for some time to be. Under these conditions any teacher dealing with the labor problem is under special obligation to avoid partisanship, in particular to avoid any such partisanship as would make any appreciable part of his class question the fair-mindedness of his guidance in the study of the controversial problem.

But suppose this teacher in company with other teachers

has already by explicit professional organization aligned himself on the side of labor. Has he not thereby so committed himself in advance to one side of the controversial areas to make it difficult for either side among his pupils to accept his full impartiality? Will not the labor pupils expect him to side with them at least inwardly if not openly? And will not the anti-labor pupils similarly expect him to side against them, at least inwardly if not openly? Under such conditions how can he hope to steer a boy or girl who comes from a strong anti-labor home to an honest facing on their real merit of the hard and unpleasing facts of the ill treatment of labor. If he try, will they not by his very effort be the further convinced of his unfair commitment? Has he not in fact by his act of affiliation exactly loaded the dice against his success at teaching?

Lest the young teacher get too biased a view from Kilpatrick's statement, it seems appropriate to quote from one of the greatest men of all time in American Education, none other than John Dewey:

> I do not believe that any educational organization is more ready or better prepared to take a courageous view of the present situation than is the American Federation of Teachers. It has never been a body to take the cheap and easy way; it has never cultivated illusions about the seriousness of the work to be done. It has recognized that together with its larger organization, the American Federation of Labor, it has a cause that demands, and that has obtained, and will continue to obtain alertness of observation and planning, and solidarity in action. It knows, from experience, that these things bring their own reward with them. Confidence and courage grow with exercise. There are many fields of labor within the American Federation of Labor. There is none in which the need, the opportunity and the reward are surer than in that of teaching.[4]

And again, from John Dewey:

> I would urge teachers to ally themselves with organized labor. Teachers in the public schools are public servants. Those who engage and dismiss them have great power. It is often exercised irresponsibly, and in many places there is a process of subtle or overt pressure and even intimidation. In order to get courage to revise instruction, teachers need the active support not only of organization among themselves but

[4] Address at the 1949 Convention of the American Federation of Teachers in Milwaukee, Wisconsin.

in connection with the elements of the community that have common ends with them and that are already organized. Both the depression of the thirties and the inflation of the forties have hit the teachers and children of the country with great severity.

Business interests concerned with reducing their own load of taxation have long been active with measures of so-called economy that are crippling public education. Teachers have learned that they are in the wage earning class. They are now more ready than in the past to act in behalf of a change of conditions that, in protecting the wage-earner, will also protect not merely their personal interests but the youth of the country and the future of society. The opportunity must be taken advantage of and teachers with social insight should take the lead.[5]

The foregoing statements are given in the hope that the prospective teacher will see the sincerity in differing points of view of men eminent in the profession—men whose views are highly respected by all who read them. They may serve as background for further thinking and provide perspective for making decisions that inevitably face the teacher on many occasions. In the final analysis the teacher will have to make up his own mind on how he can best serve his profession and retain his own personal integrity and freedom. The choice and the responsibility for that choice are his. The only limitation to this freedom is the attitude of those with whom he works in the community he serves. However, even then it is his choice to seek to serve elsewhere if he finds the resistance more than he prefers or the environment not conducive to his best and most sincere efforts.

Other organizations to which teachers belong. Up to this point the organizations that have been discussed have been those that are committed to aggressive activity for improving schools for American society and working conditions and status of teachers. Other organizations that invite teachers to membership are far too numerous to mention by name. There are those, in almost every special area in teaching, whose membership is limited to persons who by virtue of their special qualifications are invited to belong. Their purposes are quite idealistic and their efforts are usually extended toward improving the scholarly background of the mem-

[5] Pamphlet published by the League for Industrial Democracy, 1949.

bership and toward coordinating the intellectual effort of the members for their mutual benefit.

Three professional organizations of teachers—one for men, one for women, and one for both, and all general enough in nature to be mentioned—are Phi Delta Kappa, a men's honorary professional organization; Pi Lambda Theta, a women's professional honorary organization; and Kappa Delta Pi, a professional honorary organization for both men and women. These three organizations limit their membership to outstanding personnel in the field of education. Their aims are to develop leadership and render service to the profession. Other benefits, of course, are the friendships that are promoted by close association in the organization. Any teacher who is invited to join one of these organizations will do well to consider the invitation carefully. The membership is made up of outstanding people in the profession, and those who make up the list for membership will have examined the qualifications of the candidate carefully before extending the invitation. The contribution that the organization could make in the individual's professional experience would be both worthy of attention and professionally satisfying.

Some general considerations. The teaching profession needs those individuals who are committed to a lifetime of service, but not all children could be served if only those who are committed to permanency in the profession were employed. Many excellent teachers work for a short term and then leave to become homemakers or to go into other kinds of work. Teaching has long been a background of experience for other occupations. It would be most shortsighted to wish that those who work for shorter periods be deprived of the privilege to serve. Some who plan to stay in teaching only a short time change their minds and stay in teaching. Others who leave return and devote many fruitful years to the profession. This is all good for boys and girls and good for the profession.

But those who go into teaching to make it a lifetime of service must expect to carry the burden of effort, time, expense, and professional intelligence for the teaching profession. They are the ones who will benefit most. They are the ones who recognize the challenge most clearly. They are the ones upon whom society depends to bring the skill of teaching to the high level it has attained.

Teachers can expect to be harshly criticized by those who do not want to pay the cost of supporting education. Many individuals in a society wish to reap all the benefits without paying the cost. Education is one of the first to be attacked, and unfortunately until recently only the profession itself seemed organized to withstand those attacks. Lately citizens' committees at local and national levels have become awakened to the need to defend the schools and are becoming a powerful force. The National Congress of Parents and Teachers has become a power that bids well to exert all its strength for schools. With forces such as this to join the organized profession of teachers, steps can be taken to make schools what they should be and to give every boy and girl better chances. When the young man or woman decides to be a teacher, a vital decision that soon follows is the decision to join organizations that promote and protect education as a force in American society. It becomes not a question of "Shall I join?" but "Which ones give me the opportunity to exert my best efforts?" Only through organization can these efforts be effective and the profession reach its deserved status. Never before have so many people been convinced that the schools must have better support if youth are to be educated in the most helpful manner. Today's youth must be taken care of now. An aroused public is supporting the teachers and their professional organizations to see that the schools come first in our thinking.

SUMMARY

Teaching is professional work! This statement is based upon the premise that teaching is a social service, the qualifications necessary for teaching being based on both general and specialized education leading to certification, or some other professional standard. If one subscribes to the statement that teaching is a profession, then all the organizations to which one belongs that promote the members' welfare while improving the educational opportunities of those whom the members serve are professional organizations.

These professional organizations are of two kinds: First we have the local, state, and national teachers' associations, to which any teacher may belong for a membership fee. Usually the teacher belongs to all three branches of this type of association, more of course belonging to the local and state than to the National Education Association. The purposes of the three branches of the Association are much the same, differing largely at the levels at which they operate. The local association concerns itself more with local salary conditions, providing welfare services, and improving educational services in the local corporation. The state and national associations serve the membership, and again those whom the profession serves, through legislation at the state and national levels and through developing professional standards at each of these levels. Research service, codes of ethics, and other truly professional services are stressed at both the state and national levels. The American Federation of Teachers similarly operates at these same three levels, but it seems fair to say that the emphasis is more on the help to the membership itself than the wider point of view of the Associations. Some may disagree with this statement.

The second group of organizations is made up of those professional fraternal organizations, both branch and national, dedicated to strengthening the membership professionally, membership in which enables the individual to be a stronger person in the profession. Membership is limited and invitational and, unlike the Association or the Federation, one must be elected to membership.

Membership in all of these organizations is an honor, and a teacher strengthens himself by his membership, participation, and support. The teacher who expects to widen his horizons and render a career of service seeks wide membership in such organizations.

Competences that are worthy of consideration in this area are:

1. The ability to find ways of rendering distinguished service at each level of the Association or Federation, or both.

2. The ability to be discriminating in the organization to which one belongs.

3. The ability to measure one's own time and energy so that one is able to make a maximum contribution to those units in which one claims membership.

4. The ability to work in harmony with the professional codes of the organizations to which one belongs.

5. The ability to utilize the services rendered by the organizations to which one belongs as a professional person.

6. The ability to represent the professional organization effectively among groups outside the organization.

7. The ability to explain the purposes of the organization to those who seek to learn more about the organizations.

8. The ability to know what it means to be a member of the profession and so always to work with honor to the profession.

PROBLEMS

1. *Go to the president of the local classroom teachers' association and find out for yourself what the major purposes of the local association are claimed to be. Find out what you can do as an affiliated person with the association.*

2. *Make a study of the SNEA program in your institution. If there is no SNEA take steps to find out about organizing one. It is your way of beginning early to affiliate with your profession.*

3. *Go to the leader of the local Federation, if there is one in your community, and find out what its purposes are as he sees them. If this is not an available source go to the library and read any reports that are available. Use the bibliographical reference at the end of this chapter.*

4. *Go to state teachers' association annual sessions as an affiliate member from your own college and attend some programs that have vital interest for you. Determine for yourself what a state teachers' association can mean to you.*

5. *Secure a copy of the constitution of a state teachers' association in the state where you live and acquaint yourself with the state association organization.*

6. *Send to the research department of your state association and secure materials that are available to you. If you are not able to secure materials, ask a member of the state association to lend you materials from the research department.*

BIBLIOGRAPHY

Grim, Paul R., and John U. Michaelis, *The Student Teacher in the Secondary School*. Englewood Cliffs, N.J.: Prentice-Hall, Inc., 1953. Chaps. xii and xiii.

Klausmeier, Herbert J., Katharine Dresden, Helen C. Davis, and Walter Arno Wittich, *Teaching in the Elementary School*. New York: Harper & Brothers, 1956.

Lieberman, Myron, *Education as a Profession*. Englewood Cliffs, N.J.: Prentice-Hall, Inc., 1956.

McNerney, Chester T., *Educational Supervision*. New York: McGraw-Hill Book Company, Inc., 1951.

Michaelis, John U., and Paul R. Grim, *The Student Teacher in the Elementary School*. Englewood Cliffs, N.J.: Prentice-Hall, Inc., 1953.

Organizing the Teaching Profession, The Story of the American Federation of Teachers by the Commission on Educational Reconstruction. The Free Press, Glencoe, Illinois, 1955.

Staff Relations in School Administration, 33rd Yearbook, American Association of School Administrators. Washington, D.C.: 1201 Sixteenth Street, N.W., 1955.

Teacher Education for a Free People. Oneonta, N.Y.: The American Association of Colleges for Teacher Education, 1956.

The Teacher and Professional Organizations, 2nd ed. Washington, D.C.: National Education Association, 1956.

Wesley, Edgar B., *NEA: The First Hundred Years: The Building of the Teaching Profession*. New York: Harper & Brothers, 1957.

18

Looking ahead

All during your school years you have been getting ready to go to work. You have chosen one of the oldest and most honored professions. There is something quite special about you, or you would not have chosen to be a teacher. You want to be helpful to your society. If you teach your normal forty years, the length of service upon which many retirement programs are based, you will greatly affect the lives of boys and girls of two twenty-year spans, reaching across two new generations.

That is the great opportunity that awaits you. Those are the boys and girls that will be waiting for you—one generation already born, a second yet to be born. The first generation will have a great share in making you a mature, experienced teacher. All through that first generation, you will still be increasing in professional stature and in the pay you get. Throughout the second twenty years, when you have matured, you will have reached your peak salary. Your salary will advance during the last twenty years only as you increase in professional degrees or in the type of position you hold. That is the way it is now, and so it is likely to remain.

Getting that first position. You have a service to sell. Each community has its own price that it pays for that

448

service. That community might like to pay more than it does, but communities, like people, have financial limitations. After all, a community is just people—people of every kind—the kind you've had for neighbors all your life. Some pay great amounts in taxes; others pay very little. Strangely enough, communities that pay smaller amounts may be the ones that will use your services most. They may be the ones that bear the most children, and children are your professional business.

In some manner those who represent that community must find out about you. You have a professional service to sell, and they must fill a need by purchasing that service. In almost every teacher-education institution like yours, there is a placement director or official whose responsibility it is to help you meet the representatives of a community in which you might choose to work.

It is the job of the placement officer, a trained specialist, to get the right teacher in the right community.

Courtesy of Ball State Teachers College Photo Service

The placement service is an advantage you earn as a student in teacher education. There is usually no fee for helping you find a position. The contacts of the placement director are nation-wide. He can help you get a position in a far-off state almost as easily as he can in your own. He is eager to get you the position that suits you best and in which you will be most likely to succeed. It is no pleasure to a teacher-education institution to have even one of its graduates fail to succeed. For that reason you should contact the placement service early in your senior year and find out what credentials are needed in order for him to serve you best. He will need recommendations from several of your professors. You need to select those professors carefully. Select those who know you best, whom you have liked most, and who have liked you and appreciated your efforts. An influential citizen from your home community will be helpful. The minister of your church, unfortunately, is not your best person. He is expected to say good things about everyone, and an employing official would know that the minister would not be too discriminating. Your high school principal is a good reference. Others who know you best might well be your neighbors. At any rate, select someone who knows you and can write intelligently and favorably about you.

With the understanding that your credentials are in good order, try to make up your mind early and be ready to interview prospective employers by not later than March of the year in which you expect to begin work. School administrators know their staff needs for the year ahead and want to fill those positions early. In large school systems the exact positions may not be known, but those interviewing will know the number of teachers they will need in various areas. Your chance to get into the particular community you desire will be much greater if you make up your mind early.

The nature of your interview. The interview will be arranged by the placement office, and you will meet someone designated by the employing school system to interview prospective teachers. It might be a person from the personnel office, if it is a large city school system. It might be a city or county superintendent of schools or an assistant superintendent. It could be a principal, a supervisor, a department head, or even a teacher. You can be sure that it will be someone who has been authorized by the board of education through the superintendent to help select teachers for the system.

The interviewer will want to learn more about you than your credentials show. He will want to see you as a person and study your personality. You should dress attractively but not gaudily. If you are a woman, some color on the lips will help, but it should not be too showy. Moderation is always the safe practice. Be talkative, but with reserve. Talk about the things you know best, and be prepared to discuss the things you believe in the area of teaching. Avoid gushing, but demonstrate a sincere interest in boys and girls. Be prepared to discuss your philosophy of living in a sincere, open manner. You may be asked what you eventually hope to become. It would be well if you are prepared to discuss your future plans.

If you smoke do not deny it. It would be well not to smoke during the interview and certainly not to offer the interviewer a cigarette. If he offers you one, use your own judgment about accepting. If you are asked about drinking, be honest. It is likely that if you are asked about drinking the interviewer would not be able to report favorably about you if you do drink, so the truth had better be known. All things being equal, the person who does not drink is a more favorable candidate in all communities. Very few schools can use a teacher who drinks; even parents who drink do not want their children's teacher to use alcoholic drinks.

If you are a woman and inquiry is made about your marital status, be straightforward. If you have marriage plans for the year of your contract, say so. Most communities have no opposition to married teachers. Those that do are quite definitely opposed, and would consider you unfair if you had plans and did not reveal them. If the plans are indefinite, say so. In other words, be uncompromisingly honest throughout your interview. Avoid selling yourself double. That is, if you are a husband, avoid trying to get the school corporation employing you to employ your wife also. If you are a wife, it is a safe bet that the school corporation doesn't need a husband. After you have worked in a school community, the situation could be different. If you are determined about being employed as a husband-wife combination, find the community that is looking for that kind of combination, and everyone will be happy.

Be prepared to ask questions too. Find out all you can about the socio-economic conditions in the community. Is it a growing community? If it is, are they building schools? Is the community favorable to good schools? Do they have a salary schedule? Do they have a rapid turnover in teaching personnel, or do teachers like to stay? How do they induct new teachers? On what basis do they assign teachers? What is the attitude of the community toward teacher tenure? Is recognition given in the salary schedule for advanced degrees? Are there any phases of the educational program that the community is divided upon? This is only a suggested list of questions and you can add or alter them in light of your own interests. But be sure to ask questions—intelligent questions. Doing so will impress your interviewer favorably.

When the interview has ended, be gracious about thanking the interviewer for his time. If he should offer you a contract either ask

Representatives of schools make regular calls at placement offices seeking good candidates for positions.

Courtesy of Ball State Teachers College Photo Service

for a few days to think it over or ask for a chance to come to the community to see the school. If it is a long distance away you probably could not do this unless the school corporation paid your expenses, and they likely would not. It is usually best to take a few days anyway to think over a problem so vital to you as employment. If you are then favorably disposed, return the contract signed.

Once you have signed the contract quit looking for something else. Close the situation for one year. The profession suffers from job-shoppers. Contracts are signed to be honored. Your future is dependent upon your faithful respect to the contracts you sign. If you do not wish to sign the contract, return it with a short, courteous letter. Deport yourself so that your future is clear. It is your professional future that is at stake, and you can do more about it than anyone else.

The problem of tenure in a teaching position. It is important that one sign his contract and make up his mind to be happy with his position. Truthfully, it would help one professionally to think in terms of two years as a minimum without attempting to look elsewhere. It takes time for anyone to become accustomed to a community and really come to appreciate it. One cannot become a real citizen of a community in one year; the first year is spent getting acquainted. Looking upon a position as a two-year proposition will give stability to the new teacher's total attitude. If he is planning to move, the latter third of the school year is spent in thinking about a new position while attempting to render top service in his present position. It is difficult to do. If you reveal your future plans you tend to lose status. If you don't, you are not professionally honest.

This business of settling down to one's job is a task of self-discipline. Some people are always looking for greener pastures and consequently are seldom completely happy. Others can move in and make a place their home in almost no time. If you take a job with the intention of being happy and staying, you will put out all of your teaching materials, make your room take on the air of permanency, and settle down to work. Friday and Monday are just like any other day to you. The one who doesn't quite commit himself to an attitude of permanency often leaves on week ends, looks longingly for vacations so as to get away, and gets impatient for the school year to end.

So if you would be happy, move into your community and get a place to live that you can call home. Find a place to eat that will give you variety, or better still share an apartment with a compatible friend. Then eat many of your meals at home. Open an account at a convenient bank. Open up a savings account. Go to the church of your choice and if you like to sing, join the choir. If there is a young people's club, supper club, civic club, or bridge club that invites you, go, and if they appear to give you wholesome contacts, join one or more of them. These are the ways you become a citizen of a community. Make the community so definitely your home that you can vote in it. You will grow in professional and civic stature.

Certification is an important part of teacher education. Every state issues a license or certificate permitting the teacher to teach the subject or grades specified on the certificate. The state department of education issues the certificate upon the recommendation of the institution that educated the teacher. States differ in the qualifications of teachers, but within a very short time a four-year course will be required for all beginning teachers.

The certificate is the state's guarantee that the teacher is qualified to teach in the area or subject for which he is employed. If the teacher is not teaching in the area for which he has been certificated, the state can refuse to permit the local school corporation to issue a check in payment for his services. Another safeguard is in the accreditation of the school. Accreditation is based partly on the training of the teachers. A minimum is established in each of the teaching and administrative areas, and accreditation is withheld when these minima are not met.

So it is to the teacher's advantage as well as the local school system's to make sure that his certification is in good order and to see that he is properly certificated to teach what he is teaching. Some school systems ask that the certificate be filed in the office of the superintendent as long as the teacher is in the school system's employ, while others simply record the serial number and other pertinent data.

Each state has its own special minor requirements for certification, but the relationships between states with comparable certification minima is quite reciprocal. Two- or three-year permits are issued to out-of-state candidates in lieu of the certificate. During this period the teacher makes up local deficiencies. Hence a teacher with a degree and his own state certificate can quite easily transfer from one state to another.

Securing a permanent certificate to teach. Certification programs are built upon training and experience. States with forward-looking certification programs do not grant life or permanent certification without further training, culminating in at least a master's degree and supported by a minimum of five years of successful teaching experience. This program is sound because it more nearly insures good teachers for boys and girls and it serves as a safeguard against poor material getting permanently into the profession. The five years of successful experience and an extra year of specialized

An artist demonstrates techniques for a group of mature teachers, who will perhaps adapt them for pupils' use.

Courtesy of Ball State Teachers College Photo Service

professional education should serve as an effective screen to weed out undesirable or weak teachers.

If you look upon teaching as a career, the sooner you get your master's degree the more adequate will be your background and the more secure will be your appointment and salary. As stated earlier, salaries are tied up with experience and training. Tenure is also attached, since the school board wishes to give permanency of employment to those that have the highest qualifications.

Unless you are attempting to get certification in another field or in supervision and administration, your additional year should be set up to strengthen you in your teaching field. If you are an elementary teacher, take work in elementary education to make you a stronger teacher. If you are an English teacher, take a major in your master's

Teachers continue to add to their personal growth and repertoire of skills after entering active teaching work.

Courtesy of *The Muncie Star*

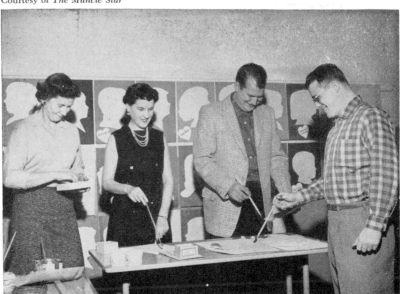

work in English with a minor in an allied area or general education for breadth. Study your needs and take work in the light of them.

After the master's degree and permanent certificate, what then? Conferences, workshops, field courses, and travel are your way of keeping abreast of the times. Professional magazines and books in your field add to your continual effectiveness as a teacher. The good teacher does not rust. He keeps himself alert by associating with other students of his professional problems, either by personal contact or through literature.

Moving from one state to another. Society has more invested in the total education of a teacher than the teacher himself. This is as true in private or church-related institutions of higher education as in state colleges or universities. The student pays a higher tuition rate in private institutions, but even there the part the student pays is only a fraction of the total cost in most cases. In the publicly supported institutions of higher education, the state has invested much in the teacher's education. The assumption is made that the student will in turn strengthen the state by rendering it a service in teaching. Thus, a question is sometimes raised whether a teacher should accept the taxpayers' money in Pennsylvania through its tax supported institutions, and then go to Illinois and teach.

If you have real convictions about your civic and social obligations to your own state because of its investment in you, you should not leave the state until you have taught enough to satisfy your conscience. Another way of looking at the matter is that citizenship is nation-wide and that your civic responsibilities are wider than the state lines. Furthermore, populations are very fluid and the teachers move back and forth across state lines the same as other people. A state loses, but it also gains. There is a tendency for teachers to migrate to where salaries are more attractive or living conditions more favorable. The teacher does not have a moral obligation to stay in the state where he was educated at a personal sacrifice to himself. The state must compete with other states for the services of teachers, and this includes physical plants, living conditions, working conditions, and salaries. This problem causes many people to look at public education as a national problem instead of a local or state problem. You may find yourself faced with helping to study and solve this problem. It will not be an easy one.

One must decide what he is worth. The problem of salary is a serious one. The teacher has postponed earning a livelihood almost four years longer than the person who has not gone to college. Statistics show that the college graduate earns on the average significantly more than the one who has not gone to college. That is somewhat misleading to the college person who goes into teaching, because teachers' salaries have not kept pace with the salaries of other professional people. But the teacher must bear it in mind that he does not invest big amounts in a personal library or professional equipment as do physicians and lawyers, and the length of training is not quite as great. The retirement and security programs for teachers are also factors. Physicians and lawyers must provide their own retirement programs. Quite attractive teacher retirement programs have been set up in almost every state, and there are other fringe services such as group insurance programs that are excellent for teachers. Too often teachers fail to think of these things when they think of salaries and really these are a part of a lifetime consideration. The annual retirement income should be roughly sixty per cent of one's annual salary at retirement. Teachers as a group are a preferred-risk group. They live longer than the average person.

The teacher does not have the bargaining power that other groups have in society, but he can know that school systems compete with other systems of similar size and with other communities with similar cost-of-living factors. The community that has relatively lower salaries must have some drawing factors, or it does not attract teachers with better training or hold them very long. Roughly the highest salary on a salary schedule should be double the beginning salary, and the maximum salary should be reached in about fifteen years or less. The better communities have established salary schedules and use them as part of the drawing power. The beginning teacher should scan a salary schedule carefully, because it is an indication of the way the community feels toward teachers.

Aside from the salary factor in deciding one's worth, there are numerous other heavy factors in one's deciding where to render teaching service. The facilities for teaching are important. Are there adequate libraries and supplementary materials for teaching? Are teaching supplies adequate and does the teacher share in determining what supplies shall be furnished? What is the normal pupil load per teacher? Teachers cannot be expected to render excellent and effective service if the teaching load either in number or size of classes is unreasonably heavy. The salary can be somewhat lower if the conditions under which one works are excellent. Money is not the only important factor with the professional person. His sense of pride in being able to do his work effectively under pleasant conditions is an equally heavy consideration. These are part of the problem when he decides how much his services are worth.

How does the young teacher use his first salary? The young teacher approaches his first position with a real longing to earn his own living. Most teachers come from the middle socio-economic group of society. They have known what it has meant to live frugally. Fully one-half of all teachers earn part or all of their way through college. This has not hurt them, and in fact it has made them more stable. Easy living does not usually produce backbone for social, civic, or moral viewpoints. Perspective seems to be tied up with man's struggle with the economic factors of livelihood, as long as they do not overwhelm him disastrously.

So when the teacher begins to earn, he immediately thinks of all those lean years when he longed for more and better clothes and the little luxuries he has not been able to purchase. His first pay check will not be nearly as large as he had thought it would be. In fact, his membership dues to his national, state, and local teachers' associations will ordinarily come out of that first pay check, totaling approximately twenty-five dollars. Also, withholding taxes will be approximately eighteen per cent of each pay check. These are real roadblocks to spending. The withholding tax will be taken each time, as well as social security and retirement. He will not be asked whether or not he wishes to join social security or the retirement program. These are already established and he automatically becomes a member of the systems. They will take roughly another twenty-five dollars per month of a ten-pay-check school year. All of these are taken out before he gets his check. A four hundred dollar pay check can easily be reduced to three hundred dollars take-home pay. But there is no reason for getting depressed or excited. Nearly everyone else has the same thing happening to his pay check too. It is typical of our present way of financing old age and paying for the rights to be citizens of our country.

On top of that is the agent for life insurance who, now that you are earning, knows you are a potential purchaser. Your biggest problem with him will not be whether or not to buy insurance; it will be a defensive attitude so as not to be over sold. Avoid mortgaging your future too heavily in insurance. It is a good investment, but your limits are exacting and severe.

Your financial obligation for your education may be to your father and mother. That obligation needs to be paid off, especially if you have other brothers or sisters. Begin immediately to set aside regular amounts, and pay off that debt as quickly and regularly as possible. Even pinch yourself some to get it paid off. You'll always be glad you did. It is even more important if your obligation is to a bank or to the college loan service to get your loan paid off. Your future credit is at stake, and you establish your credit only by being prompt in paying your obligations. Your credit is one of your greatest assets; make sure that you start to build a good credit reputation immediately on becoming an earner. Teachers as a group enjoy good credit.

This piece of special advice is to the young lady who intends to teach only two or three years and then get married: Your husband-to-be will love you doubly if you purchase a sewing machine, an electric sweeper, an automatic washer, and have savings enough to purchase a dryer and refrigerator. These are luxuries that you may have to do without for longer than you think if you don't use your own money to buy them. If you don't marry you will need them anyway. They are solid, substantial requirements that make your life more pleasant. These are the fringe luxuries that you can do without but that make life more worth living.

Much could be written about the salesman who would sell you a set of encyclopedias on twenty-four easy payments or the new car salesman who would sell you a new car for nothing down and thirty-six months to pay, throughout much of which you owe more than the depreciated value of your automobile. But maybe this is enough to alert you to the facts of life for the beginning school teacher. A school teacher's salary has real limitations. Can you live within them?

Helping to improve those with whom you teach. The principal is no better than his teachers make him. One of your very first challenges is to help make your principal strong. He is a sincere, hard-working, honorable person. It is his duty and responsibility to defend each one of his teachers professionally without fear and without the slightest sign of wavering. Some teachers will not deserve that kind of allegiance, but he cannot have a really good school and do less. You must strive to make sure that you are worthy of that kind of faith. He will defend you when you are not around to defend yourself. He will tell of your strengths and virtues and defend the weaknesses that both of you know that you possess.

What does he ask in return? Only that you teach the boys and girls in your care with the greatest consideration at your command. He wants you to give consideration to the educational needs of each of your pupils and do the most you are able to do toward that end. He wants you to be fair, kind but firm in your management of your responsibility. He wants you to know that he is standing ready to support you in problems of control, but he wants you to be strong enough never to be forced to call upon him. He wants to be able to defend you in the face of the harshest critic without the slightest fear of being contradicted by anyone. He needs to know that you would do no less for him. This kind of understanding and professional faith builds a team that can work for the good of the school in any community.

What has been said of your relationship with your principal holds equally true for the teacher across the hall, the supervisor, the school nurse, the custodian—anyone whose efforts are part of the combined services of the school where boys and girls present themselves to be taught. Reciprocal acts of faith and confidence make for teamwork. It is your responsibility to make sure that you are always going that second mile to demonstrate your willingness to show that you believe in those with whom you work.

The professional responsibilities of the one who quits teaching. This problem faces especially the young woman who quits teaching to become a homemaker and rear a family. The mother who has been a teacher feels especially close to the teacher of her children. Fortunately the children of teachers usually do well in school. The current joke that preacher's and teacher's children are brats is not true. They are usually the stronger in class because they come from homes that believe in the cultural values of life. So the young woman teacher can relax, knowing that her children will likely do better than average in school, providing she chooses a good husband to father her children. That chance is better than average because she will have chosen him from among her peers in college, and college students form an intellectually select stratum of society.

If you retire from teaching while your children are in school, be a leader in your community for improving your schools and giving educational and moral support to your teachers. They should know they can always depend on you. They can know that at the grocery, in the church circle, and over the bridge table there is one who can intelligently interpret the schools to the group. It is your chance to make your school strong.

If and when your children or husband need you less, offer your services as a substitute teacher. Every school needs a core of good substitutes, and you are one of the better qualified to serve your school in that capacity. You have been a part of your school-community. You have been a teacher with experience. You know and understand children. As a substitute you have a responsibility for being more than a baby-sitter. You need to go in and get things done. A teacher's absence should not be a total loss to the pupils. They are entitled to have a substitute who helps them use their time effectively. You can be that kind of substitute. The pay is ample, but to you that is no longer the important factor. Service is your real contribution now. The school needs you.

With the vital shortage of teachers, the school is constantly in need of full-time and part-time regular teachers. If you have the energy and time to devote a few more years after your family has grown up, offer your services to your community. It is a way to undergird your financial security, but greater still, it is your added contribution to service. Be sure to see that you are one of the best. Refresh yourself in college courses, go back to college or take field courses to insure that you are up-to-date, and be as good as the best. Married teachers are good teachers, and school systems will continue to look with favor upon them as long as they ask no quarter but step out and take their share of leadership in keeping themselves abreast of the teacher education program.

While all this may seem remote to a college student who has not yet graduated or begun teaching, the time to contemplate the future is now. The time to resolve as many of your strengths as possible is now. What you eventually do stems from the attitudes you build while on the way. Becoming is a continuous process. Your ultimate is determined by how you come to feel toward all the responsibilities of citizenship. If you become a teacher you can never completely run away from your professional interest in the social contribution a teacher makes. It is a vital part of your citizenship.

The art of maturing as a teacher. Whereas one starts out as a beginner, one does not remain so. All of the things that one does as a teacher become part of one's professional kit. You have been collecting materials that are going to be more and more a part of you. Some you may discard, but if your files are ample you will keep them. The alert school system encourages teachers to be collectors of teaching materials by providing filing cabinets in which the teacher can file his materials in his own classroom. As the teacher adds to his years of experience this file becomes more valuable and he becomes more skilled at knowing just what he wants for each situation that he approaches.

He not only gathers material and resources for his own use, but he helps the other teachers in his school, especially the new or young teachers who either teach in his building or teach the same courses

Wherever teachers go they are always searching for new materials; publishers' exhibits serve thousands yearly.

Courtesy of *The Indiana Teacher*

he does. The mature teacher is not selfish with his talent and material, but knows that he will be helping boys and girls and doing a professional service through a younger teacher.

This problem of being a professional source of help to other teachers leads directly into an entire philosophy of education that one develops for himself as a teacher of boys and girls. It involves being not only willing but eager to discover new and modern ways of doing one's work. It includes willingness to explore and experiment with method and organization of content areas, and constant alertness to processes that lead to improvement in teaching throughout one's teaching career. Improving one's self entails open-mindedness and the willingness to exchange ideas and recognize the fact that new ideas are just as common in the field of education as they are in

The effective teacher is always on the lookout for various kinds of new materials with which to teach better.

Courtesy of *The Indiana Teacher*

any of the other professions such as medicine, engineering, or dentistry.

In fact, the school has as one of its chief goals that of bringing about adaptation between man and his social environment. There are many people who are busy at changing the environment of man but seem to favor the school's remaining static, and deplore its not doing as good a job as it once did. The school cannot avoid change, and it is up to the teacher to see that the interpretation of society to youth and adaptation of youth to their society is as intelligently accomplished as possible. The teacher must be constantly a student of everything about him if he is to succeed in this important task. This alertness is a maturing characteristic of the really good teacher.

Finally, the teacher comes to see the full meaning of living and working democratically with his pupils. He sees in an increasingly clear manner that, as each year moves into the one following, better citizens are developed when they are able to participate in the evolving processes of social and political change that in turn affect their total way of living. Sharing, participating, and contributing all become a way of life in the school and out. It ceases to be a problem of teaching the answers, but working together to find the answers. Thus the maturing teacher becomes the bridge that connects the growing boy or girl with the social order of which he becomes a significant part.

It is your greatest challenge! Teaching will advance as a profession and society will regard the teacher as one of its strongest forces only as the service that the teacher renders makes each individual a more effective person in that society. The public will not take teachers on faith. The teacher must produce. That need not mean that the school must succeed magnificently regardless of the quality of the individual who presents himself to be educated. It does mean that the school should approach its maximum within the potential limits of each individual. It does not mean that all will reach the same high level. It means that differences may become even greater but the general level of all society will become higher.

Inasmuch as a greater percentage of all youth go to school and stay longer than at any previous period in our history, the school has a greater chance to reduce illiteracy. It will mean that those who a generation or so ago did not even go to school now go and stay, and the school is expected to make them literate. And the school will do more with each succeeding generation, raising the upper limits and likewise the floor. But as this takes place it requires even better teachers to meet this seemingly impossible demand.

Society and the profession itself will by this process be forced to make teaching increasingly attractive so that the most intelligent and the most educable will want to teach. You who enter the profession of teaching will be called upon to help make this a reality, else we shall bog down by weight of numbers and lack of competent teachers to take care of the demands society puts on its schools. That is society's greatest challenge of the twentieth century.

SUMMARY

We have attempted to look into the days and years ahead for the person who aims to make teaching a life's work. There is also the person who teaches for a while and goes into other work, as well as the person who teaches before becoming a homemaker. But later such a person is available as a mature woman experienced as a mother and ready again to render excellent teaching service in her own community. In the interim it should be she who is a leader in the community, helping to interpret the school to the community. It is she, when there is misunderstanding about the purposes of the school, who can talk intelligently about the school as a social force. Schools continually need financial support and the people must decide how much they want to spend for schools. Who is better able to be a leader in discussions where financial support is being discussed? The person who was formerly a strong teacher is now a strong community leader.

This chapter started with a description of the teacher going out to secure his first position. It involved the teacher in making an impressive interview. The warning against agreeing to teach in a community before all the facts are known was emphasized. But equal emphasis was placed on honoring a contract once a contractual relationship has been established.

Then came the problem of how one looks at his first income—making it do all the things one wants to do and paying off one's debts. A creditor is most patient as long as one is not earning; but as soon as one becomes an earner the creditor becomes a different person. People expect the earner to be able to manage his finances so that obligations are met.

The problems of tenure—how one feels about moving from one position to another, how one feels about his obligation to the state that provided much toward his education—become factors in one's thinking about the position he takes.

The problem of becoming an experienced teacher and being helpful to those with whom one works becomes increasingly significant. The new teacher, the teacher across the hall, the teacher of the same subject or grade level in another school, all become more interdependent as one becomes more skilled himself. How one feels toward his principal or his supervisor, even how one feels toward being a supervising teacher working with the students in teacher education—these too are career shaping factors.

The problem of continuing one's educational program into the graduate level—what one shall take and what further certification to seek, even the problem of permanent or life certification—are increasingly important as one matures and establishes new and changing values in his professional work.

Finally, the problem of permanency in the profession becomes a real issue with many who have tempting offers in other fields or choose to quit to be homemakers and rear families. How closely one continues to relate himself to professional activities and how he can best serve the profession and the youth of his community are important problems, which anyone educated and experienced in teaching does not throw off lightly. It is a great help to society and its schools that so many citizens have had a share in the operation of those schools.

Competences that are worth while include the following:

1. The ability to carry on an intelligent discussion with a prospective employer.

2. The ability to adapt one's questions to the inter-

viewer so that one can find out the important factors in the community seeking his services.

3. The ability to select a position and be happy once the choice has been made.

4. The ability to honor one's contract and stay by it even when it may mean some sacrifice.

5. The ability to decide how much is a reasonable salary and then to seek out a position that meets one's demands.

6. The ability to budget one's personal finances so that a real measure of financial security is established.

7. The ability to seek out those with whom one works and help them to be professionally more competent in their positions.

8. The ability to study one's educational needs so that an effective program of graduate work, travel, in-service education, and other educational experiences can be organized to round out one's professional education.

9. The ability to serve in the community as a lay person effectively so as to strengthen the community and the way the school can serve to be more effective.

10. The ability to maintain good relations so that even after a period of years one can step back into service and be a superior teacher.

PROBLEMS

1. *Go to the placement office in the college where you are in training and secure the necessary forms to complete your file as a prospective candidate for teaching.*

2. *Ask your placement office to secure an interview with a prospective employer. After the interview go to the placement director and discuss the details of the interview with him.*

3. *Sit down and add up all of your probable financial obligations when you take your first teaching position. Determine approximately what your probable income will be. From these two factors decide your living expenses and make up a personal budget. Stay with it during your first year as a teacher.*

4. *Find out what the attitude of officials is at the state level toward certification of out-of-state teachers. Study the problems of certification that you would have in one neighboring state. Now compare the two states. Could there be reciprocity in certification?*

5. *Discuss the problems of re-entering teaching with a good teacher in your community who has recently returned from temporary retirement. Find out all the problems that were encountered.*

BIBLIOGRAPHY

Chandler, B. J., and Paul V. Petty, *Personnel Management in School Administration*. New York: World Book Company, 1955.

Curtis, Dwight K., and Leonard O. Andrews, *Guiding Your Student Teacher*. Englewood Cliffs, N.J.: Prentice-Hall, Inc., 1954.

Eye, Glen G., and Willard R. Lane, *The New Teacher Comes to School*. New York: Harper & Brothers, 1956.

Revlin, Harry N., *Teaching Adolescents in Secondary Schools: the Principles of Effective Teaching in Junior and Senior High Schools*. New York: Appleton-Century-Crofts, Inc., 1948.

Schorling, Raleigh, and Max Wingo, *Elementary School Student Teaching*. New York: McGraw-Hill Book Company, Inc., 1950.

Part Seven

Initial experiences
in working
with children

Introduction

The person preparing to be a teacher seeks and finds many ways of working with learners. The classroom in the school is, of course, one of the richest places to work with learners. It should be kept in mind, however, that one can observe and work with children wherever they may be. In Chapter 19 we shall confine our thinking to the school that is specifically organized to help train new teachers.

In teacher education, all the places about the school where pupils are having experiences that advance their development are known as the laboratory. All the experiences that the person preparing to be a teacher has with these learners are known as laboratory experiences. Participation, observation, *practicum*, and student teaching are all laboratory experiences in teacher education. The situation presented here relates only to the early experiences.

The person who is employed to direct the learning experiences of the pupils in the school is ordinarily known as the teacher. In order to differentiate between this person and the one who is preparing to be a teacher we have been calling the one in charge the supervisor because he really is supervising the entire educational program for that particular group of learners. The one who is in the process of becoming a teacher, we have called the teacher. This carries real significance to him who would become a teacher.

Once the person comes into the presence of learners and gets even a relatively insignificant role of helping, he becomes a teacher in the eyes of these learners. How really gratifying this is to anyone who sincerely wants to work with boys and girls and wishes to acquire skill in teaching!

The supervisor will be an experienced master teacher directing the learning of boys and girls and at the same time guiding the experiences of the one who comes into his classroom seeking practical experience in working with or among learners. Truly, this becomes a laboratory for teaching!

19

Beginning to work
with learners

For many teachers, the experience of practice-teaching will
be the first opportunity to take part in teaching where they
may be observed and receive direction from a person highly
skilled in the art of teaching. The teacher-education institution strives to provide supervisors with excellent qualifications and facilities for teaching that are normal and adequate. It is essential that the supervisor be superior in
working with pupils and teachers. His is a dual purpose—
that of teaching children, and that of helping young teachers
progress toward their own goals.

Zeal and concern on the part of the teacher are necessary
if this experience is to be an effective force in his professional growth. He must recognize that when he works with
learners he bears important responsibilities. It is essential
that he become fully aware of this fact. To be late in arriving or to be in a rush in leaving detract from the esteem
that learners have for him and from his ultimate ability to be
helpful. He is now getting his first opportunity to work with
learners and it is important that the learners feel that he is
vitally interested in working with them. Enthusiastic, helpful concern will carry the teacher a long way toward
success.

Some common emotions of new teachers. One of the most common fears of teachers now in laboratory experiences is not being able to answer questions that pupils ask. The teacher may expect to be asked many things that he does not know. Children learn much through travel, television, radio, and printed materials available to them so that their range of interests and their stock of knowledge are a constant source of amazement. If a question is asked, it is best to answer it only if the teacher is reasonably certain that he is correct. If not, there are several alternatives from which to choose.

More frequently than not, questions that are related to the teaching job at hand, but that go beyond the ordinary consideration given the topic, can be turned to a real advantage. Assuming that the question is of general interest to a number of pupils in the class, a planning session can be held by the teacher and pupils in an effort to arrive at an answer. This is a valuable opportunity to teach problem-solving methods. In some cases this special problem may be the concern of only a part of the class. In either event the teacher will plan with those interested. When a solution has been found he will provide an opportunity for it to be shared and discussed by all of the class.

Not every question that arises will merit this much attention. Some questions will be asked in an effort to attract attention; others will require only a reference to a source where it may be possible to find an answer. There are times when the teacher will want to look up a point to make certain he is correct and will agree to do so and answer at a later date.

A similar source of worry to the new teacher is the possibility of making a mistake and being "caught" by the class. Human frailty being what it is, mistakes are bound to occur now and then. Children who are highly motivated to learn will note many of the mistakes that are made. Many things contribute to the errors that are made with factual information. It is not uncommon for the direct experience program to begin before all subject-matter content courses have been completed. In this case, extra effort in preparation will be required to compensate for the lack of needed information.

Mistakes are often due to distractions, moods, health, and outside conditions that limit the effectiveness of teaching. The teacher may find himself feeling "pushed" by the number of extra duties, new situations, or even personal problems. In the event that the class group has not been carefully motivated and organized to assume partial responsibility for classroom activities, there may be distractions arising from one group while the teacher works with another. Some children create problems by their conduct and represent a continual source of concern for the teacher who must constantly divide his attention because of them. Parents and other visitors may come in unexpectedly, and while they are welcome, they are to some extent a distraction. Experienced teachers find it easy to make errors under these conditions. To a beginner, the whole situation is a distraction! It is all very confusing for a while, and therefore errors may occur.

In the majority of cases, pupils are in sympathy with their teachers until they have reason to feel otherwise. This desirable state of affairs can be maintained by two means: In the first place, it is reasonable to expect the teacher to make careful preparation for the lesson, covering all aspects of the work that can be anticipated. This care on his part added to a strong background of study in his own teaching area will remove most of the chance that he will make errors of the kind under consideration. In the second place, the teacher will be absolutely honest about mistakes, demonstrate his eagerness to correct them, and will, under no circumstances, resort to bluffing. Children will continue to be sympathetic so long as the teacher adheres to these policies.

If one finds himself in possible error, he should first make sure of the problem. It is possible that he was misunderstood, or momentary confusion may cause him to feel that he is wrong. Sometimes a pupil does not understand a word or fails to follow directions. It may be that the teacher misunderstands the question. Time should be taken to identify the problem, to make sure that an error is present. If it is, he should simply correct the error and proceed. Apologies are not necessary. If the teacher becomes frightened, he lays himself open to making even more errors.

Another area of emotional involvement that often develops in the laboratory situation is the restraint that the teacher feels. He often feels that he could do much better if he were free to set up his classes and carry out his plans in his own way. In most laboratory situations, the teacher finds in operation a program that has acquired considerable stability. It is necessary that he enter this situation with the knowledge that he will not be able to make much change in the general framework. The supervisor has the situation going and the teacher must fit into it.

After consideration of the problem the teacher will readily understand that the school must go on with as little interruption as possible. To allow each teacher great latitude would lead to an impossible situation and would hinder the progress of the children who must be educated. The extent to which experimentation is possible will depend upon the supervisor, the teaching situation, and the extent of the teacher's readiness to teach. Supervisors are responsible for the educational welfare of their pupils as well as the growth of the person who is preparing to be a teacher. As the teacher becomes more familiar with teaching-learning processes, he will recognize many unexpected opportunities to use his originality. The tendency to look upon teaching as mass instruction gradually changes until much teaching is viewed as individual instruction. As this conception of his function becomes clearer the teacher will find endless opportunity—indeed, constant necessity—to experiment with ways to help pupils. The nature of the learners is so varied from one individual to another that it presents a continuous challenge to be inventive.

A frequent source of disappointment is the fact that teaching practices do not always yield expected outcomes. There are no cure-alls, for example, for the discipline problem. The use of certain devices as stopgap measures must be followed by more careful diagnosis of causes and repeated efforts to relieve the causes. So it is with learning activities. There are no magical methods that will insure the desired results in all cases. Many beginners go through the motions of teaching only to find that little has been learned and that little only in scattered instances. Practices that bring good results with one group may not be so effective with others. If an individual is not learning, it will often be necessary to engage in diagnosis and replanning.

In this section some of the common emotional tensions experienced by beginning teachers have been anticipated. The list is by no means exhaustive. It is hoped, however, that by recognizing them early the teacher will be able to devote his energy to making the most of the many educational opportunities that are present rather than suffer in a constant state of frustration because of a desire to do things that are not possible at the moment. In spite of all that is done, problems may arise that are hard to reconcile. In that case the teacher should identify as nearly as possible what is causing his fears, his feelings of frustration, or lack of accomplishment, and talk the situation over with his supervisor and college instructor. In some cases it is good to ask for a chance to discuss problems of this kind with a college class of which he is a member. Often members of such a class can be mutually helpful.

What the teacher does the first week. One of the teacher's first concerns will involve his meeting the children with whom he is to work. They are naturally interested in his name and how he looks. Now that he is a teacher it may be desirable to decide whether he will be Mr. Smith or Tom. A new role has been assumed. The supervisor will attempt to be helpful here and will introduce the teacher as Miss or Mister. But the supervisor will not be around always and pupils may be inclined to be more informal. The burden of establishing appropriate pupil-teacher relations is not so much on the supervisor as directly upon the new teacher. He is the one who will provide guidance for the learners in achieving these relationships. He will try to do it in a kindly, honest manner that will cause the pupils to do the things that make the most desirable learning situation.

The matter of pupil-teacher relations reaches far beyond the manner in which pupils address their teacher. The tone of the whole situation begins to take shape the first day and develops into an increasingly wholesome but clear understanding of roles and relationships as time goes by. Control and classroom management are most productive when pupils participate to the maximum in decision making and assume responsibility for conditions for good learning.

Before going to the school the teacher may be helped by giving consideration to certain general items. Among these considerations will be the total impression he will make upon his pupils in his early contacts with them. A question often arises whether he will dress better than usual. Extremes in dress are avoided but unusual items such as ties and jewelry may lead children to ask about them. This makes for easy conversation and may help in getting acquainted. The teacher may also want to recheck directions to reach the classroom and make sure he has the supervisor's name. Extra time should be allowed the first day to insure arriving in plenty of time.

Upon arrival at the school, the supervisor will introduce the teacher to the class at the first opportunity. In an elementary class-room, he may invite the teacher to sit with the group with which he is working. In any case, it is desirable to start learning the names of the children by whatever means possible. If there is regular seating, a chart of names will help. Learning names is difficult but very necessary.

The teacher puts himself wholeheartedly into the laboratory experience. By necessity he will be evaluated upon his activities that reflect this attitude. The plans he makes and the work he does will improve as they reflect determination and enthusiasm. The teacher is expected to do things. If a problem of management arises—materials needed from the stockroom, adjustment of lighting, absence of the supervisor—the teacher has an opportunity to assume his proper role as a helper or leader. In the primary and kindergarten grades there are many little things with which small children need help, such as wraps, shoes, and materials. A child may ask for help with any of these things or may ask the teacher to do some of his work for him. Some children will pretend to need help to gain one's attention or to avoid the necessity of doing things for themselves. The supervisor should be consulted, if there is doubt. The teacher is looking for real opportunities to help children and will soon learn to recognize what are the more important things.

Early opportunities to take part in class activity may include helping individuals and small groups, distributing materials, and similar tasks. When the teacher has become sufficiently familiar with the work that is going on, he can assist with marking papers and preparing materials. In certain class situations, there will be need for reference work, checking the availability of films, and giving make-up tests, as well as other activities that will provide needed experience and be genuinely helpful to the supervisor and the pupils.

Outside the realm of formal class work the teacher will watch for opportunities for friendly conversation with children. The majority of children naturally like teachers. They will be receptive to a smile or a friendly bit of attention. They will repay it with big dividends in their response to the teacher who likes them and shows it. These little acts of kindness can be extended in classes, on the playground, or in the gymnasium. The same general principle holds for adolescents except that they are more sensitive to approval in public. The recognition given them will be on a more mature plane and only at appropriate times. There are some children of all grade levels who resent imposition of adult attention.

After working with the class for a time, the teacher will find short lessons to be taught. This "bit" teaching often gives just the right amount of experience and he should be prepared for these opportunities. The job to be done may consist of listing new words for spelling or hearing a group read a story or involve giving a report to the class on a personal experience or giving a current events lesson. No matter what it is, as long as it consists in being responsible for something that a teacher must do, it is a significant opportunity for teacher growth.

Observation of various pupils at work and attempts to help them will lead to an early recognition that certain ones have problems in learning and in their total relationships with the school and the group. With the aid of the supervisor, the teacher may select one or two pupils at a time for study. Through this intensified effort to find out as much as possible about these particular learners, he will find that there are many possible reasons for the problems that they exhibit or the kinds of social relationships that are noticed. As these reasons become apparent, new approaches for helping these pupils often accompany increased understanding. The study of children is an important part of teaching for the reason that it does lead to more effective growth and learning. In selecting pupils for study, it is not desirable to pick extreme deviants whose cases have baffled the school faculty over a long period of time. The teacher may be interested in such cases, but at this stage will profit more from undertaking the less difficult problems. By so doing he will be more likely to see results of his efforts than if he undertakes cases where progress is often measured in terms of years of effort.

Every school has certain general practices established that become, in effect, a set of rules to be observed. For example, narrow corridors may make one-way traffic a necessity. Such plans are worked out and established to provide the maximum convenience for the most people. It is a desirable thing for the teacher to learn about all such rules and customs of the school as early as possible. While it may not be his primary responsibility to enforce the regulations, he will certainly want to govern his own actions in accordance with them.

In case nothing is said the first day or two about what activity is planned for the teacher, he should ask the supervisor what he can do to be helpful. Some supervisors have a technique of waiting to see what initiative the teacher will show. This is not always the case. The class activity at the moment may be such that there isn't much to do except participate in the assignments and observe everything that is going on. However, it is best to find out what is expected and to be alert to unexpected opportunities to help. It is nearly always possible to see little housekeeping chores to be done, such as picking up paper, watering flowers with the children, and straightening up desks. In such cases, doing things with the children is helpful and important. It is possible and desirable to bring in stories, books, insects, and other things of interest, or ask pertinent questions in discussion.

Children can be very helpful to the teacher. For instance, an opportunity to guide him about the school plant is good experience for them, and gives the teacher added insight into the characteristic ways that pupils think. It is very possible that more value will be derived from the side remarks of the guides as they go about the school than from the information that they give.

In the pupil-guided tour about the school building, the teacher will see the classrooms used by other departments or teachers, the shops, the gymnasium, the lunchroom, the library, and the laboratories of the home economics, art, industrial arts, and science departments. The teacher may ask to be introduced to the custodian, the school nurse, the school secretary, and the principal. He can also find out when the various organizations meet, when and where the athletic teams practice, the schedule of orchestra rehearsals, and the times of student council meetings. All of these points of information will add much to rapid assimilation of the school's total operation and to the feeling of security so important in the work to follow. Assuming responsibility for part of the orientation in this manner is helpful to teachers and pupils alike.

The teacher has important work. It is reasonable to expect that the teacher will maintain a high level of preparation of his work as a preliminary to assuming increasing responsibility. Assuming that he is assigned to an academic class in high school, the job he can do most readily is to prepare the regular assignments and use the material that the class uses.

It is good if the teaching situation is one in which the supervisor and the teacher may fit into the roles of co-workers, with each other and with the pupils. While this relationship may be achieved in any field, it is perhaps more natural in elementary classrooms, laboratory subjects, and physical education. It is relatively easy in such cases for the supervisor to provide experiences for the teacher in working with individuals and groups, gradually increasing his reponsibility as he grows in self-confidence and gains acceptance as a teacher in the group.

Supervisors often arrange groups of pupils in the shop, typing rooms, art rooms, and home economics laboratories and require them to check first with the teacher assigned to the group about any problem that comes up. This not only makes it possible for the supervisor to observe the way the teacher works with pupils, but also places the teacher in a vital relationship to the whole program. The elementary room also lends itself well to this early integration with the program. Small children readily take the teacher into the group. In such classes, especially at the high school level, teachers frequently find themselves an integral part of the situation earlier than in the more formalized academic activities.

As the opportunity presents itself, it is to the teacher's advantage to distribute his efforts and select activities that will provide the richest possible experience. Many supervisors welcome an intelligent suggestion from the teacher as to the variety and kinds of experiences he needs. A program of activity worked out cooperatively will usually be superior to one which the supervisor must provide alone. Even the best supervisors often find themselves unable to give enough time to planning the best experiences for the teacher. Furthermore, a cooperative program results in a series of experiences for the teacher that more closely approaches his immediate needs.

Supervisors sometimes are able to arrange for their teachers to attend faculty meetings with them. At these meetings they are introduced to other members of the faculty and participate in the social hour that is often a part of the meeting. Others make it possible for the teacher to accompany them on a home visit. A fine opportunity is presented when the teacher is able to share lunchroom duty with his supervisor or to act as an assistant in chaperoning a social activity.

It is desirable for the teacher to seek new experiences as he attains proficiency in his initial ones. Prolonged activities of the same type, such as typing, duplicating materials, officiating games, and marking daily practice papers, reach a point of diminishing returns. All of these things have value if they do not become mere routine to the exclusion of other types of activity from which the teacher could learn more.

Help can be obtained from the supervisor. The opportunity to learn many things from the supervisor is an important phase of the teacher's professional preparation. Some suggestions follow that will enable him to obtain maximum value from this important contact. In the first place the teacher should know the limitations placed upon the supervisor's time by the many duties and responsibilities he carries. Due to the size of the school or its organization, the extra-class load may be greater than usual. The supervisor carries committee responsibilities and other types of professional obligations that he must meet. A share in community responsibilities is also a part of the supervisor's load. Recognition of these responsibilities will lead the teacher to be considerate of the supervisor's time and arrange for conferences at his supervisor's convenience.

Supervisors want to give time to teachers because this is a portion of their work that gives them great professional satisfaction. It is not expected, however, that they will be required to waste time waiting for teachers. The supervisor has every right to expect the teacher to master class assignments or be familiar with the activity planned for the day. If the teacher can be counted upon to be thus prepared, the supervisor can find many opportunities in which, otherwise, it would not be possible to share responsibility. By so doing, the teacher will be building for the best working relations and may expect to reap the benefit of added responsibility.

The extent to which one can accept suggestions and discuss them objectively has much to do with the value of supervision. It is easy for some persons to weigh their own plans and ideas against those of a supervisor and come up with an improved procedure. When the teacher is able to free himself emotionally from an idea and honestly seek constructive help, the supervisor is encouraged to give him maximum assistance. As a corollary to this attitude, the teacher will seek the help he honestly needs. There are many perplexing problems in teaching. The new teacher will often need help and it is his responsibility to ask for it.

As another means of capitalizing upon the help of the supervisor, the teacher uses opportunities for conferences. In a great many situations it is possible for the teacher and supervisor to have short informal talks during or immediately after classes. Sometimes these conferences are the most profitable kind. However, there is generally a need for longer, planned conferences from time to time. This is especially true when it is necessary to make long-range plans for teaching in the early laboratory experiences or when numerous points of orientation are discussed. Some supervisors find it necessary to schedule weekly conferences with several teachers at a time when their own schedules will not permit more intimate short sessions.

As the teacher observes the work of his supervisor, his general perspective of teaching will be broadened. In general, the supervisor

Teacher and supervisor find it best to work out their problems together, as team members in the teaching area.

has been selected because of his versatility in teaching procedures and his continuing interest in the improvement of these techniques. He has demonstrated an understanding of the total process of education, the growth and development of children, and good relations with parents. In addition to these personal and professional qualities, he often has a wealth of teaching materials and resources which may be examined and noted for later reference.

If close contact is kept with the supervisor's work, the teacher will be informed of the intended use of specific procedures. Discussion of the way the supervisor's plans worked out following the observation and the supervisor's analysis of a situation is a most valuable experience. In such conference sessions, the teacher and supervisor together analyze the learning that seemed to occur and the things that seemed to go wrong. The supervisor contributes much to the teacher's professional growth through these interpretations of the actual happenings in a teaching-learning situation.

Simultaneously with observing teaching, the teacher is encouraged to read in the areas of educational psychology and methods. He will find that the use of professional books as references to help explain what he is seeing will be much more interesting than a chapter-by-chapter approach. Professional reading at all stages of the teacher's career reminds him of principles which help to clarify problems and suggest new ideas for their solution.

The teacher cultivates a professional manner. If the teacher can realize from the start how integral a part of the school's operation he really is, he will be eager to assume his share of the responsibility. This motivation is the first step toward the development of a professional manner. The supervisor integrates the teacher's assistance into his plans in such a way that an unexpected absence of the teacher may seriously disrupt the day's work. Events often occur from one day to the next which create unexpected opportunities for service. A set of papers checked by the supervisor may indicate a need for special instruction with a group. A committee meeting or a conference with the principal may cause the supervisor to plan to be out of the classroom. In such cases he may confidently expect the teacher to be on hand. The teacher may be sure that his presence and his assistance do count and that when he is absent he is missed by the pupils and the supervisor.

An effort is made early in the laboratory experience to cultivate the appearance of being at ease. There is a certain amount of showmanship to effective teaching. Relaxing the diaphragm, controlling breathing, and smiling all help. One of the best things the teacher can do, in addition to preparing adequately, is to plan his time so that he arrives early. Nothing reduces the confidence of even the most seasoned teacher more than being late to class. Stairs to climb, materials to arrange, blackboards to clean, personal appearance to be checked—all suggest the desirability of early arrival.

An asset of the teacher that is often overlooked is the fact that he has been a pupil and therefore has a general notion of what is to be done. Many teachers have had experience with children's work in churches, camps, parks, scouting, and in the home and neighborhood. Any previous experience where children were learning socially desirable things is helpful to a person who finds himself in his first teaching situation.

The development of a professional manner includes interest and enthusiasm for whatever the job is at a given time. Every opportunity to help boys and girls is important; every activity that promotes learning is important. Every responsibility that the teacher can assume adds its part to his professional growth. Responsibility calls for action necessary to carry it out. For example, instruction and directions should not be undertaken when a large segment of the class is not listening. Beginners sometimes try to ignore the confusion by going through the motions of "presenting the material," as they say, rather than first taking some action to improve the learning situation. A brief statement made in a positive, enthusiastic, but firm manner about the need for attention and what the lesson has in it for the pupil who does listen will generally suffice. It is futile to proceed with instruction until conditions are right. There are tricks for temporarily recapturing the class such as stopping briefly, dropping the voice, or asking a question. However, these measures are most effective when followed by dynamic teaching using a maximum of planned pupil activity. One thing is certain: the person is lost who tries to "outshout" a roomful of pupils. The most promising teachers stand out because of their positive actions in their undertakings.

Preparing to teach is approached as a full-time job. Many of the activities of teaching and the preparation of materials are very time-consuming. The teacher has assumed a new responsibility as he enters the classroom; that is, he is now directly in contact with children and responsible for a share of their learning experiences. From a professional viewpoint, everything else is secondary. This means, for example, that if outside work to earn money is necessary, the credit load at the college will be reduced. A thoughtful teacher presents himself for duty with children with a rested body, relaxed nerves, and a determination to be patient, considerate, and kind in his dealings with them.

Generally it is wise for the teacher to avoid too hasty conclusions about the group with which he is to work, and about the school in general. An accurate opinion about the characteristics of a group of children cannot be formed in a single day. Even those who seem the most affable in the beginning may be the very ones who seek to take

Children are led toward making many interesting discoveries with the aid of a thoughtful, resourceful teacher.

Courtesy of *The Indiana Teacher*

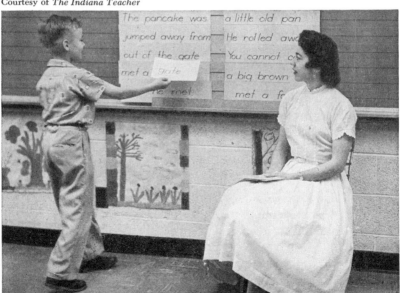

advantage of the new teacher at a later time. Nearly all groups of children will bear acquaintance; that is, the more that is known about them, the better they are liked. The same is true of the school as a whole.

Effective classroom teaching can be accomplished in many different ways. This fact adds to the desirability of approaching the new situation with an open mind. Supervisors expect a fair chance to demonstrate that the things they do are good practices. It is not necessary that all the policies and practices of the school be completely understood immediately. Often, classroom procedures that seem strange or unnecessary at first are found to have a reason in the situation. Certainly the teacher will want to learn the reasons behind practices that differ from his own school experience, and will avoid emotional involvement and argument.

Differences in practice between what the teacher concluded from his college courses and what the supervisor actually does will often be observed. In such a case of difference, the teacher carries out the practices desired by the supervisor. It is advisable to talk over the matter in conference in order to understand why the difference exists. College instructors are forced to generalize, while the characteristics of a particular class often require special treatment. There is always the added possibility that the teacher has not correctly interpreted some particulars of the college course. The supervisor is entitled to this amount of consideration, and the teacher will do well to avoid referring too much to what his college teacher said.

A teacher learns to attach significance to minor disturbances in proportion to their importance. Until considerable experience has been acquired, he may be oversensitive about little things. He learns to be sure that the disturbance is significant and likely to recur before an issue is made of it. If the situation persists to a point of interference, however, the teacher will not hesitate to act within the framework upon which he and the supervisor have agreed. He will remember that he is expected to maintain satisfactory working conditions. He has everything to gain and nothing to lose by talking to the group and asking their cooperation in carrying out the job at hand.

The teacher will learn not to show shock, alarm, consternation, or reactions of extreme disfavor to the things children do. Children will often say and do things to try themselves out to see whether or not they are growing up. Some of the things they say and do are not in keeping with approved adult standards. It is best to be calm and be sure what the standards are for children. One is working for behavior in terms of standards appropriate for children. Repeated offenses are certainly not to be overlooked, but should receive treatment as symptoms of need for help. The action selected to render assurance is then taken on the basis of reason, and not on impulse.

An attitude of quiet reserve in relations with pupils will be best in the new situation. The teacher may as well face it; he is a generation removed from his pupils. The few years' difference in age between a college junior and a high school senior are significant in terms of maturation. Added to this is the fact that the teacher is now assuming adult responsibilities. He must at times take a stand in support of the policies and practices of the school. These policies reflect the community's beliefs about the education of the young. Until he has shown himself capable of supporting these policies as an adult, the teacher must accept the fact that a certain amount of remoteness will exist between him and his pupils.

Each person who works in a school has certain personal and professional relationships with people who work under him, on a level with him, and above him. These relationships require much tact and consideration. Many individuals develop finesse that makes for the greatest harmony in these important human contacts. Many supervisors have developed great skill in the democratic process of group discussion and planning that has resulted in better work and better teacher morale. The teacher will be helped as he observes such qualities and skills and makes an early attempt to incorporate them into his own professional manner.

Some of the more obvious attributes of the teacher which indicate to his co-workers a growing sense of professionalism include mastery of subject matter, socially acceptable conduct, correct English usage, appropriate dress, and good grooming. There are other general areas in which he should examine his proficiency. Is he familiar with the usual behavior of the age group with which he is to work? Does he know what play activities will appeal to them? Is he becoming familiar with the more common routines of the group while they are at school? To what extent does he understand the accomplishments that are expected at this level? Does he know how to carry on conversation appropriate to the age group with which he is working?

In addition to such general considerations the teacher will be learning about the particular group with which he is working. Grade rooms and high school class sections alike will be found to differ in the way they respond and the way the members affect each other. The teacher will come to know some of the group characteristics of his class from early conferences with the supervisor and from direct observation. In some schools, sections are determined upon the basis of general intelligence tests. Other schools do not attempt to use ability grouping throughout the program but only in relation to certain skill subjects, such as mathematics or English. If the teacher is working with a group selected because of special needs for help

Teacher and pupils have fun learning to read, and the skill of reading is one of the school's major concerns.

in reading, for example, it is expected that he will learn very early about the part he is to perform.

The development of a professional manner may be guided by the code of ethics of the teaching profession. The National Education Association has developed a statement of this code (see page 429 ff.) to which members of the teaching profession often refer for help in setting their patterns of behavior with the community, the pupils, and their fellow teachers and administrators.

In general, the teacher gradually forms the habit of conducting himself so that his concern for the rights and feelings of all the persons with whom he deals as a teacher will be apparent. This development is more readily accomplished if every opportunity is taken to know pupils, parents, and other teachers personally.

Activities for continuing work. Earlier sections of this chapter concentrated upon the very early activities that may be utilized in a teaching situation. Not all of those suggested will be desirable for every teacher, nor will desirable experiences be restricted to that list. Following such initial activities as are selected, the teacher and supervisor will settle upon a program of work for the remainder of the time available. The following sections will suggest some of the kinds of things to be considered in this continuing activity and some helpful principles.

As a general principle, the teacher is entitled to a clear understanding of what is expected of him in major areas of responsibility. If he can anticipate with the supervisor some of the things that could occur and reach a clear understanding of what he is expected to do, he will remove the cause of much worry and possible bad management. Areas requiring attention include the expectations of the supervisor, ranging from the simple matter of distributing needed materials before the class arrives to the more complex problems arising should the supervisor be unavoidably detained or called from the room after the period begins. These eventualities are all unpredictable. The teacher will want to know the extent to which his responsibility is understood by the pupils. Knowing what his responsibilities are, the teacher may proceed with greater confidence to meet the problems that arise positively and more effectively.

Another area of understanding which the teacher and supervisor will want to work out in due time relates to plans for teaching. For example, if extensive pre-planning for units is expected or if written reports of such pre-planning are required, the teacher will want to know the form and time of delivery desired. When teaching plans are to be made, the form in which they are to be presented and the extent of detail are matters to be decided in conference sessions. There are many variations of form for lesson plans; the amount of detail desired will be determined by the teacher's need and the nature of teaching to be done.

With their supervisors teachers can discuss profitably the available sources of recorded information about the pupils they teach, and the manner in which such information is to be used. The extent to which records can be made available varies from one school to another. In the final analysis, schools are governed by the degree to which teachers demonstrate their ability to use confidential information properly.

The location of needed supplies and the right procedure for obtaining them for use is a matter of information which the teacher may be expected to learn. It is especially important to know what equipment must be shared and with whom. For example, there may not be enough maps of a particular kind in a social studies department for every teacher to have one. The teacher can contribute to good staff relations and more effective teaching if he knows that other teachers expect to use materials from his room, and if he knows what is available for his use from other rooms.

Every person who plans to be a teacher is alert to the possibilities of helping boys and girls lead normal lives and should expect to aid in directing activities that contribute to well rounded development. Insofar as the things that children do at school can be self-generating, the situation will become more satisfying to them. It is important that the daily learning activity be centered around the concerns and likes of the pupils. This means that the teacher will seek to build the learning that is to be done around interesting activities which the pupils have had a definite part in planning. Often a project of a physical nature accompanies this type of activity.

Learning takes place wherever children live and act; the laboratory of a teacher is any place where children are learning. A bird in a tree, a moth under a street light, a builder at work on an unfinished house, the corner grocer—all of these contribute to and become a part of the teacher's material if he takes advantage of all that is at his disposal. It will require some conscious effort on the part of the teacher to keep these things in mind, as he may be prone to consider learning activities restricted to the classroom.

In order to appreciate fully the importance of informal learning situations, the teacher will be interested in learning about the out-of-class phases of the school program. Earlier mention has been made of the desirability of assisting the supervisor with such activities as a club, a committee, student council meetings, convocations, social and athletic events, and lunchroom supervision. It is necessary that he extend his laboratory experience into this field to appreciate its value in the total educational program. His own experience as a pupil or college student in extra-class activities provides a resource, as far as it goes, but there is a difference of viewpoint to be considered. The activity program is now looked upon as a teaching

The teacher discovers the interests of children and how she can utilize her own strengths to their advantage.

Courtesy of *The Indiana Teacher*

opportunity, a means of providing further assistance to boys and girls in growing up.

The most effective work of the teacher is enhanced by his knowledge of the community. To the extent that he knows something of the community and of the individual parents, he can predict and explain significant behavior of certain pupils. Teachers need to know a great deal about the homes from which the children come, the way the family earns a living, the religious beliefs prevalent in the locality, how the family feels about various forms of entertainment, and even their political affiliations.

The backgrounds of education of the responsible citizens of the community become apparent in the program of the school and the facilities that are provided. The new teacher in the community will find it necessary to begin with conditions as he finds them. As he goes about his work, if he is aware of the life around him, he can gradually bring about a realization of the importance of education to the community. Sometimes this can be achieved by finding ways in which the school can be of service.

All of the areas of concern mentioned in this chapter will come early in the laboratory experiences of the teacher. The person with creative imagination who seeks ways of being helpful or of broadening his experiences will find many and varied opportunities not mentioned here. Such a person will find enough to keep exceedingly busy even without direction from the supervisor, but the supervisor can open many gates to excellent opportunities for experiences with learners. The two—the supervisor and the teacher—will soon cooperatively seek new adventures in teaching.

SUMMARY

The teacher new to the laboratory, where direct experiences with learners give him a rich and varied opportunity to test his ability, will approach his work with enthusiasm. His success will depend upon those competences which he carries into the learning situation as well as those which are acquired or strengthened during his stay there.

Some of the more significant competences that he will want to check in making a self-appraisal are given as a reminder.

1. The ability to utilize content background material to enrich learning experiences for children.

2. The ability to admit when he doesn't know the answer and to be at ease in suggesting to the learners that he will work cooperatively with them in search of answers.

3. The ability to groom one's self appropriately and attractively.

4. The ability to accept school regulations already established and to fit into the situation easily.

5. The ability to see things that need to be done and to go about doing them efficiently and effectively.

6. The ability to learn names easily and use them to good advantage.

7. The ability to build up good room control without being dictatorial.

8. The ability and desire to work in extra-class activities.

9. The ability to converse with children of all ages and abilities.

10. The capacity to accept all of the members of the group.

11. The ability to seek out community resources.

PROBLEMS

1. *Upon being assigned to a supervisor in a teaching situation make a list of the school regulations that the pupils are expected to observe. Use them as a basis for being in harmony with accepted school regulations throughout the assignment.*

2. *Over a period of several days wear unusual or attractive jewelry or accessories and note the reaction of pupils and the comments that are made. Check your ability to elicit comment.*

3. *Try calling the class roll and check your accuracy in remembering names and faces. Utilize devices that fit you.*

4. *Rearrange bulletin board and plant arrangements in the classroom and note reaction of children. Check with supervisor before embarking upon this project.*

5. *Check yourself as a resource person by building up background materials on topics or objects that are of interest to learners.*

6. *Carry on conversation with pupils of different ages and interests and check your difficulties and strengths in the situation.*

7. *List the pupils you accept most readily and those who seem not to get along well with you. Then determine what attracts you to some while others seem to affect you in a negative manner. After this analysis work diligently to correct your feeling toward those you seem to reject. Teachers must respect all of their pupils.*

8. *Make a survey of the resources that you will find educationally helpful in your immediate school community.*

9. *Attend and take part in several extra-class activities and determine the ones to which you are able to make a distinct contribution. If you find yourself weak in some in which you should be stronger, go about building up resources for them.*

10. *During a five-minute period, observe a pupil and write down everything you see. Examine and analyze what you have obtained. In four weeks do the same thing, and compare your notes with the previous notes. How have you grown?*

BIBLIOGRAPHY

Bossing, Nelson P., *Principles of Secondary Education.* Englewood Cliffs, N.J.: Prentice-Hall, Inc., 1949.

Burr, James B., Lowry W. Harding, and Leland B. Jacobs, *Student Teaching in the Elementary School.* New York: Appleton-Century-Crofts, Inc., 1950.

Cottrell, Donald J., *et al., Teacher Education for a Free People.* Oneonta, N.Y.: The American Association of Colleges for Teacher Education, 1956.

Curtis, Dwight K., and Leonard O. Andrews, *Guiding Your Student Teacher.* New York: McGraw-Hill Book Company, Inc., 1950.

Feyereisen, Katheryn, and Verua Deickman, *Guiding Student Teacher Experiences.* Lock Haven, Pa.: Association for Student Teaching, 1952.

Grim, Paul R., and John U. Michaelis, *The Student Teacher in the Secondary School.* Englewood Cliffs, N.J.: Prentice-Hall, Inc., 1953.

Michaelis, John U., and Paul R. Grim, *The Student Teacher in the Elementary School.* Englewood Cliffs, N.J.: Prentice-Hall, Inc., 1953.

Schorling, Raleigh, and Max Wingo, *Elementary School Student Teaching.* New York: McGraw-Hill Book Company, Inc., 1950.

Index